# Biopolitics After Neuroscience

Also available from Bloomsbury

*A Philosophy of Comparisons*, by Hartmut von Sass
*Nietzsche's 'Ecce Homo' and the Revaluation of All Values,* by Thomas H. Brobjer
*The Ethics of Generating Posthumans,* edited by Calum MacKellar and Trevor Stammers
*The Futility of Philosophical Ethics*, by James Kirwan

# Biopolitics After Neuroscience

*Morality and the Economy of Virtue*

Jeffrey P. Bishop, M. Therese Lysaught and
Andrew A. Michel

BLOOMSBURY ACADEMIC
LONDON • NEW YORK • OXFORD • NEW DELHI • SYDNEY

BLOOMSBURY ACADEMIC
Bloomsbury Publishing Plc
50 Bedford Square, London, WC1B 3DP, UK
1385 Broadway, New York, NY 10018, USA
29 Earlsfort Terrace, Dublin 2, Ireland

BLOOMSBURY, BLOOMSBURY ACADEMIC and the Diana logo are trademarks of
Bloomsbury Publishing Plc

First published in Great Britain 2022
This paperback edition published 2023

Copyright © Jeffrey P. Bishop, M. Therese Lysaught and Andrew A. Michel, 2022

Jeffrey P. Bishop, M. Therese Lysaught and Andrew A. Michel have asserted their
right under the Copyright, Designs and Patents Act, 1988, to be identified as Authors
of this work.

For legal purposes the Acknowledgments on p. viii constitute an extension of
this copyright page.

Neuroscience, Fibre optics carrying data around the brain
(© Westend61 GmbH / Alamy Stock Photo)

All rights reserved. No part of this publication may be reproduced or transmitted in
any form or by any means, electronic or mechanical, including photocopying, recording,
or any information storage or retrieval system, without prior permission in writing from
the publishers.

Bloomsbury Publishing Plc does not have any control over, or responsibility for, any
third-party websites referred to or in this book. All internet addresses given in this
book were correct at the time of going to press. The author and publisher regret any
inconvenience caused if addresses have changed or sites have ceased to exist, but
can accept no responsibility for any such changes.

A catalogue record for this book is available from the British Library.

A catalog record for this book is available from the Library of Congress.

Names: Bishop, Jeffrey Paul, author. | Lysaught, M. Therese, author. |
Michel, Andrew A., author.
Title: Biopolitics after neuroscience: morality and the economy
of virtue / Jeffrey P. Bishop, M. Therese Lysaught and Andrew A. Michel.
Description: London; New York: Bloomsbury Academic, 2022. |
Includes bibliographical references and index.
Identifiers: LCCN 2022004450 (print) | LCCN 2022004451 (ebook) |
ISBN 9781350288447 (hardback) | ISBN 9781350288485 (paperback) |
ISBN 9781350288454 (pdf) | ISBN 9781350288461 (epub)
Subjects: LCSH: Ethics. | Cognitive neuroscience–Moral and ethical aspects. |
Cognitive science–Moral and ethical aspects. |
Neurosciences. | Neoliberalism. | Biopolitics.
Classification: LCC BJ45.5.B57 2022 (print) | LCC BJ45.5 (ebook) |
DDC 170–dc23/eng/20220323
LC record available at https://lccn.loc.gov/2022004450
LC ebook record available at https://lccn.loc.gov/2022004451

ISBN: HB: 978-1-3502-8844-7
PB: 978-1-3502-8848-5
ePDF: 978-1-3502-8845-4
eBook: 978-1-3502-8846-1

Typeset by Deanta Global Publishing Services, Chennai, India

To find out more about our authors and books visit www.bloomsbury.com and
sign up for our newsletters.

*For Cynthia, Madeleine, Isabel, and Lydia*
*For Bill, Sam, Meg, and Bear*
*For Corinne, Josiah, Miriam, Benjamin, Jesse, and Easton*

*Between the subject and the object there exists a third thing, the community. It is creative like the subject, refractory like the object, and dangerous like an elemental power.*

~Ludwik Fleck

# Contents

Acknowledgments — viii

Introduction: The Age of the Brain — 1
Prelude to a Neuroscience of Morality: Of Science and Social Imaginaries — 20

## Part I  The Neuroscientific Narrative of Morality

1. The Neuroscientific Narrative of Vice — 31
2. The Neuroscientific Narrative of Virtue — 57
3. Popular (Neuro)Science and Other Political Schemes — 77

Interlude between Neuroscience and the Economic Imaginary:
Of Capitalists and Criminals — 100

## Part II  The Evolution of an Artifactual Being

4. The Neoliberal Narrative of Morality — 113
5. Springs of Action and the Political Management of the Poor — 142
6. Bacon, Smith, and the End of Virtue — 168

Concluding Un(neuro)scientific Postlude: Between Beasts and Angels — 196

Notes — 215
Selected Bibliography — 265
Index — 283

# Acknowledgments

When we began this project in 2010, little did we know that we were embarking on a quest. We began with an original idea that, as with all authentic research and quests, brought us into conversation with unexpected interlocutors, opened new avenues for inquiry, and took us to places we could not have imagined.

We set out funded by a grant from the Templeton Foundation's "Science of Virtue" program administered at the University of Chicago. We intended to examine what we saw as four interrelated questions. First, we were intrigued by the rhetoric around poverty and vice in the United States. Second, we wanted to understand emerging findings around poverty and biology to which, we thought, the neurosciences might add helpful depth and precision. Third, we wanted to press the Western virtue tradition, to begin to tease out the as-yet unexamined ways that virtue/vice, economics, embodiment, and community interact in this tradition. Fourth, we posited that doing so would enable us to trace counter-traditions in Western virtue theory that complicate received wisdom on poverty/vice and wealth/virtue. Having examined these four streams—public rhetoric, neuroscience, virtue theory, and counter-traditions—we planned to articulate a richer understanding of virtue attendant to poverty and wealth in light of what we took to be important neuroscientific findings.

What we discovered was quite different than what we expected. We discovered that troubling rhetoric around poverty and vice—rhetoric that surged into public view in new ways over the course of this project—is rooted in a longer history that traces its roots to earlier centuries and other lands. We discovered the presuppositions of this rhetoric embedded within neurobiological research, where we found an entirely new—and entirely strange—discourse on virtue and vice. Tracking the roots of this discourse took us not to the Western virtue tradition but to the history of economics, which opened a door into an entirely different trajectory of the interplay between science, bodies, politics, epistemology, and ultimately, metaphysics.

Along the way, our inquiries were deeply shaped by our colleagues and interlocutors. We owe a debt of gratitude to Amy Laura Hall, one of our original co-PIs. Much of the inspiration for the social philosophy of science that shaped the project came from her mantra, "follow the money." Presaging our discovery of Ludwik Fleck, Amy Laura would note that every active feature that shapes society will shape what the scientist has to say about the object of inquiry. We are grateful for the two years she journeyed with us on this work.

We are also grateful for the directors of the Science of Virtue program, Jean Bethke Elshtain and Don Browning. Their guidance during the grant and their gracious and rigorous advice on our project encouraged us to find that which animated the activities of neuroscience, forcing us to dig deeper and to extend our research into domains that are not properly neuroscientific. They also curated an outstanding cohort of philosophers, political philosophers, theologians, neuroscientists, psychologists, social psychologists, and economists in a conversation that was engrossing, sometimes contentious, but always rich. Wrestling with each other's nomenclatures, discourses, and methods illuminated many things, not the least of which was the various ways the term "science" functions within the spheres of science, epistemology, and metaphysics. We, along with the fields of philosophy, social theory, theology, and virtue ethics, continue to feel the loss from their deaths in 2013 and 2010.

Beyond the project, our queries were aided by a host of colleagues. We are grateful for our various engagements with the late Peter Lawler, Laura Brock, Erin Dufault-Hunter, Jean-Pierre Fortin, Easton Hebert, Kelly Johnson, Warren Kinghorn, Christina McRorie, David Michelson, Cory Mitchell, and Dan Rhodes. A special thank-you to our graduate assistants at Saint Louis University, who helped to track down papers, create annotated bibliographies, fix our footnotes, and search out page numbers for cited texts: Emily Trancik, Boaz Goss, Ysabel Vandenberg, Martin Fitzgerald, and Jordan Mason.

Words cannot express our debt to Jade Grogan at Bloomsbury Academic who saw the merit in this project and shepherded us through the final editing process. We are especially thankful to the anonymous reviewers, whose resounding encouragement helped to push us through to completion.

We are also thankful to Max Bonilla of the Joseph Ratzinger/Benedict XVI Vatican Foundation, who encouraged us to submit this project, in its yet-to-be-published form, for consideration for The Expanded Reason Awards. We are humbled that we received this Award in 2021.

Finally, we would like to thank our spouses—Cynthia Bishop, Bill Riker, and Corinne Michel—who indulged us with their patient and good-humored forbearance for what turned out to be more than a two-year project, and for their support of our fascinations with it. Joining that pit crew were our children, some of whom were in fact children when the project began and are now adults, and some of whom were not yet born. We are born into a world and into projects not of our own choosing, and we are pulled along by others into projects we may or may not understand. It is always good to have those whom we love most and those who love us the most walk alongside us into these unexpected terrains. We are thankful to them for accompanying us on a journey not of their choosing and for their indulgence of our passions.

Sine his nihil.

# Introduction

## The Age of the Brain

Since the turn of the new millennium, popular literature exploring connections between neuroscience, human identity, and particularly morality has mushroomed. Consider, for example, Barbara Oakley's *Evil Genes: Why Rome Fell, Hitler Rose, Enron Failed and My Sister Stole My Mother's Boyfriend*, which uses "cutting edge images of the working brain to . . . shed light not only on dictators far afield, but on politics at home, as well as business, religion, and everyday life";[1] or Dean Haycock's *Murderous Minds: Exploring the Criminal Psychopathic Brain: Neurological Imaging and the Manifestation of Evil*, which draws findings from neurological imaging and behavioral studies to probe the putative biological basis of evil.[2] Kent A. Kiehl's *The Psychopath Whisperer: The Science of Those without Conscience* similarly uses fMRI studies to show how prisoners' brains work differently from our own.[3] And the list could continue.[4]

Evil, theft, sexual liaisons, murder, conscience—these have traditionally been the purview of moral theory. But where historic moral traditions long understood these behaviors, capacities, or characteristics as products of social formation, habituation, and will, contemporary neuroscience straightforwardly locates morality in the brain. Thus, we find Walter Sinnot-Armstrong's three-volume series on moral psychology—recast as biological cognitive neuroscience—with each volume focusing on some aspect of morality.[5] Or Patricia Churchland's *Braintrust: What Neuroscience Tells Us about Morality*[6] or Ralph Mecklenburger's *Our Religious Brains: What Cognitive Science Reveals about Belief, Morality, Community and Our Relationship with God*.[7] Again the list could continue.[8] Tome after tome promises to tell us who or what we are and why we do the things we do.

This presumption that morality is a product of brain chemistry is not simply an artifact of the popular press or mass media. Rather, these popular titles capture a central thrust of the scientific-industrial-government complex that is contemporary neuroscience. On April 2, 2013, US president Barack Obama announced the BRAIN (Brain Research through Advancing Innovative Neurotechnologies) Initiative (BI), a twelve-year, public–private collaborative that seeks to "revolutioniz[e] our understanding of the human brain."[9] Aims of the BI range from the ambitious—mapping the estimated ten billion neurons in the human brain—to more the preliminary—developing a "functional connectome."[10] Target costs for the BI are estimated at approximately $4.5 billion solely for the portion of the project earmarked for the National Institutes of Health (NIH).[11]

The BI is the most recent Big Science project, shifting cultural and scientific momentum away from the Holy Grail of the Human Genome Project (HGP). Where the second half of the twentieth century has been characterized as the Age of the Gene, captured in the iconic image of the double-helix, the twenty-first century thus far has become the Age of the Brain, conveyed in the now-ubiquitous image of the fMRI brain scan.[12] Since the late 1990s, we have witnessed the exponential growth of scientific journals, popular books, research centers, and more, all focusing on the untapped potential of the brain.

The BI reprises its predecessor—the HGP—both explicitly and implicitly on a number of levels. Repeatedly, we hear that the BI has the potential to do for neuroscience what the HGP did for genomics.[13] So tight are the parallels between them that Francis Collins, NIH director and former director of the HGP, accompanied President Obama in his April 2013 announcement.[14]

Eliding the HGP's rather flat-footed delivery on its initial therapeutic promises, the BI envisages similarly bold prospects for improving the well-being of millions—perhaps billions—of human beings globally.[15] As Obama declaimed:

> But think about what we could do once we do crack this code. Imagine if no family had to feel helpless watching a loved one disappear behind the mask of Parkinson's or struggle in the grip of epilepsy. Imagine if we could reverse traumatic brain injury or PTSD for our veterans who are coming home. Imagine if someone with a prosthetic limb can now play the piano or throw a baseball as well as anybody else, because the wiring from the brain to that prosthetic is direct and triggered by what's already happening in the patient's mind. What if computers could respond to our thoughts or our language barriers could come tumbling down.[16]

Where the HGP promised to cure diseases like juvenile diabetes, Parkinson's, or rare single-gene disorders, the BI seeks to "uncover the mysteries of brain disorders" that affect millions of Americans, including Alzheimer's, Parkinson's, depression, and traumatic brain injury.[17] Like other Big Science projects from the *Apollo* missions to stem cell research, the benefits of the Initiative are portrayed as enormous, far exceeding any monetary price tag.

However, President Obama did not lead off with the medical benefits that the BI will bring humanity. Rather, the BI was framed primarily as an economic stimulus package, guided by the directive of the State of the Union address: to invest in things that power the economy.[18] "Ideas," Obama noted, "are what power our economy."[19] The BI was designed to stimulate and invest in America's innovators, those "dreamers and risk-takers" who have made the United States an economic superpower.[20] Such innovation fuels the US economy as a whole.[21] Here, again, the BI will reprise the HGP: "And every dollar we spent to map the human genome has returned 140 dollars to our economy. One dollar of investment, 140 dollars in return." In the same way, via private sector partnerships, encompassing leading companies, foundations, and research institutions, the BI promises to create new jobs for millions of Americans in new fields.[22] Like Jesus's parable of the sower, the BI promises to yield 100-fold or more. The BI was also announced just four months after the European Union announced that their own Human Brain Project would be funded to the tune of 500 million euros. The United States must compete in the international marketplace.

Thus, the BI is deeply intertwined not only with US economic interests but with its national and political interests as well. Alongside the mainstream government centers of biomedical research—the NIH and the National Science Foundation (NSF)—an equal partner in the BI is the Defense Advanced Research Project Agency (DARPA). Established in 1958 by Dwight D. Eisenhower in response to the Soviet launch of *Sputnik*, DARPA sits within the US Department of Defense and explores the usage of emerging technologies for military purposes; technological inferiority to other countries is an issue of national defense. Similarly, the HGP—often referred to as "the Manhattan Project of biology"—was deeply interwoven with questions of national security.[23]

A final parallel between the HGP and the BI must also be mentioned. Following the model established in 1990, the BI earmarks funds for the Presidential Commission for the Study of Bioethical Issues to explore the now-standard ethical, legal, and social implications of the Initiative, in order to ensure that the science is done responsibly.[24] The Commission issued two reports, both cutely entitled *Gray Matters*, and recommended the tight integration of neuroscience and ethics within research programs.[25] It further targeted three key areas for ethical analysis: "cognitive enhancement, consent capacity, and neuroscience within the legal system."[26] Like the HGP, brain research raises unique ethical issues because, in the words of Commission Chair Amy Guttmann, it "strikes at the very core of who we are."[27] More specifically, "it has the potential to lead to a deeper understanding of our cognition, emotion, imagination, behavior, memory, learning, and social interactions."[28]

Just as the HGP "gave us the ability, for the first time, to read nature's complete genetic blueprint for building a human being,"[29] the BRAIN Initiative promises to go one step further and discover "*the very core* of who we are." In doing so, it seeks to find the biological loci that have, to date, largely eluded genetics, seeking to pinpoint the source of our thoughts, behavior, and social interaction—in short, our morality—no longer solely in our genes but now in our brains.

Thus, the popular literature cited earlier is but a megaphone for commitments built into contemporary neuroscience. But it amplifies more than just a search for the biological basis of morality. It amplifies particular conceptualizations of morality and the human person. For it is no accident, we will argue, that the BI was designed to stimulate the economy and to advance US geopolitical interests. Philosopher Charles Taylor has identified the economy as one of the dominant social imaginaries of the twenty-first century.[30] Ineluctably, this social imaginary animates contemporary neuroscience, tacitly infusing the field with philosophical commitments about the nature of the human person and action. The genesis of this subterranean philosophical anthropology reaches back 400 years, the most recent chapter in an ongoing project seeking to link so-called biological foundations of moral behavior to certain theories of political economy.[31]

As a result, neuroscientists are less engaged in the act of discovery than in the act of constructing—of finding in fMRI and PET scans, neurotransmitters, and neural pathways the regnant projections of late modern Western culture. In other words, we see in neuroscience who and what we imagine ourselves to be. As we will argue in this book, neuroscience maps a certain late modern, Western philosophical anthropology onto the brain and then claims to have discovered therein the truth about human morality and human nature. It is a kind of inverse phrenology, in which the source of certain political and economic behaviors is "found" in the genome, which codes for brain structure and brain function.

But the aim here is not simply self-knowledge. Rather, if—as the story goes—morality and political economy emerge via a pathway from the genome to the brain, once we understand morality's biological foundations, we will know how to build the great society. Per certain thinkers like Adrian Raine or Sam Harris, it is only a matter of time before we discover which kinds of genomes and brains are diagnostic for which problematic social behaviors. Armed with such knowledge, we will be able to deploy the *innovative neurotechnologies* funded by the BI to engineer moral persons and moral societies. Techno-science will save us from the frailties of biology.

To frame this argument requires some background. In the remainder of this introduction, we briefly overview the emergence of the field of neuroscience, theorizing more deeply its recursive formation with its cultural context. We then spotlight a striking characteristic of both neuroscientific and popular rhetoric on morality, namely, the ways they are perfused with economic language and concepts. We close by framing a key aspect of this rhetoric, namely, its laser-like focus on intervening in human bodies to improve not only individual performance but economic productivity—in other words, its biopolitics.

This book, then, is about the neuroscience of morality, or, more specifically, it is about what one has to believe about human morality in order for the findings of the neuroscience of morality to be true. Put differently, in this book, we will argue that neoliberal political economy shapes what it is possible to say about the neuroscience of morality.

## Ecce Neuroscience

The term "neuroscience" emerged only in the late 1960s, concurrent with the founding of the Society for Neuroscience in 1969.[32] Despite, or perhaps because of, its recent advent, the field of neuroscience has sought to establish a longer history, with some even valiantly tracing its origins to the ancient Egyptians in 4000 BCE.[33] These efforts to establish itself have been wildly successful. Within a short span of fifty years, the field now boasts some 150 international journals aggregated under this heading,[34] a multibillion-dollar federal initiative with international counterparts, high school courses, a college major, and has become, as one commentator has called it, "a pop culture fixation."[35] The "neuro-turn," as historian Stephen T. Casper calls it, has infused public consciousness, spawning new subdisciplines—neurohistory, neuroeconomics, neurocriminology, neuroethics, neurotheology, and so on—in striking succession.

How did the staid American Physiological Society give rise to this new thing—the neurosciences—in the 1960s, and how do we account for its rapid ascendance as a cultural trope? The answer lies in the deep symbiosis between scientific projects and their cultural contexts. This symbiosis is complex. We provide initial sketches of its pieces in the next three sections, narrating how our own research questions led us to discover a complex and subterranean nexus of interactions.

We began our study with a question: how is morality conceptualized within the neurosciences? We quickly ran into a complication: studies published in scientific journals are very careful to appear morally neutral. With the exception of futuristic thinkers who call for moral enhancement, rarely are neuroscientific studies so bold as to define morality.[36] Rather, we discovered, most neuroscientific researchers carefully seek to avoid morally charged language in an attempt to be—or appear—unbiased in their observations and conclusions. In lieu of putatively archaic terms like "morality" and "immorality," or even "virtue" and "vice," this subfield uses terms that sound more scientific, such as "empathy" or "sociopathy," or "prosocial" or "antisocial" attitudes and behaviors.

Yet, despite this scientific veneer, such terms often serve as proxies for concepts and traits formerly encompassed within moral theory. They presume much of the content of traditional moral theory, often without acknowledgment, while melding it with other social commitments. These social concepts are then operationalized for measurement. Thus, while seemingly more clinical or "objective" than traditional moral language, the constructs that neuroscience seeks to study are deeply informed by our cultural context, and they carry, as we shall show, powerful moral, political, and economic valence.[37] Moreover, as the result of their scientific "findings," neuroscientists of morality presume and forward particular understandings of morality without recognizing that they are products of a particular history and social context, a particular political economy, and a presumed philosophical anthropology.

Subsequently, as we saw at the opening of this chapter, these proxies are frequently translated back into the commonly understood moral language of the larger social community, especially via popularized versions of neuroscience. So, the movement of these neuroscientific terms begins in the larger thought-community of a culture with a presumed social imaginary (for our study the culture of the late, Modern West); they are reconceptualized and operationalized by the discipline of neuroscience in order to become standardized and studied; they are then given back to the community transmuted into the language of neuroscience, carrying a new social, political, and moral valence.

For us, this raises two concerns. First, we are concerned that this move from neuroscience back into communal concepts of morality is made in too facile a manner. Too often, those speaking from the neuroscientific thought-community to the larger society proceed as if neuroscientific language is clear, straightforward, and unproblematic, because, after all, it is (supposedly) morally neutral; it is *science*. Yet, second, implicit in the new neuroscientific accounts of morality is a moral anthropology—a vision of the human person as a new kind of moral being. But this moral anthropology is not one that is discovered. Rather, it is the moral anthropology that has animated the political economy of the West for over three centuries. Put differently, the scientific articulation of neuroscientific facts about morality now reifies in the brain the political economy and the regnant anthropology of the late modern West.

Consider but one example. Over against traditional understandings of the human person, one of the most challenging neuroscience-based assertions concerns the erasure of human rationality and human agency in moral behavior. In November 2011, *The New York Times* published an opinion piece by philosopher Eddy Nahmias entitled "Is Neuroscience the Death of Free Will?"[38] The answer, according to several major thinkers in the neurosciences, was: yes. In an odd mix of science and journalism, "thought-leaders" like Sam Harris,[39] Daniel Wegner,[40] and Jerry Coyne,[41] along with "thought-makers" like reporters Jeffrey Rosen[42] and Tom Chivers,[43] informed the public of the shaky ground of free will, calling into question fundamental concepts of moral and legal responsibility. They suggested that our subjective experience of conscious awareness of world and self are little more than illusions, neurological processes that can only objectively and accurately be seen or understood from the perspective of someone standing outside of the moral actor, someone in the scientist's position; subjective agency, in other words, is not a causal force in human behavior. Viewed by those in the know—those with expertise in the neurosciences—there is no free will.

Our legal and moral life is based on the assumption that we have control over, and thereby responsibility for, our behavior. Thus, if the account proposed by those like Harris, Wegner, Coyne, Rosen, and Chivers is true, then rational arguments for acting in accord with legal and moral norms fail. How can we hold people responsible for behavior they did not choose to enact? How can we exhort others—our children—to act and live morally if the ability to choose such actions is, in fact, determined by their neurobiology and is not, in reality, within their power? And more importantly, can we avoid a machine-like society that would intervene upon the brains of individuals deemed "antisocial" in order to promote the good of society?

Were such claims confined to lofty, in-house banter between philosophers, the stakes would be low. Yet such claims enter into popular rhetoric with surprising ease. It is no coincidence that Rosen's essay appeared in *The New York Times Magazine*. As the titles cited at the opening of this chapter make clear, the popular media—from papers and news media to high-culture magazines and blogs—feature a steady stream of items translating the latest finding in the neurosciences into lay terms. Such pieces move quickly from the science to its possible implications, spinning scenarios of peril and of promise. With the backing of an unimpeachable "neuroscience" and images of brains with different regions "lighting up" when a task is done or an idea is thought, these media products subtly exert a formative power over a public imaginary ready to hear that we might have no control over our desires to satisfy our impulses. After all, why fight against "nature" and "natural" urges when one's agency—one's ability to choose one's actions—is an illusion? Regardless of whether neuroscientists really understand the neuroscience of morality, the popular rhetoric around such findings is already affecting behavior. Recent research suggests, for example, that research subjects who are simply exposed to scientific claims that free will is an illusion make more frequent decisions to cheat,[44] suggesting that there is something subtly yet powerfully formative about scientific public rhetoric.

How and why did this anthropology come to be? What interests might drive this erasure of such a long-standing central characteristic of human identity? For that, we turn to a second question.

## Imaging Economics: Whose Virtue? Which Science?

When we embarked on this project, we were not only interested in how the neurosciences conceptualized morality. We were also struck by a recurrent trope in popular discourse, linking poverty and vice.[45] Media pundit Bill Cunningham megaphoned the position pointedly:

> I cannot say it too often or too many times. Nothing FDR did in the 1930s stopped or alleviated the Great Depression . . . There's nothing LBJ did in '64, '65, and '66 that helped the plight of African-Americans; in fact, it hurt them. Almost all their actions brought about the law of unintended consequences. The goal of model cities, Section 8 housing, and food stamps was to give the poor people money, not understanding that poor people were not and are not poor because they lack money. *They're poor because they lack values, ethics, and morals.* All that the mid-'60s and '70s did to the black community was to pay black fathers money on condition that they not be involved in the lives of their children and that black mothers were told that if you married, it would have a painful consequence. If, on the other hand, you acted irresponsibly by producing children out of wedlock, you would have a positive consequence, because government would fund bad behavior.[46]

Cunningham's racist rant stands in a tradition that locates the source of economic failure in individual moral failure. Poor people lack morals, not money. Cunningham's implicit definition of "values, ethics, and morals" is clearly economic, racialized, and sexualized. Virtue, by implication, equals sexual restraint and "responsible" reproduction, which enables economic production. The wages of such sin is to have no wages, or at least to have insufficient income to support oneself and the too many children that one has produced. Importantly, Cunningham elides "the poor" and "African-Americans," conveniently obscuring the fact that most of "the poor" in the United States are Caucasian or Hispanic.[47] This racializing of the relationship between poverty and vice has been a constant dimension of public rhetoric in the United States since the 1960s.

We had originally hypothesized that given emerging studies correlating poverty and economic inequality with physiological effects—higher levels of cortisol, embedded traumatic responses, and the growing literature on the social determinants of health—the neurosciences would provide data for nuancing and complexifying both popular and scholarly accounts of virtue ethics.[48]

Yet it did not. Rather, we found ourselves in an unexpected landscape. Echoing Cunningham, economics was everywhere intertwined with the neurosciences in overt and subtle ways. In addition to the BI's unapologetic and explicit linking of neuroscientific progress to economic boom, three quick examples trace the pattern. First, we discovered that economics maps the social location of many with neuro-expertise, imbues study design, and shapes research questions. As Chapter 3 details, key popularizers of neuroscience find their professional homes in business schools or claim expertise in newly created fields such as "neuroeconomics." In recent neuroscientific studies of morality, economic transactions are used as model for the study of moral concepts, like trust. And certain neuroscientists boldly claim Adam Smith as their intellectual forebear. Yet where Adam Smith's theory of morality informed development of his economic thought, now certain theories of economics—theories that have moved far afield from Adam Smith—shape how neuroscientists conceptualize morality. "Wealth creation," as we will see, is posed as the exemplar of "prosocial behavior" while moral action has become reconfigured as equivalent to an economic transaction, circularly providing a basis for equating morality with capitalist economics.[49]

Second, economic ideas serve as markers for a psychiatric diagnosis. Consider the DSM-5 (*Diagnostic and Statistical Manual of Mental Disorders-5*) definition of antisocial personality disorder. In defining this mental disorder, the DSM lists the following "objective" clinical criteria:[50]

A) A pervasive pattern of disregard for and violation of the rights of others occurring since age 15 years, as indicated by three (or more) of the following:

1 failure to conform to *social norms* with respect to lawful behaviors as indicated by repeatedly performing acts that are grounds for arrest;
2 *deceitfulness*, as indicated by repeatedly *lying*, use of aliases, or conning others for personal profit or pleasure;
3 impulsivity or failure to plan ahead;
4 irritability and *aggressiveness*, as indicated by repeated physical fights or assaults;
5 *reckless disregard* for safety of self or others;
6 consistent *irresponsibility*, as indicated by repeated failure to sustain consistent work behavior or honor financial obligations;
7 *lack of remorse*, as indicated by being indifferent to or rationalizing having hurt, mistreated, or stolen from another.

Clearly, the "clinical" criteria for this psychological condition are largely moral failings: lying, greed, imprudence, intemperance, stealing. What might escape casual notice is the way that the DSM-5 subtly slips into this definition certain forms of economic behavior—"conning others for profit," "repeated failure to sustain consistent work behavior or honor financial obligations," stealing—as key markers of this condition. Intriguingly, here in a single space, neuroscience, morality, and economics are inextricably intertwined.

What is more, this nexus transcends this single definition of antisocial personality disorder. Across the literature of psychopathology, a key variable that neuroscientists seek to correlate with antisocial behavior is socioeconomic status (SES). In study after study, researchers ask repeatedly: what is the effect of "environment" on gene expression and/or correlated neural signatures and/or behaviors? The scientific proxy for "environment" here is SES. In other words, built into many neuroscientific study designs is an assumed relationship between SES—a.k.a., class—and behavior or morality. Here the neurosciences echo an ongoing argument in the larger, mainstream community of US culture and its history: does SES (poverty) shape neural pathways so as to result in "antisocial" behavior (vice), or is it that genetics shapes neural pathways resulting in behaviors (vice) that lead to low SES (poverty)? The debate is not a new one.

As we will discuss in Part II of the book, this intertwining of morality and economics emerges from a long history dating back to the invention of the distinction between the "deserving" and "undeserving" poor in the mid to late eighteenth century. This context shaped the trajectory of both moral theory and scientific thinking through the nineteenth and into the twentieth centuries. Alasdair MacIntyre, in his landmark work *After Virtue*, insightfully notes that "every moral philosophy presupposes a sociology."[51] His work over the last forty years has illuminated how the Anglo-American understanding of ethics is the product of a nineteenth-century sociological phenomenon—namely, the reimagining of ethics no longer as praxis but as an applied science known as "moral theory." No longer primarily a tradition of reason-giving, with the rise of empiricism and the deployment of Humean skepticism, theorizing about ethics reshaped itself around two scientifically grounded strands—rationalist (Kantian deontology) and empiricist (utilitarianism). In *After Virtue*, MacIntyre finds that Nietzsche's critique of both Kant and the "English psychologists" (a term Nietzsche reserves for all of English reflection on morality) is correct. All post-eighteenth-century moral theory, he concurs, is just a mask for the will to power. However, unlike Nietzsche, MacIntyre lays the blame not at the feet of Socrates and Greek philosophy, but with this pseudo-scientific turn. Thus, by the early twentieth century, philosophers are characterizing moral behaviors as if they are tastes, for which there can be no accounting, no reason-giving. MacIntyre names this development emotivism.[52]

While we find his account compelling, he oddly stops short in *After Virtue* of an in-depth exploration of emotivism's sociological roots. He begins to glimpse them in *Ethics in the Conflicts of Modernity*. Over against Hume's pretense of empiricist universality, MacIntyre finds in the Scot and his heirs a lack of honesty about British culture's normative role in their thought. As he notes, "the sentiments that Smith and Hume catalogue and describe with such care and wit are in part not sentiments shared by all humankind, but sentiments praised and cultivated by eighteenth-century commercial and mercantile humankind and often enough by their present-day heirs."[53] Likewise, the virtues they extoll are derivative of this same context and not part of the fabric of being human. In this study, we push MacIntyre's argument further. For it is not just that Hume reflects his time; more strikingly, we find that wealth—whether inherited or gained through commercial activity—assumes a peculiar place in Hume's ethics, a role it surprisingly does not play for Smith. Moreover, we find that Hume's heirs are deeply shaped by a century-long argument about the English Poor Laws and the poor. The Poor Laws, which reified the notion of the deserving and undeserving poor, in concert with Hume's valorization of wealth through the centering of utility, inflect a critical mutation in moral anthropology.

In other words, Cunningham's diatribe reprises the masked economic roots of modern moral theory, inflected via two of the most powerful social imaginaries in the United States—neoliberalism and race.[54] David Stedman Jones succinctly defines neoliberalism as "the free market ideology based on individual liberty and limited government that connected human freedom to the actions of the rational, self-interested actor in the competitive marketplace."⁵⁵ Neoliberal economics is associated most strongly with a set of policies implemented around 1980 by the governments of Margaret Thatcher and Ronald Reagan, often referred to as "The Washington Consensus," putatively in response to a series of threatened loan defaults by governments of developing countries.⁵⁶ These policies, often referred to as the pillars of Structural Adjustment—deregulation, liberalization, and privatization—sought to eliminate or limit government regulation on businesses and the economic activity of individuals; to "liberalize" or "free" international markets from any "barriers" impeding the free and efficient flow of capital and trade, through the removal of tariffs, changes in local labor laws and minimum wage requirements, and so forth; and to privatize government-owned and government-managed services (e.g., utilities, health care, education), leaving such goods in the hands of private entrepreneurs or individuals. As neoliberalism evolved throughout the 1990s and into the twenty-first century, additional commitments emerged, namely financialization; as well as the givenness—or perhaps necessity—of economic inequality.⁵⁷

Yet neoliberalism is not simply an economic theory. As pastoral counselor and theologian Bruce Rogers-Vaughn notes in his important book *Caring for Souls in a Neoliberal Age*, it has become "a cultural process" better referred to as "neoliberalization." Not only does this term capture the way in which neoliberalism is constantly changing, adopting "hybridized and mutated forms as it travels around the world."⁵⁸ It also foregrounds how neoliberalism has morphed, in the words of political theorist Wendy Brown, into:

> a normative order of reason developed over three decades into a widely and deeply disseminated governing rationality [that] transmogrifies every human domain and endeavor, along with humans themselves, according to a specific image of the economic . . . [It is a distinctive mode] of the production of subjects, a "conduct of conduct," and a scheme of valuation. It names a historically specific economic and political reaction against Keynesianism and democratic socialism, as well as a more generalized practice of "economizing" spheres and activities heretofore governed by other tables of value.⁵⁹

Brown and others detail how, since the early 1970s, the elements of neoliberal logic have transformed the social, political, cultural, moral, interpersonal, and psychological spaces of our lives and culture. Rogers-Vaughn traces how neoliberal commitments become translated into scientific, academic, and professional principles. Privatization, for example, underlies a new focus on "methodological individualism"—which seeks the causes, and therefore, solutions, for all behaviors within individuals rather than in social structures. Likewise, liberalization grounds society's increased commitment to "economic efficiency"—privileging technologically "cost-effective" product-based interventions that generate profits for corporations rather than practitioners. Privatization linked with radical individualism also fuels a dismantling of social institutions; David Harvey cites Margaret Thatcher's now-infamous phrase:

> There was, as she declared "no such thing as society, only individual men and women"—All forms of social solidarity were to be dissolved in favour of individualism, private property, personal responsibility, and family values.⁶⁰

There is no such thing as society; only individuals. The market seems to be the only community that is possible. Beyond infiltrating all aspects of contemporary culture with its principles, neoliberalization goes one step further. As Brown succinctly puts it, now: "All conduct is economic conduct; all spheres of existence are framed and measured by economic terms and metrics, even when those spheres are not directly monetized." This pervasive economization of spheres of life previously is, for Brown,

> a process of remaking the knowledge, form, content, and conduct appropriate to these spheres and practices . . . That is, we may (and neoliberalism interpellates us as subjects who do) think and act like contemporary market subjects where monetary wealth generation is not the immediate issue, for example, in approaching one's education, health, fitness, family life, or neighborhood. To speak of the relentless and ubiquitous economization of all features of life by neoliberalism is thus not to claim that neoliberalism literally marketizes all spheres, even as such marketization is certainly one important effect of neoliberalism. Rather, the point is that neoliberal rationality disseminates the model of the market to all domains and activities—even where money is not at issue.[61]

All domains of human life and human behavior can be examined through the lens of neoliberal economics, including—we argue in this book—the "discoveries" of the neurosciences. What one finds in the neurosciences of morality is this neoliberalized subject—an abstract anthropology of a being at the mercy of its desires and emotions, which are directed by an omnipresent invisible hand via genes and brains, developing in an environment imagined in economic terms. Whether this cocktail consigns the person to antisocial (anti-economic) or prosocial (pro-economic) behavior, either way, what has been lost is freedom.

## Embodying Politics, Scanning for Morality

How convenient, one might note, that at the moment economics discovers free will to be an illusion—so do the neurosciences. Can this be a coincidence? We think not. In fact, it is not only that both the neurosciences and morality have been economized; the neurosciences have assumed two key roles in furthering the neoliberal project. The first is the project of naturalization. As David Harvey notes, since the 1970s, neoliberalism has been increasingly perceived "as a necessary, even wholly 'natural,' way for the social order to be regulated."[62] It has become "the air we breathe . . . a necessary part of the natural world."[63] Neuroscience "naturalizes" neoliberalism in that most solid of grounds—the human body, the brain. As the DSM makes clear, the characterization of antisocial personality disorder—like other psychological diagnoses—brings together violations of morality (lying, stealing), economics (failure to work or honor financial obligations), and politics (violating others' rights, disrespecting laws, failure to conform to social norms). Then, via brain imaging, genetics, and gene-by-environment studies, neuroscientists seek to find the causative locus of failure to conform to these socioeconomic norms in the human body. Whether by this *via negativa* or through studies in positive psychology, the neoliberal subject (who we name *Homo capitalus*) is discovered as already there in the biological nexus of neural pathways. Once it is found,[64] it is a but a short step to declare free will a myth—rather, we will have no choice but to agree that human behavior as *Homo capitalus*—whether a person fulfills this natural *telos* or misses the mark—is completely determined by economic laws grounded in the biology of the human brain.

A second role assumed by a neoliberalized neuroscience is that of governmentality. A term coined by Michel Foucault, governmentality refers to "the thousand and one different modalities and possible ways that exist for guiding men, directing their conduct, constraining their actions and reactions, and so on" that transcend direct political oversight.[65] Here Foucault is referring to the myriad subtle, often invisible, modalities by which society polices individual behavior, or, more powerfully, creates mechanisms by which individuals themselves. When these modalities engage with human bodies to effect their policing function, Foucault refers to them as techniques of "biopolitics." They are a form of hegemony that does not look like a hegemony, one often forwarded under the rhetoric of freedom and liberation "even as [they] shackle the human soul."[66]

Again, these functions for a seemingly apolitical branch of science are not new. Since the advent of genetics in the early 1900s, the Western mindset has been committed to the belief that science will provide a clear view of the landscape of human behavior, a true view where all factors in human behavior will be known, and, in being known, can be deployed to help the human estate. If we just know where in the body—or now, in the brain—our moral failings are situated, and the ways in which the brain functions to produce failed moral behavior, we will have found the material fulcrum by which to leverage human action into the moral behavior that society needs. If we understand the "Moral Molecule," as it is called by one researcher,[67] we will be able to not only understand morality, but moral markets, and that confounding behavior known as altruism. By assisting those with antisocial traits, we quite optimistically believe that we can build better and stronger, more economically and politically stable societies. If we know the origin of economic, moral, and political problems, we will know where to act to have better political dialogue, or a more moral society, or how to make better investment or economic decisions—the key moral occupations in Western, educated, industrial, rich, democratic (WEIRD) societies.

Neuroscientists of morality may object that the point here is not to control behavior, but instead to relieve suffering, particularly for those burdened with antisocial personality traits, to treat them for a medical condition. Certainly, most researchers do want to help people. Certainly, the justification for this research is to relieve the suffering of patients, or to alleviate the social ills that emerge from antisocial and immoral behaviors.[68] The scientific hope is that by identifying the environmental and neurobiological determinants of antisocial traits, society might be able to intervene in order to prevent or disrupt antisocial behaviors, the proxy for vice, or to promote prosocial behavior, the proxy for virtue.[69]

In other words, there is a political or moral imperative to intervene to make people with antisocial traits more moral, or politically safe.[70] As we unpack and analyze these studies, we will elucidate not only the understanding of antisocial or prosocial behavior held by these researchers but also the moral and political valence of such endeavors. Neuroscientific research is not only driven by the pursuit of knowledge for its own sake but also seeks practical outcomes. This pragmatic and immanent *telos* seeks interventions, usually aimed at the level of the body or brains of those who have become pathological—or, perhaps better, who have been made pathological—to fit into society. Likewise, the study of the neural substrates of virtue—that is to say, prosocial attitudes and behaviors—seeks to discover the relevant neurotransmitters and relevant brain areas so as to intervene and to promote virtue.[71] If morality—having evolved through human history as a natural, biologically instantiated mechanism—is driven by neuromodulators within neural substrates, then neuroscientists can dissect the functional anatomy underlying the antisocial or prosocial behavior to lay bare the nature of human morality; or so the story goes.[72]

Thus, the neuroscientists of morality are chasing after virtue and vice. Their quest is to master and control morality, particularly the vicious—the antisocial—those who do not fit easily into the modern-day *polis* constructed by biopolitical economy. Some imagine preventing the vicious from coming into being through "genetic virtue" programs; others imagine medical and technological interventions to curb and hopefully to master the antisocial, or to set them outside the normal protections of the *polis*. This desire is born from a particular kind of culture, born in a particular sociohistorical moment on a large island in the north Atlantic, translated across an ocean to find its apogee in North America, where it has transformed the world.

## The End of Morality

Is this the story we want to live? If this is the story being told by contemporary neuroscience, have we reached the end of "morality"? If our analysis is correct, that may well be the case—we may well have reached the end of the moral theory derivative from Hume.[73] And this, we believe, is all to the good. Reaching the end of moral theory so construed, however, does not mean we have reached the end of ethics. Rather recognizing that we have reached the end catalyzes us to re-envisage new ways of thinking about who we are as persons and what it means to live rightly and well in communities of human flourishing. We hope this book provides just such a catalyst.

To do so, however, we need to more carefully understand how we have reached this point in history. We believe that a careful analysis of the contemporary neuroscience of morality provides a window into the often-invisible factors that have contributed to the current understanding of ethics. We mount this critique not only to raise concerns about the social location of the neurosciences and the broader political economy in which contemporary scientific research is inextricably enmeshed. We offer this argument as a lens through which all of us—philosophers, theologians, economists, scientists, physicians, psychologists, pastors, among others—should critically examine our own lives, projects and theoretical frameworks and the ways in which our contexts inchoately inform and shape our own work.

The overall argument of this book is quite simple: contemporary neuroscience of morality does not so much discover human morality or human nature so much as it imagines and enacts what the larger community of society already holds to be true about nature and human morality. These imaginings and enactments emerge from the larger social imaginary, which Charles Taylor defines as an inchoate conception "of the moral order of society."[74] It is a kind of metaphysical moral order that sets the boundaries on what it is possible for a community to imagine and to think, and thus to enact. The neuroscience of morality emerges out of this social imaginary.

While this is true of the neuroscientific research enterprise as a whole, in this book, we focus one subset of the enterprise, what we name *the neuroscientific narrative of morality*. It would be impossible to do an exhaustive and detailed survey of this literature, and such a survey would undoubtedly try our readers' patience. Thus, in what follows, we are intentionally selective in our approach, but we believe that we have selected representative and highly cited studies of neuroscience of morality as our exemplars. Via these exemplars, we demonstrate not only the tenuous grounding of what is often presented as fact; we will also trace an historical thread that runs through the whole of neuroscience, namely, the ways in which this scientific thought-style is grounded in larger social orders. In other words, in this book, we critically engage neuroscience.

If one is going to critically engage a particular science, one first must ask: what counts as a science? This question is more complicated than one might imagine. Ludwik Fleck, a scientist and philosopher of science, in his book *Genesis and Development of a Scientific Fact*, describes four different types of science: popular science, textbook science, journal science, and *vademecum* science. Popular science is the science of nonexperts. It is science as it exists in the culture of generally well-educated adults.[75] Textbook science is for beginners, constructed as if there are no controversies, as if everything is settled.[76] It is derived from an untold myriad of journal science findings put together without eye to how this knowledge emerged. Though Fleck does not say it, we would argue that textbook science is a creative work of philosophy, because it is the synthesis of a worldview of the subject treated in the textbook. Journal science is just as it sounds—the science that has been scrutinized and found to bring novel insights into relief. These insights must stand in some strong relationship to previous bodies of knowledge, but other scientists judge whether that relationship with the larger body of acceptable knowledge is sufficiently strong, whether it confirms or challenges that previous body of knowledge. Journal science is refined, circumscribed, and circumspect; it is narrow and pushes into the unknown. *Vademecum* science is the messy science of the scientist's notebook. It is personal knowledge, but it also carries with it notes of what is previously known on a subject, combined with personal musings about the subject. It might list the methodologies at the scientists' fingertips. It records the novel data generated by the scientist, and brings that data into a very messy conversation with the previously settled opinion. In some sense, it represents the messiness of doing science.

Our project will engage both journal science and popular science. However, circulating in the background is not just formal science in these four forms. Beyond the messy doing of the science itself, and the messy interchanges between these types of sciences, neuroscience itself is mish-mash of different sciences interacting and intersecting. Often referred to in the plural ("the neurosciences"), the work of neuroscience is interdisciplinary. It attempts to combine and correlate the findings of several distinct sciences, including psychology, psychiatry, neurology, neuropsychiatry, sociology, economics, behavioral politics, economic behavior, genetics, and neurobiology. Each separate domain of science—for example neurobiology and sociology—has its separate theories, its separate methods, its distinct objects, and its distinct purposes, all of which combine to give us the results and conclusions of a particular scientific investigation. Thus, neuroscience is a fusion of several sciences into a single scientific domain, which is further complexified by being practiced in popular, textbook, journal, and *vademecum* forms.

As we describe in the prelude to Part I drawing further on Fleck's work, these different scientific subdisciplines that have been concatenated under the domain "neuroscience" can also be described as different scientific "thought-communities" (e.g., neurobiological imaging and behavioral economics). What we see is an attempt to forge a new, neuroscientific thought-community, one that correlates the findings of the neurobiological thought-community with the findings of the social scientific thought-communities. We include under social sciences things like sociology, psychology, and economic science. When these two domains are brought together under the umbrella of a single experimental protocol, each science has points of contact with the other but also vast areas that do not overlap. There is significant slippage between the two domains.

Even greater slippage occurs when one seeks to draw conclusions from experimental studies about social and moral behavior. This occurs not only in conclusions drawn by those in the neurosciences about social behaviors and morality, for example, with Peter Giarnos, Stephen Manuck, Essi Viding, Uta Frith, and Andreas Meyer-Lindenberg (i.e., journal science), but particularly when one takes up multiple studies where two or more domains of science are brought together especially in popular works like those by Jonathan Haidt, Sam Harris, Simon Barron Cohen, Paul Zak, and David Eagleman (popular science). These works seek to synthesize the findings of science into philosophies. Thus, in order to critically engage "neuroscience" we will not only examine journal studies, asking questions of the purpose of study, which we take as important for understanding the findings of the scientific studies. We will also be analyzing the works of the popularizers of science, those who want to claim the mantle of science, but who are more accurately engaged in philosophical endeavors, and who do so for a myriad of other purposes.

In this book, then, we move between and across disciplinary boundaries and explore the interstices of the various disciplines and the scientific domains that generate and synthesize knowledge. We explore both journal science and scientists and popular science and popularizers. As we move along this study, we point to the areas of slippage between their domains of knowledge, each with its separate theories, its separate methods, and its distinct purposes, and thus with its unique philosophical construction. We then broaden the lens to critically examine the here-to-fore unacknowledged cultural, political, and economic assumptions that structure the way these neuroscientific studies are conceived and constructed. Every question is already on a quest, emerging from a social location and looking for something for its own distinct purposes. As we will see in the case of neuroscience, each scientific study and each synthetic linking between the various findings carries with it its own moral, political, and economic assumptions, and then reifies them in the brain, or in the genome, or in the society. For the reasons outlined earlier, we were particularly intrigued by the implicit assumptions of economic theory that shape the concepts of virtue and vice that are operative in these neuroscientific studies. We show how the relationship between economics and virtue in contemporary popular and neuroscientific discourse presupposes a mutation in the relatively recent construct of the *Homo economicus*. Complicating these neurobiological stories are unacknowledged assumptions about poverty and wealth, and a much more complicated story of the relationship of economic theories to our concepts of virtue and vice and prosocial and antisocial behaviors.

In Part I of this book, we explore the neuroscientific narrative of morality. Before setting off on this journey, we provide more background on the work of Fleck and his monograph *The Genesis and Development of a Scientific Fact*, where he provides a compelling account of the dynamics of the social dimension of scientific knowledge. In a short essay penned shortly before his death, he concisely states his operative thesis: "Between the subject and the object there exists a third thing, the community. It is creative like the subject, refractory like the object, and dangerous like an elemental power."[77] This Prelude to a Neuroscience will lay out the relationship of individual scientists to the community of scientists and how the thought-style of a group of scientists establishes a thought-community. Moreover, the thought-community of scientists has a relationship with the larger community, what Fleck calls the exoteric community of society at large. Fleck's insights about the flow of knowledge between these various thought-communities will assist us as our argument develops.

Part I of the book explores the way that vice is pathologized and virtue is prescribed within the neurosciences. Of course, there are various ways in which virtue and vice are conceived and operationalized in the various studies. No scientist really wants to define good and bad, moral and immoral, or virtue and vice per se. Instead, what we find is that the neurosciences have developed proxies for virtue and vice—prosocial and antisocial attitudes and behaviors, respectively. In Chapter 1, we examine the growing body of research at the interface of neuroscience and antisocial behavior. We explore various studies of brain and environment, or gene and environment in relation to antisocial behavior. Here "environment" is captured almost exclusively by economics—be it socioeconomic status or socioeconomic positioning. What is more, the neurobiological narrative of vice—that is to say, antisocial behavior—is anchored in the DSM and carries with it the power of the institution of psychiatry. It is a story that emerges from a very particular thought-community with a particular historical force in a particular historical moment. Shaped by its historical context, it presumes that genes make brains and brains make behavior. In doing so, it forwards a particular anthropology that animates its quest.

Where in Chapter 1 we engage the neuroscientific story of vice, Chapter 2 engages the neuroscientific story of virtue. Here we explore the discourses on prosocial attitudes and behaviors, as they are emerging from the much more recent and therefore more limited literature on both psychopathology and positive psychology. As we shall show in Chapter 2, the study of the neural substrates of virtue—that is to say, prosocial attitudes and behaviors—seeks to discover the relevant neurotransmitters and relevant brain areas so as to intervene and to promote virtue.[78] With their counterparts in Chapter 1, the neuroscientists of virtue tell a specific story: genes beget brains, and brains beget behaviors. Sometimes those behaviors are antisocial;[79] sometimes they lead to poverty.[80] The hope is that, by intervening via medical science at the level of the brain—through psychopharmacology or selective genetic moral enhancement— we can improve behavior and performance in the social and economic arenas.[81] Occasionally, gene-by-environment studies complicate the neuroscientific story: genes interacting with the socioeconomic environment beget brains, and genetically and socioeconomically shaped brains beget behaviors.[82]

Chapter 3 completes the neuroscientific narrative of morality, as we connect the neuroscientific research—diagnostic tools, research methodologies, operationalized inventories—with popularizers of neuroscience who deploy economic game theory in behavioral research to ground the narratives of vice and virtues more deeply in market theory. It quickly becomes clear that standing behind the neuroscience of morality is an anthropology—a late-twentieth-century variant of *Homo economicus*, that we will call *Homo capitalus*, where the human has become and is in service of capital. This anthropology is biopolitical in two ways. First, it presumes that the *bios* (genes and brains) produces the behaviors that shape the *polis*. As such, the human animal is incapable of free will and choice. There are several levels at which reformers aim their interventions to regulate the chaos of malfunctioning genes and brains, through technology and medicine but also through programs of reform and penal systems. For this reason, then, the *polis* must create a social, moral order designed to control the behavior of those who do not conform as productive members of the contemporary political economy—to eliminate behavior deemed antisocial and to promote behavior deemed prosocial.

In order for this popularized story of science to be taken up by the mainstream, it has to align with a regnant set of assumptions that governs the way people imagine their social existence, how things fit, move, conform to or challenge expectations— Taylor's shared social imaginary.[83] But the vector points both ways. Where Part I traces the neuroscientific narrative of morality as it moves from journal science into the broader cultural imagination, both Fleck and Taylor point us to the more critical dynamic: that it is the social imaginary or the imagination of the larger social thought-community that lies behind the very possibility and parameters of the scientific quest. The imagination of scientists—and therefore the practice of science—is first shaped by the broader assumptions of the cultures in which they are embedded. In Part II, then, we explore the primary social imaginary that has shaped the quest of the neuroscientific narrative of morality—economics. Part II traces the genealogy of *Homo capitalus* from Its roots in the empirical sciences as they developed in a specific culture, namely, that of late-eighteenth-and nineteenth-century British philosophy and political economy. It is this social imaginary that has shaped the evolution of the neurosciences, and this political economy that the neurosciences then reify as a biopolitics of morality.

To explore this social imaginary, we trace the genealogy backward. We move from the present-day situation to the past for several reasons. First, by starting with the various features operative in the present, we can more accurately trace these backward to the operative elements in the recent past and then the distant past, which animate our present neuroscientific questions about morality. Second, and following MacIntyre, moral theory is intricately tied to the social fabric of society. By tracing it backward, we are not only following MacIntyre in *After Virtue*, but we are able to show the further development of moral theory as it has cashed itself out in economic theory. In other words, we trace economic theory back to the rise of Mill's positive science, which is intricately linked to his and Bentham's utilitarianism, and which itself emerges out of a concern for social enterprise. Put differently, by tracing the history backward, we can more easily illustrate the social milieu out of which the positive science morality and economics arises.

We begin Chapter 4 with the story of neoliberalism as advanced by the Chicago School of Economics. The Chicago School marked a shift in political economy from its nineteenth-century forebears in three key ways. It made its mark by advancing the concept of economics as a science. This required not only the positing of *Homo economicus* as a normative figure. It also required the putatively explicit severing of economics and ethics. Once severed, we find economics subtly usurping what had been the domain of ethics. We watch as economics becomes the governing logic of the state, society, and then "the hidden side of everything." And we watch how *Homo economicus* mutates, in the work of Gary Becker, into the fictive being *Homo capitalus*, the human person as at once capital and enterprise unit. The resonance between the language and concepts of neoliberalism and the neuroscientific narrative of morality here become transparent.

But this is only half the story. In Chapter 5 we move backward into the nineteenth century, describing how *Homo economicus* emerges, not as a discovery of science but from the development in the philosophy of science, particularly in the work of John Stuart Mill. *Homo economicus* is not a reality but is an abstraction, a fictive creation of economic scientists that conveniently fits into an overarching machinery of an economized society. We show the relationship of Mill's economic theory to his science of ethology and his father's science of psychology, and how all of that emerges from Jeremy Bentham's penchant to imagine social science in the service of social engineering. Bentham believes that David Hume's skepticism permitted a novel approach to science, such that the science would reveal the social physics according to which the "principles of morals and legislation" can be deployed.[84] These emergent principles of morals and legislation would permit the deployment of the right "springs of action" to be deployed such that society could become a well-functioning machine.[85] We also show how the social science of David Ricardo and Thomas Malthus, inspired by the work of Joseph Townsend, were informed by a new consciousness of the poor, with the reification of the notion of the "deserving" poor, who could become free through their industry, and the undeserving or "beastly" poor. Essentially, we have the prosocial, who become *Homo economicus*, and the antisocial, who are a burden to society.

In Chapter 6, we trace the emergence of the concept of economic "man" back to David Hume and Francis Bacon, not Adam Smith. Just as Mill's positivist science contributes to the production of *Homo economicus*, Hume's and Bacon's empirical science sets the trajectory of WEIRD societies. Bacon's and Hume's skepticism about knowledge of causes called into question regnant cultural notions of moral anthropology, leaving our imaginings about human nature abstract, simplistic, and feeble. Hume denatures human nature. We show that Smith, in revisions of his *Theory of Moral Sentiments* at the end of his life, was attempting to give a richer and thicker account of moral anthropology directly as a response to the simplistic and simple-minded anthropology of Hume. What this means of course is that *Homo economicus*, a figment of the imagination of the early twentieth century, does not originate with Smith, but with Hume and Bacon. And that means that the political economy that is operative in the north Atlantic from the middle of the eighteenth century to our day builds a stark and violent lifeworld aimed at grinding "rogues honest, and idle men industrious."[86] It is this global biopolitical economy that we live in today.

Finally, we conclude un(neuro)scientifically. We claim that we must return to what Smith attempted to do in challenging Hume's anthropology. That is not to say that Smith's moral anthropology is correct, but he seemed to see Hume's failings and to aspire more deeply toward a communal human identity. Even Mill understood that the human actor cannot be reduced to *Homo economicus* or *Homo capitalus*, an abstract being, a being born in the imagination of economists and mutated into a cog in the wheel of capital production. While not embracing Smith's or Mill's anthropology, we hope our study contributes to a cultural conversation about the nature of the human, one not exhausted by scientific renderings but that rather embraces the nobilities and beauty of being human, despite all of our failings and frailties, which are opportunities that necessitate social cohesion and the care of the least of these. In other words, as a society we must open spaces of non-reductive, philosophical dialogue for the good of all humans and their thought-communities.

# Prelude to a Neuroscience of Morality

## Of Science and Social Imaginaries

Every scientific question is already a quest. When a scientist asks a question, she seeks to discover something that is unknown. Yet, scientific questions are not asked blindly. The scope of acceptable questions is defined by a dominant paradigm—a set of concepts, ideas, theories, and methodological approaches shared by members of a particular scientific field. Such theories emerge from a worldview committed to particular assumptions about the fundamental nature of reality. As such, the trajectory of every scientific quest to discover the not-yet-known is marked by two key characteristics: it is set within a space delimited by the known, and *contra* cultural depictions of individual researchers pursuing their work in lonely labs, it is a deeply social enterprise.

As we move to examine the neuroscientific literature, we want to pause for a moment to consider this social nature of even the "hard" sciences. As a fusion of two scientific domains—neurobiology and the social and psychological sciences—neuroscience seeks to discover the not-yet-known by correlating methods and findings from two distinct research domains. Yet, we will argue, it has largely failed to recognize the ways in which each of these research domains is shaped by a more fundamental worldview that informs the questions asked and delimits what can be discovered. In other words, neuroscience has a history (a time, so to speak) and it has a social context (a space), both of which will inevitably shape the kinds of truth claims it makes.

In this prelude to Part I, we point to three different ways that science is a social endeavor—from the nature of cognition itself to its communal practice and its embeddedness in a cultural milieu that ineluctably shapes and informs its conceptual apparatus. To frame this discussion, we draw on the work of Ludwik Fleck, a Polish-Jewish physician-scientist who developed the first system of historical philosophy and sociology of science.[1] Writing thirty years before Thomas Kuhn's landmark book *The Structure of Scientific Revolutions*, Fleck's groundbreaking work *The Genesis and Development of a Scientific Fact* gives a compelling account of the social processes that lie behind the practice of science and generation of scientific knowledge.[2] Fleck provides a powerful framework for illuminating the development of neuroscience, particularly how history and social context have shaped the objects of its investigations into human morality.

The primary exemplar Fleck uses to articulate his theory is that of "the carnal scourge," which by the end of the fifteenth century had spread to epidemic proportions. Until the end of the nineteenth century, the "carnal scourge" was perceived as a single disease. For a number of historically contingent reasons, scientists in the late nineteenth and early twentieth centuries began to understand the carnal scourge as a conglomeration of diseases.[3] Eventually, several diseases were disambiguated from this more global diagnosis and were established as discrete disease entities, including the entity that we now know as syphilis. In his case study, Fleck traces not only the social processes by which syphilis was disambiguated from other diseases, but also how the scientific community succeeded in translating its new ideas to the widest possible community—society—so that the entire configuration of syphilis as a medical and scientific phenomenon became culturally taken for granted. In other words, Fleck describes how syphilis emerged as a medical and scientific "fact." To be clear, no one now denies that the spirochete *Treponema pallidum* is a real thing in the world. But Fleck demonstrates that the emergence of the spirochete as a new object of scientific knowledge required a social process of knowledge generation, winnowing, and articulation.[4] He outlines moreover how, given the ways bodies respond to the spirochete, different aspects of syphilis's medical presentation resulted in various ways of imagining the disease and forged the creation of new scientific projects.[5]

We will focus on three key components of Fleck's analysis—the nature of cognition, his notion of thought-collectives (which we will call thought-communities), and the ways that thought-collectives interact in the development of scientific knowledge. We begin with cognition. We often imagine thinking to be a solitary activity—captured so well in Descartes's depiction of the cogitator discovering his lone self, co-extensive with his own mind. Fleck upends this Cartesian myth by recognizing that thinking itself is inescapably social. As he notes:

> Cognition is the most socially-conditioned activity of man [*sic*], and knowledge is the paramount social creation [Gebilde]. The very structure of language presents a compelling philosophy characteristic of [a] community, and even a single word can represent a complex theory. To whom do these philosophies and theories belong?[6]

In other words, our embeddedness in social realities thoroughly perfuses every component of thinking—each word, our very linguistic structures, the "philosophies" that inchoately accompany those linguistic structures, as well as the range of theories required for scientific discovery. All of these we acquire only from other people.

Fleck is interested not only in the social constructedness of the building blocks of our cognition. He is in fact more interested in tracing the social dynamics of its movement, development, and creativity. Unpacking how thought circulates and is refined, he further asks:

> Whose thought is it that continues to circulate? It is one that obviously belongs not to any single individual but to the collective. Whether an individual constitutes it as truth or error, understands it correctly or not, a set of findings meanders through the community, becoming polished, transformed, reinforced, or attenuated, while influencing other findings, concept formation, opinions, and habits of thought.[7]

Thus, thoughts, concepts, ideas, and theories circulate through a community of like-minded persons, who are engaged in a collective process of sharing, shaping, developing, affirming, and transmitting this material to others. In other words, a theory only exists as the set of ideas held by like-minded persons: "What actually thinks within a person is not the individual himself but his social community."[8] In this way, even what counts as an object for scientific investigation emerges from the conceptual work of the community of scientists.

This communal dynamic of scientific inquiry intrigues Fleck the most. He traces the lively debates about what we now know as syphilis as they ebbed and flowed over four centuries, from those inclined to differentiate syphilis as early as the fifteenth century due to responsivity to mercury treatments to those physicians who doubted its existence altogether. For example, as late as the end of the nineteenth century, Josef Hermann, a leading researcher, believed that constitutional syphilis did not exist, claiming that, what we now call syphilis was simply a sequelae of gonorrhoea and chancre and that it is "simple, local disease which never spread to the human blood, is completely curable, never leaves permanent effects, and is never propagated by procreation and heredity."[9]

It was finally at the turn of the twentieth century, in the early years of the development of many different scientific techniques, methodologies, and approaches to biological disorders, that syphilis began to be disambiguated as a scientific fact. Microbiology, immunology, public health, and practical medical approaches were at work, all developing different approaches to understanding the carnal scourge, forwarding approaches that were often at odds with each other.

As Fleck's account makes clear, scientific endeavors are notoriously conservative. While the ideas and concepts of a larger, mainstream scientific community are at once malleable and resilient, science at heart is a conserving discipline. Once ideas and concepts and theories have gained a foothold, they resist being pushed aside:

> Once a structurally complete and closed system of opinions consisting of many details and relations has been formed, it offers enduring resistance to anything that contradicts it. A striking example of this tendency is given by our history of the concept of "carnal scourge" in its prolonged endurance against every new notion. What we are faced with here is not so much simple passivity or mistrust of new ideas as an active approach which can be divided into several stages.[10]

Why do dominant scientific concepts so strongly resist modification or abandonment? Fleck gives five main reasons for the resistance of conceptual frameworks:

> (1) A contradiction to the system appears unthinkable. (2) What does not fit into the system remains unseen. (3) Alternatively, if it is noticed, either it is kept secret, or (4) laborious efforts are made to explain an exception in terms that do not contradict the system. (5) Despite the legitimate claims of contradictory views, one tends to see, describe, or even illustrate those circumstances which corroborate current views and thereby give them substance.[11]

In the end, it takes a lot of data to overthrow an established theory. When new data arise that do not fit a particular theory, rather than overthrow the theory, it is not uncommon for scientists to come up with ad hoc hypotheses to save a theory from the discordant data. It is easier to convince the larger community of scientists of an ad hoc hypothesis than to convince the group that the theory might be wrong. Because of their social nature, theories are too strong to just overthrow with every novel finding. In other words, theories circumscribe what can be thought. The novelty of a new scientific finding is still bounded by older and traditionally accepted truth claims of the community of scientists.

Fleck refers to this community of scientists as a *Denkkollectiv*, a thought-collective. A thought-collective simply is "a community of persons mutually exchanging ideas or maintaining intellectual interaction."[12] Despite the cognitive nomenclature, a thought-collective has a constant dynamism and a sort of three-dimensionality. As Sady notes:

> Members of that collective not only adopt certain ways of perceiving and thinking, but they also continually transform it—and this transformation does occur not so much "in their heads" as in their interpersonal space.[13]

For Fleck, thought-collectives infuse all areas of human interaction. They may be as fleeting as an individual conversation or last over generations in the form of religious movements, folk traditions, art, science, and more. As Sady notes, "long-lasting collectives create social institutions which enable and regulate the method by which next generations are added to a given collective: educational systems and social rituals accompanying the admission of new members."[14]

Thus, scientific thought-collectives—or as we will refer to them going forward, thought-communities—are for Fleck one manifestation of the broader category of thought-communities. They could be as large as the community of scientists or as small as a community of microbiologists or neurobiologists, or even as small as a group that specializes in a particular methodological approach within microbiology or neurobiology. Regardless of size, thought-communities depend on the shared language, assumptions, and understandings that permit the thought-community to get on with its work.

What emerges from a thought-community, particularly if it perdures over time, Fleck names a thought-style. A thought-style is the way in which a thought-collective thinks together about questions. Sometimes a thought-style emerges from a particular kind of scientific community, sometimes from a different set of methodologies, sometimes from a different set of theories, or even from various models of the entity being studied. It provides a shared set of theories, models, and methodologies within which one scientist's ideas are put to the test by other scientists. Of necessity, these tools shape the kinds of questions asked and the kinds of facts that emerge from their investigations. A thought-style enables the work of a scientific thought-community to advance, given what they have already accepted as true.

When a thought-style becomes sufficiently refined and specialized, the thought-community forms what Fleck calls an "esoteric circle"—a variety of specialists who gatekeep and advance that particular thought-style. One of the largest groups within an esoteric scientific community are mainstream scientists, who largely resist modification and will struggle to maintain the coherency of the concepts generated by that style of thought in the face of contradictory information, even as the style itself incrementally changes over time. Thus, thirty years prior to the publication of *The Structure of Scientific Revolutions*, Fleck described the conservative dimension of what Thomas Kuhn calls normal science.[15] What Kuhn labels "normal science," Fleck refers to as the main body of the esoteric scientific community. The normal science generated by scientists fits within the structure of what it is possible for the group to think. Anything that does not fit, if it is noticed at all, is unthinkable, not seen, suppressed, or explained away.

Thus, when scientists begin to question theories, they do so carefully. The thought-style of a mainstream scientific community defines the space and delimits (and even constricts) what can be thought. Yet when "laborious efforts" are made over and over again to explain discordant data that seems to contradict the system—in other words, to save a particular theory—some scientists become dissatisfied. They are willing to set aside the theory and to play with new configurations. In doing so, they are often scorned by their colleagues in the thought-collective who adheres to the regnant theory of the day. They cordon themselves off into smaller groups that push the boundaries, hoping to overhaul what the larger community of scientists think they know to be true. Fleck refers to these outlaws who abandon the circumscribed thinking of the larger community of mainstream scientists as the vanguard. This vanguard—which in some way might be seen as an esoteric circle within an esoteric community—share together a thought-style that they all understand, however small this circle might be. In challenging the thought-style of the larger thought-community, their ideas are often considered unpredictable, radical, or even dangerous.

Vanguard scientific thought-communities arise all the time, especially in moments where data are discordant with extant theories or when science is in crisis.[16] Sometimes these creative, small, thought-communities will find no novel insights; and at other times, they will give birth to innovative approaches to their questions or to break through theoretical insights, as when, in the history of physics, quantum physics began to push against the limitations of Newtonian physics. While a successful vanguard community begins small, it imagines the possibilities in ways that the mainstream scientific community could not have done. The creative scientist will throw caution to the wind and imagine hitherto unthought of solutions to the questions and puzzling data, and possibly even imagine other questions that the dominant thought-community could not. But until the vanguard circle produces data, they will be thought foolish, or at times utterly ridiculous. The constriction of the mainstream scientific thought-community's thinking results in a kind of irrational conservatism that resists the evidence produced by the smaller group of radicals.

As such, thought-styles not only define an intellectual identity for a coterie of scientists; they also provide a marker by which a particular scientific community demarcates itself from others. Depending on the proximity of shared thought-styles, scientists from different thought-communities may be able to communicate with each other and with non-specialist communities to varying degrees. Sometimes a thought-community is very esoteric, comprising only a small number of people. But if it is successful, its ideas begin to percolate into ever-widening circles of different thought-communities. Fleck calls these exoteric communities—those who "are under the influence of the [thought] style but do not play an active role in its formation."[17]

The largest exoteric community is society itself. What had been accepted as the "carnal scourge" by the larger community became a question in the esoteric community of scientists, until more and more knowledge came to light, calling the accepted fact into question in a way that only the esoteric thought-community could understand. Then over time the facts about syphilis move back into the larger exoteric community, where it remains today for us, a fact.

Put differently, the vector is not unidirectional; influence does not move simply from the esoteric community to the exoteric community. While often invisible, the exoteric community recursively forms and informs esoteric scientific communities. At times this influence drives scientific conservativism. As Fleck narrates in vivid detail, throughout its history, the medical-scientific conceptualizations of syphilis were deeply interwoven with ethical-religious-mystical frames. Notions of "a change in blood" intertwined with convictions that "the disease [was] a punishment for sinful lust," sent by "God, Who has sent it because He wants Mankind to shun the sin of fornication."[18] Such religious—and even astrological—beliefs inhibited mainstream scientists from thinking differently about the disease.[19]

At other times, however, it is the exoteric community that enables radical innovations or new ways of seeing within a particular scientific discipline. As Sady notes:

> Sometimes new ideas come from unexpected directions and without any relation to science itself. This is how Fleck explains the discovery of spermatozoon which happened together with the fall of political absolutism and popularization of the idea of individual freedom understood mainly as freedom of personal movement. One could not discover spermatozoon just looking through a microscope. However, someone, who thought about a free person, could notice freely moving—so "free"—spermatozoa. This was the influence of environment which created a restless mood necessary for searching for something new. And a new mode of thinking created in a different domain of life allowed one to perceive, distinguish, and describe it in a way which would stimulate reflections of others— those participating in revolutionary social changes as well.[20]

In other words, often the spark behind novel scientific insights comes from new ways of thinking—social, religious, philosophical, artistic, and more—derived from the broader social contexts in which both science and scientists are immersed.[21]

This larger exoteric community might also be referred to as possessing a social imaginary. Sociologist John Thompson coined the term "social imaginary," defining it as the "creative and symbolic dimension of the social world, the dimension through which human beings create their ways of living together and their ways of representing their collective life."[22] Philosopher Charles Taylor, in his book *Modern Social Imaginaries*, further fleshes out the idea of a social imaginary as "the ways people 'imagine' their social existence, how they fit together with others, how things go on between them and their fellows, the expectations that are normally met, and the deeper normative notions and images that underlie these expectations."[23] Thus, social imaginaries are rather inchoate and squishy. They can be carried in "images, stories, and legends."[24] Larger communities, cultures, and societies hold to these imaginaries and make possible common practices. Standing behind them is a kind of metaphysical moral order that is often imprecisely defined but nonetheless present.

Taylor notes that scientific theories are informed by social imaginaries even if a social imaginary is itself not a theory.[25] Scientific theories move into the social imaginary, as Taylor notes, through the activity of elite thinkers in a society. These popularizers in turn begin to shape the social imaginary of the larger society, while the social imaginary makes possible the interplay between the scientific community and the mainstream community.[26] A social imaginary makes it possible for science to emerge from a society, and it makes it possible for the science to shape society and the social imaginary itself.

Certainly, reality exists, but how we envisage, conceptualize, and then respond to that reality emerges within a community of shared understanding. Fleck helps make clear that science is primarily a social endeavor. Put differently, even the facts of a real entity, the spirochete *Treponema pallidum*, for example, emerge through a social process; that is to say, facts are socially constructed. To say that facts are socially constructed does not deny the existence of the entity that we call *Treponema pallidum*, but it turns our attention to those broader social factors that enable particular "facts" to gain the status of scientific truth and to, then, reinforce the elements of the social imaginary that originally made them possible.

But what of the process of establishing facts about those things that exist in a different way than something like *Treponema pallidum*, things like "morality" or "virtue" or "vice" or the "economy"—if they can be called "things" at all? This is a bit more complicated. These "things" emerge through what Michel Foucault calls regimes of truth. Fleck, writing at a time when Foucault was a mere child, already anticipates the problems that Foucault would spend his life trying to understand. How does the practice of psychiatry establish madness as a thing to be treated and investigated? What does the medical subject contribute to the objects—diseases—upon which it gazes? How does criminality emerge as an object of scientific investigation out of the practices of incarceration? How does knowledge create power that is then leveraged for the creation of new knowledge?

Apropos to our project that pieces together the thought-communities that make possible neuroscience, Foucault says of his work in his lectures published as *Birth of Biopolitics*:

> The point of all these investigations concerning madness, disease, delinquency, sexuality . . . is to show how the coupling of a set of practices and a regime of truth form an apparatus of knowledge-power that effectively marks out in reality that which does not exist and legitimately submits it to the division between true and false . . . [T]he moment when that which does not exist is inscribed in reality, and when that which does not exist comes under a legitimate regime of the true and false, marks the birth of this dissymmetrical biopolarity of politics and the economy. Politics and the economy are not things that exist, or errors, or illusions, or ideologies. They are things that do not exist and yet which are inscribed in reality and fall under a regime of truth dividing the true and the false.[27]

Put differently, Foucault wants to understand how it is that something that does not exist in the same way as, say, an entity like *Treponema pallidum* or a brain, comes to be thought of as a "thing." In a way, our task in this book is to try to see how neurobiological things—genes, amygdala, prefrontal cortex—are correlated to socially scientifically constructed things—virtue, vice, morality, economy. Only by getting behind these processes will we discover more precisely how the neuroscience of morality is engaged in establishing a regime of truth that can then be operationalized to control human behavior.

Prior to analyzing the discourse on the neuroscience of morality, we first had to ask: what do we mean then by the term "neuroscience"? Following Fleck, it seems logical to begin with the esoteric thought-community (the neuroscientific community) that shares a thought-style. Yet, as quickly became clear, this is a rather difficult task, insofar as neuroscience is not a distinct discipline as such. Rather, the emergent field of "the neurosciences" as it has taken shape since the late 1960s is an interdisciplinary mélange. It attempts to combine and correlate the findings of several distinct sciences, including psychology, psychiatry, neurology, neuropsychiatry, sociology, economics, behavioral politics, genetics, and neurobiology.[28] Each of these separate domains—for example neurobiology and sociology—has its separate thought-style, its theories, its separate methodologies, its experimental models, its distinct objects of inquiry, and its distinct purposes, all of which combine to give us the results and conclusions of a particular scientific investigation. Neuroscience is an attempt to bring these distinct thought-communities together into a single thought-community. Thus, as we proceed, we will use the term "neuroscience" to indicate this new field that is creating a new thought-community; it is struggling to find its thought-style, and as we will see in the course of this book, there are difficulties in doing so not only insofar as they are attempting to meld a diversity of thought-communities; they are further attempting to find correlations between two very different sorts of things—biological entities and human moral behavior.

To be certain, neurobiology deals with things like brains, neurons, and brain structures such as the amygdala, or the cortex, or the prefrontal cortex—things that exist independent of our knowledge of them. Yet, we can ask whether a structure like the amygdala should be thought of as a separate entity, since it is interconnected with other structures that together perform a function that exceeds what the amygdala could do alone. Neurobiology also deals with things like genes or brains, which exist as entities even if we do not know about them. Yet, we can still ask the question about whether genes that have mutations should be thought of as different things from "normal" genes, or whether genes should be thought of as a constellation of genes that qua constellation should be thought of as an entity.

However, as important as these questions are, our task here is to explore how neuroscience sets for itself the task of correlating neurobiological things with the psychological and social "things," specifically "things" like virtue, vice, morality, and economy. As we will show, these social scientific "things" must be understood as emerging from thought-communities that have different thought-styles. So, while there are neurobiological thought-collectives and social scientific thought-collectives, neuroscience is itself emerging as a community of two different thought-collectives.

Throughout this book, we will refer to these different thought-collectives adjectivally, as neurobiological, or social scientific, or neuroscientific thought-styles, thought-collectives, and thought-communities.

In addition, as Fleck pointed out, these thought-styles do eventually rise to the level of society as a whole. Insofar as neuroscience has become part of the scientifically sophisticated culture of the late modern West, it imbues the exoteric lay, mainstream thought-community. Books like *Evil Genes* or *Murderous Minds*, or *The Righteous Mind*, or *The Moral Landscape*, or *The Moral Molecule* make sense because to some extent "neuroscience" has made its way into the exoteric community such that neuroscientific approaches to moral matters can make sense to nonscientific audiences. The reason that neuroscience can move easily from the neuroscientific thought-community into the mainstream thinking of Western cultures is because they share something in common, namely a social imaginary.

Part I of this book describes this process by which scientific ideas move from the vanguard of the esoteric community to the larger exoteric community. It sets out the neuroscientific narrative of morality and traces how that narrative moves seamlessly into our broader social context. Chapters 1 and 2 set out the ways that the thought-communities make possible the neuroscientific understanding of vices and virtues, respectively. Chapter 3 describes how neuroscience is popularized and moves into larger, mainstream culture by what Fleck refers to as general specialists. At the end of Part I, we will claim that this movement of neuroscientific concepts into the mainstream community is possible not only because the exoteric community and neuroscience share a social imaginary. We will claim that this movement is possible because the shared social imaginary has seeded the matrix of ideas, concepts, and philosophy that has made the neuroscience of morality possible. Taylor has identified "the economy" as the dominant way that social imaginary of the twenty-first century makes itself known.[29] Part II of this book will make this social imaginary explicit and trace how it has come down to us today from the eighteenth, nineteenth, and early twentieth centuries as "economics," framing our understandings of both science and morality. This task of establishing this economic social imaginary sets the agenda for the quest that is neuroscience.

Part I

# The Neuroscientific Narrative of Morality

# 1

# The Neuroscientific Narrative of Vice

We live in a cultural moment when a mixture of scientific and popular imagination has created a buzz around neuroscience and moral behavior. With popular titles like *The Science of Evil: On Empathy and the Origins of Cruelty* and *The New Evil: Understanding the Emergence of Modern Violent Crime*, our culture seems enraptured with vice.[1]

Yet this popular literature amplifies a conversation that begins in the specialist, esoteric thought-community of neuroscience. For example, in a 2006 commentary titled "Genes for Susceptibility to Violence Lurk in the Brain," Essi Viding and Uta Frith, two leading developmental neuropsychologists, summarize findings from a study by Andreas Meyer-Lindenberg et al.[2] Here, healthy volunteers with a functional polymorphism in the promoter region of the monoamine oxidase-A (MAOA) gene showed smaller and more hyper-responsive amygdalae and less active cingulate cortexes, brain regions correlated with emotional regulation.[3] Viding and Frith characterize these findings as "exciting" because they seem to show the missing link between genotypes and impulsive, violent behavior; that missing link is the brain. Viding and Frith claim that genes (the MAOA gene among others) leave a so-called neural signature on the brain that predisposes individuals to impulsive aggression—in other words, "genotype differences show in the brain."[4] They find studies like Meyer-Lindenberg's to provide "an important theoretical advance in our knowledge about the brain basis of reactive violence."[5] Connecting these findings with other studies that have analyzed genetic factors, Viding and Frith hypothesize that antisocial traits manifest behaviorally when brains are marked with neural signatures. Put differently, genes "make" the brain; genes confer "bad" behavior; the source of antisocial behavior—what was classically referred to as vice—is in the brain.[6]

Thus, for some in the field of neuroscience, the hunt is on for genetic or neural "signatures" that indicate a predisposition to socially disadvantageous traits. This chapter unpacks this literature, examining how the neurosciences theorize vice in relation to the brain and the environment. If morality—having evolved through human history as a natural, biologically instantiated mechanism—is driven by neuromodulators within neural substrates, then neuroscientists can dissect the functional anatomy underlying antisocial behavior to lay bare the nature of human morality; or so the story goes. This story we name *the neuroscientific narrative of vice*.

We noted in the Introduction that it is complicated to track notions of morality in scientific journals, as they attempt to avoid evaluative moral language in order to appear morally neutral. Thus, we will argue, within the neurosciences, "immoral behavior" or "vice" takes as its proxy "antisocial behavior." Likewise, we will see in Chapter 2, "moral behavior" or "virtue" takes as its proxy "prosocial attitudes and behaviors." It is not simply that evaluative language is stripped from the neuroscientific gaze; rather, we argue that neuroscience translates complex moral discourse into terms that match its objectifying, and arguably thinned, aims. Once neuroscience has recast moral discourse in its self-serving terms, each of these constructs—antisocial and prosocial behaviors—is then operationalized, or harnessed, for measurement.

Although seemingly more clinical or objective than more traditional moral language, these constructs have powerful moral valence.[7] They carry with them tacit social, political, and economic assumptions that inevitably color the science. Neuroscientific research is driven not only by the pursuit of knowledge for its own sake, but it also seeks practical outcomes, often couched in terms of helping those who are suffering from psychopathologies. Neuroscience hopes that by identifying environmental and neurobiological determinants of antisocial traits, society might be able to intervene in order to prevent or disrupt antisocial behaviors, the proxy for vice. These interventions, ideally, would be aimed at the level of the body or the brain of those who have been pathologized. Humanity, via scientific prowess, can fix itself.

Yet as the very proxies themselves make clear, this conceptualization of morality itself is not strictly scientific. Thus, in this chapter, we begin to illuminate the moral, political, and philosophical assumptions that constitute the neuroscientific narrative of vice. We examine the ways that social scientific concepts are correlated to neurobiological concepts. The neuroscientific narrative of vice brings together two distinct scientific thought-communities with distinct thought-styles—the thought-community of neurobiology and the thought-community of the human sciences.[8] As such, the neurosciences run into the challenge faced by all human social sciences, namely, finding ways of naming their objects. The leading method for defining objects of inquiry in the human sciences is known as conceptual funneling. We demonstrate this process by analyzing two key concepts adopted by neuroscience from the human sciences—namely, socioeconomic status (SES) and antisocial personality disorder (ASPD). As ASPD has become a proxy for vice, the proxy for "environment" in the search for neural signatures is operationalized as SES. But the conceptual funnel is always dependent upon the social context in which it is developed. Thus, we briefly recount here the broader histories of the concepts of SES and ASPD as well as of the field of psychiatry in order to demonstrate the ways in which the truth about human behavior is inevitably politically and morally charged.

## The Socioeconomic Brain—a Tale of Two Sciences

The emergent field of the neurosciences seeks to fuse multiple scientific disciplines typically categorized under the two broad domains of the biological and human sciences. To illustrate how this works in practice, we begin by describing several neuroscientific studies carried out by a research group at the University of Pittsburgh. Peter Gianaros, a neuropsychologist, typically examines the interface between structural and functional brain anatomy and SES. Stephen Manuck, also a neuropsychologist, typically uses neurohormonal and neurotransmitter activity to study brain function in relation to SES.

While the neuroscientific literature is vast, we have selected the work of Gianaros and Manuck as representative—and, in fact, exemplary—for a number of reasons. First, through the work of their respective labs, both researchers have compiled a portfolio of rather careful neuroscientific studies. Their neurobiological work is solid and well respected, and their use of the human sciences represents well the interests, objectives, and methods of that domain. Second, their work seeks to discover an interface between social factors, specifically SES, and the physical and mental health of individuals; thus, they provide an exemplar of how neuroscience fuses the social and biological sciences. Third, the types of studies they do exemplify a key focus of the neurosciences, namely, the relationship of environment-to-brain and brain-to-environment. For Gianaros and Manuck, the arrow of causation moves from social-environmental influences to the way that the brain functions, which then might shape social behaviors. For other neuroscientists, the vector points in the opposite direction, as they seek to discover the ways that genes shape brains and that brains subsequently shape behavior, resulting in social context. Finally, their work—separately and together in collaborative studies—demonstrates how the environment, imagined as economics and operationalized as SES, has become a primary research variable posited as causative of behavior.

Before turning to their specific studies, let us provide a brief overview of neuroanatomy and neurophysiology, as a basic understanding of the neurobiology of genes, neurotransmitters, and brain structures is required in order to follow the research we engage in Part I. Some simple conceptions of human brain anatomy, which will be sufficient for our purposes in this work, conceive of the brain as a tripartite structure. The *brain stem* allows for autonomous functions such as breathing and temperature regulation. Above and surrounding the brainstem, deeper structures of the cerebral hemispheres, sometimes referred to as the *"reptilian"* or *"limbic" brain*, allow for quick-time (unconscious) reactive processes in response to environmental demand (such as threat). The outer, so-called *cortical areas* of the hemispheres are associated with higher-order cognitive processes like language and cognitive control (including autobiography, self-awareness, and underlying unconscious response to threat and/or modulation of emotions generated from limbic areas).

Our work will concentrate on the limbic and cortical areas. These areas work in such intricate association that it would be difficult to define an exact boundary point between them, and the areas of research we will elucidate are often focused along this seamless boundary. In fact, this transitional space is sometimes simply called *the corticolimbic area*. Structures associated with the corticolimbic areas of the brain include: the amygdala, hippocampus, nucleus accumbens, and cingulate gyrus. These are known to play an important role in emotion and behavioral regulation. The amygdala—an almond-shaped limbic brain area—is sensitive to affective and contextual cues, especially those having to do with the response to threat and fear (popularized as the "fight or flight" response). These regions are intricately connected to the hypothalamic-pituitary-adrenal (HPA) axis and regulate the function of peripheral hormones, like prolactin (PrL), oxytocin, dopamine, adrenaline, and corticosteroids.

This is the brain structure at a "macro" level. At the "micro" level, neurotransmitters, as instruments of communication, are vital to that most basic interaction that happens between one nerve cell and the next. For instance, serotonin (alongside dopamine and norepinephrine) is one of several dominant neurotransmitters. As will be discussed later in this chapter, serotonin's role in emotion and behavior has been followed closely since investigations in the mid-twentieth century found that its activity and metabolism played a major role in human physiology and pathophysiology (including early hypotheses about its implication in the evolution of mood disorders, such as the early monoamine hypothesis of depression).[9] Serotonin is produced in the raphe nucleus of the brain stem, and from there it is distributed widely to cortical and especially limbic areas of the brain. Serotonin's variable metabolism and activity have been correlated with trait variation in impulsiveness, negative affectivity (or neuroticism), and aggressive disposition. Serotonin metabolism and brain responsivity to serotonin figure highly in research focused on depression, anxiety, substance abuse, impulsive aggression (including criminal violence), as well as ASPD. For example, persons with histories of attempted or completed suicide show low cerebrospinal fluid concentrations of 5-hydroxyindoleacetic acid (5-HIAA), a metabolite of 5-HT (serotonin), when compared to control subjects.[10]

Likewise, outward aggression, especially of an impulsive, unpremeditated nature, has been associated with poor central nervous system (CNS) serotonin responsivity.[11] Variability in CNS serotonergic responsivity is thought to reflect an enduring trait-like neurobiological dimension of individual differences.[12] That is to say, people who are depressed to the point of suicide and people who are impulsive in anger responses tend to have lower activity in the HPA axis and thus have lower PrL levels in their blood. The degree of serotonergic responsivity, researchers suggest, links to psychological traits like neuroticism (or negative affectivity) and impulsivity. Such traits have been implicated in the development of various personality disorders, such as antisocial personality.

But serotonin itself cannot be measured. Thus, to study brain serotonergic responsivity, neuroscientists often use the neuropharmacological stimulator fenfluramine. Fenfluramine stimulates serotonin-releasing neurons or neurons expressing serotonin receptors to increase serotonergic neurotransmission. In persons with a typically functioning HPA axis, giving fenfluramine will stimulate the HPA axis and increase the level of PrL secreted; PrL can be measured in blood very easily and thus serves as a good biomarker for activity in HPA axis. Thus, via a fenfluramine challenge, neuroscientists can measure the activity of the corticolimbic system and the HPA axis. As such, the fenfluramine challenge serves as an index for the way the serotonin system functions physiologically in vivo and for indirectly tracking serotonergic response.

Several studies use the fenfluramine challenge.[13] Among these are the work of Gianaros and Manuck. In a series of studies published between 2004 and 2010, these neuroscientists—separately and together—explored the relationships between neurophysiology, neuroanatomy, and SES. Here we see the findings of one thought-community (neurophysiology and neuroanatomy) correlated with the findings of another thought-community (social science). Individually, they hypothesized that prolonged stress of low SES would mark or change the physiological neurotransmitter response of the HPA axis, rendering it less functional than in those persons living without the stress of low SES. SES, in other words, would leave a signature on the brain in both its structure and function. In order to show that the HPA axis is marked in those living in poverty in a society, they tested the HPA axis of subjects who had grown up in poverty by giving them a dose of fenfluramine. Low SES, they hypothesized, should cause a disruption in the working of the HPA axis, which would be indicated by lower PrL levels when given fenfluramine.

We begin with Manuck. In a 2004 paper, Manuck and colleagues explored the relationship between SES, serotonergic responsivity, and a polymorphic gene for serotonin reuptake.[14] This study showed that persons living in lower SES—as measured by educational and income levels—exhibited smaller PrL responses after a fenfluramine challenge. Other studies have confirmed this relationship of SES and serotonergic response.[15] This study suggests that something about SES shapes the way that the corticolimbic system and the HPA axis have been trained to respond. However, in this study, the only subjects that showed this lower level response were those with a genetic polymorphism of the serotonin transporter gene (5-HTT). A polymorphic gene is not an abnormal gene; rather, it is a gene that produces a protein that is functional, but just functions differently than the gene present in most people in a population. In other words, *all* people living in lower SES did not have attenuated activity of the corticolimbic system and the HPA axis. Only those subjects living in lower SES who *also* had a genetic variant showed that SES further affected PrL levels.[16] To summarize, a gene that appears to produce lower levels of the serotonin transporter, interacting with an environment of influence (low SES), modulated the expression of a neurobiological trait, serotonin responsivity, relative to controls.

Behind this hypothesis is the assumption that growing up in poverty affects brain development and function, which then affects behaviors. As noted earlier, diminished serotonin responsivity has been associated with negative affectivity, impulsivity, and antisociality, a point to which we shall return more forcefully later. Manuck et al. did not, however, *show* that low SES resulted in negative affectivity, impulsivity, and antisociality in their study population. Rather, they only showed that those subjects with a polymorphic gene who lived under conditions of low SES had downregulated PrL levels. Yet despite the fact that they did not assay the link between this polymorphism, corticolimbic system/HPA axis responsivity and behavior, Gianaros and Manuck *infer* a possible connection to negative behavioral traits. To make this inference, they draw on the work of other scientists. Some have noted an association between "a 44-bp insertion/deletion polymorphism in the 5_ regulatory region of the serotonin transporter (5-HTT) gene [and] behavioral phenotypes as diverse as anxiety-related personality traits, various psychopathologies (e.g., affective disorders, alcoholism, bulimia nervosa, autism), late onset Alzheimer's disease, and cardiovascular reactions to psychological stress cardiovascular reactions to psychological stress."[17] Other labs have observed lower PrL levels in patients who have attempted suicide relative to non-suicidal controls following a fenfluramine challenge.[18]

Manuck and colleagues subsequently conducted a second study in 2005 entitled "The Socioeconomic Status of Communities Predicts Variation in Brain Serotonergic Responsivity."[19] This study is unique in its careful probing of SES along lines that go beyond typical individual or subjective measures of SES. In this study, Manuck and colleagues measured a different set of indicators to focus on what they termed "community SES." They used census tract data as an index of area-wide SES. Area-wide data included things like costs of housing, median household income, rates of poverty and unemployment, as well as indicators of social fragmentation, such as the number of single-person households, pensioners, or unmarried individuals residing in a community. In other words, in this study SES is pegged according to nonsubjective and non-individual measures of SES.[20]

In this 2005 study, Manuck and colleagues used the same *individual* measure of SES as they had used in their 2004 study, but also added different and unique *community* measures of SES. Results from the study suggested the following: "When compared with residents of more advantaged communities, individuals living in census tracts having a lower median income, higher rates of poverty, unemployment, and public assistance, higher costs of renting (relative to income), and lower property values showed diminished CNS serotonergic responsivity, as indicated by a blunted PrL response to the serotonin agonist, fenfluramine."[21] These effects were in addition to impacts at the individual level of socioeconomic position (income level and years of education) from prior studies. Not only were individuals' serotonin responsivity blunted by their individual SES, but their serotonin responsivity was additionally diminished by a unique and separate factor—the SES of the community in which these individuals resided. This community-based impact on serotonin responsivity was, however, independent of the serotonin transporter gene polymorphism. Undeterred, they opine that "it is possible, of course, that genetic variation elsewhere equally influences the community association with brain serotonergic responsivity."[22]

While this fascinating research suggests that one's census tract (traditionally called the neighborhood or community) has an impact on an individual's neural functioning underpinning the dynamics of emotional and moral life, again Manuck et al. did *not show* that people living in communities with lower SES or that individuals with variations in the 5-HTTLPR (serotonin transporter) gene display more negative affectivity, impulsivity, or antisociality. Nonetheless, they conclude that "These findings may be relevant to reported effects of low community SES on the prevalence of psychiatric disorders or behaviors associated with dysregulated central serotonergic function, such as depression, impulsive aggression, and suicide."[23] In fact, most of their introduction to this article outlines these correlations. Moreover, in their discussion, they engage research correlating community SES with the NEO Personality Inventory, noting that persons living in less-advantaged communities tended to describe "themselves as less conscientious on a scale that taps characteristics such as resourcefulness, persistence, self-discipline, and achievement, motivation."[24] Thus again, despite a lack of direct causality, this research on the relationship between SES, genes, and neurobiology is set within a larger project seeking to infer connections between morality, neurobiology, and economics.

In 2007, Manuck teamed up with Gianaros and other colleagues to take a different approach. In this study, they examine SES's *structural* and functional impact on the brain here using a different mode of analysis, namely, MRI and fMRI.[25] In addition, rather than an objective measure of SES, this study used a subjective measure of SES, the MacArthur Scale of Subjective Social Status.[26] It asked subjects to mark their own perceived level of SES.[27] The results were mixed. People who reported that they perceived themselves in a low SES had a smaller volume of gray matter in the anterocingulate cortex, a part of the corticolimbic system, as well as the HPA axis. However, there was no correlation between objective individual SES and gray matter volume in the anterocingulate gyrus, nor between community SES and gray matter volume. In other words, the studies using MRI and fMRI did not show a robust correlation between SES and activity of the corticolimbic system.

Nonetheless, Gianaros and Manuck spend most of the discussion section of the paper speculating on possible alternative mechanisms to correlate these entities and further with negative behavioral traits. As they conclude:

> To build on the present findings, an important next step will be to determine the social, environmental and possibly genetic factors that characterize individuals who perceive themselves as holding a low social standing and who exhibit structural changes in the pACC *that may reciprocally relate to maladaptive forms of behavioral and physiological reactivity* to psychosocial stress. More broadly, we hold that in the context of vulnerability and resilience to psychiatric and other medical disorders, it is unlikely that the pACC functions independently of other networked corticolimbic areas, such as the amygdala and hippocampus, whose net activity mediates complex neurobehavioral processes.[28]

In other words, in spite of lack of evidence supporting this thesis, the connection between SES, neurophysiology, and "maladaptive" behaviors continues to be presumed and pursued.

In 2010, Gianaros and Manuck bring their work together with that of others in a jointly authored review article entitled "Neurobiological Pathways Linking Socioeconomic Position and Health."[29] Here they survey a series of neuropharmacological, molecular genetic, and neuroimaging studies that explore: (1) correlations between SES and the reactivity of certain brain regions, particularly the corticolimbic system—which, as we noted earlier, is essential for a person's engagement with the social environment; and (2) correlations between SES and the physiological mechanisms of the HPA axis—which depends on both genetic expression of various neurotransmitters (in this case serotonin) and the function of those neurotransmitters. Most of the research reviewed preceded and is presumed by their previous work outlined above, so there is little by way of new scientific findings.

Here they also acknowledge that the science on SES's structural impact on the brain as examined by MRI and fMRI is not very strong. Only Gianaros's own study, cited earlier, suggested an effect. But rather than seeing this finding as problematic for their thesis that SES marks the brain, Gianaros and Manuck conclude that what is needed is a finer grained objective standard for assessing SES. SES is just not a sufficient measure. They acknowledge that assaying social determinants of physical and mental health is not a straightforward matter. They engage in a robust discussion of the distinctive measures, including objective and subjective measures of SES. Arguing that multiple factors across a person's life in time, place, and development across a lifespan will shape their brains, they propose reconceptualizing SES as what they now term "Socioeconomic Position" (SEP).[30] In other words, here they suggest that it is one's *position* within the larger community (and not just one's *status*) that impacts the functioning of the brain.

They also note that many genetic and epigenetic phenomena are at work in this process, pointing specifically to the way that one's background community SES also participates in shaping health outcomes, including mental health outcomes, like depression, impulsivity, and antisocial personality traits. Gianaros and Manuck use a graphic representation to map the complexity of the interactions of SEP at the individual level up to the country level, across the life span of the individual, and as it relates to biological, genetic, psychological, and environmental/social levels, and as it relates to different subjective vs. objective measures of that position. In the midst of this representation they place an image of an individual's brain that is embedded in "multidimensional, multilevel, and life span considerations."[31]

But in the end, Gianaros and Manuck do not let weak data refute their hypothesis. Over against the fMRI studies cited, they find hope in functional neuroimaging evidence that points to perhaps the amygdala—another corticolimbic structure controlled by the anterocingulate gyrus—as the neural locus that may be affected by childhood socioeconomic factors. Again, moving to inferences beyond their research, they note that social information processing models in the brain suggest that people raised in disadvantaged socioeconomic environments seem to develop an early sensitivity to social threats, leading to dysregulation of emotional processing, which are the product of the corticolimbic system. In other words, if as a child one lives in an environment that is insecure, one might have trouble with emotional processing, resulting in antisocial and other behaviors. They also note that a different neuroimaging study showed a correlation between subjective perception of parental SEP and greater amygdala reactivity.[32] The amygdala is involved in the automatic fight or flight mechanism. In other words, people who perceived themselves as having been raised in lower SEP, had a more reactive amygdala when interpreting threatening faces. The thesis is that those raised in lower SEP are more likely to interpret social cues as threatening, and therefore more likely to lash out in impulsive antisocial ways.

Thus, given that the HPA axis and the function of the corticolimbic system seem to be involved in emotional regulation, and given that SES seems to have effects on the brains of people who suffer the stressors of low social status and poverty, there has been a push to understand the causal direction of these correlations. Gianaros, Manuck, and their colleagues are not alone in how deeply the larger frame imagining social functioning impels them to extrapolate from the conclusions of their research to implications for individual behavior. As we shall see later in this chapter, the neuroscientific narrative of vice seems to be rooted in the dysregulation of the corticolimbic system. For Naomi Sadeh and her colleagues, antisocial personality traits are traced to a function of serotonin uptake receptors and socioeconomic factors. But as Gianaros and Manuck clearly state: "The conceptual argument adopted here and elsewhere is that *the expression of socioeconomic health disparities depends on the embodiment by the brain* of socially stratified biological, psychological, social, and environmental factors linked to health and mortality across individuals, particularly in interaction with predisposing genetic risk and epigenetic plasticity."[33]

However, even when researchers are very careful, the ways they posit the interactions between genetic polymorphisms and socioeconomics, and in turn how they imagine these polymorphisms and socioeconomic factors to shape brain function and, therefore, behaviors, present numerous problems. One difficulty lies in defining SES. Gianaros and Manuck's shift from SES to SEP illustrates the importance of the social scientific conceptualization. It also points to the power of the larger, social, exoteric thought-community. Lacking a correlation between objective measures of SES and gray matter volume, Gianaros and Manuck conclude not that socioeconomic dimensions of the environment have no effect on the brain, but that what is needed is a new and better measure of socioeconomics.[34]

Additionally, there are difficulties in defining antisocial behavior. As we have noted, thought-styles in the human and social sciences are very different from neurobiological thought-styles, creating methodological missteps when researchers try simply to correlate findings. Different assumptions, theories, methods, and models animate each science, and they often do not overlap. But of equal concern is the creation of social scientific concepts themselves. Social scientific concepts are not easily disentangled from their social and political histories—in fact, such disentanglement may well be impossible. Yet two social scientific concepts lie at the heart of these studies—SES and ASPD. In the next section, we unpack the history and development of these concepts in order to better understand how they complicate neuroscientific claims.

## The Development of Concepts in Human Sciences

To posit a correlation between social environments and neurological functionality (through examination of the HPA axis or fMRI) requires the development of a theoretical interface between two distinct scientific domains—the human sciences and the biological sciences—with their concomitant different thought-styles, theories, models, and methods. Gianaros, for instance, uses a particular method of neuroimaging and analysis known as Voxel-based morphometry.[35] Utilizing Voxel-based morphometry to examine gray matter volumes is based on a host of other foundational physical sciences that suggest that Voxel-based morphometry is reasonable; it coheres, given what is accepted. Brain physiology and the techniques used to stimulate the corticolimbic and HPA axis in Manuck's studies or to image the functional anatomy in Gianaros's studies depend on a whole set of more basic scientific findings that equally derive from a web of foundational scientific theories, models, and methods, and ultimately a set of foundational assumptions in ontology. The same holds for foundational social, psychological, and economic scientific measures and concepts. Here, a distinct set of theories, models, and methods give legitimacy to, for example, objective or subjective measures of SES as well as discrete behavioral disorders such as ASPD. What is more, social, psychological, and economic scientific theories, models, and methods have their own idiosyncratic histories and are animated by their own implicit anthropologies, as we shall see in Chapters 4–6.

In other words, neuroscience—in seeking to fuse two domains of science—presumes that the conceptual apparatus of the physical sciences and the conceptual apparatus of the human sciences can simply be juxtaposed with one another without further articulating the theoretical and methodological interface between the two. This complexity is rendered even more confused by the multiple new modes of understanding brain science, including systems neuroscience methods that focus on complex interconnectivity via metaphors to computer program networking. These multiple and various discourses in the social and neurosciences do not easily correlate or overlap with one another and sometimes compete or contradict one another.

Consider, for example, the model used for studying serotonergic reactivity that is related by contemporary neuroscience to a clinical disorder—ASPD. On the one hand, we have a discourse that grows out of a focus on the micro-level of neurotransmitters at the level of the neural synapse—serotonin responsivity, which has its origin story in the catecholamine hypothesis of depression. On the other hand, we have a theorized psychiatric medical condition—ASPD—which grows out of the tradition and discourse of clinical psychiatry that is trying to understand an anomalous phenomenon in human social behavior, a clinical tradition, and explanatory framework that does not consider neurotransmitters directly. Contemporary neuroscience is then trying to link these disparate discourses and origin stories in a way that makes them cohere in one narrative. But does the story ring true? At best, this synthesis between neurobiology and any particular human science remains conceptually unexplored. Or put differently, a robust neuroscientific thought-style is only now beginning to emerge.

Thus, in order to situate contemporary research on the interface of neuroscience and morality, we need to give a brief history of the development of operative notions like SES and ASPD, both of which arise at the same time as the catecholamine hypothesis of psychiatric disorders, in the middle to latter half of the twentieth century. Given the purposes of this book, this history cannot be exhaustive. However, a brief history will allow us to explain some of the puzzling philosophical features in the development of *any* concept in the human sciences, whether SES/SEP or ASPD. Moreover, given the neurobiology described by Gianaros and by Manuck in their respective studies, we also must unpack the social history of the development of the catecholamine hypothesis of affective disorders in conjunction with the development of the *Diagnostic and Statistical Manual of Mental Disorders* (DSM) and the concept of ASPD.

## The Creation of a Social Scientific Fact: Conceptual Funneling

Social or psychological concepts, like SES or ASPD, do not exist in the world as obviously as do rocks, or spirochetes, or even brains. As "objects" of the human sciences, they exist in a very different way compared to objects of the physical or biological sciences.[36] Yet, in order to study a given concept X, researchers in the human sciences require a validated, conceptual definition of X. To generate such definitions, they rely heavily on a process referred to as conceptual funneling. Earl Babbie, Catherine Marshall, and Gretchen Rossman provide a helpful overview of how conceptual funneling works. First, one needs a general conceptual definition—for example, an economic status.[37] Such conceptual definitions can emerge from prior philosophical reflection, cultural presuppositions, or even folk philosophical commitments—in our case, from a philosophical claims about the nature of economics (here meaning something like "means to cover the costs of living") and status about the hierarchy of the means. These conceptual definitions are then refined, filling in content, sometimes by appeals to history or by appeals to ethnographic exploration—for example, by asking actual people to fill in their folk definitions. This iterative process of specification funnels the *nominal* concepts down to something manageable and that seems to "represent some consensus, or convention, about how a particular term is to be used."[38]

Yet a nominal definition is not enough for any concept because one has to establish a link between the concept and instances of the concept as it manifests in the world. As such, a second step is needed; the human scientist must create an *operational* definition and establish the operations by which the scientist can pick out an instance of the concept in the world. Operational definitions allow concepts like SES or ASPD to come into relief. Thus, as Babbie notes, for the social sciences, "conceptualization is the refinement and specification of abstract concepts, and operationalization is the development of specific research procedures (operations) that will result in empirical observations representing those concepts in the real world."[39]

The final step in the process is to put the operations to the test, usually by validating the operational definition by administering the operationalized instrument to numerous people. Several of the operational items on the instrument might not survive the process of validation, which is a statistical process complex enough to make sure the operations are actually related to the conceptual object it hopes to isolate. Thus, as a first operational definition, something like SES might start out with numerous items (or operations); but various of these operational items may be dropped because they do not disambiguate one SES from some other area of social life, or because they do not capture every instance of the concept in the world. If there is significant enough discordance between the operational definition and the real-world instances, the conceptual definition itself might need to change.

Thus, the process goes like this: conceptualization, operationalization, validation, refinement of the operational or conceptual definition and, in extreme instance, reconceptualization altogether.[40] This looping process is referred to as the conceptual funnel, a refining process that produces a standard definition, a part of the tradition of the human sciences. Of course, the circularity of the process could also be conceived as an epistemological circuit floating independent of anything in the world, a mere abstraction that has very little to do with the realities that it hoped to pick out, because it can be infinitely refined.

The concept of SES provides an excellent example of conceptual funneling in action. Not only does Babbie himself use SES as an example; we have also seen this process unfold as Gianaros and Manuck shift their language from SES to SEP. While we will elaborate on both of these examples shortly, we first want to complicate our social scientists' accounts. This funneling process, at least per Babbie, Marshall, and Rossman, is portrayed as somewhat ad hoc, a technique that social scientists use simply to create "working definitions" to focus their research. Babbie differentiates nominal definitions from "real" definitions:

> trying to specify the "real" meaning of concepts only leads to a quagmire: It mistakes a construct for a real entity . . . A *nominal definition* is one that is simply assigned to a term without any claim that the definition represents a "real" entity. Nominal definitions are arbitrary . . . but they can be more or less useful.[41]

Thus, careful social scientists understand that concepts in the human sciences are socially constructed, that there is an arbitrariness or bias built into social scientific concepts, and that there is a distance between concept and reality that ought not be ignored. Yet critical distance from the esoteric thought-style of the social sciences seems largely absent as social scientific concepts are appropriated by the emerging neuroscientific thought-community and by the larger, emerging mainstream thought-community of society itself.

## The History of a Social Scientific Concept: Socioeconomic Status

While Babbie, Marshall, and Rossman accurately and forthrightly articulate the process by which concepts are specified in the human sciences, their account overlooks one critically important factor: the historical influences on the development of social scientific concepts. Fleck makes clear that this process of conceptual funneling is deeply informed by historical and cultural factors, both intrinsic and extrinsic to particular thought-communities. Here SES is particularly instructive.

The concept of SES developed out of a renewed interest in the concept of poverty that began to emerge in the post–Second World War era. As historian Gertrude Himmelfarb has noted, prior to the mid-eighteenth century, while social, religious, and political discourse is redolent with concern for the poor, there was no concept of "poverty." As we will see in Part II, as the early-nineteenth-century debates about the British Poor Laws unfold—spurred by the contributions of Jeremy Bentham, Thomas Malthus, and David Ricardo—individual poor people began to disappear into the background of the abstraction that is poverty.[42] The concept of poverty as an abstract condition is dependent upon the rise of the statistical sciences and our trust in numbers, which, as Mary Poovey has noted, depends on the curious way in which numbers come to be seen as marking out particulars, while at the same time acting as universals.[43] Drawing insight from Poovey, we will further explore the history of Malthus and the Poor Laws, but for now, it is important to note that the concept of "poverty" emerged at a particular historical time-point as a result of a specific confluence of events in British politics, the emergence of capitalism, and the advent of the positive human sciences.[44]

Economist Martin Ravallion marks 1955 as a historical time-point for a second significant awakening to the notion of poverty in scholarly and popular culture, what he refers to as a second Poverty Enlightenment.[45] Prior to the 1960s, sociologists had begun to focus on "social problems."[46] But the 1960s saw an "initial sharp rise of interest [in poverty, which] peaked in the early 1970s."[47] Such attention may have been catalyzed by Michael Harrington's 1962 landmark book *The Other America* that documented pervasive poverty within postwar United States.[48] Harrington's book is largely credited for prompting Lyndon B. Johnson's "war on poverty" and the passing of the Economic Opportunity Act of 1964. In the years surrounding 1964, numerous books on poverty were published in the sociological literature.[49]

In 1965, Assistant Secretary of Labor Daniel Patrick Moynihan also published his landmark study of Black families and poverty in the United States, "The Negro Family: A Case for National Action."[50] Moynihan's work catapulted the relationships between social class, social status, race, and poverty more fully into public consciousness, highlighted by the social upheaval of racial protests and the white-on-Black violence that rose to the surface with the Civil Rights movement. The moralizing attitudes on both sides of the political spectrum came into stark relief. A la Bill Cunningham's remarks in the Introduction, the right suggested that the putative self-destruction of the Black family resulted from a Black penchant for vice which resulted in poverty; those on the left located responsibility for the impoverishment of Black communities in US social and economic policies.

It was in this milieu that August B. Hollingshead created what has become the most-used and the most-cited measure to assess SES in the history of sociological research—the Hollingshead Four Factor Index of Social Status (FFI).[51] In his early work at Yale, Hollingshead strove to develop simple measures of social classification for use in survey research. His first, a three-factor tool based on area of residence, occupation, and years of school completed by the head of household, was first deployed to study social class and mental illness in an urban community.[52] Early results from the study were published in 1953 and, as he recalled, "Shortly afterwards, I began to receive requests from sociologists, social workers, social psychologists, and a few psychiatrists for copies of the detailed procedures we had used to stratify the 5 percent sample of households and the psychiatric patients in the psychiatric census."[53] In response, he subsequently refined it to a two-factor instrument, dropping area of residence.[54]

The cultural and social scientific milieu of the 1960s prompted Hollingshead to conceptualize and operationalize instruments that would better assay social and economic status. He continued to focus on education and occupation, which was finessed from an originally somewhat random list to "a detailed list of occupations based on U.S. Census classifications."[55] These were now complemented by attention to sex and marital status. In 1975, he wrote a whitepaper introducing the FFI as a measure of social status. Notably, this whitepaper was never published in a peer-reviewed journal, but it received immediate acceptance.[56] While other instruments measure SES, none have gained wide acceptance as Hollingshead's FFI.[57] Notably missing from the FFI is income. Hollingshead did include income in his original white paper with a table showing the correlation of occupation to income level, and thus concluded that income was part of his instrument. Notably, Hollingshead, never included in his instrument a dimension of race.

Over time, Hollingshead's instrument, which was originally known as the FFI for Social Status, came to be known as the FFI for SES. A number of points are important to note here. First, Hollingshead's work is an excellent example of the conceptual funneling process in action over a twenty-five-year period, as he shifts and refines the operational measures in response to attempts at validation. At the same time, we see a subtle shift, with enormous ramifications, in the concept itself, as the language shifts from a focus on "poverty" in the 1960s (see the titles in note 47) to a different abstraction "socioeconomic status." Third, Babbie notes that while the funneling process is an accepted part of social scientific research, there is a certain dimension of arbitrariness to it:

> Wishing to examine socioeconomic status (SES) in a study, for example, we may simply specify as a combination of income and educational attainment. In this decision, we rule out other possible aspects of SES: occupational status, money in the bank, property, lineage, lifestyle, and so forth. Our findings will then be interesting to the extent that our definition of SES is useful for our purpose.[58]

In other words, as the popular adage goes, "what you measure is what you get." Instruments like the FFI bring certain variables into view, but obscure or render invisible what they do not measure—such as race. Fourth, the funneling process also demonstrates Fleck's account of thought-communities. Nurtured within the esoteric community of sociologists in the 1950s, Hollingshead's emergent concept of social status as a measurable entity is first picked up in the 1960s by the esoteric community of psychology/psychiatry. But equally, the concept is influenced by its broader, exoteric context—for example, the new measure of "marital status" channeling the 1960s preoccupation with the brokenness of Black families rather than the effects of sociopolitical practices like redlining, employment discrimination, Jim Crow, and the federal highway program on Black communities.[59] It carries with it—and reinforces—these ideological commitments as it expands beyond sociology in exponential fashion to the entirety of the social sciences, medicine, and society in the 1970s onward.

And, as the human sciences are fused with the biological sciences with the advent of neuroscience, the accepted facticity of SES continues to expand and—as we saw with Gianaros and Manuck—the funneling process continues. Oddly enough, most neuroscientific studies examining SES as a variable do not use validated instruments of SES, including the 2004–7 studies by Gianaros and Manuck outlined earlier. Yet despite this fact, Gianaros and Manuck call for a new and more textured understanding of SES, renamed and reconceptualized as SEP. This more broadly defined concept, they hope, might show a greater correlation to neurobiological markers, whether through correlations with studies on the HPA axis or through correlations with fMRI studies.

Yet problems immediately become apparent. First, Gianaros and Manuck seek to reconceptualize SES not because it insufficiently captures the realities of social factors like social status and economic power, but because SES does not correlate with brain findings. They want a social marker that might actually correlate to their neurobiological findings. Put bluntly, since the measure is not giving them what they want, they hope to change the measure.

Second, they call for the reconceptualization of SES as SEP (hoping that it will take into consideration "multidimensional, multilevel, and life span considerations"[60]) without ever giving or defending a robust conceptual definition. Nor do they operationalize their new, supposedly more textured concept of SEP. In fact, they sampled SES via a questionnaire that asked subjects to report income range; for those who did not report an income range, Gianaros and Manuck simply inferred income status from reported educational status.

Third, they extracted census tract data for the locations within which the participants lived. The tract data for their subjects included:

> median household income; proportion of households receiving public assistance; proportion of households beneath the federally designated poverty level of income; percentage of individuals in the work force who were unemployed; median value of owner occupied housing units; median gross rent, as a percentage of household income; and proportion of residents over age 25 years lacking a high school diploma.[61]

In Gianaros's and Manuck's studies, each dimension is its own variable. Because each acts as a variable, they do not come close to capturing anything that could be thought of as a social scientific object, namely, SEP. Thus, for the work of these neuroscientists, neither SEP nor SES (as they use the terms) is a concept that captures a holistic reality, despite the fact that they use these concepts as if they are holistic, robust concepts that mark something in reality. While we admire the work done by Gianaros and Manuck (both their separate and combined work), we are concerned that what they call for increased texture begins to look more and more like conceptual chaos.

Leaving its use in neuroscience aside for the moment, it should be clear by now that SES or SEP are complex concepts that have their own histories, related to and developed for research in very specific social and economic contexts, which are themselves also historically constituted. These concepts developed out of a particularly troubling time in American history, and may or may not name something, which may or may not have an impact on the structure and function of the brain, which may or may not have something to do with antisocial behavior. To be clear, we are not at all suggesting that the economic or social environs within which a child is reared have no effects on brain development. Nor are we suggesting that the traumatic conditions under which many people live do not similarly have neurological and physiological sequelae. As research on the social determinants of health makes clear, certain social, political, or economic environments negatively impact the health, wellness and flourishing of the people who live in those environments. It is plausible that aspects of these environments might likewise have some effect on brain development and brain function. It is also plausible that these elements might have some influence on social behaviors. However, finding the specific social or economic factor or factors that can be systematically identified and correlated to brain structure, brain function, and—via the brain—to social behaviors cannot even get off the ground until something like SES or SEP can be conceptually defined, operationalized, validated, and confirmed. Thus, we are a long way from drawing robust conclusions on how something akin to SES or SEP might affect brains and behaviors. And thus, the conclusions that Gianaros and Manuck and other neuroscientists hope to draw cannot be taken as the fact of the matter.

## The History of a Social Scientific Fact: Antisocial Personality Disorder

For the neurosciences, as we have seen for Gianaros and Manuck, the brain serves as a node connecting two elements: SES and behavior. Most often behavior is conceptualized as a particular form of mental illness, such as depression, anxiety, substance abuse, impulsive aggression, criminal violence, and suicide. Yet these diagnoses are, like SES, concepts of recent vintage, "facts" that have emerged only recently, and have done so out of a similar—and in fact, correlated—process of funneling with a specific historical development shaped by their cultural milieu. Understanding this history is crucial for critically analyzing the neuroscientific endeavor to locate the cause of behavior in the brain. We narrate it here alongside the development of what is also thought to be a straightforward scientific concept—ASPD, which emerges from the psychological and psychiatric thought-communities.

The story of ASPD begins with the development of the catecholamine hypothesis in neurobiology. Serotonin, a catecholamine, emerged as a major player with the rise of the catecholamine hypothesis of affective disorders in the 1940s. In the mid-twentieth century, several coinciding scientific discoveries began to focus on the major neurotransmitter-molecules such as glutamate, GABA, serotonin, norepinephrine, and dopamine as causally related to mental illness. Sero*tonin* was discovered in the 1930s and noted for its constrictive properties in vascular and gastrointestinal tissues, thus one aspect of its name that has to do with vascular *tone*.[62] It was in 1948 that serotonin became recognized as a major neurotransmitter in the brain. In 1951, two researchers at Sea View Hospital on Staten Island, Irving Selikoff and Edward Robitzek, were studying two new drugs for the treatment of tuberculosis—isoniazid and iproniazid.[63] In addition to anti-tubercular effects, they noted that these antibiotics also induced "a subtle general stimulation . . . the patients exhibited renewed vigor and indeed this occasionally served to introduce disciplinary problems."[64] The mood-enhancing property of these drugs was soon harnessed for clinical trials in the treatment of clinical depression.[65]

This serendipitous finding in the context of tuberculosis research served as the impetus for the so-called psychopharmacological revolution of the 1950s.[66] It led to further investigations into the mechanism of action of the mood-enhancing effects of these drugs, which seemed to work by inhibiting monoamine oxidase-A (MAOA), an enzyme responsible for the degradation of major neurotransmitters, including serotonin and norepinephrine. These investigations culminated in early speculation about the monoamine hypothesis of depression, as found in Joseph Schildkraut's sentinel paper "The Catecholamine Hypothesis of Affective Disorders."[67] Schildkraut, writing in 1965, associated low levels of neurotransmitters with clinical depression. While a simple monoamine hypothesis for depression did not hold up to further rigorous scientific study, this early thesis animated much of the biological revolution in psychiatry, and the major neurotransmitters remain important in the study of psychiatric illness, even if relegated to having moderating influence on human behavior.

Despite increased interest in pharmacological solutions, the dominant approach to mental illness in mid-century emphasized social factors as the source of psychiatric problems. This approach, which came to be known as "social psychiatry" flourished in the 1960s, fueled by the work of major figures such as Harry Stack Sullivan, Karen Horney, and Erich Fromm.[68] It was no accident, therefore, that Hollingshead developed and tested his initial indices for SES in the context of a ten-year study of mental illness. Within this framework, successful treatment required not only treating the patient but "treating" society as well.[69] "Community psychology," embodied in the Kennedy administration's support of community health centers as a public health strategy, prospered.

But then, "suddenly," as Bruce Rogers-Vaughn notes, "during the 1970s, everything changed."[70] According to the received narrative, patients and families, alongside clinicians and researchers, had become somewhat disillusioned with purely humanistic interpretations—including psychodynamic interpretations—of abnormal human behavior, especially notions that placed the full onus of responsibility for psychiatric disorders on developmental concerns, such as the idea of "refrigerator mothers" causing autism in children. Rogers-Vaughn, however, posits a different thesis, linking the revolutionary "biological" turn in psychiatry to the ascent of neoliberalism.

In his book *Caring for Souls in a Neoliberal Age*, Rogers-Vaughn details the ways in which neoliberalism underlies the contemporary epidemic of mental illness growing exponentially across the globe as well as the ways in which it has reshaped the field of psychiatry in its own image, redefining the conceptual apparatus of the field and coopting it in support of the expansion of the burgeoning market for psychopharmacological medications.[71] He traces the methodological shifts in the field of psychiatry beginning in the late 1970s to key neoliberal commitments, namely, methodological individualism and economic efficiency. Methodological individualism shifts responsibility for both achievements and problems from social or political structures to individuals; in the case of psychiatry, this meant a shift from social problems research to a focus on "biological origins and person-specific treatments."[72] Indeed, once a testable scientific hypothesis for psychiatric disorders had been posited, there was a push to operationalize definitions that led to the creation of a neuropsychiatric research paradigm in the 1980s, funded by the National Institutes for Mental Health (NIMH). This push shifted research commitments toward the neurosciences beginning in 1980, enhanced when George H. W. Bush designated the 1990s as "the decade of the brain." This new field of inquiry was accompanied by the introduction of the American Psychiatric Association's DSM-III in 1980. Most interpreters of psychiatric history would say that the DSM-III represents a watershed moment that shifted psychiatry into a paradigm that located the etiological loci of mental illness within specific individuals.

It is in the DSM-III, for example, that "major depressive disorder" was officially defined for the first time, for example. Having defined depression as biologically rather than socially mediated, psychiatry then needed a biological intervention. Prozac, the first major SSRI for the treatment of depression, entered the market in 1986, providing an individually and biologically targeted remedy that largely obviated the need for slow, time-consuming interventions like psychotherapy. Pills are less costly and more efficient. They likewise more quickly restore or enhance individual happiness or desire, freedom, and personal initiative, all of which are essential for a robust market; "happy consumers and producers are better consumers and producers. Reducing depression thus makes the entire system more efficient and profitable."[73] Thus, psychiatry scored a major political achievement, ensuring its position within the medical-industrial complex by serving the interests of neoliberal economies.[74]

It appears to be no accident that since the ascendency of neoliberalism in 1980s, the incidence of depression—as well as most other categories of mental illness—has skyrocketed both nationally and internationally.[75] Among the conditions on the rise are personality disorders, including antisocial personality.[76] It is in the DSM-III, III-R, -IV, and -5 that ASPD becomes a "real entity" alongside other psychiatric disorders, like major depressive disorder and schizophrenia. ASPD, like SES, also required conceptualization, operationalization, and validation in order to be sure of a robust standard for this diagnosis. What is more, that is precisely why DSM-III developed: to conceptualize, operationalize, and validate diagnoses so that new drugs emergent from the catecholamine hypothesis of affective disorders could be tested.

Yet, as with all of the entries in the DSM, the category of ASPD has a history of development. In 1980, psychologist Robert Hare developed the Psychopathy Checklist (PCL), which operationalized early conceptual notions of antisocial behavior as set forth by psychiatrist Hervey Cleckley in his book *The Mask of Sanity*.[77] Cleckley's book, first published in 1941, identifies and describes people who, though appearing completely reasonable and sane—even charming—turn out to lack a moral sense and to engage repeatedly in manipulative and destructive behaviors toward others. In Hare's operationalization, he lists traits of the disorder as glibness, grandiosity, pathological lying, absence of remorse or guilt, lack of empathy, callousness, impulsivity, and irresponsibility—including a persistent violation of social norms. The descriptions given by Hare and Cleckley are far more clinical than scientific or philosophical. Eventually these clinical descriptions come to ground a definition of ASPD.

We see the retention of these early concepts in DSM-III, -IV, and -5 in the criteria for ASPD. As we saw in the Introduction, the DSM conceptualizes ASPD in its most recent iteration as follows:

A) A pervasive pattern of disregard for and violation of the rights of others occurring since age 15 years, as indicated by three (or more) of the following:

- failure to conform to social norms with respect to lawful behaviors as indicated by repeatedly performing acts that are grounds for arrest;
- deceitfulness, as indicated by repeatedly lying, use of aliases, or conning others for personal profit or pleasure;
- impulsivity or failure to plan ahead;
- irritability and aggressiveness, as indicated by repeated physical fights or assaults;
- reckless disregard for safety of self or others;
- consistent irresponsibility, as indicated by repeated failure to sustain consistent work behavior or honor financial obligations;

- lack of remorse, as indicated by being indifferent to or rationalizing having hurt, mistreated, or stolen from another.
B) The individual is at least age 18 years.
C) There is evidence of conduct disorder with onset before age 15 years.
D) The occurrence of antisocial behavior is not exclusively during the course of schizophrenia or bipolar disorder.[78]

Note that this iteration (from DSM-5) has slight distinctions from DSM-IV. Interestingly, the word "deception" is altered to "deceitfulness" in this latest version. Also, the diagnosis of ASPD is retained in DSM-5 but is no longer on a separate axis from other mental disorders, purportedly giving it equal status with more "biological" diagnoses, like major depressive disorder. These seemingly subtle shifts, unnoticeable to casual consumers of mental health nomenclature and technologies, are further evidence that psychiatry is a living tradition in evolution and, at times, in conflict and contradiction with itself.

In this way, the early notions of psychopathy and sociopathy are folded into the DSM-III (and beyond) as ASPD. Interestingly, in the lead-up to adoption of the DSM-5, there were rival systems of conceptualization of personality disorders and much debate regarding possible more radical changes, which illustrates the shifting nature of the conceptualization of these disorders.[79] Interestingly, DSM-5 now includes a second, alternative proposed system of diagnoses of personality disorders in a Section III. It reports the following rationale for this:

> The current approach to personality disorders appears in Section II of DSM-5, and an alternative model developed for DSM-5 is presented here in Section III. The inclusion of both models in DSM-5 reflects the decision of the APA Board of Trustees to preserve continuity with current clinical practice, while also introducing a new approach that aims to address numerous shortcomings of the current approach to personality disorders.[80]

So the history of this "conceptual funneling" of ASPD continues into the present.

In sum, then, the serendipitous discovery of mood-enhancing drugs that function according to the catecholamine hypothesis, alongside emerging hypotheses about psychopathology and in accord with the development of instruments that operationalize concepts like ASPD in a sociopolitical context that had radically shifted to neoliberalism, led to the disorder's codification in the DSM-III. As already discussed, the particular diagnosis of ASPD emerged in the context of dynamic changes in the discipline of psychiatry that ultimately led to a paradigm shift away from psychodynamic theories of antisocial behavior to the currently regnant biomedical model of psychiatry. A watershed moment in this history was the adoption in 1980 of the *Diagnostic and Statistical Manual-III*, which laid the foundation for the modern psychiatric clinical and neuroscientific research enterprise and attempts to define and operationalize clinical diagnoses in a manner that would enable scientific investigation.

Interestingly, the aspirations of the biological movement in psychiatry, represented by the DSM-III and beyond, have not been fully realized, calling into question the entire enterprise. With the publication of DSM-5 in 2013 a robust dissent arose, including dissent by many who have called for various reforms or have expressed concern over the growing elasticity of criteria for psychiatric disorders that encompass the increasing terrain of the human condition. Serious researchers increasingly hold that DSM clinical criteria, which developed themselves out of a period of disillusionment with psychoanalytic models of mental illness, have not enjoyed thoroughgoing scientific validation. Thus, the foundational paradigms and assumptions of the DSM tradition are being reconsidered in favor of new, alternative models for making sense of psychiatric illness. Correlatively, neuroscientific researchers are increasingly unsatisfied with the DSM enterprise as it has not led to the increasing validity of underlying concepts. In this context, the NIMH unveiled a new set of standards known as the Research Domain Criteria (RDoC) where the focus is more on endophenotypes (including imaging findings) as vantage points for further psychiatric research.[81] Such innovative models are increasingly attractive to basic neuroscience researchers who hope they will be of greater utility and yield findings that conceptualize more clearly the neuroscientific basis of mental illness.

In other words, the whole process has itself become circular. The purpose of the DSM enterprise was to establish robust conceptual definitions of various psychological and social disorders, so that operational criteria for picking out something like ASPD in the world might be consistent, allowing for correlations to neurobiology to be made, and allowing for biological targets for therapy to be created. The idea was that once something like ASPD was consistently identifiable in the world, then we would be able to find correlations—or better, causal mechanisms—between these antisocial behaviors and brain physiology, and then create innovative pharmacological technologies to treat neurobiological targets. Yet, increasingly, researchers are claiming that social scientific definitions are so slippery that almost anything can be labeled a psychiatric disorder. In other words, social scientific definitions are so problematic that it almost makes science impossible. To remedy this situation, the NIMH created the RDoC, seeking to start with the brain and to move outward toward the behaviors, establishing a set of criteria that emerge from certainties about the brain. In other words, they want to start with the brain in order to find differences in brain physiology and hope to then construct the behaviors as pathological.

The investigative powers of this ongoing and dynamic enterprise have been enhanced by advances in genetics and neuroimaging technologies, advantages on which the work of Gianaros and Manuck have capitalized. The neurobiological work utilized to understand the neurophysiology of the brain seems more real precisely because we can point to findings in the brain. Yet there is a huge disconnect between these findings and establishing causation from brain to behavior, without any robust way of categorizing the behaviors. In other words, the whole enterprise of the DSM had hoped to secure brain findings by establishing a robust social scientific definition of ASPD. When this project failed, the RDoC hopes to establish a robust social scientific definition in the brain, and prior to the brain in the genes that "make" the brain. This move seeks to get away from the failed circular reasoning of conceptual funneling, but as we shall see, it presents a whole host of new problems. It is to this work that we now turn.

## From Genes to Brains to Antisocial Behavior[82]

We turn now to Viding and Frith. As you recall from the beginning of this chapter, these leading developmental neuropsychologists argue that "Genes for Susceptibility to Violence Lurk in the Brain."[83] At the center of their argument is a finding by Andreas Meyer-Lindenberg et al., who noted that a functional polymorphism in the promoter region of the MAOA gene has been correlated with aggressive behavior and is associated with observable differences in neural circuitry.[84] Where for Gianaros and Manuck, the arrow of causation moved from social factors interacting with genes to neural changes resulting in social misbehavior, for Viding and Frith, the vector is different, moving from gene to brain to social misbehavior.[85] They are far from alone in their search for genetic or neural "signatures" that predispose persons to socially disadvantageous traits that can be managed pharmacologically.

Let us begin by looking more closely at the study done by Meyer-Lindenberg et al., entitled "Neural Mechanisms of Genetic Risk for Impulsivity and Violence in Humans," in their search for one of the most antisocial of behaviors—violence.[86] As mentioned earlier, MAOA and the gene coding for it are elements of intense interest to neurobiologists and neuroscientists because of the role of the major neurotransmitters in emotional regulation. MAOA breaks down the monoamines implicated in emotional regulation. In some persons, the gene coding for MAOA harbors a genetic polymorphism in its promoter region; this polymorphism is a common variant in the human population. It can be easily assayed in human research studies via genotyping. Typically, the variation is characterized in terms of low-efficiency alleles versus high-efficiency alleles, and any individual can carry one of several combinations.[87] Because this gene is X-linked, men are hemizygous, meaning that they carry either one low-efficiency or one high-efficiency allele. Women can carry two low-efficiency alleles, one low-efficiency allele and one high-efficiency allele (the heterozygous condition), or two high-efficiency alleles.

Meyer-Lindenberg et al. studied the correlation between individual genotype and neural structure and function.[88] They summarize their findings as follows:

> Here, we have studied the impact of a common functional polymorphism in MAOA on brain structure and function assessed with MRI in a large sample of *healthy* human volunteers. We show that the low expression variant, associated with increased risk of violent behavior, predicted pronounced limbic volume reductions and hyperresponsive amygdala during emotional arousal, with diminished reactivity to regulatory prefrontal regions, compared with the high expression allele.[89]

In other words, in this study of ninety-seven *healthy* volunteers, low expression of the gene encoding for MAOA, which has elsewhere been associated with antisocial traits, correlates with smaller, but more reactive limbic structures—centers of emotionality.[90] In addition, they also noted diminished reactivity of the cingulate cortex, which modulates emotional arousal. In other words, the corticolimbic system differs in both structure and function in those who have the polymorphism relative to controls. To be specific, healthy volunteers with the functional polymorphism of MAOA showed smaller and more hyper-responsive amygdalae and a less active cingulate cortex.

Yet, while discrepancies in neurotransmitter levels have been shown to correlate with behaviors and conditions such as depression, suicidality, aggression, anxiety, and impulsiveness,[91] it seems that we should take seriously the fact that these *healthy* volunteers showed no signs of diagnosis of ASPD or trait. The conclusion drawn by Meyer-Lindenberg et al. that "genotype differences show in the brain," which certainly appears to be true, elides the fact that these individuals were *healthy*, not sociopaths.[92] Despite their enthusiasm, Viding and Frith nuance the conclusions drawn by Meyer-Lindenberg et al., noting that "it is unlikely that genes directly code for violence; rather, allelic variation is responsible for individual differences in neurocognitive functioning that, in turn, may determine differential *predisposition* to violent behavior."[93] Yet they still posit a correlation.

Yet even this more nuanced conclusion is not warranted by the Meyer-Lindenberg et al. study, as many other variables are at work. As geneticists have come to understand, not only do genes encode for protein products, they also interact with a host of other biological structures, including other genes and their protein products. Moreover, genes are not merely conduits of information. Genes are also themselves three-dimensional structures that interact within a biological and physiological milieu. Most importantly, geneticists increasingly hold that gene expression is influenced not only by the biological and physiological environment but also by the social environment, as Gianaros and Manuck have suggested.

Beyond these multiple strains of research endeavor, yet another related body of research centers on what are known as gene-by-environment studies that seek to correlate genetic and environmental influences to antisocial behavior, in much the same way as Gianaros and Manuck. Environment seems to mean here all influences that are *not* genetic, but not just the physiological environment of genes and brains, but also the social environment of human animals. Many other factors beyond SES (or SEP) have effects; historical life events, often negative ones (such as abuse or neglect) also leave their mark on behavior.

An oft-cited landmark study in this genre was published in 2002 by Avshalom Caspi et al., entitled "Role of Genotype in the Cycle of Violence in Maltreated Children."[94] This study correlated environmental influences—abuse or maltreatment—with a polymorphism in the promoter region of MAOA gene and future diagnosis with antisocial personality traits. They suggest that environmental differences could moderate or exacerbate the manifestation of antisocial behavior. This study utilized the Dunedin Multidisciplinary Health and Development Study where a cohort was constituted when investigators enrolled 91 percent of consecutive live births in Dunedin, New Zealand between April 1972 and March 1973, some of whom were later genotyped at age twenty-six. Those individuals with the low-efficiency polymorphism in the promoter region of the MAOA gene who had sustained severe maltreatment as children were more likely to be diagnosed with antisocial traits in adulthood than were those with the high-efficiency allele.[95] In order to quantify maltreatment, researchers derived a "cumulative exposure index," which counted the number of "maltreatment experiences" from ages three to eleven using behavioral observations (including early mother-child interactions), parental reports (including a "harsh discipline" checklist), and exposure to child physical and sexual abuse via retrospective reports. According to this index, 64 percent of the children experienced no maltreatment, 28 percent experienced one indicator of maltreatment, referred to as "probable maltreatment," and 8 percent experienced two or more indicators of maltreatment, referred to as "severe maltreatment."

However, individuals with the low-efficiency genotype who had not sustained childhood maltreatment were no more likely to be diagnosed in adulthood with antisocial traits than the general population without the polymorphism.[96] Caspi et. al. conclude the following:

> Until this study's findings are replicated, speculation about clinical implications is premature. *Nonetheless*, although individuals having the combination of low-activity MAOA genotype and maltreatment were only 12% of the male birth cohort, they accounted for 44% of the cohort's violent convictions, yielding an attributable risk fraction (11%) comparable to that of the major risk factors associated with cardiovascular disease. Moreover, 85% of cohort males having a low-activity MAOA genotype who were severely maltreated developed some form of antisocial behavior. Both attributable risk and predictive sensitivity indicate that these findings could inform the development of future pharmacological treatments.[97]

Therefore, they suggest that a non-abusive environment moderates the effects of the low-efficiency alleles. First, it should be noted that gene-effect alone is insufficient to produce the behavioral outcome, meaning that Meyer-Lindenberg et al.'s finding of neural signatures may not be as important of a contributor to behavior as Viding, Frith, and Meyer-Lindenberg et al. suggest. It is the gene in the context of the environment in formative periods of a person's life that predisposes that person toward antisocial behavior. Second, the way that Caspi et al. state their claim seems odd. They claim that a good (nonviolent) environment has a protective effect, rather than that a bad (violent) environment had a detrimental effect. This still assumes a robust genetic ontology, presupposing that the gene is the most important contributor, and if not for the environment, the patient would be a sociopath. The really important bit is the gene.

Other types of environmental stress, including that of low SES, have been studied in relationship to neurotransmitters and genetics. For example, in 2010 psychologist Naomi Sadeh et al. published the results of two studies in a paper in the *Journal of Abnormal Psychology* entitled "Serotonin Transporter Gene Associations with Psychopathic Traits in Youth Vary as a Function of Socioeconomic Resources."[98] These two studies explored the possibility of a correlation between a gene that coded for a less effective serotonin transporter protein and future diagnosis of personality disorders relative to SES. SES was defined by creating a composite score from Hollingshead's FFI and the parental income of the subjects. In the results of the first study, Sadeh et al. write, "Youth with the l/l genotype who lived in low-SES environments exhibited relatively higher levels of callous-unemotional and narcissism features than did youth from high-SES environments."[99] The study was replicated in a different demographic in a second study performed by Sadeh et al. and suggested again that psychopathic tendencies in youth, such as narcissistic and callous-unemotional traits, vary as a function of SES. As before, the corticolimbic system and the theory of serotonergic responsivity are in the background of Sadeh et al.'s study.[100]

These are but a few examples of the kinds of studies seeking and positing correlations between genes and behaviors that develop relative to environments. This kind of research often portrays itself as merely descriptive. Yet, it is aimed at intervention. The Meyer-Lindenberg et al. study is a case in point. As they state: "Our data identify differences in limbic circuitry for emotion regulation and cognitive control that may be involved in the association of MAOA with impulsive aggression . . . and point toward potential targets for a biological approach toward violence."[101] Although their study only identifies correlation between gene and neurological structure/function—a correlation in a healthy population sample—they draw a directional cause-effect relation that leads from genes to neural structure, to neural function, and finally to violent antisocial behavior. They imply that, given the psychopharmacological revolution, simple therapies for violence or antisocial personality are just around the corner. Likewise, Viding and Frith introduce their commentary with a moral imperative for this neurobiological research:

> Preventing violence is one of the most important global concerns. The political, social, or economic causes of violence are well studied, but more recently the awareness has grown that biological causes, which may explain individual differences in predisposition to violence, also need to be investigated.[102]

If we could just better understand the genetic-neurobiology of violence, then we would have the leverage to do something about it once and for all, by focusing on the "potential targets for a biological approach toward violence."[103] Where political, social, and economic interventions have failed, neuroscience can finally succeed by targeting the defective brains of sociopaths, through techno-scientific control of antisocial behaviors.

## The Neuroscientific Narrative of Vice

Within the neurosciences, then, a significant subset of research seeks to find causal mechanistic solutions for behaviors deemed problematic, particularly antisocial personality or impulsive violence. This instrumentalist-therapeutic trope for solving social problems, which includes socioeconomic problems, can be found much more widely than the specific studies we have covered in this chapter.[104] Terrie Moffitt, a prominent social psychologist, states, for example: "Behavioral science needs to achieve a more complete understanding of the causes of antisocial behavior to provide an evidence base for effectively controlling and preventing it."[105] Adrian Raine, a neurocriminologist, calls for a massive social campaign to do away with the cancer of criminality that plagues the body politic.[106]

Although science claims moral neutrality, the operational definition of ASPD includes terms like criminality, violence, deception, impulsivity, sloth, grandiosity, despondency, lack of remorse or guilt, and lack of concern for others, all of which betray the moral valence that is part of the definition. As the DSM makes clear, seemingly clinical terms such as ASPD—like other psychological diagnoses—are simply umbrellas that bring together a range of behaviors traditionally understood within a moral framework: violations of morality (lying, stealing), economics (failure to work or honor financial obligations), and politics (violating others' rights, disrespecting laws, failure to conform to social norms). Subtly here, traditional moral categories—located within coherent social and philosophical frameworks—have been transmuted into neuroscientific categories. Traditionally, such traits were the object of community-based behavioral interventions theorized around habituation, a *telos*, and a particular moral anthropology of the human person. Within the neurosciences, the primary pathway to behavioral change is instead via intervention on pathological brains, giving the whole story an urgent imperative.

These interventions, however, equally presume an anthropology, one quite different from traditional understandings of the human person.[107] This masking of vice behind neuroscientific proxies is embedded in a larger deterministic anthropology that tells a story of how genes make brains and brains make behavior. Neuroscientists work backward from biological research findings to hypothesize a causal nexus in the complex milieu from genes and environment to brains to antisocial behavioral traits. The causal link between genes-within-environments to behavior is grounded in the brain—in fact, within the corticolimbic system. As noted, neuroimaging research has shown that the prefrontal cortex and the anterior cingulate cortex are involved in inhibiting the responsivity of the amygdala. A person with a hyper-responsive amygdala—whether determined by genetics or whether the genetics combined with environmental factors—might interpret what is typically described as a neutral face as one that is threatening, and act out violently.[108] It is thought that in people with hyper-responsive amygdalae, the internal response of the brain drives emotion out of proportion to the environmental threat, thereby potentially catalyzing impulsivity, violence, and antisocial personality traits. Alternatively, genetic or environmental impairment of the amygdala might result in the opposite—an absence of fear conditioning, such that the person does not develop what would have traditionally been called a conscience, making it easier for the person to violate moral norms. The person is labeled instead as callous. Conscience understood in the neurobiological narrative of vice is simply the consistent operation of an underlying neural circuitry, one formed by the conjunction of genetics and environment, rather than being understood as a higher-level construct, one that is a crucial aspect of human personhood (in particular, human morality).

The studies we have reviewed—from Gianaros and Manuck to Sadeh et al.—all employ a metaphor of "bottom-up" causation where the "bottom" (genes/biology interacting with the environment) produces the "up," violence or antisocial personality. For Meyer-Lindenberg et al., the bottom is merely genetics that moves upward to the brain and then to behavior. For Gianaros and Manuck, as well as for Caspi et al., and Sadeh et al., the environment (often imagined as SES or SEP) contributes something, either protection or potentiation, to the way the brain develops, which in turn shapes behavior. The model remains one of determinative causation—an efficient causal mechanism—akin to a physics of human sociobiology where A (genes) plus B (environment) leads to C (neural structure and function), followed by D (behavior). Genes and environment interact to form the brain that together "make" behavior. No one, in this narrative, suggests that cognitive aspects of higher reasoning can work downward on brains or genes or environments.

In addition, while the neuroscientific narrative of vice has attempted to remove the overtly moralistic language typically associated with vice, the moral, political, and even economic dimensions of this new narrative lurk beneath the surface of the scientific text. These modern studies reproduce the simple trope we noted in our Introduction—that vice results in poverty, or vice versa, that poverty results in vice. As such, the anthropology is not only deterministic; it locates economics at the heart of the human and moral enterprise. So normative has economics become that the neurosciences are configured as a new regime of behavioral control, through social manipulation, or perhaps even engineering. The BRAIN Initiative was launched, in the words of the acronym, to "advance innovative neurotechnologies." And the purpose of those neurotechnologies? Gianaros and Manuck sum it up succinctly:

> Privilege, power, prestige. How does the brain come to represent these and other dimensions of socioeconomic position (SEP)? . . . More importantly, could these representations, in part, beget socially stratified patterns of behavior and biology that undermine equities in physical health, psychological well-being, and even longevity across individuals? If so, would this inform the design of brain-based preventative strategies, interventions, or social policies aimed at reducing the human cost of chronic medical conditions and psychological disorders that track a socioeconomic gradient? These questions are neither new nor exhaustive, but they remain open and pressing, as developing nations and those with economies of scale confront ever-increasing challenges in allocating limited resources to the public and widening socioeconomic health disparities that are arguably unjust.[109]

Here the nexus becomes clear: the intersection of "brain-based preventative strategies" and social policy.

What we see in the neuroscientific narrative of vice is a story told by bringing together these two distinct thought-communities of scientists with their distinct thought-styles—on the one side the thought-community of neurobiology and, on the other, the thought-community of the human sciences. Yet, the human scientific arm of neuroscience inevitably runs into the problems that all human sciences have, namely, finding ways of naming its objects through the process of conceptual funneling. Because the conceptual funnel is always dependent upon the social circumstances of its development, finding the truth about human behavior will inevitably be politically and morally charged. We will make the political and economic dimension of these thought-communities clearer in Chapters 2 and 3, and then we will turn in Chapter 4 to unpack the way these communities are constituted by the larger social forces of the social imaginary of the late modern West. But first, let us complete our neuroscientific narrative of morality by turning to the counterpart of vice, namely, the neuroscientific narrative of virtue.

2

# The Neuroscientific Narrative of Virtue

As we noted in the Prelude, some innovative scientific approaches, which at first appear esoteric and bizarre, produce novel and revolutionary insights that transform the entire scientific thought-community. Other novel approaches flourish for a time and then die quietly; still others wreak havoc and enter into the lore of scientific triumphalism, only to have their ideas seep into the unconsciousness of a thought-community. One such idea is highlighted among "Milestones in Neuroscience Research" on the University of Washington website: "1808 - Franz Joseph Gall publishes work on phrenology."[1]

Although phrenology is now dismissed as a pseudoscience, Gall is hailed by many as the founder of psychology as a biological science.[2] With his colleague Johann Gaspar Spurzheim, he remains a "seminal figure in psychology, psychiatry, criminology, education, and even philosophy."[3] Gall theorized that mental functions and psychological characteristics were localized in discrete brain locations or "organs." The prominence of a particular trait in a person, he proposed, was proportional to the size of the organ, which would be manifest in the shape of the skull. "Hence," as Donald Simpson notes, "a large cerebral organ was associated with a cranial protuberance or bump."[4] By "palpating" a person's skull and "reading" these protuberances, a trained professional could diagnose a person's psychological qualities, assess their intellectual aptitudes, and predict their character. For example, as John van Wyhe notes, "a prominent protuberance in the forehead at the position attributed to the organ of Benevolence was meant to indicate that the individual had a 'well developed' organ of Benevolence and would therefore be expected to exhibit benevolent behavior."[5]

Phrenology, as a scientific (and therefore cultural) practice, flourished as one of the leading psychological theories through the late nineteenth century. By the 1840s, twenty-eight phrenological societies in London alone boasted over 1,000 members.[6] It became a cross-continental cultural phenomenon, infusing many aspects of popular culture from cheap street corner pamphlets to royal courts.[7] Some advocated using phrenology to address social and economic problems. Mid-nineteenth-century employers might "demand a character reference from a local phrenologist to ensure that a prospective employee was honest and hard-working."[8] It was used as a scientific basis for justifying racial and gender discrimination, most notably being used by Belgian colonizers in the 1930s as the basis for asserting the superiority of the Tutsis over the Hutus in Rwanda.[9] It also played a significant role in criminology, often supporting efforts to study criminality and in support of penal reform by differentiating between those who could be rehabilitated and those who should never be released.[10] Although its influence waned in Europe by roughly 1860, it continued to flourish in the United States through the early part of the twentieth century.

As with Hollingshead, Gall drew largely on psychiatric patients and criminals to develop his theory. For example, as Simpson notes: "Gall localized the organ of sexuality in the cerebellum on the basis of case studies, including examination of a nymphomaniac widow."[11] Thus, the subtle and implicit interweaving of morality, psychological disorder, and social burden in neuroscientific research traces an even longer history.

However, phrenology was not only about vice. In fact, some of the twenty-seven traits Gall localized to various brain regions were virtues, including love of children, friendship, goodness, moral sense, conscience, and "comparative sagacity."[12] In this chapter, we focus on this strand of the story, which we name the neuroscientific narrative of virtue. While the bulk of contemporary research on the neuroscience of morality has its origins in psychiatry and has historically tended to focus on the narrative of pathologized vice, more recent work has begun to focus on the arena of positive psychology. Positive psychology focuses on non-pathological features of human personality related to human behavior, function, or emotions, such as wisdom or gratitude or happiness, ideas historically tied to the traditional virtues.

In their now oft-cited 2009 paper, "Neurobiology of Wisdom: A Literature Overview," psychiatrists Thomas Meeks and Dilip Jeste describe wisdom as a "unique psychological trait" and set out to hypothesize its neurobiological basis. Like their counterparts Viding and Frith, Meeks and Jeste's work is also driven by a social motivation and justification. As they note:

> Wisdom is considered an important contributor to successful personal and social functioning. Understanding the neurobiology of wisdom may have considerable clinical significance. For example, knowledge of the underlying mechanisms could potentially lead to development of preventive, therapeutic, and rehabilitative interventions for enhancing wisdom, including those designed for persons with relevant neuropsychiatric disorders (e.g., frontotemporal dementia).[13]

Meeks and Jeste are engaged in a project meant to prevent, treat, and rehabilitate those who are prone to violence and those, who by accident, have been left with neuropsychiatric disorders.[14]

They are joined in this project by others. Martin Seligman and Christopher Peterson, for example, seek to develop a DSM-like manual—the CSV, *Character, Strengths, Virtues: A Handbook and Classification*.[15] Their book details the positive aspects of psychology, promoting wisdom/knowledge, courage, humanity, justice, temperance, and transcendence, while they also attempt to give conceptual definition to the positive character traits. Positive psychologists are not attempting to articulate descriptions of pathologies, that is, vices, but virtues, and thus they are "moving the spotlight from disease to health, from treatment to prevention, and from risk factors to protective factors."[16] Like their counterparts in Chapter 1, they objectify normal, virtuous phenomena and behavior, seeking to localize wisdom and the traits that are its "subcomponents" in the genome and in the brain. Where their counterparts in Chapter 1 generally substituted more clinical and neural proxies for traditional references to vice, those working in positive psychology do both. They interweave more highly abstracted proxies with traditional virtue language, referring to "virtue," "morality," or "character," to components of traditional virtue theory (such as happiness or wisdom), or to particular traditional virtues, such as gratitude, courage, justice, and temperance. This difference will be important to probe as we move forward. Notably, while traditional language is retained, traditional definitions of the virtues are not.

Yet, what exactly are they defining, and what exactly are they operationalizing and reifying? In the following, we will carefully unpack Meeks and Jeste's work in order to elucidate the assumptions that animate their normative claims about wisdom, which center on behaviors labeled as "prosocial." We could choose any number of works from any number of researchers. We choose to analyze Meeks and Jeste in detail for four main reasons. First, their work is heavily cited in neuroscientific studies. Second, paralleling Gianaros and Manuck, they attempt to marshal different kinds of studies and thereby provide a window into the larger landscape of research in this area. Third, they attempt to formulate a robust conceptual definition of wisdom, which is necessary for further human scientific study of the "virtues." Fourth, by seeking to show correlations between the psychology of wisdom and the science of neurotransmitters, the genome, and the brain, they demonstrate how the neuroscience of virtue attempts to combine psychological research on wisdom with neurobiological research, embodying the pattern we noted in the Introduction by which the new thought-community that is neuroscience emerges.

In the "Neurobiology of Wisdom," Meeks and Jeste proceed in a manner much like their counterparts in Chapter 1. Through a funneling process, they first attempt to generate a conceptual definition of wisdom and its subcomponent virtues. Once armed with this conceptual definition, they attempt to show how each subcomponent maps onto the realities of neurotransmitters and the genetic control of those neurotransmitters. They then explore structural and functional neuroimaging, looking for the location of each subcomponent in the brain.

Here again, we draw attention to the political dimensions of the neuroscientific narrative of morality. As with antisocial traits, we show how the subcomponents of positive psychology—the virtues if you will—are socially constructed, deeply informed by the particular cultural context of the late modern West. We show how the literature moves quickly from "findings" in the brain to calls for social policies and interventions designed to enhance morality (or, perhaps, eliminate those who pose a threat to social well-being). And we show how, again, a key aspect of the conceptual framing of this research endeavor is economic. The literature forwarding this neurobiological narrative of virtue is of more recent vintage than the narrative for vice (or antisocial behavior); there has, to date, been less research into how environments of influence might impact on prosocial behavior in the context of genetic predisposition, though heritability patterns would suggest a similar relationship between gene and environment as seen in antisocial behavior. Rather than cross-mapping the virtues and SES, however, we find in the broader conversation an implicit presumption between virtue and wealth as well as the emergence of an elision of human agency that aligns, not surprisingly, with contemporary developments in economic theory. We then show the way in which these virtues are mapped onto the genome and onto the brain creates the conditions for a new kind of phrenology.[17] This new science of phrenology draws, not on bumps in the skull, but on genomic analysis and fMRI studies.

## The "Scientific" Construction of Virtue

As noted in Chapter 1, any human scientific study must first develop a conceptual definition. Conceptual definitions can develop in many ways. They can originate from philosophical or religious commitments; or they can be discovered in ethnographic work or in grounded theoretical approaches that attempt to get at folk definitions. Meeks and Jeste open their survey with a brief review of the philosophical and religious origins of the concept of wisdom. They note that wisdom is "a unique attribute, rich in history dating back to the dawn of civilization." They cite the classical Greek writings which focused on rationality, Eastern traditions in India and China which stressed "emotional balance," and Gall's trait number 20, "comparative sagacity."[18]

Yet oddly, after this rehearsal, these intellectual traditions play no role in their conceptual definition. Rather, the authors turn primarily to contemporary psychological research on wisdom in order to identify the definitional subcomponents. That is to say, their new conceptual definition emerges from their own thought-community. To craft this definition, they selected ten different works in the social science literature that propose "a definition or description" of wisdom; the criteria by which these works were chosen are not provided.[19] Each of these publications offers a conceptual definition of wisdom developed through wildly different processes. Meeks and Jeste take each of these ten definitions, break them down into subcomponents, and then cross-reference the subcomponents from one definition with the subcomponents from the other nine, looking for points of commonality. If any three of the ten definitions shared the same subcomponent—for instance, emotional homeostasis or prosocial attitudes—then Meeks and Jeste included that subcomponent as part of their definition of wisdom. They proffer that this approach provides a "meta"-perspective on the psychology of wisdom and allows them to propose a slightly broader—and therefore new—definition.

Using this process, Meeks and Jeste distill six subcomponents to constitute their conceptual definition of "wisdom":

(1) prosocial attitudes/behaviors,
(2) social decision-making/pragmatic knowledge of life,
(3) emotional homeostasis,
(4) reflection/self-understanding,
(5) value relativism/ tolerance, and
(6) acknowledgment of and dealing effectively with uncertainty/ambiguity.[20]

Again, they claim that at least three of the ten sources included the above six subcomponents, though not all ten included all six characteristics.[21]

Paralleling the narrative of vice, these subcomponents act as proxies for virtues. For example, in describing the first subcomponent—prosocial attitudes and behaviors—they state: "One of the most consistent subcomponents of wisdom, from both the ancient and modern literature, is the promotion of common good and rising above self-interests, i.e. exhibiting prosocial attitudes and behaviors, such as empathy, social cooperation, and altruism."[22] Notably, they do not derive this subcomponent from ancient literature but solely from contemporary psychological literature. As the psychiatric literature assumes that *antisocial* personality traits are roughly equivalent to vices, it is not surprising that Meeks and Jeste's definition of wisdom includes *prosocial* attitudes and behaviors—a virtue. Further, as with the narrative of vice, here we find the virtues captured under a putatively more clinical and morally neutral umbrella category.

However, Meeks and Jeste contribute their own conceptual work to this definition in part by creating new language to capture what in the ten source definitions is much more differentiated and nuanced. For example, Meeks and Jeste claim that "prosocial attitudes and behaviors" constituted part of the definition of wisdom in five of ten source definitions: (a) Richard Sternberg includes "achievement of a common (social) good" as one element of his definition;[23] (b) P. B. Baltes et al. state that there exists an "implicit idea that wisdom serves a common good";[24] (c) Scott Brown and Jeffrey Greene performed a technique called factor analysis to conclude that altruism is a dimension of wisdom;[25] (d) Monika Ardelt notes that affective wisdom includes "positive emotions and behaviors toward others and absence of indifferent or negative emotions toward others";[26] and (e) Jason et al. include "warmth" as one of five dimensions of wisdom.[27]

Notably, then, none of the works mined for the definition of wisdom actually or explicitly uses the language of "prosocial attitudes and behaviors." Rather, each of these five studies names a term—for example, common good, warmth, altruism. Meeks and Jeste then collapse this variety of specific features into one concept—"prosocial attitudes and behaviors." As a result, the concept includes odd-bedfellows (e.g., "warmth" and "the common good"). Abstracting from the substantive meaning of the terms used in the actual studies results in a subcomponent with little conceptual coherency, a cipher that can be filled with multiple meanings.

In order to demonstrate this, let us further unpack each of the five sources on which Meeks and Jeste draw to ground this notion of prosocial attitudes and behaviors. Sternberg's concept is developed in a book that combines implicit theories that are operative in many psychological studies of wisdom with his own explicit theory of wisdom. Derived from both conceptual and empirical work, it is not meant to be a conceptual definition at all, but rather one that takes other operational definitions and attempts to redefine the original concept. In the process of conceptual funneling, Sternberg uses validated operational criteria to reflexively redefine the original concept upon which the operational definitions ride. Thus, Sternberg is not so busy defining wisdom as he is trying to show that wisdom is:

> the application of successful intelligence and creativity as mediated by values toward the achievement of a common good through a balance among (a) intrapersonal, (b) interpersonal, and (c) extra-personal interests, over (a) short and (b) long terms,

in order to achieve a balance among (a) adaptation to existing environments, (b) shaping of existing environments, and (c) selection of new environments.[28]

Wisdom then is a time-sensitive balancing of interests directed by and at one's environment, with the ultimate *telos* being the common good. We will return to this concern for balancing interests in Chapter 4. Thus, where Meeks and Jeste place prosocial behavior as a mere subcomponent of their definition of wisdom, for Sternberg the common good is the *telos*, the end sought by all wise people; it is, for Sternberg, that for the sake of which all wise people act.

Baltes, Smith, and Staudinger are also cited as including prosociality within their definition. Meeks and Jeste reference their paper presented in 1991 at the Nebraska Symposium on Motivation. In addition to this paper, Baltes has had a long and distinguished career conducting research on wisdom. However, much of the work done by Baltes and the Max Planck group in Berlin has focused on wisdom as expert knowledge, as a cognitive human capacity. They distinguish between the cognitive mechanics and the cognitive pragmatics of wisdom.[29] Cognitive mechanics refers to the hardwired or biological aspects of wisdom, and the cognitive pragmatics of wisdom refers to the "software," or wisdom's cultural and informational aspects. On this account, wisdom is a kind of intelligence, in both form and content.

The Berlin Group derives their account of altruistic behavior from folk definitions of wisdom but theorize it in cognitive terms. Wisdom, on their definition, always seems to be knowledge directed at the good for oneself or others.[30] It is "an expertise in the conduct and meaning of life,"[31] particularly in the "fundamental pragmatics of life."[32] Included in these pragmatics are:

> knowledge about the conditions, variability, ontogenetic changes, and historicity of life development as well as knowledge of life's obligations and life goals; understanding of the socially and contextually intertwined nature of human life, including its finitude, cultural conditioning, and incompleteness; and knowledge about oneself and the limits of one's own knowledge and the translation of knowledge into overt behavior. Equally central to wisdom-related knowledge and judgment are the "spiritual" incomprehensibilities of life, such as the mind-body dynamics or the existence of a divine being.[33]

Without displaying all the background here, we should note that this comprehensive definition is the result of extensive theoretical work informed by extensive empirical work in developmental psychology. Baltes and the Berlin Group have done massive work on the conceptual definition of wisdom, conceptualized first out of implicit or folk theories about wisdom, and then operationalized and measured empirically, to create an explicit cognitive theoretical definition of wisdom. The definition appears to be highly refined and to have evolved over twenty-plus years of psychological work. It is not clear why Meeks and Jeste cite solely a paper presented in Nebraska, rather than the vast body of work produced by Baltes and the Berlin Group.

Still, the Berlin definition is not without its critics. In fact, one of these critics is the researcher Monika Ardelt. Ardelt's definition of wisdom is also one of Meeks and Jeste's ten sources. Ardelt, a social psychologist, states that, as part of the affective characteristic of wisdom, one finds "positive emotions and behaviors toward others."[34] However, her definition stands as a critique of that given by Baltes and the Berlin Group. She is highly critical of their cognitive focus and their exclusion of personalized definitions. Her essay unpacks the way that the Berlin Group conceptualized and operationalized their definition of wisdom.

Ardelt's critique is astute, but we would argue that she misses a far more critical point. She notes that the Berlin Group found that clinical psychologists performed better on an inventory designed to measure wisdom and, in fact, that those who had the highest scores on their wisdom scale, were indeed psychologists.[35] She argues that by conceptualizing and operationalizing wisdom as expertise, one would find that those with intellectual training in psychology would do better on a wisdom inventory. However, we would argue that perhaps the Berlin Group finds psychologists to be wise precisely because psychologists conceptualized and operationalized a particularly cognitive psychological definition of wisdom. Thus, it seems that the conceptual funneling process of the Berlin Group is better described as an epistemological circuit, a point missed by Ardelt. Suffice it to say that as part of Meeks and Jeste's ten sources, the subcomponent of "prosocial attitudes and behaviors" is uncritically derived from two theoretically opposed and mutually critical research groups.

A fourth definition upon which Meeks and Jeste relied for the subcomponent of prosocial behavior was that of Scott Brown and Jeffrey Greene. Brown and Greene are psychologists working in a university setting. They derive their definition from research on college students. They began with conversations with ten doctoral students using a qualitative social scientific research method called grounded theory.[36] Brown's initial work in 2004 is akin to describing the implicit or folk theories of these doctoral students. In-depth interviews of these students resulted in a definition that Brown believed to be grounded in the real world. This study attempted to give an overarching view of how these ten students perceived development across their four years of college and beyond.

Brown and Greene take the developmental definition described in the 2004 grounded theory study and operationalize it in their 2008 study. This study, cited by Meeks and Jeste, was an attempt to validate the operationalized definition using the instrument developed in the 2004 study.[37] Yet in this article, Brown and Greene were simply developing an inventory test. Their study was not intended to set out a conceptual definition but to validate an operational definition.

Finally, Meeks and Jeste cite the work of L. A. Jason et al. Like Brown and Greene, Jason et al., set out first to describe wisdom using grounded theory to uncover a folk definition. Forty-three people with whom the researchers were acquainted participated in the initial qualitative study. The subjects were asked to name and describe people who they thought were wise. It should be noted that one of the forty-three subjects named herself as the wisest person she knew and another named a "free-roaming whale."[38] Taking the characteristics of wisdom articulated by these forty-three people, the researchers were then able to construct a 38-item "scale tapping the construct of wisdom," which was then used in a second study.[39] In other words, Jason et al. designed an operational definition from a folk conceptual definition of wisdom.

In a second study by Jason et al., which set out to validate the operational scale, 242 college students enrolled in introduction to psychology classes at DePaul University, were given the 38-item scale called The Foundational Value Scale. The study was primarily one in which a scale was being validated both internally, by statistical comparison of the thirty-eight items to one another, and externally to five other psychological and social scales: the Center for Epidemiology Studies Depression Scale (CES-D), the Perceived Stress Scale (PSS), and the Life Orientation Test (LOT), Interpersonal Support Evaluation List, and the Marlowe-Crowne Social Desirability Scale.[40] The researchers hypothesized that "wisdom might operate as a protective factor, leading to enhanced feelings of optimism and support, and reduced stress and depression."[41] Of the original thirty-eight items, only twenty-three were included in the factor analysis. Factor analysis demonstrated five items that loaded heavily across other items. These five components were harmony (nine items), warmth (five items), intelligence (three items), connecting to nature (four items), and spirituality (two items). Meeks and Jeste took Jason et al.'s second component (warmth) to be akin to their notion of prosocial attitudes and behaviors.

This closer analysis of the five sources used by Meeks and Jeste to foreground "prosocial attitudes and behaviors" as a subcomponent of wisdom makes clear that this subcomponent may be on somewhat shaky ground. They draw from synthetic work done by Sternberg, from longitudinal cognitive behavioral work done by the Berlin Group, from Brown and Greene's inductively grounded folk definition, and from Jason et al.'s validation studies. Moreover, Ardelt's emotive approach is in direct competition with that of Baltes and the Berlin Group. We could, of course, do a similar analysis of each of the other five subcomponents of Meeks and Jeste's meta-definition of wisdom, such as emotional homeostasis or value tolerance.[42] That analysis would render a similar verdict.

Each of these research groups has a slightly different thought-style, with different fundamental theories and sometimes conflicting theories at work. Meeks and Jeste proceed as if one can simply take different concepts and operations that emerge out of different thought-styles and posit a new conceptual definition. Yet in the neuroscience of wisdom, the "Neurobiology of Wisdom" remains a landmark paper, advancing the project of establishing the new thought-community of neuroscience.

## Inverted Phrenology

Armed with this conceptual structure, Meeks and Jeste then move to correlate wisdom with neural structures. They do so by linking specific subcomponents of their definition with brain structures and functions, as well as associating the human science with genetic signatures and neurotransmitters. They do not do so by performing empirical studies. Rather, they turn to the extant empirical literature and attempt to locate something akin to "emotional homeostasis" or "prosocial attitudes and behaviors" in previous studies in order to determine which neurotransmitters or brain regions might be implicated. However, the bulk of empirical neuroscientific work focuses on negative traits and disease states (the vices). Therefore, rather than citing studies that find a positive correlation between a given subcomponent and neurobiology, they instead base their argument on literature that correlates negative traits with brain structure and function.

Take, for example, the trait of emotional homeostasis.[43] As we noted in Chapter 1, the corticolimbic system—particularly a smaller volume amygdala, a hyper-responsive amygdala, and lack of cingulate gyrus modulation of the amygdala—has been correlated in emotional impulsivity and violence. Studies of clinical depression have shown a dysfunction in the neural circuitry connecting the amygdala and the anterior cingulate such that the amygdala is hyperreactive and the cingulate is under-reactive.[44] Consequently, Meeks and Jeste draw on *these* findings to hypothesize that *opposite* traits—emotional impulsivity rather than emotional homeostasis—will be located within the same structures but differently configured. The neurobiological basis of wisdom, in other words, will be located at least in part in brain systems that inhibit negative emotion (such as anxiety or fear) and promulgate positive ones (such as gratitude or happiness). They note: "A key overarching concept in emotional homeostasis is the ability of PFC [prefrontal cortex] to inhibit limbic reactivity."[45] Continuing, they state: "Reframing negative emotional experiences as less aversive may involve recruitment of PFC regions (lateral, medial, and orbito-frontal) to dampen amygdala activity."[46] In other words, they are attempting to correlate human scientific concepts—derived as they were in a haphazard and quasi-systematic way, as described earlier—with neural substrates. Notably, these correlations are made entirely via inference, without any direct, empirical data.

Once traits have been correlated with neural structures, the next step is to link those traits to their genetic substrates. As we saw in Chapter 1, differential amygdala-cingulate activity has been associated with genetic differences in the serotonin transporter gene, which is hypothesized to be an important mediator in the causal pathway leading to emotional impulsivity and antisocial traits.[47] Meeks and Jeste, therefore, *theorize* that "controlling reactions to aversive stimuli is also related to optimal monoaminergic functioning, especially variations related to dopamine and serotonin and genes associated with monoaminergic activity."[48] In other words, they *speculate* that those with high-efficiency alleles in the MAOA gene are better able to maintain emotional homeostasis and to avoid aggressive behavior. Furthermore, they write: "partly underlying emotional regulation is impulse control, which . . . is also relevant to decision making."[49] Thus, they take a posited subcomponent—emotional homeostasis—and find studies, both genomic/neurotransmitter and neuroimaging studies, that seem to be getting at something akin to emotional impulsivity. Yet, in order to draw an inference to emotional homeostasis, they have to invert the findings on emotional impulsivity relative to the dysregulated corticolimbic system. In other words, the method employed here draws on the social and psychological literature to create a quasi-systematic definition of emotional homeostasis and then correlates it to various existing findings of genomic/neurotransmitter and neuroimaging studies about different characteristics. This method is presented as a plausible way of locating emotional homeostasis in the genome and the brain. Meeks and Jeste follow these same steps with each of the other subcomponents of wisdom.

Their main focus, however, is directed at "prosocial attitudes and behaviors," which emerge as the most important subcomponent. As they remark, "sociopaths, who may exhibit exquisite social cognition and emotional regulation that actually facilitate their selfish motives, would not be considered wise."[50] To substantiate their claim, they draw on three areas of research—mirror neurons, the prefrontal cortex, and neurotransmitters. They begin with the recent discourse surrounding mirror neurons. Mirror neurons, first discovered in primates and later uncovered in the human inferior frontal gyrus, are activated when one person observes another doing some action. For example, if one sees a professional tennis player perform a backhand stroke, mirror neurons fire in a pattern corresponding to this motor movement in the same way that they would if the observer were actually performing a backhand stroke. Neurobiologists have theorized that these neurons represent the rudimentary neurobiological elements of human empathy—the capacity to intuit another's experience. Citing a study by Decety and Jackson, which showed that "persons with greater unconscious somatic mimicry have higher ratings of self-reported altruism," Meeks and Jeste suggest that mirror neurons serve an important role in the underlying neurobiology of prosocial behavior.[51]

However, empathy is clearly more than physical mimicry; it is also connected with intuiting the internal emotional experience of another. Other research, borrowing from the psychological literature's notion of "theory of mind," has correlated the capacity to take the perspective of another person—their mental and emotional state—with activation in the medial prefrontal cortex (MPC).[52] Meeks and Jeste take this work on empathy and the MPC to the next level, linking it with other studies which examine the MPC and social interactions, specifically a 2004 article by Decety et al., "The Neural Basis of Cooperation and Competition: An fMRI Investigation."[53]

Here Decety et al. examined empathy—what they term "mentalizing"—using a psychological game paradigm to examine the underlying neurobiology. In this study, research participants engaged in a computerized game in which each subject played independently, cooperated with another in playing the game, or were placed in competition with one another. In the competitive conditions, the researchers found the MPC to be activated to a statistically significant difference when compared to other game conditions. They theorize that the competitive stance elicited increased activity in the MPC because the subject is motivated to understand the intentions of the other—to "mentalize" the competitor's stance.[54] In contrast, those subjects involved in cooperative game play showed activation in the orbitofrontal area—an area associated with reward value. Decety et al. suggest that "the reward value stems from the psychological satisfaction of reaching a common goal through interaction with a conspecific [friend or foe in the game]."[55] In other words, positive feelings of reward are stimulated during cooperation whereas brain centers focused on identifying the intentions of others are activated in competitive interactions. They conclude that "cooperation provides a social incentive and is associated with right orbitofrontal involvement, and competition requires additional mentalizing resources and is associated with an increase in medial prefrontal activity."[56] Put differently, while cooperation is more pleasurable, competition requires one "to read the mind" of one's competitor, to be more empathic with one's competitor in an odd sense. While this seems counterintuitive, it is highly compatible with competition-based economies, a point to which we shall return in Chapters 3 and 4.

Citing these studies, Meeks and Jeste seek to ground prosocial attitudes and behavior neurologically. However, they do not critically assess how empathy in this psychological game may well be less associated with knowing the other for that other's good than it is with knowing the other in order to serve one's interest in winning the game (the opposite of altruism), a point to which we shall return in future chapters. Furthermore, if the MPC and orbitofrontal area are correlated with positive social interactions, one might expect to find opposing brain functionality in those with antisocial traits. In fact, another study, entitled "Neural Correlates of Social Cooperation and Non-cooperation as a Function of Psychopathy," published in *Biological Psychiatry*, finds that "persons with high sociopathy ratings showed (relative to comparison subjects) decreased amygdala response while being uncooperative during social cooperation task and less orbitofrontal cortex activity while cooperating, suggesting a lack of aversive emotions while violating social norms and a lack of positive emotions while exhibiting social cooperation."[57] In other words, sociopaths found competition pleasurable, while finding cooperation unpleasurable.

Meeks and Jeste draw on this study to suggest that in the pathological state—sociopathy—orbitofrontal impairment renders positive emotions blunted and conscious activation impaired, whereas in the prosocial condition, the orbitofrontal cortex generates positive emotions thereby delivering the reward for virtuous behavior. Prosociality, enabled by a well-functioning brain, appears to lead to feeling good. They cite other evidence in the field of neuroeconomics to confirm this hypothesis. For instance, Moll et al. found that donating money is associated with activation in reward circuitry, mainly the nucleus accumbens (associated with pleasure). This reward circuitry is the same neural system thought to go awry in substance use disorders. Moll et al. suggest that prosocial behavior (and altruism) is connected to base biological drives toward pleasure.[58] Of course, it is no coincidence that we are speaking of "prosociality" and "antisociality" in terms akin to monetary transaction. As we shall show in later chapters, there is a tendency to conceive of altruism as a kind of economic transaction, one that is not really selfless, but instead pays dividends in making one feel good.

The neurobiological underpinning of prosocial attitudes and behaviors would be incomplete without linking the circuit from neural function to the underlying genetics and neurotransmitter mechanisms. As before, various neurotransmitter systems have been implicated, including those of dopamine and oxytocin—which are thought to be the "pleasure" hormone and the "altruism" hormone respectively. In a 2005 study published in *Molecular Psychiatry*, neuropsychologist Rachel Bachner-Melman and her colleagues associated a polymorphism in the gene coding for D4 dopamine receptor with self-reported selflessness—also described as altruism. In this study, 354 non-clinical families with multiple siblings were genetically tested for a polymorphism in the gene encoding the D4 receptor and were also asked to complete a Selflessness Scale, which purportedly measured "the propensity to ignore one's own needs and serve the needs of others."[59] Bachner-Melman et al. hypothesized as follows:

> We examined two dopaminergic genes in these subjects that we hypothesized might contribute to prosocial or altruistic traits based on the role a single variant

of these genes plays in attention deficit hyperactivity disorder (ADHD), often comorbid with antisocial behavior. Meta-analyses[60] show that the dopamine D4 receptor (DRD4) exon III 7 repeat (D4.7) and the DRD5 148 bp microsatellite variant have both been associated with ADHD in some but not all studies. We reasoned that if one variant contributes to antisocial traits, then conversely the absence of this variant or the presence of other variants might contribute to altruistic behavior.[61]

The D4 genetic polymorphism is therefore identified because of its relationship to psychopathology, specifically ADHD, and researchers test the inverse hypothesis that the alternative genotype (D4.4) will confer prosociality, the flip side of the coin. The study found that subjects who carry the D4.4 version of the gene versus the D4.7 version of the gene were more likely to self-report selflessness on psychological inventories intended to capture altruistic behavior.

The dopamine system is further linked to reward pathways associated with the mesolimbic system, including the nucleus accumbens and medial prefrontal cortex, again areas of the brain found to be associated with psychological tests for empathy. Although they do not test the relationship between D4 genotype and these brain structures, Bachner-Melman et al. conclude with the following conjecture:

> The balanced maintenance of both the D4.4 and D4.7 repeats in human evolution[62] is related to the need for diverse behavioral phenotypes in human populations partially determined by this gene, altruistic and prosocial (D4.4) vs a more aggressive, novelty seeking or perhaps even antisocial type (D4.7) ... We also suggest the notion that the linkage between reward and altruistic attitudes provide the neurochemical substrate and "hard wiring" needed to drive acts that benefit others even at the expense of reducing one's own fitness. We "feel good" and rewarded by a dopamine pulse when doing good deeds. Selection for specific polymorphisms that "reward" altruistic acts via brain dopaminergic pathways is the grist for the evolutionary mill.[63]

As in the neurobiological narrative of vice, here the neurochemical explanation for virtue derives from the material of the gene. It is the gene that "makes" the brain that manifests empathy (prosocial emotionality) and altruism (prosocial attitudes), which are emergent behavioral properties.[64]

## Biopolitics and the Social Control of Vice and Virtue

Meeks and Jeste's six subcomponents of wisdom seem almost uncontroversial. Yet, a closer look makes clear that these subcomponents carry a moral and even a political valence in two key ways. First, the subcomponents of wisdom reverberate the political values of leftist political liberalism—pragmatic decision-making, value tolerance, ambiguity. These are the political ideals of a particular segment of powerful people in the West.[65] No liberal democrat would disagree with these subcomponents. Yet, one can easily imagine the subcomponents of wisdom that a libertarian might posit: personal responsibility, self-motivation, freedom, suspension of moral judgment. And yet a different set of virtues would be envisaged by a group of people more concerned with security than liberty: deference to authority, meekness, the good of the many outweighs the good of the one; or again in a small tribal community: communitarian commitment, sharing, constancy, and so forth. Would it not be possible to find the virtues of different political communities in the neural circuitry and even the genes of the citizenry?

In other words, the list of virtues in Meeks and Jeste's definition of wisdom is socially constructed, characteristics that resonate with the dominant science emerging out of liberal societies. They have been gleaned from psychological studies drawn from slightly different, but overlapping, subgroups of the neuroscientific thought-community. Moreover, these characteristics, more often than not, begin with *folk definitions* from people hailing from a very narrow social demographic—largely college-educated, economically upper-middle to upper-class, likely predominantly white and male community, in short, those who are socially "successful." The characteristics of wisdom or happiness or virtue identified by such a cohort, "refined" via conceptual funneling, are then redefined as novel virtues, no longer "temperance" but rather "emotional homeostasis," no longer "prudence" but variants on "social decision-making/pragmatic knowledge of life" or "tolerance of ambiguity." These new, putatively neutral clinical and scientific trait, pro*social* behavior, supposedly shorn of their moral baggage but derived from the morality of a dominant Western political ideal, are not "found" in the brain or in the genome. They are political values that are mapped post hoc onto fMRI studies or onto genetic studies of neurotransmitters. Supposedly located in and therefore reified in the genome and the brain, neuroscience claims to have discovered the true biological foundations of a therefore universal morality.

Yet not only does the content of the neuroscience of morality carry political valence; as we saw in Chapter 1, the leap from identifying particular "loci" associated with a behavioral trait and calls for sociopolitical programs to intervene at these neural and genetic sites is almost immediate. In the case of the neuroscience of virtue, the practical implications lead to the imaginings of technological moral bioenhancement.[66] Arguing against what has been termed the bioconservative position—a position that finds it morally improper to enhance human biology—philosopher Thomas Douglas argues for the moral permissibility of morally enhancing oneself.[67] He rejects any moral prohibitions that would prevent one's brain from being manipulated in order to redirect one's psychological motivations for the good. Ingmar Persson and Julian Savulescu go much further, arguing that there is a moral imperative to enhance ourselves morally—now that we can enhance our intellectual capacities, we may create humans who are capable of destroying the world, and we must have moral capacities that prevent that from happening.[68] Moreover, they claim that without moral bioenhancement—literally intervening in the brains and genomes of people—we may not have the moral motivation to change our behaviors that will stop climate change.[69]

More than one thinker has issued a call to screen for and to select out those genes that seem to be involved in violent behavior.[70] Adrian Raine, as we have pointed out in Chapter 1, and Sam Harris, as we will show in Chapter 3, both call for active measures to weed out those with brain disorders—through various social mechanisms or technological brain interventions—that may lead to violence. Likewise, Mark Walker has suggested that, since we morally enhance through socialization and educational programs, and since we seem constantly to fail to improve, perhaps the problem lies in our human nature. Thus, he proposes a Genetic Virtue Project anchored in our genes. According to Walker, nearly all personality traits have some degree of heritability, implicating genetic factors in that subset of traits identified as virtues.[71] He explores the genetic origins of truthfulness, justice, and caring attitudes. While citing scientific evidence for each case, none of the studies that he cites are really designed to test truthfulness, justice, or caring per se. For instance, as with most of the studies we have reviewed regarding the neuroscience of virtue, his claim about truthfulness is made indirectly through appeal to literature on antisocial personality disorder, which has "lying" as one of its component features. He cites papers claiming that there are moral contracts among primates and that there are "neurological structures . . . for detecting those who cheat on social contracts."[72]

As with truthfulness and justice, Walker does not cite actual genetic studies showing a genetic link to something akin to care, but points to studies in primates that suggest something akin to caring.[73]

Based on these correlations, Walker proposes a pragmatic course of action:

> Having identified the relevant genes, the practical execution of the GVP [Genetic Virtue Project] . . . could proceed in at least two different ways. In the first instance, preimplantation diagnosis could be used to select those embryos that have profiles consistent with the potential for learning virtuous behavior. In the second, genetic engineering techniques could be employed to alter extant embryos to exhibit more of the desirable genes (and fewer of the undesirable genes).[74]

Most geneticists would roll their eyes at such grandiose suggestions. Yet Walker believes that there is no scientific or theoretical reason why his GVP will fail—only practical, political problems stand in the way. While finding state-mandated virtues problematic, he opines that states in liberal democracies would be less likely to implement GVP as they tend to remain neutral on robust conceptions of the good.[75] Parents, perhaps, might like to select for these virtuous personality traits much like they would select for intelligence or longevity or having robust immune systems.[76] However, even here there will be political problems because parents who have genetically enhanced the virtue of their children may not want to expose them to the vicious children who have not been enhanced.

Yet for Walker, the political dimension only becomes important after we ("we") decide to implement a particular set of virtues through the genetic manipulation. He ignores the fact that there is a political dimension inherent in the virtues he wishes to genetically enhance. Such naïveté with regard to politics also plagues other proposals for moral enhancement as well those the entire project of the neuroscience of morality. Thus, from Viding and Frith to Meeks and Jeste, we must conclude that researchers are engaged in a new inverted and prospective phrenology, this time couched in the powerful rhetoric of neuroscience. While claiming to discover the roots of our behaviors, they are in reality reading that behavior backward into the brains. Now, instead of feeling bumps on the skull and correlating them with traits mapped onto cerebral anatomy, we read fMRI scans that "light up," signaling the presence or lack of socially normative behaviors, propensities, and potentialities. The ground for this new phrenology is more scientifically secure and predictive in the way the old phrenologists had hoped their science would be. All the while, as with their predecessors, the social and political assumptions of these scientists are enacted into social regimes of control by the new phrenologists.

In the end, whether attempting to translate "neuroscientific findings" into social policies and programs to find "cancers on the body politic," as Adrian Raine has called them,[77] or to enhance prosocial correlates, as Walker or Meeks and Jeste hope, we see that neuroscience is a deeply Baconian project.[78] Following the vision of Francis Bacon for whom the purpose of science was "first and foremost the amelioration of the human condition and the 'relief of man's estate,'" through technological interventions designed to build a great society where humans can flourish.[79] Yet here the vision exceeds even Bacon. It becomes clear in these proposals that the biological material of the body politic is the body—the genome and/or the brain—of the individual. That is to say, the social ills that afflict us are no longer understood to reside in the will of those who perpetrate violence and vice against the body politic; nor is it thought to be in the political or economic structures. Instead, the social ills are rather understood as embedded in the "bad" genes or "bad" brains of those bodies that are the subcomponents of the body politic.

What goes unnoticed is a subtle eugenic and triumphalist thrust that animates these political and technological imperatives to morally, and thus politically enhance the citizens; for the story maintains that the demise of society is written in our genes and in our brains. It becomes imperative to intervene to protect the populace from rogue antisocial elements whose neural substrates do not promote the common good. The story asserts that it is for their own good that we should intervene upon these defective brains. In short, we have a biopolitics, in which the political economy of the dominant and powerful create new knowledge that further reinforces the dominance of those in power. Government supports research aimed at curing social ills; neuroscientists tell us the neurobiological narrative of vice; pharmaceutical and technological research is directed at curing these defective genes and brains and behaviors, and promoting social and political harmony; the media pick up these triumphalist stories convincing the body politic of their truthfulness. Neuroscience aims at techno-scientific control; it participates in a biopolitics of morality, controlling *bios* for the sake of the *polis*. All the while, we ignore the fact that the so-called common good is a product of those who have created and who sustain this biopolitics, those in political power, those powerful enough to tell us stories about genes, and brains, and antisocial behaviors, all aimed at social behaviors that maintain the political economy.

## The Neuroscientific Narrative of Vice and Virtue

From Meyer-Lindenberg et al., to Meeks and Jeste to the vast array of neuroscientific studies, we find the intertwined fields of neurobiology, psychopathology, and positive psychology. Coming together in this powerful new thought-community, they seek correlations between what the neurobiologist sees in genes and brain structures with what the psychologists and sociologists see in human behaviors. The result is a *neuroscientific narrative of vice and virtue*. This narrative tells the following story. Certain genes, sometimes combined with environmental factors imagined largely in economic terms, give rise to neural structures and functional features of brain activity, typically centered in the amygdala, anterior cingulate, and ventromedial prefrontal cortex. Neural pathways linking these regions of the brain give rise to psychological traits, such as empathy or negative affectivity, which in turn, influence behavior, including moral behavior toward others. Some of these moral behaviors are antisocial—they are vicious—and others are prosocial—virtuous. The functioning system can go awry at several steps along the way. One can have polymorphisms at the genetic level; one can be reared in abusive or impoverished socioeconomic environments.[80] Either genes alone, or genes under environmental influences, can lead to small and hyperreactive amygdalae that are not under the direct control of a hyporesponsive cingulate gyrus, resulting in emotional lability such that one acts out in an antisocial manner. Alternatively, a larger amygdala better controlled by the cingulate results in emotional homeostasis—a prerequisite for the display of wisdom, which is made manifest in prosocial behaviors.

It does not take much creativity to note the key points of intervention—genes, neurotransmitters, brain loci (amygdala, cingulate, ventromedial prefrontal cortex), and neural functioning. To get better impulse control, one simply has to intervene upon the amygdala or to increase the control of the various regions of the cingulate gyrus to prevent the impulsive or violent behaviors. Those like Viding and Frith suggest that if we understand these pathways, we might be able to develop interventions to curb antisocial behavior and reduce violence. Those like Meeks and Jeste, who imagine a world where peace and harmony are possible, propose promoting positive prosocial behaviors by targeting those regions of the brain responsible for prosociality. They imagine a techno-scientific approach to social control.

Where Meeks and Jeste had to search far and wide to find the neuroscientific virtues, the vices come ready made. The neuroscientific vices find their ground in the DSM, which reifies pathologies through its systematic attempts to connect concepts of antisociality to research regimes. Where Meeks and Jeste's virtues are tenuous, the vices seem more secure because they carry the systemization of a very powerful neuroscientific establishment: psychiatry. The DSM designation of antisocial personality disorder has been biologized in the catecholamine hypothesis, operationalized in antisocial personality indexes, and validated on untold numbers of inmates, among others. In fact, in many states within the United States, one cannot be paroled if one scores poorly on Hare's psychopathy test.[81]

Yet, we must ask: why is *this* the narrative told by the emerging thought-community that is neuroscience? After all, alternative narratives are possible. For example, is the notion of emotional homeostasis as construed by Meeks and Jeste compatible with righteous anger? In anger, homeostasis gives way to an up-regulation of emotionality directed at an injustice existing outside the biological parameters of the individual person. Meeks and Jeste do not distinguish between righteous anger engaged passionately against an injustice (prosocial behavior) and an impulsive anger run amok in destructive rage (antisocial behavior). More subtly, their logic cannot account for how an individual brain might be disrupted by traumatic experience yet display wisdom in the face of such brokenness. The experience of PTSD as recounted by combat veterans, whose neurobiology has apparently been altered by the experiences of war, may be judged as failing in critical ways, and yet these lives of these persons may also represent an embodied narrative of the costs of war—perhaps a hidden source of wisdom, not only for the sufferer but also for society.[82]

Moreover, it is unclear how the neuroscientific narrative of vice and virtue can help differentiate between the ways that similar neurological processes might result in a particular trait—for example, impulsivity or risk-taking—being assessed differently in different social contexts. For example, how do we distinguish between the impulsivity required by the soldier who reacts in a combat situation, saving the lives of his comrades-in-arms—a prosocial action; but when he returns home and exhibits the same impulsivity toward violence, he is deemed antisocial. Or between the impulsivity that leads a person to assault someone (again labeled as "antisocial") and propensity toward "risk-taking" involved in venture capitalism? And is there not a kind of emotional regulation needed to carry out a Ponzi scheme, which at least at the beginning seems to have the appearance of prosociality in its claims to be creating wealth?

Let us dwell on this point for a moment. For as we saw in Chapter 1, the neuroscientific narrative of vice has been shaped from its very beginning by a cultural assumption correlating low SES (i.e., poverty) and pathology or antisociality. Although less studied by neurobiology, a broad cultural presumption posits the inverse: that the virtuous—who are self-disciplined, work hard, and control their reproductivity (though not necessarily their sexual activity)—will prosper economically. Behind this is a second cultural assumption that sees the act of wealth creation as a virtue. Shortly after the 2008 economic crash, Lloyd Blankfein, former CEO of Goldman Sachs, defended the work of the financial industry:

> Banks are really serving the greater good. We help companies to grow by helping them to raise capital ... Companies that grow create wealth. This, in turn, allows people to have jobs that create more growth and more wealth. It's a virtuous cycle. We have a social purpose.[83]

When asked whether one could make too much money, Blankfein replied that he was "doing God's work."[84]

Yet a series of post-crash studies are beginning to suggest that these "prosocial" multibillionaires possess many personality traits that outside the context of venture capitalism are pathologized as antisocial. The entrepreneur—a new character in the MacIntyrean sense—and the addict, it seems, are hard to distinguish. As Johns Hopkins neuroscientist David Linden notes:

> the psychological profile of a compelling leader—think of tech pioneers such as Jeff Bezos, Larry Ellison, and Steven P. Jobs—is also that of the compulsive risk-

taker, someone with a high degree of novelty seeking behavior. In short, what we see in leaders is often the same kind of personality type found in addicts, whether they are dependent on gambling, alcohol, sex, or drugs.[85]

Not only do they share similar traits, evidence suggests that many "great men" have in fact been "addicts." These traits, which can be harnessed to great business and financial success, often lead those same successful entrepreneurs to cross the boundaries between the legal and illegal, not infrequently committing financial and drug crimes as well. It is as if the "virtue" of making exorbitant amounts of money or launching highly successful businesses is understood as offsetting what might in others be deemed vices.

Or consider David Segal's story, "Just Manic Enough: Seeking Perfect Entrepreneurs."[86] Segal argues that "a thin line separates the temperament of a promising entrepreneur from a person who could use, as they say in psychiatry, a little help." He describes a young entrepreneur making a pitch to an angel investor. The man, he notes:

> displays many of the symptoms of a person having what psychologists call a hypomanic episode. According to the Diagnostic and Statistical Manual—the occupation's bible of mental disorders—these symptoms include grandiosity, an elevated and expansive mood, racing thoughts, and little need for sleep.[87]

As with the addictive personality argument, Segal cites the usual range of local heroes—Teddy Roosevelt, George Patton, David O. Selznick, Henry Ford, and Steve Jobs—as exhibiting this "hypomanic temperament."

A third set of studies has looked at the relationship between successful financial traders and psychopaths. Composite profiles of those drawn to and successful in the fast-paced, high-pressure environment are found to have parallels with psychopathic personality, particularly around gregariousness, impulsiveness, dishonesty, and lack of empathy. Studies cited note that "professional stock traders actually outperform diagnosed psychopaths when it comes to competitive and risk-taking behavior . . . and that the traders were surprisingly willing to cause harm to their competitors if they thought it would bring them an advantage."[88] These studies reprise others that began emerging in the early 1990s that compared stockbrokers with the seriously mentally ill and the brain damaged.

Other studies look at other traits. A series of studies have sought to correlate wealth and compassion. While the presumption is that those who are richer would be less likely to lie, cheat, and steal, evidence suggests that the opposite is true—that increase in social status correlates with a decrease in compassion.[89] Moreover, one study found that wealth also changes one's perspective on virtue itself: "that wealthier people are more likely to agree with statements that greed is justified, beneficial, and morally defensible. These attitudes ended up predicting participants' likelihood of engaging in unethical behavior."[90] Along the same lines, researchers have found that "Participants who indicated greater endorsement of utilitarian solutions had higher scores on measures of psychopathy, Machiavellianism, and life meaninglessness."[91]

Yet for some, the payoff does not mask the fundamental dynamic. Economist Jeffrey Sachs correlates those addictive, antisocial traits mentioned earlier that make for success with criminality. As he notes,

> The world is drowning in corporate fraud, and the problems are probably greatest in rich countries—those with supposedly "good governance." Poor-country governments probably accept more bribes and commit more offenses, but it is rich countries that host the global companies that carry out the largest offenses. Money talks, and it is corrupting politics and markets all over the world.
>
> Hardly a day passes without a new story of malfeasance. Every Wall Street firm has paid significant fines during the past decade for phony accounting, insider trading, securities fraud, Ponzi schemes, or outright embezzlement by CEOs. A massive insider-trading ring is currently on trial in New York, and has implicated some leading financial-industry figures. And it follows a series of fines paid by America's biggest investment banks to settle charges of various securities violations.[92]

The moral evaluation of behaviors, prosocial or antisocial, is possible only outside the story told by neuroscience.

This returns us to our preceding question: why is the narrative we have traced—this neuroscientific narrative of morality—told by the neuroscience thought-community? Here we recall Fleck. We have shown, in these first two chapters, how this new field of neuroscience—a new entity born by forging together two different sorts of sciences—tells a neuroscientifically shaped, socially constructed story of moral behavior. This story—that moves from genes (molded in a social environment) to brains to behavior—is not simply an objective account of scientific fact. Neuroscientific observations do not begin with genes; neuroscientific observations do not begin with brains. Neuroscientific observations begin with behaviors that are already grounded in a socially predetermined relationship between the pathological and the normal, behaviors that are deemed desirable or undesirable by the larger social context. In the mode of discovery, one does not in fact start with the genes, nor with the neurotransmitters, nor with the neural structure or functioning. One begins with behavior, which is thought independently of science to be bad or good, moral or immoral, vicious or virtuous, antisocial or prosocial, according to the political economy of those in power to make such decisions. The conceptual funneling process begins in the definitions created by a larger, societal thought-community. Conceptual funneling is in fact an epistemological circuit created by the experts in neuroscience.

Yet, the vector flows in both directions. Just as neuroscience has been deeply shaped by its broader cultural context, the findings from this scientific thought-community (Fleck's esoteric community) have, from the beginning, moved almost seamlessly into the elite levels of society. Here, translated into popular language, "the neuro" has ever-increasing cultural purchase and interpretive power. Without this mutually reinforcing relationship, neuroscience would be simply another esoteric scientific thought-community. Yet why, we must ask, has neuroscience and particularly its narrative of morality been amplified so readily and resoundingly by the power-brokers of US and Western culture?

In order to answer that question, we must first demonstrate the extent to which this narrative has moved into popular culture and how that uptake has further shaped it. To this task we turn in Chapter 3. At the heart of this story, there are several contradictions found in the political economy of the late modern West. One is that this neuroscientific narrative of vice and virtue seems to eliminate a critical component of the traditional account of the virtues, namely, individual agency. As we noted earlier, A (genes) + B (social environment) leads to functional neuroanatomy, which leads to behavior—a mechanism of bottom-up causation. Traditional understandings of vice and virtue have top-down mechanisms, in which a rational agent, habituated in the virtues of her society, exercises some degree of top-down control over her own biological activities, in habituation, for example, but also on her own behaviors. In contemporary neuroscience, such agency is construed as a convenient illusion, posited *post hoc*, giving us a false sense of control. Neuroscience suggests that the *perceived* sense of agency, "the *feeling* that we are the cause of our actions and their consequences" is generated by the inferior parietal cortex, and that moral rationality is a *post hoc* explanation of our actions.[93] Thus, our sense of ourselves as acting agents is ultimately deemed to be an illusion, simply a product of the gene and brain, perhaps interacting with the environment. Does it make sense to speak of morality (virtues or vices) without agency? Does neuroscience not have a moral anthropology unto itself?

As noted earlier, the neuroscientific narrative claims not to be engaged in a moral endeavor. It is in the popular neuroscience that the elision of moral agency comes most clearly into relief. That which is implicit in the emerging neuroscientific thought-community becomes explicit in the attempt to translate neuroscience into the broader thought-community of contemporary society. Here, as we shall see, we are called to imagine there is no downward control, no rational agency that can push back against the biological and social influences on behavior. This trend conveniently aligns with recent developments in our dominant political economy, which has shifted from an account of persons as free economic agents as motivated by rational self-interest to those who only act based on what feels good and whose self-interest is predetermined by the market, which is the new agent of freedom. Popular neuroscience reproduces these fault lines grounded in the history of Western political economy. We turn now to the popularizers of neuroscience to complete the narrative.

# 3

# Popular (Neuro)Science and Other Political Schemes

According to Scimago Journal Rankings, *Nature Reviews Neuroscience* was the top neuroscience journal in 2018 with an H-index of 375 (tied with *Nature Neuroscience*) and an average of 32.24 citations per document (two years).[1] Yet even in the era of the internet and open source publishing, few regular people—even few scholars outside the field of neuroscience—read articles from *Nature Reviews Neuroscience*. Or, for that matter, from any of the 149 other neuroscience journals ranked by Scimago. Yet in the twenty-first century, all things are neuro. One can now find Neuro Coffee that "supports brain health," the Neuro line of products from Paul Mitchell that will "revolutionize how you style your hair with innovative tools," and Neuro Drinks, hyped by none other than Kim Kardashian.

fMRI brain images are now as familiar to children and the public at large as the double-helix. "The neuro" has become the dominant cultural icon of the twenty-first century. How has this happened? Certainly, federal projects like the BRAIN Initiative play a role. But findings from the insider discourse of the neuroscience thought-community do not land in the ordinary citizen's inbox or Twitter feed unaided. Rather, as Fleck noted, to become established as a scientific fact, findings must move beyond the small, scientific thought-community to a wider public. In the first two chapters, we examined the esoteric discourse of neuroscience and unpacked the neuroscientific narratives of vice and virtue respectively. In this chapter, we begin to examine the symbiotic relationship between neuroscience and contemporary culture. In order to display how neuroscience's thought-style has infused public consciousness, we turn to the popularizers of neuroscience of morality.

More specifically, in Chapters 1 and 2, we demonstrated the way that notions of vice and virtue, which originate in and are deeply embedded in the larger community of Western culture, have been redefined and transformed into proxies by neuroscience. Neuroscience reifies these proxies by claiming to find their origin in the genome and the brain. We also showed how these proxies carry with them a subtle political valence, particularly in the ways that socioeconomic factors are conceptualized, operationalized, and then become variables that researchers hope to correlate with both brain structure/function and behaviors.

In this chapter, we examine the translation of neuroscience from scientific to popular literature, showing how these redefined and reconstituted vices and virtues make their way into the larger, exoteric community. As we move in this chapter from strictly scientific renderings to those thinkers who popularize neuroscience, the political and economic dimensions no longer remain implicit but come more fully into relief. Redolent with claims, terms, and methods infused even more overtly with political and economic commitments, the popularizers continue the larger project of the neuroscientific thought-community, recursively reifying these commitments by grounding them in the putatively objective facticity of the brain and the genome.

While it was tempting to simply review literature with titles like *Evil Genes* or *Murderous Minds*, we instead survey three of the most important and scientifically astute popularizers of modern neuroscience—Jonathan Haidt, Sam Harris, and Paul Zak. Each is a leading figure in the science of morality, and each is a prolific high-culture public intellectual, translating the science of morality to a hungry public. Each thinker is interested in morality and holds that morality can be understood scientifically. Each is also interdisciplinary in his approach, with two of them having primary disciplines outside neurobiology. Haidt is a social psychologist, whose primary interest is in moral and political psychology. Harris has PhD-level training in neuroscience, but seeks to write more as a philosopher and public intellectual. Zak is an economist by training but is interested in the psychological and the biological roots of economic and moral behavior. Haidt is the most careful. Harris is the boldest in his claims. Zak is the most reductive.

In the writings of these public intellectuals of neuroscience, we hear a common narrative. In this story, science is beginning to prove that morality is less about rationality and more about moral tastes or preferences, based in neurologically generated experiences of pleasure and pain. Rooted in our evolutionary biology, these moral tastes served to bind social groups together for the purposes of survival. Biologically grounded, these moral tastes give rise to human behaviors that are more instinctual or automatic and unconscious than we have normally understood, with rational deliberation, conscience, or choice being merely the post hoc operations of our cerebral cortex working to understand or justify our actions. As such, morality is largely not under our control. This bottom-up account of morality combined with the continuing importance of morality for society's well-being suggests, in the end, that the political and economic order must necessarily act as the regulative locus for the possibility of moral behavior, or, in other words, help us control of our animal emotions.

In order for the neuroscientific narrative of morality to be heard by the larger community of Western societies, touchstones must already exist in the larger society. We claim in this chapter that while the popularizers translate the science in a way that the public can understand, there must already be resources in circulation that permit the larger society to take up the science. These shared background assumptions are a common set of regnant beliefs about the relationship of the human actor to the social milieu. A regnant anthropology, however inchoate it may be, grounds the shared assumptions of the neuroscientists of morality, the popularizers, and the larger society. In this chapter, we bring this implicit anthropology into relief.

## Haidt's Righteous Mind: The Politics of the Brain

One of the most careful popularizers of the science of morality is Jonathan Haidt. By training, Haidt is located within the human sciences. He draws on the findings of neurobiology and evolutionary biology in order to discover the psychological roots and mechanisms of political and moral behavior. He seeks and finds the source of this behavior in psychological predispositions, which in turn have some basis in the brain.

Haidt is a social psychologist, who cut his teeth as a moral psychologist in an academic department of psychology. Since 2011, he has served as the Thomas Cooley Professor of Ethical Leadership at New York University's Stern School of Business. His research focuses primarily on the psychology of morality and the moral emotions, particularly as they apply to efficiency and ethics in economics and business. He describes his work as helping "economists and other social scientists to figure out how to make businesses, non-profits, cities, and other systems work more efficiently and ethically,"[2] "with only minimal need for directly training people to behave ethically."[3] His books include *The Happiness Hypothesis: Finding Modern Truth in Ancient Wisdom* and *The Righteous Mind: Why Good People Are Divided by Politics and Religion*, the former attempting to bring the wisdom of the ages into conversation with the contemporary science of happiness and the latter attempting to explain why we find Western societies divided by morality and politics.[4] A presenter of three TED talks, author of numerous articles in *The New York Times* and other news outlets, and guest on The Colbert Report, Haidt has impeccable credentials as one of the leading translators of the findings of neuroscience into the popular media.[5] Here we focus on Haidt's landmark book, *The Righteous Mind*, which explores (per its promo page) "one of the hottest topics in the sciences: morality." Reaching number six on *The New York Times* best-seller list in 2012, it has been translated into multiple languages; excerpts from the book have also been published as separate products in both English and translations.

Haidt is measured and thoughtful in his reading of morality, politics, and psychology, and careful at interpreting the science. He draws widely from an array of disciplines spanning philosophy, history, politics, evolutionary biology, cross-cultural studies of moral attitudes, and experimental psychology, in addition to neurobiological studies.[6] As such, his work depends less upon the technological dimensions of neuroscientific research. But, as with our previous figures, he deftly correlates neuroscientific findings with material from the other literatures, drawing inferences that ground social science theories in genes and brains. Thus, *The Righteous Mind* is a synthetic work; it should be thought of less as a work of science and more as a work of public philosophy.

The book is divided into three parts, each of which accumulates evidence for three claims about morality and politics. These claims are, as the section titles indicate:

Principle 1: Intuitions Come First, Strategic Reasoning Second
Principle 2: There's More to Morality than Harm and Fairness
Principle 3: Morality Binds and Blinds.[7]

The upshot of these principles is that morality and politics is primarily a function of emotions, of moral intuition—what Haidt calls moral tastes—and less so about rational deliberation. He calls his moral psychology *a social intuitionist* model. In order to unpack this model, we will spend more time focusing on Haidt's second principle, but we will briefly describe the evidence that he garners for each claim. We will show that his work is built on a theory of moral taste, while marginalizing rational moral agency and emphasizing the automaticity of much of moral behavior.

For each of his principles, Haidt proposes and deploys a metaphor. For his first principle, "intuitions come first, strategic reasoning second," the corresponding metaphor is the elephant and the rider: "the mind is divided, like a rider on an elephant, and the rider's job is to serve the elephant."[8] The rider is reason or rationality, and the elephant is moral emotion or taste. Haidt claims that for the past four centuries, morality has gotten this metaphor backward. Especially since the Enlightenment, theories of morality, he claims, have been too centered on rationality, as epitomized in the extreme rationalism of both Immanuel Kant and Jeremy Bentham. Setting aside his problematic claims about Jeremy Bentham, Haidt argues that morality has been the product of Western society's emphasis upon reason and the individual—or, in other words, the rider.[9] He finds this misunderstanding not only in moral philosophy but in developmental and moral psychology as well, taking to task luminaries like Jean Piaget and Lawrence Kohlberg, who have focused primarily on the cognitive development of children.[10]

For Haidt, this idea that morality is primarily about cognition is an artifact of Western individualism. He argues instead that morality is primarily driven by group identity and moral intuitions or "gut feelings."[11] As the centerpiece of this section, Haidt cites a series of psychological studies showing that cross-culturally (or "universally") many decisions are made strictly based on disgust or a violation of some rule that appears not to have any aspect of harm.[12] In these studies, subjects were presented with behavior many might deem disgusting and asked if they found it moral or immoral. For example, they might be presented with scenarios like this: "A man goes to the supermarket once a week and buys a chicken. But before cooking the chicken, he has sexual intercourse with it. He then cooks and eats it."[13] The subjects were then asked about the morality of the man's actions and challenged as to why they found the action immoral. Other studies asked subjects to reflect on the morality of particular scenarios while standing next to foul-smelling things—like dog excrement—to see if subtle negative sensory (read: emotional) contexts shape people's moral deliberations. For Haidt, these studies indicate that certain levels of disgust—and therefore unconscious emotional responses—can change how we behave and what we think about the morality of a situation.

The scenarios used in these studies were carefully crafted to ensure: (1) that they included an action which typically registers to people as disgusting; and (2) that by that action no harm was done to the actor or to another person. The man who has sex with his store-bought chicken before he eats it is not causing harm to himself, others, or the chicken.[14] Yet many respondents, even those in Western societies, will make a moral judgment that this behavior is wrong. Others will initially claim it to be wrong, but they will gradually come to realize that they cannot figure out what is wrong about it, and subsequently conclude that they just don't like it. In Western liberal or libertarian societies, many more respondents will conclude that the behavior is odd but not necessarily a moral failing on the part of the man.

Haidt concludes from such studies that our sense of right and wrong has more to do with feelings, like disgust, than with rationality, and seems more grounded in the emotional centers of our brains, rather than the rational and cognitive centers. He thus concludes:

> *the mind is divided, like a rider on an elephant, and the rider's job is to serve the elephant.* The rider is our conscious reasoning—the stream of words and images of which we are fully aware. The elephant is the other 99 percent of mental processes—the ones that occur outside of awareness but that actually govern most of our behavior.[15]

In other words, our moral judgments are primarily driven by the way the elephant—our feelings of disgust and desire—intuitively perceives and responds to a situation; we are only marginally able to control the elephant with our rationality. Drawing on cross-cultural studies, he claims that these feelings of disgust or desire are innate and not strictly speaking cultural. However, culture can and does shape our moral deliberations because most Westerners participating in these studies will eventually conclude that the behavior is not immoral because no one is harmed. Thus, culture has something to do with the final assessment of the behavior.

Haidt notes that, in fact, if morality were primarily a function of reason, the world would be full of psychopaths. "Psychopaths," he asserts, "reason but don't feel ... babies feel, but don't reason."[16] In other words, psychopaths reason perfectly but lack any sign of empathy. It is the empathic dimension, for Haidt, that makes an action moral.

> Psychopathy does not appear to be caused by poor mothering or early trauma, or to have any other nurture-based explanation. It's a genetically heritable condition[17] that creates brains that are unmoved by the needs, suffering, or dignity of others.[18] The elephant doesn't respond with the slightest lean to the gravest injustice. The rider is perfectly normal—he does strategic reasoning quite well. But the rider's job is to serve the elephant, not to act as a moral compass.[19]

Haidt's claim that psychopathy is not based in nurture seems only partially correct in light of studies by Caspi et al. and by Sadeh et al., which we cited in Chapters 1 and 2. Also note that his thinking follows the typical bottom-up causal arrow, from genes to brains to behavior. Thus, "[i]ntuitions come first, and strategic reasoning comes second," functioning more like a press secretary (a second metaphor he deploys frequently throughout the book), attempting to give explanations for the way that one has behaved, but only after the fact.

In Part II of *The Righteous Mind*, Haidt turns to his second principle: "*there's more to morality than harm and fairness.*"[20] This second principle spotlights a key problem of generalization in moral psychology and much of neuroscience: can we conclude universally valid moral insights from a predominantly Western scientific and philosophical framework deployed primarily on Western subjects? Here Haidt makes an important cultural observation. He notes that Western, Educated, Industrialized, Rich, and Democratic (WEIRD) societies[21] have, at least since the 1700s, privileged normative moral frameworks focused on harms and fairness, the two great moral principles from modern Western thought. Such mores, Haidt claims, correlate with individualism. Haidt points to evidence from the cross-cultural moral psychological literature, showing that in more traditional sociocentric cultures, harm and fairness are only two moral intuitions, embedded within a wider embrace of more dominant moral commitments, particularly loyalty, authority, and sanctity.[22] As we suggested at the end of Chapter 2, if moral psychological and neuroscientific studies were to be conducted in non-WEIRD cultures, other moral principles would likely emerge as operative, principles more concerned with the social rather than an individualist dimension.[23] Yet, he again asserts that these non-Western moral principles are equally not so much rules but rather intuitions grounded in the affective or emotion centers of the brain. In other words, the brain's emotional centers, not its rational centers, are the primary drivers.

In fact, for Haidt, it is a misnomer to even refer to notions of fairness (justice) or harm as principles. Rather, he maintains that Western moral psychology has uncovered fairness and harm as important moral *tastes*. The concept of moral tastes provides the core of Part II of *The Righteous Mind*. By moral tastes, Haidt means something akin to the notion of "moral senses" advocated by eighteenth-century-philosopher David Hume. As we will see in Chapter 6, for Hume, sense experience could be both pleasurable or noxious; similarly, Haidt's moral tastes also appear in binaries. Like our other five senses, Haidt asserts that our moral tastes are biologically grounded, though he is not interested in pinpointing their exact neural location, seeing them as primarily psychological concepts.

In his seventh chapter, "The Moral Foundations of Politics," Haidt identifies and discusses at length each of five moral tastes: Care/Harm, Fairness/Cheating, Loyalty/Betrayal, Authority/Subversion, Sanctity/Degradation. After an interlude describing his work correlating these tastes with people's stated political preferences in the tumultuous US context from 2005 to 2011, he adds in his eighth chapter "The Conservative Advantage" a sixth taste: Liberty/Oppression. He outlines how each of these moral tastes has led to evolutionary survival benefit for the contemporary human animal, and then postulates how they now serve as a foundation for morality and politics. Thus, he uses the phrases "moral taste" and "moral foundation" interchangeably.

As noted, in modern Western liberal democracies two tastes—Care/Harm and Fairness/Cheating—rise above the others. The Care foundation allows the human animal to survive in the face of evolutionary pressures. Whereas many organisms survive by producing numerous offspring, humans survive by investing more energy in the form of care in each individual offspring.[24] The Fairness/Cheating foundation also promotes survival in the face of evolutionary threats by allowing social bonds to overcome the so-called "selfish gene" phenomenon. Rather than a human acting solely to save his own hide or the hides of those who share his own particular genes, certain socially active emotional pressures "triggered" by acts of reciprocity and cooperation keep the human from acting selfishly. Haidt's language here is important to hear:

For millions of years, our ancestors faced the adaptive challenge of reaping these benefits without getting suckered. Those whose moral emotions compelled them to play "tit for tat" reaped more of these benefits than those who played any other strategy, such as "help anyone who needs it" (which invites exploitation), or "take but don't give" (which can work just once with each person; pretty soon nobody's willing to share pie with you).[25]

Such practices of exchange (or economics), Haidt argues, allowed humans to move beyond the "selfish gene" to altruism that promoted group survival.[26] Given the political contingencies in the West, where individualism reigns supreme but where political agreements also navigate (in theory) between extreme individualism and group survival, it is no wonder that Care/Harm and Fairness/Cheating are essential to Western political arrangements, and thus they take precedence in Western moral psychology. Care and fairness are prosocial; harm and cheating are antisocial.

While these two moral tastes take precedence in the West, all six moral tastes remain operative and likewise ground moral beliefs and political commitments. The Loyalty/Betrayal foundation has evolutionary benefit in that loyalty permits group bonding, and therefore promotes survival in the face of threat. Betrayal is thought to be one of the most hurtful of emotions. The strong emotional response to betrayal and the subsequent judgment of the community might force the perpetrator out of the community. Thus, the strong desire to avoid the negative emotional response to betrayal acts to encourage loyalty, and the exclusion from the community, might give an evolutionary selection benefit to those who remain loyal.[27]

Like chimpanzees, humans also demonstrate deference to authority, and we expect leaders to demonstrate some sort of responsibility to care for those lower in the hierarchy, which in turn encourages loyalty. However, overly authoritarian leaders trigger the negative side of the Authority/Subversion foundation, inciting subversion and revolt giving group members the ability to take charge when a leader has overstepped his bounds. This can help to keep leaders from becoming tyrannical. The balance between the two poles of this moral taste helps to keep group cohesion.[28]

Haidt's fifth moral/political foundation is the Sanctity/Degradation taste. This foundation, he claims, is the hardest for Westerners to understand and accept. It is born out of seeing certain aspects of human life as dignified and worthy of praise, or as degrading and thus disgusting. Haidt notes that there is some evolutionary benefit to this foundation, like steering clear of certain foods that may be dangerous or the setting aside of bodily wastes. But there is also the positive element as well, namely, the setting apart of some aspects of life, or some culturally important group of people, as sacred. These sacred people—shamans, for example—are set aside for certain kinds of tasks that will in turn promote social cohesion. This foundation also gives us a sense of the importance of human beings as set apart from other animals. For instance, eating another human being elicits disgust, even if done out of a need to survive. This action triggers a sense of the violation of the sacred.[29]

Haidt's sixth moral/political foundation—which he developed after attempting to operationalize the first five—is also posited as downstream in evolutionary history. As humans began to evolve such that they could use tools—or more particularly weapons—

and as they evolved language, he speculates that the predisposition for the powerful to lead became less of an evolutionary plus for survival. With the development of weapons and linguistic cooperation, concentrated power was less necessary for survival, and thus the Liberty/Oppression foundation emerged. This foundation allows people to notice and to resent crass domination; it creates bonds between the oppressed such that they can organize and attempt to overthrow the tyrant. According to Haidt, "[t]his foundation supports the egalitarianism and antiauthoritarianism of the left, as well as the don't-tread-on-me and give-me-liberty antigovernment anger of libertarians and some conservatives."[30] Thus the political arrangements in technologically advanced cultures give birth to a new moral taste, according to Haidt.

These political bonds, to which all the tastes contribute, gives rise to Haidt's third principle: "*[m]orality binds and blinds*." In Part III, to capture this principle, he deploys a third metaphor: "human beings are 90 percent chimp and 10 percent bee," meaning that we form troops or ideological camps and promote those camps over cooperation with other camps. Here he is attempting to reclaim and explain one of Darwin's insights, "that morality was an adaptation that evolved by natural selection operating at the individual level and at the group level. Tribes with more virtuous members replaced tribes with more selfish members."[31] Haidt does not define what he means by "virtuous" here, but we suspect that here, as for the thinkers we discussed in Chapter 2, virtuous behavior is equivalent to prosocial behavior. He goes on to describe the group-level genetic adaptations for "ultrasociality," "group-mindedness," and "shared intentionality" that must be considered.[32]

He is challenging here those like Richard Dawkins and George Williams who argue that the "free rider problem" disproves group selection. But he pushes Darwin even further to argue for what he calls "the hive switch": "the ability (under special circumstances) to transcend self-interest and lose ourselves (temporarily and ecstatically) in something larger than ourselves."[33] To theorize this *collective emotional* experience, he turns to sociologist Emil Durkheim, who describes how participation in group rituals generates an experience of self-transcendence wherein people lose a sense of themselves as individuals, become "simply part of a whole." Durkheim names this experience of self-transcendence as the sacred, crediting it for the widespread phenomenon of religion.[34] Religion, for Haidt, was one way of binding us together as teams to meet the evolutionary vicissitudes at hand:

> Religions and righteous minds had been coevolving, culturally and genetically, for tens of thousands of years before the Holocene era, and both kinds of evolution sped up when agriculture presented new challenges and opportunities.[35]

For Haidt, religion is not necessary; nature, raves, sporting events, drugs (like mescaline and LSD) can generate the same experience. This newly evolved ability to hive-switch is rooted in "neurons, neurotransmitters, and hormones."[36] Lead candidates are oxytocin and mirror neurons: "Oxytocin bonds people to their groups, not to all of humanity. Mirror neurons help people empathize with others, but particularly those that share their moral matrix."[37] These enable "the suppression of free riders" and the promotion of prosociality.

However, this team approach creates insiders and outsiders, and thus the morality built up around religion also "blinds people to the motives and morals of their opponents."[38] It "binds us," he claims, "into ideological teams that fight each other as though the fate of the world depended on our side winning each battle. It blinds us to the fact that each team is composed of good people who have something important to say."[39] Here Haidt suggests we are essentially geared to perceive threats to our group and to respond vigorously to those threats to improve survival, in much the same way that a chimpanzee troop might in order to overcome a threat. However, we get ensnared in the "moral matrix" of the group and do not reach out beyond ideological partners. He ends the book for a call to cooperation, that we all become more bee-like, widening the net to include the insights of others who have a different set of operative moral tastes.

In the end, Haidt's descriptive project is admirable, and it problematizes much that is taken for granted in WEIRD societies. His explanation of the battles of political partisans can be refreshing, and we appreciate his attempt to advocate for a more civil politics based on solidarity, cooperation, mutual understanding, and dialogue.

Haidt not only draws on the literature represented in our first two chapters, but embodies much of what we encountered there. He clearly exemplifies Fleck's account of how "facts" move from the emerging neuroscientific thought-community to the broadest kind of thought-community, namely, society. Trained as social and moral psychologist, he draws from the neurobiological sciences to amplify the findings of the neurosciences in public consciousness. Not only does he draw from the psychology and neurobiology—he draws from an almost dizzying array of subdisciplines. In doing so, he moves quickly, relying on inferences, correlations, and suggestive connections rather than hard evidence. He amplifies the concern we raised in Chapter 1 about methodology, by using the ready-made conceptual definitions, which as we showed emerge from the shared assumptions of social scientists and the broader society. Prosociality is a stand-in for virtue; antisociality is a stand-in for vice.

He also shares the same difficulties encountered earlier in conceptualizing "morality." For example, when he begins to try to map political liberals and political conservatives onto his six "tastes" or "foundations," his research leads him to conclude that political liberals tend to draw on three moral tastes—the Care/Harm, Fairness/Cheating, and Liberty/Oppression tastes—where political conservatives tend to draw from all six.[40] Yet as he discusses how people from different camps align with these "foundations," he is forced to incorporate into each axis quite opposite elements. For example, as he notes,

> Everyone—left, right, and center—cares about Liberty/Oppression, but each political faction cares in a different way. In the contemporary United States, liberals are most concerned about the rights of certain vulnerable groups (e.g., racial minorities, children, animals), and they look to government to defend the weak against oppression by the strong. Conservatives, in contrast, hold more traditional ideas of liberty as the right to be left alone, and they often resent liberal programs that use government to infringe on their liberties in order to protect the groups that liberals care most about.[41]

He is attempting to strike a neutral stance, but it is also clear that the conceptual funneling process has not sufficiently refined his conceptual or operational definitions. After all, liberty implies more than a small rider atop the emotional elephant.

As with most of our interlocutors in the first two chapters, Haidt shares the belief that the arrow of causation moves, in his words, "From Genes to Moral Matrices." In fact, to ensure that the point is not missed, he outlines this causal vector as a three-step sequence, called out as subheads in his final chapter—"Step 1: Genes Make Brains," "Step 2: Traits Guide Children along Different Paths," and "Step 3: People Construct Life Narratives."[42] These narratives, he notes, "are not necessarily *true* stories," but they are "saturated with morality" and ground political identities.

As with his counterparts, Haidt moves from his aggregated findings from the array of sciences to explore implications not only for individual persons but for the broadest possible subject: the body politic. In doing so, he is careful to adopt an air of neutrality with regard to any political position. He finds strengths and weaknesses in both liberal thinkers and conservative thinkers.[43] But as he moves into his final chapter, his allegiances begin to appear, particularly his allegiance to capitalism.[44] Corporations are cited earlier as an exemplar of "hives at work," "new superorganisms" that can be sites where individuals become "*united into one body*" and—under transformational leadership—can achieve a certain level of transcendence.[45] He shifts from a discussion of morality to one of "moral capital," citing Edmund Burke, Frederick Hayek, and Thomas Sowell.[46] He argues at length the claim that "Markets are Miraculous,"[47] puzzles over liberals' rejection of Adam Smith, and returns repeatedly to a theme that runs through the book, that of "the free rider" problem.

In fact, his next project, which he envisages as "a sequel to *The Righteous Mind*, will explore the relationship between capitalism and morality."[48] His goal is to "depolarize capitalism," for "if economic conversations become less polarized and more pragmatic, economic policies will get better and prosperity will rise." Toward this end he has already begun to explore capitalism's moral narratives, its relationship to "moral evolution," and "How Capitalism Changes Conscience."[49] He has also helped launch EthicalSystems, Inc., which provides training and consulting services to businesses and other organizations.

Again, despite his claims of moral neutrality, Haidt himself remains dependent upon a moral anthropology that originates in the West. His appeal to moral tastes places him firmly in the British empiricist tradition of moral philosophy, in line with Adam Smith, David Hume, and Frances Hutcheson, as we will describe in chapter six. Political and moral foundations arise in moral intuitions or moral sense or, as he prefers, moral tastes. Haidt credits Hume with metaphor, which was omitted from the third and subsequent editions of his *Enquiry Concerning Human Understanding* (1748):

> Morality is nothing in the abstract Nature of Things, but is entirely relative to the Sentiment or mental Taste of each particular Being; in the same Manner as the Distinctions of sweet and bitter, hot and cold, arise from the particular feeling of each Sense or Organ. Moral Perceptions therefore, ought not to be class'd with the Operations of the Understanding, but with the *Tastes* or Sentiments.[50]

Like Hume, Haidt does not place virtue in human nature but holds that it is derivative from sense perception, namely, pleasure and pain. "The Righteous Mind," Haidt claims, is unapologetically "evidence for Hume's claim . . . [written] in 1739 that 'reason is, and ought only to be the slave of the passions, and can never pretend to any other office than to serve and obey them.'"[51] He pays homage to Hume throughout the book.

Thus, to say that Haidt has little place for rational moral agency would be an understatement. He refers to those who would reverse Hume's claim to be engaged in "the ultimate rationalist fantasy" or better laboring under a *"rationalist delusion"*;[52] per Hume, reason is "only fit to be the servant of the passions."[53] Rather than rationality guiding our moral behaviors, we find that moral tastes, acting independently from a rational free will, are foundational. Combined, these moral tastes ground our moral and political arrangements and together promote the survival of the group in the face of threats from nature or other animal and human aggressors. Haidt does not explore whether political systems exert evolutionary pressures, nor does he give an explanation for how evolutionary pressures resulted in *these* pairs of moral tastes. He does not touch on whether all the tastes are fixed for the species or how political systems act to enculturate these tastes and promote certain tastes over others. He also does not explore whether certain tastes might work within some political systems and not work so well in others. Moreover, he does not give any sense of whether or how the rational mind might exert pressure on the moral tastes. For instance, the rational mind might be fully active in tamping down the emotional content of the moral tastes, thus itself exerting an evolutionary pressure.

In the traditional construal of the virtues, the rational mind works to habituate one's behaviors such that the emotional dimension does not outrun the rational dimension. The rider, to continue Haidt's metaphor, tames the elephant.[54] Haidt is not alone in his reliance on Hume. As noted by Alasdair MacIntyre in *After Virtue*, Hume's theory of moral sentiments animates much of the Western cultural milieu when it comes to moral, political, and economic thinking. Haidt, as well as Sam Harris and Paul Zak, picks up this extant theory of moral sentiment that animates much of Western politics and economics. In this sense, other popularizers of neuroscience do not stray far from Haidt. Thus, the milieu of the late modern West shapes what it is possible for a moral psychologist like Haidt to say. Whereas Haidt desires only to describe moral tastes, in a rather un-Humean move, two other thinkers are willing to say what *ought* to be the case based on the findings of neuroscience.

## Harris's Moral Landscape: Toward a Moral Physics

One of the most prolific popularizers of the neuroscience of morality is Sam Harris. Harris, trained as a cognitive neuroscientist at UCLA, was for ten years the CEO of Project Reason, a nonprofit foundation he co-founded, which was "devoted to spreading scientific knowledge and secular values in society."[55] Like Haidt, Harris is a frequent voice on the public intellectual circuit, regularly gracing the pages of major newspapers, blogs, and presenting two TED talks.[56] Per his own website, Harris has authored five *New York Times* best sellers, been translated into twenty languages, hosts the "Making Sense" podcast that was selected by Apple as one of the "iTunes Best" and has won a Webby Award for best podcast in the category Science and Education.

Harris's primary agenda, as one of the leading figures in the New Atheism movement, is to debunk religion. Where Haidt (and, as we shall see, Paul Zak) sees religion as having played a powerful, functional role binding humans together, Harris sees religion as primarily blinding humans to the realities of morality. Harris's early work explored the neurobiology of religious belief.[57] He has continued to champion this project in a series of books, including *The End of Faith: Religion, Terror, and the Future of Reason*, which won the 2005 PEN Award for Nonfiction, *Letter to a Christian Nation*, and *Waking Up: A Guide to Spirituality without Religion*.[58] Harris's scathing comments on religion have not been limited to Christianity; he has been accused of Islamophobia and inciting violence toward Muslims.[59]

It is difficult to tease Harris's work on the neuroscience of morality apart from his agenda to debunk religion. In fact, Harris sees them as two sides of the same coin. While we will focus primarily on the ways in which he translates neuroscientific findings regarding morality into public discourse, his constructive work is always in dialogue with religion, and thus we will also be referencing some of his work on religion. We take as exemplars his 2010 book *The Moral Landscape*, as well as *The End of Faith* and his short book *Free Will* published in 2012.[60]

In *The Moral Landscape* Harris sets out to convince a public benighted by religion that the real grounds for articulating a true science of morality can only be found in reason and experiment. Despite this conviction, he does not appeal to scientific literature directly, but instead writes in the spirit of materialist science; nor does he do actual neurobiology or even work in the human sciences. His writings, thus, are works of public philosophy more than works of actual neuroscience.[61] Nonetheless, he identifies as a neuroscientist, presents his work as that of neuroscience, and is acknowledged as such by the public neuroscientific community. Neuroscience is his thought-community. While Harris claims that his account of human moral behavior is objectively true, as we will demonstrate, he simultaneously (and contradictorily) remains deeply emotivist and deeply deterministic. Moreover, when pressed, it becomes clear that his putatively objective morality serves a more foundational commitment to a kind of Western exceptionalism. In illustrating this, we will again show how the neurosciences are informed by a certain late modern, Western understanding of political economy.

Harris's fundamental thesis in *The Moral Landscape* is that "human well-being entirely depends on events in the world and on states of the human brain."[62] By studying the brain, we can discover the neuroscientific facts that ought to inform human values.[63] Equipped with a detailed map of these morally relevant brain states, the neurosciences can ground an objective, scientific, and universal account of morality. This neuroscientific study of morality, thus, can be as certain as the study of physics. Because this moral physics is discoverable, Harris eschews moral relativism and moral pluralism. Moral truth is scientific truth. If we cannot say that something is wrong, how can we ever be outraged at something like the attacks on the World Trade Centers?

Thus for Harris, science provides not only descriptive information (which for many researchers is the only legitimate project); it can also serve the normative project as well. Studying neuroscience should:

help us understand what we *should* do and *should* want—and, therefore, what *other people* should do and should want in order to live the best lives possible. My claim is that there are right and wrong answers to moral questions, just as there are right and wrong answers to questions of physics, and such answers may one day fall within reach of the maturing sciences of the mind.[64]

Science, thus, not only solves the problem of moral pluralism or relativism; more importantly, it frees us from moralities based in faith commitments.

While admitting that all science is founded on some form of belief or intuition, Harris is quick to point out the difference between faith—which he defines as an unfounded religious belief—and belief founded on empiricism. "Belief, in the epistemic sense— that is, belief that aims at representing our knowledge about the world—requires that we believe a given proposition to be *true*, not merely that we wish it to be so."[65] He notes that once we see that our beliefs are really attempts to represent the world, "we see that they must stand in right relationship to the world to be valid."[66] Thus, beliefs are justified insofar as we can give reasons grounded in the empirically observable world. Any belief, then, that originates from the received wisdom of the past, anything that depends on "faith," is a problem. By definition, since religious faith can never be empirically anchored, moral precepts of religious faith are not, in fact, moral. Religious faith is an epistemological black hole, sucking the scientific light of truth out of the world. It is "still the mother of hatred here, as it is wherever people define their moral identities in religious terms."[67]

Freed from religion, what then is the empirical starting point for morality? Since all science begins in sense experience, all moral science should begin in the relevant *moral* senses. For Harris, these are the sense experiences of pleasure and pain. The constitution of moral truth, in other words, must begin in the morally salient intuitions. He notes:

> A rational approach to ethics becomes possible once we realize that the questions of right and wrong are really questions about the happiness and suffering of sentient creatures. If we are in a position to affect the happiness or suffering of others, we have ethical responsibilities toward them—and many of these responsibilities are so grave as to become matters of civil and criminal law. Taking happiness and suffering as our starting point, we can see that much of what people worry about under the guise of morality has nothing to do with the subject.[68]

Thus, he grounds moral knowledge in the empirical—the phenomenal states of pleasure and pain. From there, we can work backward to discover the brain states that are responsible for the sensations of pleasure and pain, a.k.a. the neurobiological experience of happiness or suffering. By understanding how the objective brain produces such experiences, we can then extrapolate to the ways we can promote pleasure and reduce pain, which is the sum total of morality. Correlatively or conversely, since we can figure out what states in the world might cause the brain to produce pleasurable or painful sensations, we are capable of objectively discerning what states of affair ought to be brought about in the world, so that they trigger the brain to produce sensations of pleasure and experiences of happiness.

Harris does not propose how one derives axiological facts from states in the world and states in the brain, but he does derive a set of imperatives from sensations of pleasure and pain. Wedding his thin utilitarianism to a version of the Kantian imperative, he asserts that: insofar as other human brains are capable of having sensations of pleasure and pain, we ought to avoid those actions that induce pain and promote those states of affairs that induce pleasure. The morally salutary imperative—the generalizable moral claim—emerges from the empirically verifiable fact that brains of similarly situated others can have sense experiences of pleasure and pain. A person should be an end in herself insofar as she can have positive emotions of happiness.

The generalization from particulars knows no limit. The happiness of another—even a distant other with whom one has no contact, but of whose suffering one is aware—becomes part of one's responsibility. This obligation emerges out of the desire to have pleasurable sensations oneself, which one will have if one produces pleasurable sensations in another. Now, through science, a person knows that certain actions will increase the amount of happiness in the brain states of another, and because this will increase the amount of pleasure she feels, an obligation emerges. "Reason," for Harris, "is nothing less than the guardian of love."[69] Love seems here to mean the desire to give pleasurable sensations not only to those close to one's personal circle but to all similarly situated beings.

"[B]ecause moral concerns translate into facts about how our thoughts and behaviors affect the well-being of conscious creatures like ourselves,"[70] Harris sees himself as a moral realist. If there are moral facts, and facts can be correct or wrong, then we can know which norms, actions, and behaviors are true, correct, good actions and which are false, incorrect, bad.[71] "Moral view A is truer than moral view B, if A entails a more accurate understanding of the connections between human thoughts/intentions/behavior and human well-being."[72] Thus, we have the moral physics—the true science of morality—around which society should be organized.

For Kant, freedom was the *a priori* condition of possibility for any action to be moral. Yet in Harris's moral physics, agential free will disappears. Scientifically discoverable causes of action precede our becoming aware that we have chosen. Thoughts, moods, and desires spring up for subjectively inscrutable reasons.

> Why did I use the term "inscrutable" in the previous sentence? I must confess that I do not know. Was I free to do otherwise? What could such a claim possibly mean? Why, after all, didn't the word "opaque" come to mind? Well, it just didn't—and now that it vies for a place on the page, I find that I am still partial to my original choice. Am I free with respect to this preference? Am I free to feel that "opaque" is the better word, *when I just do not feel that it is the better word*? Am I free to change my mind? Of course not. It can only change *me*.[73]

For Harris, our belief in free will arises only out of ignorance of prior causes; it is a trick of consciousness. Our behavioral action begins prior to our awareness of any choice or reason to act. We are only aware of the conscious thoughts, not of the series of neurophysiological causes—the real causes—that have commenced prior to the awareness of thoughts. Thus, we have the illusion that there is an "I" choosing.

Accordingly, for Harris, not unlike Haidt, giving reasons for one's action is a post hoc endeavor, solely an interpretation laid over the real cause of our action. To illustrate how causation is initiated prior to thinking in moral behavior, Harris outlines a series of cases in which one person kills another person. He challenges readers to try to identify the moral culpability of various agents. The cases are as follows:

1. A 4-year-old playing with a gun, accidently shooting someone.
2. A 12-year-old playing with a gun accidently shooting someone.
3. A 25-year-old who kills someone because he had been abused as a child.
4. A 25-year-old who killed someone for the fun of it.
5. A 25-year-old with a tumor in his medial pre-frontal cortex, who killed someone.

Harris's point here is to show the degree to which culpability could be extended; in all but one case (case 4), many are willing to say that the actor was not responsible. Yet, many would also see the 25-year old who killed for the fun of it as psychopathic.[74] Harris concludes: "It seems to me that we need not have any illusions about a causal agent living within the human mind to condemn such a mind as unethical, negligent, or even evil, and therefore liable to occasion further harm."[75]

Thus, moral deliberation and our desire to assign moral culpability is a post hoc process and a deception of our consciousness; we only become aware at a moment after the preconscious action has begun.

> But why is the conscious decision to do another person harm particularly blameworthy? Because consciousness is, among other things, the context in which our intentions become completely available to us. What we do subsequent to conscious planning tends to most fully reflect the global properties of our minds—our beliefs, desires, goals, prejudices, etc. If, after weeks of deliberation, library research, and debate with your friends, you still decide to kill the king—well, then killing the king really reflects the sort of person you are. Consequently, it makes sense for the rest of society to worry about you.[76]

This notion of harm done to the rest of society is where Harris's moral physics becomes a social mechanics of control.

With regard to those displaying "antisocial" personalities, he has no sense of an essential agent, merely a concatenation of forces that seem to coalesce around a settled voluntary intention, and which taken together seem to display a predisposition to problematic actions. Moral evaluation of such persons is not anchored on the essential agent but rather on how that agent affects the stability of the polis/society, measured by the amount of subjective suffering that he causes. Harris continues: "While viewing human beings as forces of nature does not prevent us from thinking in terms of moral responsibility, it does call the logic of retribution into question."[77] If it were the case that psychopathy could be cured via neurobiological treatment, then "our retributive impulse [would be] profoundly flawed,"[78] since the psychopath does not consciously will their evil. In fact, Harris moves a step further and claims that "the urge for retribution, therefore, seems to depend upon our not seeing the underlying causes of human behavior."[79] Our urge for retribution is not so much a moral failure as it is an epistemic one. Should we have the necessary scientific knowledge to diagnosis the human brain correctly, our sense for retribution will follow in lockstep. In general, armed with neuroscientific knowledge of moral norms, we will be equipped to relieve the human estate of suffering and to promote conditions which create brain states which produced subjective experiences of happiness. As he notes: "Clearly, such insights could help us to improve the quality of human life—and this is where academic debate ends and choices affecting the lives of millions of people begin."[80]

We find several features of Harris's popular neuroscience confusing, scientifically, philosophically, and politically. First, he is a consequentialist that places heavy emphasis on pleasure as the ground of morality and pain as the ground of immorality. It appears that his notion of good arises here. By knowing what states of affairs in the world cause pleasurable or painful phenomenal states, we can know morally what out to be done and what we ought to avoid doing. Yet, oddly, these his moral scheme is not concerned so much with these phenomenal states, because the really real aspects of pleasure and pain are not phenomenal, but are instead found in the brain states that seem at best to be coincident with the phenomenal states. In his commitment to rational empiricism, he does not unpack the mystery of sentience.

This leads to a second problem. If our experience of free will is a trick of our phenomenal conscious experience, then it would seem that pleasure and pain might also be tricks of consciousness. He seems to suggest that phenomenal experience is pretty closely linked to brain states without ever proving it—he simply asserts it as a correlation. Moreover, this correlation would not hold for those who are immoral, or for us when we commit immoral actions. Most often in these situations, agents act with blatant disregard for the pleasure and pain of other sentient creatures, and thus they create states of affairs in the world that increase pain and reduce pleasure, even while it may in fact increase pleasure for themselves. Thus, the correlation between the phenomenal experience of moral agency and the brain states collapses.

Third, as we saw earlier, for Harris psychopaths are not free to inflict pain as there is no moral agency. Their brains are not functioning properly. If we cannot get their brains to function properly either through remediation or through neuroscientific techniques, then they should be removed from society, not punished by society. Yet in fact, there are no free-willed agents at all. And if so, there are no free-willed agents to construct the morality for society. Rather, morality is to be created and enforced, but not created by individuals and enforced upon themselves, but by society, where remediation schemes constructed by the general will of society (and not the individual wills of agents) become the enforcers of the morality.

Thus, Harris's moral physics gives rise to a kind of social mechanics that seems rather totalitarian in its function. The dictates of neuroscience, seeking to understand the ways that more general happiness can be created for more individuals in society, give birth to the dictates of the general will of society.

> If our well-being depends upon the interaction between events in our brains and events in the world, and there are better and worse ways to secure it, then some cultures will tend to produce lives that are more worth living than others; some

political persuasions will be more enlightened than others; and some world views will be mistaken in ways that cause needless human misery.[81]

Where Haidt thinks that we can understand the moral tastes of humans, we can begin the work of decreasing our blindness and increasing what binds us together, Harris creates a social mechanics out of his moral physics. What cannot be controlled through techno-scientific manipulation of brains ought to be controlled through social mechanisms. *Polis* emerges from *bios*, that just is the case; but given that, on Harris's account, some civilizations are better than others, the *polis* ought to intervene on bodies. Harris's social mechanics looks very much like the modern secular West precisely because it has been formed by that same social imaginary. That is to say, Harris's thought-community is thoroughly that of Western political economy that seeks to shape behaviors via political and economic nudges. As we shall see more fully in the next section, it is the market that binds us together morally, and as neuroeconomist Paul Zak shows us, it is neurobiology, specifically oxytocin that grounds markets biologically.

## Zak's Moral Molecule: Sex, Religion, and Political Economy

If reason is love's guardian, as suggested by Harris, then Paul Zak thinks he has found the source of all love—the moral molecule, oxytocin.[82] Zak, who holds a PhD in economics, is a self-described neuroeconomist, Professor of Economics, Psychology and Management at Claremont Graduate University, and the founding director of their Center for Neuroeconomics Studies. His training in the neurosciences came in the form of a one-year postdoctoral fellowship in fMRI at Harvard. As with Haidt and Harris, Zak is a prolific media presence, ceaselessly seeking to translate neuroeconomics to an eager public. Exceeding the others, he boasts a lengthy resume of print and media placements, as well as a TED talk.[83]

Zak's research attempts to find the neuroscientific basis for human moral and economic behavior. In his book *The Moral Molecule: The Source of Love and Prosperity*, he identifies the mammalian neurohormone oxytocin as the molecule responsible for morality, as well as for love and prosperity.[84] Oxytocin is synthesized in the hypothalamus and stored in the posterior pituitary gland. It is part of the hypothalamic-pituitary-adrenal (HPA) axis discussed in Chapter 1 that is integral for the neuroendocrine system and seems particularly important in human behavior.

Zak's primary location as an economist shapes his work in three interrelated ways. First, his turn to neurobiology is driven by a desire to understand economics—both individual economic behavior and ways of advancing economics generally.[85] Second, his work (like that of Haidt) aims to be of practical use in the business environment and organizational management. He largely targets the practical applications of his work toward "neuromanagement" (another term he has coined) for business environments as well as "consumer neuroscience."[86] The mechanisms he has discovered, his website notes, "have been used by the World Bank to stimulate prosperity in developing countries and by businesses to enhance economic performance."[87] Third, Zak understands morality—or love—as a kind of economic transaction.

Zak's work on oxytocin began as an interest in the moral concept of trust as it relates to economic theory. As we will explicate further in Chapter 4, in the economic theory that dominated most of the twentieth century, rational self-interest ruled the day. Ideal economic actors were portrayed as those who rationally chose between competing alternatives in order to maximize individually determined interests. Zak's work seeks to challenge this understanding of both markets and agency. He draws on both moral psychology and economic theory to argue, like Haidt, that people often do not act rationally but emotionally and recasts markets not simply as the locus for cutthroat individual competition but rather as arenas of trust, empathy, and altruism—or morality, as he sees it. In fact, the market becomes for Zak the communal locus for moral behavior, and creates the conditions for human flourishing. As a neuroscientist, he is more explicit than most in clearly correlating his work with virtue and vice.[88]

As we noted earlier, such altruism, or acting prosocially at a cost to oneself, is one aspect of human behavior that bedevils contemporary evolutionary biologists. Whereas in the history of evolutionary theory, it was believed that selfishness would lead to the selection of the selfish, an evolutionary account of altruism offers a way to understand the realities of human cooperation which are necessary for building economic relationships. Here Zak and Haidt are in harmony with one another. Yet, if altruism is a biologically grounded phenomenon that logically must get eliminated from the gene pool as the selfless person dies in his sacrifice for the biologically grounded egoist, then how does altruism survive?

Zak thinks that he has found the answer in oxytocin. Human cooperation and economic success, he claims, are mediated by oxytocin. He tests this theory in a series of studies examining the relationship between rationality and emotionality in economics. In one study, he uses a game created by economists called the Trust Game. It works like this. Two Players A and B, who are anonymous to each other, are given ten dollars and allowed to keep whatever money they have at the end of the game. Player A is told that if he sends Player B an amount of money, the moment the money hits Player B's account, it will triple. So if Player A transfers two dollars to Player B's account, then Player B will now have sixteen dollars in his account. Player B is told that if he sends money back, the amount sent by B will likewise triple in A's account. Player B is given one opportunity to reciprocate. So if he transfers four dollars into A's account, A will now have twenty dollars and B will be left with twelve dollars. Both come out ahead. But if B does not transfer money, B could leave the game with sixteen dollars. The rational self-interest theory of economics would suggest that the best thing for Player A to do is to not transfer any money into Player B's account. He should take the ten dollars and run, because if B does not reciprocate, he could end up with only eight dollars. The theory of rational self-interest would also suggest that Player B should not reciprocate by sending Player A any money because he now has sixteen dollars. But in the vast majority of cases where Player A trusts enough to transfer money to Player B, Player B reciprocates and they both come out ahead. In practice, Player B seems always to reciprocate, taking less money for himself in order to reward Player A for his initial generosity.[89]

Zak sums it up thusly:

> In the United States the stakes in the [Trust Game] have been as high as $1,000, and in developing countries as high as three months' average salary. With large sums or small, in dollars or dinars, participants almost always behave with more trust and trustworthiness than the established theories predict that they will. In my own experiments with the game, 90 percent of those in the A-position (the trusters. . .) send some money to the B-player (the recipients. . .), and about 95 percent of the B-players send some money back, based on . . . what? Gratitude? An innate sense of what's right and wrong?[90]

Although he did not survey Players A and B to discern what motivated their decision-making, Zak claims that the players do not have a reason for their behaviors, like gratitude or an innate or rational sense of right and wrong. He instead looks for the instrumental and efficient cause—that is to say—the biochemical cause. He "finds" it in the neurochemical pathways of oxytocin. Not unlike Haidt and Harris, Zak presumes that there is more going on than rational calculation and careful deliberation moving toward discreet ends. In other words, there is less rational agency at work in neuroeconomics and in altruism than we think; through the action of oxytocin, our behaviors are more subconscious than conscious.

As he did not query the Trust Game payers as to their reasons or deliberations, Zak likewise did not measure their oxytocin levels. Oxytocin cannot be measured in vivo. Like his fellow neuroscientists, Zak works through inference and correlation. In separate studies, he gives people a nasal dose of oxytocin and measures behavioral changes; he finds that people become more generous under the influence of oxytocin.[91]

Zak describes two pathways for how oxytocin works. These are not actual neurochemical pathways but rather schemata for how oxytocin *might* produce certain behavioral effects.[92] First, he proposes what he calls the Human Oxytocin Mediated Empathy circuit, or the HOME circuit.[93] When oxytocin is released by the pituitary gland, it acts to increase the release of serotonin in the brain, which reduces anxiety. It also acts to increase the release of dopamine, the "reward" hormone, which stimulates the reward areas of the brain, which we described in some detail in Chapter 2. Thus, oxytocin acts to reduce anxiety (which arises due to threats) and to stimulate the pleasure/reward areas of the brain. The latter effect results in our desire to repeat the behaviors that resulted in pleasure.[94]

The second "pathway" Zak names the Oxytocin Virtuous Cycle (OVC).[95] In this schema, oxytocin release leads to more empathy, which in turn leads to more altruism, which in turn leads to more trust, which in turn leads to more oxytocin release. While there are certainly other hormones—like testosterone and epinephrine—that act in the opposite direction as serotonin, oxytocin, and dopamine, Zak prefers to focus on the upside of oxytocin.[96] He proposes that the HOME and OVC pathways help to create the social bonds necessary for group cooperation and therefore for the increased likelihood for group survival in the face of threats through more mutual cooperation within the clan. "The virtuous cycle, with oxytocin front and center," he avers, "is still the glue that holds society together."[97]

Due to its hypothesized role in increasing empathy and prosocial behaviors, Zak names oxytocin "the moral molecule." Likewise, he credits oxytocin for playing a key role in sex and religion. In the sex act, especially at climax, oxytocin reaches its highest levels.[98] In other forms of association, especially around religious rituals and dancing, oxytocin levels also appear to be high.[99] Oxytocin, he avers, mediates connection to other persons, to the universe, or to the ultimate things, or to God. Therefore, for Zak, what we have traditionally named God is really just a product of oxytocin, which stimulates neurological pathways around connection and community, as well as the desire to keep outsiders out. In the end, God is a story concocted to rationalize the feeling of connectedness to the group and disconnectedness to the out-group.[100] Zak describes the way in which these two desires compete for the mind and will of the person, seeking selfishly to protect one's own, but also needing to cooperate with others—including outsiders—in order to better survive.

To more clearly capture Zak's conclusions, let us outline a second set of studies that are fundamental for his thesis, namely, a set of experiments that deploy the Ultimatum Game. In the Ultimatum Game, the participants are again anonymous to each other. Player 1 is given a stack of one hundred $1 bills. She is instructed to give Player 2 some or none of the bills. Player 2 can accept or reject Player 1's division of the bills. If Player 2 accepts the division, then both Player 1 and Player 2 get to keep their respective number of bills. However, if Player 2 rejects the offer, neither player keeps the bills. Thus, it is in Player 1's best interest to offer a high enough amount such that Player 2 will not reject it, and it is in Player 2's best interest to accept any amount offered by Player 1, because any amount is better than no amount.

As it turns out, the players of the Ultimatum Game rarely act purely out of rational self-interest. As said, Player 1 if acting out of rational self-interest would keep ninety-nine dollars for herself and give only one dollar to Player 2, and Player 2 would accept it if acting purely out of self-interest. But that does not happen. If Player 1 offers anything less than about forty dollars, then more people in Player 2's position reject the amount, leaving none for either. Thus, statistically speaking most people in Player 1's position offer more than rational self-interest would dictate and more people in Player 2's position reject the offer if less than about forty dollars, meaning that they too do not act out of rational self-interest, but out of an emotion—anger.

Equipped with such outcomes, Zak seeks to justify the morality of market economies and the kinds of community and altruism mediated by oxytocin. Most people, he claims, are willing to be generous only with those who are close in kinship and friendship. Exercises like the Trust Game and Ultimatum Game, however, demonstrate that "the marketplace actually makes people *more* moral, not less."[101] Trade, Zak claims, stimulates the production of oxytocin and extends the OVC "beyond the small circumference of kinship and friendship," into the larger world.[102] It therefore takes the OVC to a new level, a third "pathway" that he calls the Oxytocin Prosperity Cycle.[103] In this schema, oxytocin produces empathy, which produces morality, which produces trust, which produces prosperity, which produces more oxytocin.

As such, for Zak, market exchange increases prosocial behavior.[104] He presents evidence showing that the more heavily integrated a person is into the market, the greater their propensity to share more of their money in the Ultimatum Game. "Market integration" is a term used by economists to mean that one is more heavily dependent on the market rather than upon farming, or hunting and gathering, etc. to acquire one's necessities for living. In other words, Zak argues that the more committed one is to the market, the more generosity increases when playing economic games. Market integration improves generosity. According to Zak, "[s]tripped to its essentials, then market exchange is a bit like coming together to worship a higher power," because like sex and ritual, participating in markets increases oxytocin, which increases morality and generosity.[105] Self-interested and altruistic behavior is in a balancing relationship. Zak notes that "prosocial behavior, which melds individual interest with the greater good, creates the virtuous cycle, then reinforces it in an endless loop. That's the model for economic behavior [Adam] Smith was talking about."[106]

This analogy between ritual and markets is not accidental. The story, according to Zak, goes that, once Adam Smith figured out that markets led to the attenuation of self-interest as much as they depended on self-interest, we began to move away from religion as the main promoter of connection, trust, prosocial attitudes and behaviors, and prosperity, and we could move to markets as the great organizing forces of the polity of modern cities and nation states. Zak states:

> In ancient times cities were built around temples, and as late as the eighteenth-century travelers in Europe or North America would have known they were approaching a city when they saw church spires on the horizon. But shortly thereafter, the telltale urban landmark became billowing smokestacks and redbrick factories. During the Gilded Age before the First World War, historian Henry Adams observed that the market had superseded religion as the central organizing principle of all modern societies. The religious energy that had once motivated the building of great cathedrals, he said, had morphed into a drive to invent and acquire.[107]

Where once sex had promoted increased connectivity and kinship bonds, and where once religion had promoted larger group connectivity beyond kinship, now the market can reach beyond lands and peoples, creating one-world in which all are connected. And this has all happened through the mediation of oxytocin. While Zak avoids the moralizing attitudes of the nineteenth and twentieth centuries toward vice (where vice produced poverty, or poverty produced vice), now the market produces human happiness by growing the economy through the feedback loops of oxytocin and social cohesion. Through the mediation of oxytocin markets are created, prosperity is created, the great city is created, political economy is created. Oxytocin is the founder of all political economies, as well as markets and prosocial behavior.

## The Political Economy of Neuroscience

The vector is now complete. We have traced the arc of the neuroscientific narrative of morality from the inner circle of the esoteric community—neuroscientific researchers exploring the biological science of vice and virtue—as it has been amplified by three popularizers of neuroscience through the channels of Western culture. For evidence that the neuroscientific thought-style has osmosed into the larger community, we have to look no further than pages of *The New York Times*, where opinion columnist Thomas Edsall recently cited Haidt's moral foundations theory as if it were simply true: "Fights about abortion, gay rights, gun rights etc. are less about policy than about underlying core values, values that for many are not up for discussion or compromise because they are deeply held — indeed, given the genetic influences on such attitudes, it's probably fair to say they are at least partly biologically instantiated."[108]

At first glance, the three popularizers analyzed here appear to be working at different projects. However, on closer inspection, the similarities are striking. Although Harris was formally trained in cognitive neuroscience, and they all make strong claims about the biological basis of morality and behavior, none of them actually conducts neurobiological research. Haidt is primarily a social psychologist, Zak is primarily an economist, and Harris functions now primarily as a philosopher. Nonetheless, they adopt the method of inference and correlation we saw practiced by the patho-neuroscientists and positive psychologists in Chapters 1 and 2. And they take it to the next level, not simply postulating practical outcomes of particular scientific studies, but by drawing on widely disparate sources to craft grand narratives about normative political arrangements, social theory, and economic infrastructure.

In doing so, they amplify and make explicit two subtle presuppositions that shape the neuroscience of morality. First, each author plants the seeds of doubt about rational moral agency, more popularly known as free will. Harris sees *no* place for free will, drawing on Libet's experiments and by appeal to a reductive account of the brain as a kind of machine produced by genes, and thus advocates for techno-scientific control of disordered genes and brains. Haidt gives some role to rational agency, but his account locates moral explanation as a post hoc rationalization of behavior motivated by emotionality. He approximates the rider's role in moral deliberation to be 1 percent. Zak does not address free will directly, but the amount of explanatory power that he grants to oxytocin suggests that oxytocin is acting behind the scenes rather than rationality. We do things that increase oxytocin. Oxytocin binds communities together, and produces forms of social organization that create conditions where there is more oxytocin, more pleasure. Reason is used by the group to create more pleasure for the group.

Secondly, our three popularizers share a common objective: to reject or reconfigure the relationship between morality and religion. Harris, again, sides with the abolition of religion; Haidt and Zak are more subtle, both narrating religion as simply a manifestation of biological processes that bind people together. Haidt's Durkheimian account casts religion as an evolutionary adaptation that, via a biologically mediated experience of self-transcendence, overcomes our inherently selfish genes to foster group cohesion, increasing the fitness and survival of particular communities. Now that we understand the function of religion, however, we find these same biological processes stimulated by a wide variety of other social practices (e.g., LSD, raves, and sports). At the same time, however, what we are now finding is that too much group cohesion can be a negative, undermining the social cohesion of the wider polis. Thus, what is needed in the twenty-first century are communal rituals that engender social cohesion but take us to a new evolutionary level by enabling us to cross group boundaries. Zak names the biological source of this self-transcendence: the molecule oxytocin. Oxytocin binds families together in that it increases in sexual activity and in that it increases in breast feeding, and in loving familial relations. It also increases in group activities like dances and liturgical activity, and other forms of religious expression in worship. Religion, however, is not universal. In fact, it divides.

However, there is another form of "worship" that binds more universally. It covers the world over in the global economy. Where familial relations and religious activity bound smaller and larger groups, we now have a new form of social organization that can bind us all together. That form of social organization we call the market.[109]

How is it, we ask at this juncture, that neuroscience—or at least, the neuroscience of morality—has become such a consistent apologist for market economics, particularly in its twenty-first-century globalized form? Certainly, the neuroscientific narrative of morality taps into, in a savvy way, social touchstones that enable the translation of specialized, scientific discourse into publicly accessible language. More deeply, neuroscience and the wider public symbiotically share a set of background assumptions, a common set of beliefs about the relationship of the human actor to the social milieu. At the center of these beliefs is a regnant, implicit anthropology and an implicit political and economic landscape, one that regardless of how inchoate it may be is shared by neuroscientists, the popularizers, and society at large. And while these beliefs certainly enable neuroscientific findings to travel the vector from the scientific community to society, we will argue in Part II that the vector as powerfully—but more invisibly—moves in the other direction: that since the beginning of the modern period, it has in fact been the regnant social, economic, and political thought-style of Western culture—Taylor's social imaginary—that has and continues to provide the conceptual framework out of which contemporary neuroscience and its precursors see the world, shape their questions, and determine their findings. To that narrative, we now turn.

# Interlude between Neuroscience and the Economic Imaginary

## Of Capitalists and Criminals

The economization of neuroscience won't surprise those familiar with Steven Levitt and Stephen Dubner's 2005 best seller, *Freakonomics*.[1] *Freakonomics*' aim, as its subtitle states clearly, is to extend economic market models to an increasingly wider array of social interactions—sumo wrestling, drug dealing, legalized abortion, parenting, naming children, and more. The book, and its sequels, make the case to an eager public that the invisible hand drives not only the market but is, in fact, "the hidden side of everything."

In Levitt and Dubner, the academic and popularizer meld. Levitt is a highly accoladed economist who holds the William B. Ogden Distinguished Service Professor of Economics at the University of Chicago, where he directs the Becker Center on Chicago Price Theory.[2] He has been awarded the John Bates Clark Medal, given to the most influential economist under forty, been named one of *Time* magazine's "100 People Who Shape Our World," served as former editor of the *Journal of Political Economy*, and founded and directed the Center for Radical Innovation for Social Change at the University of Chicago.[3] Like Haidt, he has founded a consulting company, the TGG Group, which brings together economists, psychologists, and behavioral scientists to advise businesses and philanthropies in maximizing performance and profitability.[4] Stephen Dubner is a journalist for *The New York Times* who, in 2003, reluctantly accepted an assignment to do a story on Levitt.[5] He was, at the time, working on a book on the psychology of money. From their shared interests, the Freakonomics franchise was born, expanding to a blog, a documentary film, a radio show and more.[6]

As we will see, that Levitt teaches at the University of Chicago and directs the Becker Center is essential to the story we tell. In Part II, we are particularly interested in unpacking the larger social imaginary that has subtly shaped the neurosciences, especially as this has so deeply infused the neuroscientific narrative of morality. Our study here was driven by a series of questions: Why do our popularizers, as well as other neuroscientists, so frequently cite as their forebears the late-eighteenth-century figures of David Hume and Adam Smith? Why is the neuroscientific narrative of morality so keenly interested in correlating proxies for vice with socioeconomic status or socioeconomic position? Why is this narrative so enrapt with questions of criminality? And how does it happen, as we shall see, that the person the neuroscience of morality finds in the brain is *Homo capitalus*?

In Part II, we focus on three intertwined threads of this social imaginary—neoliberalism (Chapter 4), the rise of the social sciences concurrent with political economy (Chapter 5), and the Baconian roots of Hume's innovations in moral philosophy (Chapter 6). Behind these movements lie two additional historical developments crucial to our account: the emergence of neoliberalism in the twentieth century and the reimagination of "the poor" as a social category in the sixteenth. In this Interlude, we sketch these developments.

## Neoliberalism: The Hidden Side of the Hidden Side of Everything

Neoliberalism is currently the dominant economic theory and cultural form. It traces its roots to twin birthplaces—the Ordoliberal or Freiburg School that emerged in Germany and Austria in the mid-1930s, and the Chicago School of Economics that began in the 1920s. Historians chart three phases in its development. The first phase was launched at the meeting of the Walter Lippmann Colloquy in Paris in 1938 where the term "neoliberalism" was first introduced.[7] German Ordoliberalism largely defined itself over against Nazism.[8] The German state had been in shambles since the end of the First World War, and the rise of fascism had been intertwined with economic collapse. Positing Nazism as the logical outcome of state power and economic intervention, this new movement used this unique historical moment to reorder the relationship between the state and the market, with an eye to limiting the state in order to maximize the market's hegemony.[9] In the American context, the Great Depression served largely the same rhetorical function as the Nazi state in the German context. Paul Krugman traces, for example, how the Chicago School's Milton Friedman claimed that the Federal Reserve was the sole causal factor for the Great Depression, casting the economic crisis as "in some sense a demonstration of the evils of an excessively interventionist government."[10]

Thus, neoliberals capitalized on these global crises to enact a subtle inversion in the relationship between the market and the state. No longer was the problem that defined by nineteenth-century classical liberal economics' doctrine of laissez-faire which sought simply to carve out a space for free markets by limiting the state.[11] Rather, neoliberalism sought to establish the market as the regulator of the state. The market economy becomes itself the principle, not only of the state's limitation, but of its internal organization and regulation, resulting in "a state under the supervision of the market rather than a market supervised by the state."[12] In other words, neoliberalism sowed the seeds for the market economy to become the formal principle for regulating of the state, society, and, eventually, "everything."

Notably, it is only in the 1940s to 1950s that "the economy" emerges as an objective, distinct domain.[13] As Wendy Brown notes:

> Prior to this time, "economy" (without the article) referred to seeking a desired end with the least possible expenditure of means, closer to our notion of efficiency or thriftiness today . . . It is only when the definite article is slipped in that "the

economy" is cast as a self-contained structure, one in which wealth generation becomes its own autonomous sphere. Compare this with the etymological root of economy, *oikos*, which identified for the ancient Greeks the space/place of the household, not material life as such, not the market, and not the economy. In short, the identification and reification of "the economy" as a distinct object is recent . . . This suggests that the economy, far from being a transhistorical category, may have been a brief twentieth-century event.[14]

Thus, neoliberalism introduces a second mutation—from economics conceived as practical activity (actions ordered to sustaining a household) to *the economy* as an entity, a thing unto itself. *The* economy as *an* objective domain of scientific investigation or economics as *a* body of knowledge was unknown prior to the mid-twentieth century. This shift follows a similar trend seen with other sciences. As Peter Harrison notes, from the late nineteenth into the early twentieth centuries, "science," which had been an activity of natural philosophers, became understood as a discrete body of knowledge.[15] Economics followed this same pattern; once a domain of moral philosophy, it too sought to become a science.

The second chapter in the development of neoliberalism is marked alternately by Milton Friedman's 1951 paper "Neo-liberalism and Its Prospects"[16] or by the first meeting of the Mont Pelerin Society (MPS), an institute dedicated to developing and promoting neoliberal commitments, in Mont Pelerin, Switzerland, in 1947.[17] Here Ordoliberal Friedrich von Hayek, author of the influential book *Road to Serfdom* (1944), gathered a small circle of economists, philosophers, and sociologists, including the young Friedman. Responding to Nazism and fascism in Freiburg and New Deal Keynesianism in Chicago, economists in this second phase began to argue that governments should take a more active role to protect the markets' freedom in large part by reimagining a state shaped by formal economic principles. In other words, though putatively opponents of government intervention, neoliberal economists in this phrase strongly supported—in fact, demanded—what Foucault refers to as "active, multiple, vigilant, and omnipresent" government intervention aimed at creating the possibility for a market economy.[18]

In order to advance its ideology, Hayek understood that neoliberalism had to capture the cultural imagination. Hayek, Foucault notes, argued that

> We need a liberalism that is a living thought. Liberalism has always left it to the socialists to produce utopias, and socialism owes much of its vigor and historical dynamism to this utopian or utopia-creating activity. Well, liberalism also needs a utopia. It is up to us to create liberal utopias, to think in a liberal mode . . . Liberalism must be a general style of thought, analysis, and imagination.[19]

In other words, Hayek understood that his esoteric-circle needed to move its ideas beyond the small, economic thought-collective into the larger, mainstream thought-community. Hayek proposed a very effective two-pronged strategy for fostering neoliberalism as the general thought-style of Western culture, taking cues from Edward Bernays, the Austrian-American who pioneered the fields of public relations and propaganda. First, it needed to foster a cadre of public intellectuals, "professional secondhand dealers in ideas" who "need not possess special knowledge of anything in particular, nor need even be particularly intelligent, to perform [their] role as intermediary in the spreading of ideas."[20] Second, it needed to establish centers of neoliberal thought. From the 1950s through the 1980s, various think tanks, often well financed by corporations, were established, from the Institute of Economic Affairs, the American Enterprise Institute, the Heritage Foundation, the Hoover Institute, the Center for the Study of American Business, and more. These centers funded research, published their own academic journals, and promulgated their commitments through popular media. Today, there are now over 275 free-market think tanks in seventy countries.[21]

Via these think tanks and their popularizers, neoliberalism entered its third phase in the late 1970s, conquering Keynesianism and spreading rapidly across the globe as the dominant approach to economic and political policy through the agency of the British and US governments and the international financial institutions. It remains in practice the largely uncontested dominant ideology of the global political economy. Critical to this shift was Gary Becker who developed the theory of human capital. Where the second phase of neoliberalism reconfigured the state under the aegis of the market, a space had remained carved out for individual freedom, both in terms of ethics and economics. In the third phase, this space subtly disappears. All aspects of society, all human actions, and in fact, the human agent herself, come under the general economic form of the market. "Now everything" as Foucault notes, "can be analyzed in terms of investment, capital costs, and profit—both economic and psychological profit—on the capital invested."[22]

Yet despite its utopian rhetoric, recent commentators have begun to name neoliberalism's dark underbelly. One of its first real-world experiments was, for example, the 1970s "Miracle in Chile," where the violent Chilean dictator, Augusto Pinochet, directly counseled by Friedman, his Chilean protégés, and the CIA, implemented draconian neoliberal economic reforms alongside his reign of terror against the Chilean people. The Pinochet regime killed or "disappeared" over 3,000 Chileans, tortured some 30,000, and interred almost three times that many. While eventually the Chilean economy met certain benchmarks for success (e.g., reducing the number of Chileans living in absolute poverty), a commentator living through the "shock" intentionally imposed on the country observed that the Chilean program's primary result and likely aim were to effect a massive transfer of wealth and power to a small minority of monopolists and speculators.[23] Analysts concur that this wealth transfer inflicted severe suffering on the poor and middle class, increasing and entrenching economic inequality.[24]

Based on similar outcomes inflicted globally since neoliberalism's ascendance in the 1980s, critics often characterize neoliberalism as a "more efficient regime for the global production of suffering and death."[25] Contra Zak and other free-market enthusiasts who declaim capitalism as *the* moral system, statistics make strikingly clear that the phenomenal increase in accumulated wealth that has occurred since the 1980s has been accompanied by extraordinary increases in socioeconomic inequality and exponential increases in human suffering.[26] What Pope Francis refers to as the "throw-away culture," Sakia Sassen describes as "a global system of expulsion":

In the current global economy, millions of human beings are needed for neither production nor consumption. These unfortunate souls have become a permanent underclass. The existence of an ever-expanding population of migrants, refugees, prisoners, asylum seekers, the perpetually unemployed, and other outcasts become what [Zygmant] Bauman calls "the waste products of globalization."[27]

These "expelled" challenge the narrative and truth of the neoliberal economy.

Moreover, concomitant with neoliberalism's ascendance has been the augmentation of "the contemporary security state [which] manages this population through policing and confinement—either literally or by economic segregation into 'low rent' districts—as well as by direct or indirect extermination."[28] Per Jaime Peck, a key element of neoliberalism's third phase has been the "invasive re-regulation of the urban poor."[29] Rogers-Vaughn brings this home pointedly for our neuroscience popularizers, noting:

> What we have here is nothing less than the privatization of death and violence. This allows neoliberal social orders, through what William Davies calls "the happiness industry," to foster the illusion that life within their protection is one in which "human flourishing" and positive emotions predominate. But simultaneously, it also enables them to conceal and deny their own production of terror and death.[30]

Not only does this manifest itself via proposals to pharmacologically intervene in the genetic-neural pathways of persons with low SES or to enhance the rest of us with oxytocin. Neoliberal violence is systemic, abstract, and anonymous, primarily functioning through faceless, "objective" financial mechanisms, as well as the "expansion of [the] penal state apparatus and social control policies."[31] It is not accidental, that since 1970 the US incarceration rate has increased 700 percent. Although comprising only 5 percent of the global population, the United States is home to roughly 25 percent of the world's prison population.[32] This extraordinary practice of confinement—in which one out of every three Black boys can expect to spend time in prison during his lifetime (versus one in seventeen white boys) with currently almost 40 percent of US prison inmates being Black—developed concurrently with a rapid increase in the neoliberal privatization of the prison system in the United States beginning in 2000, one component of what critical legal scholar Michelle Alexander has named "The New Jim Crow."[33]

If the critics are correct, how do we find such wildly different accounts of economics? How, more pointedly, could our neuroscientists of morality, particularly the popularizers, have missed this dark underbelly and champion the market as the apogee of morality, *the* moral system, a moral system that is putatively embedded in our biology? The answer, we suggest, lies in the correlate peculiarity of the neuroscientific narrative of morality, namely, the presumed connection between poverty and vice. As we saw with Hollingshead and others, the human sciences in the twentieth century have repeatedly hypothesized and investigated a putative relationship between socioeconomic status and the behavior of the poor. This connection between economics and morality traces a much longer history—one that is, in fact, co-extensive with the history of the human sciences.

## Moralizing the Poor: The Foundation of a Bifurcated Anthropology

As we will see in Chapter 5, from Hume to Mill, a key focus was the political task of reforming the English Poor Laws, an outcome finally accomplished in 1834. In fact, a driving factor in the development of social and human sciences was the vexing problem of the management of the poor. As Polanyi notes:

> The figure of the pauper, almost forgotten since, dominated a discussion the imprint of which was as powerful as that of the most spectacular events in history. If the French Revolution was indebted to the thought of Voltaire and Diderot, Quesnay and Rousseau, the Poor Law discussion formed the minds of Bentham, and Burke, Godwin and Malthus, Ricardo and Marx, Robert Owens and John Stuart Mill, Darwin, and Spencer . . . Pauperism, political economy, and the discovery of society were closely interwoven.[34]

Due in large part to this decades-long debate about the Poor Laws, this period—roughly 1740–90—has been identified as the first "poverty enlightenment."[35] The English Poor Laws comprised a series of legislative acts implemented and repeatedly revised from 1536 to 1834 that sought to provide relief for a precipitous and visible rise in rural pauperism. As Polanyi notes, at the beginning of this era, "the poor" were essentially synonymous with "the common people"—people who did not own land and therefore worked the common lands (or the "commons") of manors and monasteries.[36] Social consensus held that, as a Christian culture, there was a shared obligation to care for the elderly, the sick, widows, and orphans. Vexing, however, were beggars and vagrants. Early poor laws sought primarily to punish "vagabonds," "sturdy beggars," and "idlers," inflicting anything from short-term imprisonment, whipping, placing in stocks, and a return to their birth place to two years' servitude, branding with a V or burning through the ear for a first offense and death, perhaps by hanging (for repeat offenders).[37]

These punitive measures sought to "solve" the problem of the poor through discipline. Positive efforts to provide provisions for poor relief began to emerge around 1547 and were continued during the reign of Elizabeth I, culminating in her Poor Relief Act of 1601.[38] This and subsequent legislation shared key characteristics. It was administered through some 1,500 local parishes, each responsible for "their own" poor. Each parish collected local taxes or "rates" from local property owners and tenants in order to fund the program. The legislation differentiated between the "deserving" or "impotent poor" who were unable to work and the "undeserving" or "able-bodied" poor who, it was assumed, could earn their living by manual work. For the former, the law counseled parishes to set up alms houses or poor houses or to distribute money, food, and/or goods. For the latter, parishes were directed to establish workhouses or other means of putting them to work to earn their keep. Those who would not work were to be sent to newly established Houses of Correction. A key concern driving this legislation was the mobility of the poor as they left their ancestral homes to seek work in other communities. To counter this "vagrancy," the 1662 Act of Settlement required that the poor receive relief only from their local parish in which they were registered, effectively limiting their mobility.[39]

The most significant revision of the poor laws was the Berkshire Bread Act enacted in Speenhamland in 1795. In the face of increasing misery of the poor, local authorities set up a system that subsidized wages "in accordance with a scale dependent upon the price of bread, so that a minimum income should be assured to the poor irrespective of their earnings."[40] Badly conceived and badly administered, Speenhamland paradoxically both drove wages down to unlivable levels and discouraged people from working.[41] It was without dispute an economic disaster.[42] Speenhamland became the primary target and foil of the architects of the emerging political economy whose efforts contributed to the repeal of the poor laws in 1834.

But why did a need for the poor laws emerge? Why did the population of the poor increase so exponentially from the mid-1500s to the time of Hume, Bentham, and Mill? As Polanyi notes, "it was in the first half of the sixteenth century that the poor first appeared in England; they became conspicuous as individuals unattached to the manor."[43] While many reasons were proffered at the time, this detachment was driven by two primary events—what R. H. Tawney has called the "agrarian revolution" catalyzed by the rapid, large-scale enclosures of common lands and the dissolution of the Roman Catholic monasteries under Henry VIII.

First, the practice of enclosure. Prior to 1500, "commoners" were largely those who worked manorial lands through a variety of generational practices, customary tenancy, and villeinage, managed through local practices of communal oversight. Income and livelihood generated by farming, pasturing sheep, and grazing horses and livestock on the commons was supplemented by craft and other forms of local productivity at the household and village level. Beginning around 1500, and escalating exponentially from 1700 to 1850, manorial authorities—at times aided and abetted by Parliament—begin to "enclose" large swaths of the commons, in order to create massive pastures for sheep herding to support the lucrative and growing international textile industry. Not only did the process of enclosure eliminate villagers' sources of food and income; as part of the enclosure process, families or whole villages were also often evicted from their homes as the villages themselves were converted to sheep pasture.[44]

As a result, tens of thousands of people were displaced and thrown into new and appalling conditions of misery and starvation. Lacking means of support, persons formerly tied to local land and communities began to search elsewhere for work. Thus, as Tawney notes, "the new and terrible problem is the increase in vagrancy. The sixteenth century lives in terror of the tramp."[45] As before, the first response to this new problem was repression. Per Tawney:

> The distinction between the able-bodied unemployed and the impotent is one which is visible to the eye of sense. The distinction between the man who is unemployed because he cannot get work and the man who is unemployed because he does not want to work, requires a modicum of knowledge and reflection which even at the present day is not always forthcoming... It is not accepted at once as a matter of course that the destitute shall be publicly relieved, still less that the able-bodied destitute deserve anything but punishment. Governments make desperate efforts for about one hundred years to evade their new obligations. They whip and brand and bore ears; they offer the vagrant as a slave to the man who seizes him.[46]

In other words, the enclosure of the common lands resulted in a new moral order that divided and confined the poor, defining a population of persons who were in need of management and bodily control.

Simultaneously, the primary source of poor relief for local communities—the network of over 800 Roman Catholic monasteries—was dismantled. At the time of the English Reformation, Catholic institutions were among the greatest landowners who, like their manorial counterparts, supported myriads of local villages that farmed their lands. Beginning in 1535 with the Suppression of Religious Houses Act, over the next five years Henry VIII dissolved most of the Catholic monasteries in England, confiscating monastic property. In a process that historian Eamon Duffy refers to as "the stripping of the altars," in 1539 alone, "it is estimated that lands worth an annual income of £136,000 as well as portable wealth of as much as £1 million to £1.5 million was confiscated [from the Roman Catholic Church in England] and given to propertied laymen in an era in which the crown's annual income from land never exceeded £40,000."[47] This transfer of monastic property to the gentry functioned as a form of enclosure of ecclesiastical and monastic properties.

Not only did the dismantling of the monastic infrastructure deprive local commoners of their work, income, and often homes associated with the ecclesiastical properties; Roman Catholic Churches and monasteries had also long served as the primary social bodies engaged in charitable care for the poor and in the creation of communal identity. The stripping of the altars crippled the church's ability to exercise this function at the same time that the enclosures, mercantilism, and a shift to industrial economies were wreaking massive economic upheavals on the poor. With the Catholic church incapacitated for this work, responsibility for supporting the poor fell to public authorities, administering poor relief through local Anglican parishes, which were now required to collect compulsory taxes.[48]

Thus, the violence outlined earlier—alternatively concealed and visible—is not unique to neoliberalism. As Michael Perelman has detailed, state-sanctioned violence that inflicted massive dispossession and fomented widespread suffering and misery lies at the birth of capitalism itself.[49] As Polanyi notes, while the Tudors and Stuarts tried to save the common people from the worst effects of the social dislocations of enclosure, "nothing saved the common people of England from the impact of the Industrial Revolution . . . The effects on the lives of the people were awful beyond description . . . the economic advantages of a free labor market could not make up for the social destruction wrought by it."[50]

Alongside these developments lie two fundamental transitions: one in anthropology and one in axiology. First is the shift to understanding persons, land, and money as commodities. As Polanyi notes, a market economy envisages markets "not only for goods but also for labor, land, and money, their prices being called respectively commodity prices, wages, rent and interest."[51] Prior to the end of the eighteenth century, labor and land had been protected from commodification by mercantilism.[52] But "in a singular departure," by the nineteenth century, Polanyi notes, "economic activity [had been] isolated and imputed to a distinctive economic motive." To achieve this, all aspects of society needed to be somehow subordinated to the market, including labor and land. But as Polanyi notes, "labor and land are no other than the human beings themselves of which every society consists and the natural surroundings in which it exists. To include them in the market mechanism means to subordinate the substance of society itself to the laws of the market."[53]

While more details will unfold in the following chapters, what we see in the era from 1550 to 1800 is the process by which labor (some people) and land begin to become commodities—objects produced for sale on the market, "subject to the supply-and-demand mechanism interacting with price."[54] But, as Polanyi notes:

> labor, land and money are obviously *not* commodities [they have not been produced for sale] . . . Labor is only another name for a human activity which goes with life itself, which in its turn is not produced for sale but for entirely different reasons, nor can that activity be detached from the rest of life, be stored or mobilized; land is only another name for nature, which is not produced by man; actual money, finally, is merely a token of purchasing power which, as a rule, is not produced at all, but comes into being through the mechanism of banking or state finance. None of them is produced for sale. The commodity description of labor, land and money is entirely fictitious.[55]

Thus, a key intervention had been made: persons—or, more specifically, some persons—were extracted from their lands and communities, and reconceived under the abstraction labor, "the technical term used for human beings, insofar as they are not employers but employed."[56] Some persons had become commodities.[57]

The market for labor was one most strenuously resisted by English rural society and therefore the last market to be organized under the new industrial system. The Poor Laws effectively prevented the establishment of a competitive labor market; thus, the free labor market finally came into being only with the repeal of the Poor Laws in 1834.[58] As we will see, key thought leaders of the preceding decades—from Hume to Mill—were critical for laying the groundwork necessary to transform persons into labor and in doing so completely recasting moral anthropology. But key to their work was the specter of the poor, the pauper.

Concomitant with this transition in anthropology comes a transition in axiology. As Polanyi notes,

> The alleged commodity "labor power" cannot be shoved about, used indiscriminately, or even left unused, without affecting also the human individual who happens to be the bearer of this peculiar commodity. In disposing of man's labor power, the system would, incidentally, dispose of the physical, psychological, and moral entity "man" attached to that tag. Robbed of the protective covering of social institutions, human beings would perish from the effects of social exposure; they would die as the victims of acute social dislocation through vice, perversion, crime, and starvation.[59]

For as the numbers of the poor increase, a cause must be found. And the cause certainly was not going to be laid at the feet of nobles, landowners, and the extraordinarily profitable new economic system. Rather, the cause must lie in the poor themselves.

Thus, the first response is disciplinary, to recast the poor as criminals—imprisoning them, punishing them, depriving them of their freedom. And their main crime—idleness. If they would choose to work, they would not be poor and starving. Therefore, failure to work for one's sustenance becomes defined as the central vice. As the census of the poor swells, incorporating women, children, and the aged, this centrality of wage labor becomes the central discrimen, distinguishing between those who *deserve* society's care and those who do not. It also proposes the main remedy: the horrific institution of the *work*house, rendered even more dehumanizing under Bentham's watch.

Equally, contemporaries blame the endless increase in the rolls of the poor not on constant dispossession of their property and livelihoods—the rolls of the poor are increasing because they are reproducing. Thus, the second key vice of the poor becomes sexual activity. As we will see with Malthus, the poor are reprimanded repeatedly for marrying early and not curbing their sexual activity, even within marriage. Here again the charges deflect attention from the true source of the problem. At least among men, age of marriage is influenced by the age at which maximum earning power is reached.[60] Tawney poses the question:

> when a large number of agricultural and industrial workers (in the sixteenth century probably a majority) were small landholders or small masters, did the fact that they had to wait for the death of a parent to succeed to their holding, or (in the towns) for the permission of a guild to set up shop . . . tend to defer the age of marriage? . . . One may contrast the extraordinary reduction in the age of marriage of the people of Lancashire brought about by the early factory system, with its armies of operatives who had nothing to look forward to but the wages earned immediately upon reaching maturity.[61]

In other words, the problem of "overpopulation" that emerged only at the end of the seventeenth century was an artifact not of the immorality of the poor but rather changed social conditions. But regardless, biopolitical mechanisms were needed to solve the problem.

\* \* \*

Here, then, we see the roots of the fundamental anthropology and axiology that shapes the work of those figures we will meet in Part II—Thomas Malthus, David Ricardo, Jeremy Bentham, David Hume, John Stuart Mill—and that are carried forward into the social imaginary of the twentieth century and shaped the neuroscience of morality. Our task in Part II of this book is to make explicit this social imaginary and to trace its roots back to their origin. It is a complex argument. We begin by showing how it has operated to produce the implicit, but nonetheless regnant, anthropology of twenty-first-century neoliberalism—the human as capital, determined by biology and controlled by the political and economic structures with little or no agency of its own. It is the story of how *Homo economicus*—the animal that acts to maximize its rational self-interest—emerges as a product of positive social and psychological sciences in the late nineteenth and early twentieth centuries but morphs into a being equipped only with moral tastes, moral intuitions, and moral emotions, a mere product of genes and emotional brains, non-rationally pursuing its own pleasures, while avoiding pain. We call this emergent twenty-first-century being with little or no real moral agency, whose actions are voluntary yet not free, *Homo capitalus*. It is this vision of the human—the person required for the political economy imagined by Gary Becker and others—that the neurosciences "discover" in the brain.

Yet in unearthing the almost seamless alignment between neoliberalism and the neurosciences, we were pressed to look farther by a striking—in fact, slightly jarring— feature of the neuroscientific narrative of morality, namely, their frequent invocation of the towering eighteenth-century figures of David Hume and Adam Smith as their intellectual forebears. Why Hume? Why Smith? Asking these questions took us on a journey step-by-step back to the eighteenth century and the emergence of market capitalism and political economy. Here we discovered that while superficially the neuroscientific narrative of morality is, indeed, heir to Hume, their story requires a significant misreading of Smith and masks two more powerful, intertwined genealogies.

The first is an anthropology that begins with Francis Bacon and runs through Hume to two giants of moral theory—Jeremy Bentham and John Stuart Mill. Bentham and Mill were less moral theorists, less interested in moral theory, than they were political and economic operatives interested in establishing a positivist science to inform political economy. But the driver for doing so was the new configuration of wealth and property—and the attendant skyrocketing in human poverty that attended the onset of market capitalism in the sixteenth century. We shall see that the moralization of the poor—that is to say the birth of the deserving and undeserving poor which eventually wends its way into twentieth-century instruments for measuring SES—finds it origins here. The new social problems incited by the capitalist reconfiguration of British society required a new post hoc reconfiguration of anthropology and morality. As we arrive at Hume, the human has become a slave to his senses—to the moral taskmasters of pleasure and pain; only wealth and property make one free. In fact, the moral "man" can only be produced—since he has no will to self-create—by the panopticon of society as can be seen in poor law reform of nineteenth-century Britain. Thus, we will show that it is Hume, not Smith, that makes possible *Homo economicus*, and it is Hume, not Smith, that results in the mutation of *Homo economicus* into *Homo capitalus*. But this can only happen insofar as standing behind Hume is the empirical skeptic for whom all knowledge—all science—becomes a tool, a technology, for "improving the human condition," socially construed; in other words, for engineering society. That skeptic is Francis Bacon.

Part II

# The Evolution of an Artifactual Being

# 4

# The Neoliberal Narrative of Morality

Jonathan Haidt opens his account of "The Moral Foundation of Politics" with a claim that seems to distance him from the critique we have developed thus far, noting:

> Behind every act of altruism, heroism, and human decency you'll find either selfishness or stupidity. That, at least, is the view long held by many social scientists who accepted the idea that *Homo sapiens* is really *Homo economicus*.[1]

In order to demonstrate "how wrong this view is," he follows with a series of examples to test this theory, asking readers to put a price tag (from zero to one million dollars) on a series of potentially troubling actions, concluding from how he surmises the readers would answer these scenarios that *Homo economicus* is just an "economist's fantasy."

While Haidt's moral theory may not depend on *Homo economicus* strictly construed, his protest here is a deft sleight-of-hand, deflecting attention from his operative anthropology. For, as we will argue, the vision of the human person animating his account of moral behavior is not *Homo economicus* but, in fact, its most recent mutation. As we suggested in the introduction, this mutation is not the figure of the early twentieth century or even of Mill who first articulated him into being. It is, moreover, "far from Adam Smith's creature propelled by the natural urge to 'truck, barter, and exchange,'" a "creature of needs satisfied through exchange."[2]

Rather, the figure championed by Haidt, as well as Harris and Zak, is the anthropology required for the ironically emotivist "economic science" of the twentieth century that stands in the lineage of neoliberal economics, captured well in the apotheoses of the Chicago School of Economics, George Stigler and Gary Becker. Here we find the person as entrepreneur of herself, "an intensely constructed and governed bit of human capital tasked with improving and leveraging its competitive positioning and with enhancing its (monetary and nonmonetary) portfolio value across all of its endeavors and venues."[3] This anthropology—adopted blithely and wholesale by the neuroscientific narrative of morality—we call *Homo capitalus*.

*Homo capitalus* did not spring de novo fully formed from the mind of Gary Becker. Rather, this thoroughly economized human actor evolved incrementally, mutating in response to innovations in political economy. In this chapter, we trace the ascent of *Homo capitalus*, telling the story via three sentinel figures in the Chicago School of Economics who together crystalize the three main phases of US neoliberalism in the twentieth century—Frank Knight, Milton Friedman, and Gary Becker. We focus on the Chicago School for three reasons. First, the emergence of the neurosciences aligns largely with what is generally understood to be the third phase of the ascendance of neoliberalism in the 1970s. Secondly, American neoliberalism is understood to be far more radical, complete, and exhaustive than its European counterpart; Foucault in fact refers to the Chicago School as "anarcho-liberalism."[4] Third, it is the moves made by the Chicago School with regard to ethics and anthropology that appear most strikingly in our neuroscientific narrative of morality.

In tracing the development of the Chicago School via Knight, Friedman, and Becker, we focus on three specific and intertwined trajectories, of which neoliberalism is only the latest chapter. First, we want to illuminate the long and rather contested relationship between economics and ethics. Despite its scientific pretensions, economics was at one time considered to be a subdiscipline of moral philosophy. The relationship between ethics and economics was seemingly severed by Frank Knight in the early part of the twentieth century—a move that differentiated this new chapter in economics both from Adam Smith's and from Knight's nineteenth-century predecessors. This rhetorical commitment to maintaining a bright line between economics and ethics notwithstanding, it is clear that neoliberal economics has more brazenly asserted itself as a particular school of ethics.[5]

Second, Knight's attempt to carve out ethics as a separate sphere came as economics sought to establish its credibility as a discipline and a science characterized by formal, mathematical laws governing human behavior. Here Knight continued the project of his nineteenth-century forebears of founding an economic science, but during the first phase of neoliberalism (~1920s to 1950s), economists made a series of key theoretical moves that distinguished twentieth-century economics from classical liberal economics of the nineteenth century.

Third, where ethics worked primarily around questions of moral theory, generally eschewing practical matters, economics took from Hume and Bentham a penchant to focus on the practical control of human behavior. Economics sought to become a positive science of praxis. It also followed the social scientists' proclivity to distance themselves from normative morality per se, preferring to draw on seemingly neutral nonmoral terms. Doing so permitted them to adhere (for a time) to Hume's is/ought dichotomy, giving them an air of objectivity.

We begin, then, with the most recent chapter, neoliberalism. With neoliberalism, moral agency and its attendant moral anthropology, subtly undergoes a deep transformation. As we will see, vice becomes virtue, the irrational becomes rational, the unfree (actions like addiction) becomes voluntary. In the end, "choice" loses its relationship with freedom—although exercised prima facie, *Homo capitalus* is now beyond freedom, an instantiation of capital, Itself animated by a biologically driven impulse to maximize the return on its investments in the self, a micro-corporation or entrepreneurial venture swept up into the game of global markets whose rules are determined by economic science. As a result, classical understandings of free will and human agency are no longer necessary—in fact, they must be illusions. He who was once responsible is now *responsibilized*.[6]

As Foucault has noted, neoliberalism stands as one of the most subtle forms of social control yet. As he puts it: whereas *Homo economicus* had long been the one who must be left alone, freed from governmental control, the new "man," a mutation of *Homo economicus*, is he whose behavior can be shaped through the partnership of the economic and biological sciences.[7] Whereas Freakonomics and the popularizers of neuroscience claim that rationality has little control over moral behaviors, they still hold that those behaviors can be described rationally through scientific interrogation of that behavior and controlled better by political-economic manipulation. Thus, a term first coined by critics of the reductionistic anthropology posited by John Stuart Mill in his account of political economy morphs in the twentieth century from the ultimate rational actor to a creature discovered by the neuroscientific narrative of morality—one completely determined by the laws of economics.

## Gary Becker and the Birth of Human Capital

We start with the most recent chapter in the evolution of the Chicago School of Economics, specifically with Gary Becker. Becker held a joint appointment as professor of economics and sociology at the University of Chicago from 1970 until his death in 2014. He won the Nobel Prize in Economics in 1992 precisely for extending "the domain of microeconomic analysis to a wide range of human behavior and interaction, including nonmarket behavior."[8] He is also credited as the primary figure in advancing the notion of human capital that began to emerge in the 1950s. In addition to his prolific oeuvre, Becker translated his work for popular audiences first via a monthly column for *Business Week* from 1984 to 2004, and subsequently with a blog co-authored with Richard Posner.[9] Becker was at times joined in his work by George Stigler, who was also on faculty at the University of Chicago from 1958 to 1991. Stigler is best known for work on industrial organization and the effects of government regulation, and he is considered one of the most important contributors to the practice of deregulation, adopted by governments across the globe from the 1980s forward.[10]

As captured by his colleagues Levitt and Dubner, Becker inserts a profound mutation in economics: no longer is it simply that an "invisible hand" directs the market; now economics—and particularly market economics—becomes the invisible, "hidden side of everything." Or as Foucault notes, neoliberal economics under Becker aims to explain all ends through the control of means.[11] Like the neurosciences, economics takes its purview to be human behavior, which had traditionally been the jurisdiction of ethics. Like the neurosciences, Becker and his colleagues remain entranced by criminality, delinquency, socioeconomic status—and even socioeconomic positioning (SEP). Yet where the neurosciences have developed proxies for virtues and vices, Becker blithely adopts traditional ethical terminology or concepts traditionally associated with virtue or vice; as with the neurosciences, he radically inverts their meanings. Moreover, Becker's work echoes our neuroscientific popularizers, reducing all behavior—moral and otherwise—to preferences or "tastes." These tastes are all governed by the one, biologically grounded dogma of economics, the law of utility maximization, the corollary of a new anthropology of the person as human capital. Under the inescapable laws of economics, human actions remain voluntary but no longer free, an emphasis captured in the concern of neoliberal economics with social policy and social operation designed to encourage the automatic behaviors of individuals. Here we find, not *Homo economicus*, but a new being, *Homo capitalus*, the person *as* capital.

## Totalizing Economics and the Birth of Human Capital

The centrality of utility maximization in Becker's work locates him as a neoclassical economic theorist. But while using the language of neoclassical economics, Becker subtly, but significantly, shifts the scope of the terms. Neoclassical economic theory holds that human beings always act rationally to maximize individual satisfaction or utility (what classical Utilitarians called "pleasure"). But where previous economists limited their analyses to transactions and behavior that had been clearly economic, Becker's Nobel Prize-winning innovation lay in "extending a specific formulation of economic values, practices, and metrics to every dimension of human life."[12] Thus Becker, who Foucault names "the most radical of the American neoliberals,"[13] applies economic analysis beyond economic and rational conduct. It can be applied to any activity and thus becomes "the science of the systematic nature of responses to environmental variables." This, as Foucault notes, "is a colossal definition."[14]

Becker's move to make economics about everything is already signaled in his doctoral thesis on the economics of discrimination,[15] and was continued in subsequent analyses of crime and punishment;[16] marriage, family, and children;[17] drug use;[18] and more. These initiatives are summarized in his 1992 Nobel lecture, "The Economic Way of Looking at Behavior."[19] He explains that "by treating such phenomena as racism, theft, and children as 'tastes' comparable to tastes in food or fashion, economics is able not only to explain why racism persists or why some people have more babies than others, but also to predict future behavior on both individual and grand scales."[20] In applying market logic to social phenomenon, Becker inverts what had been the classical relationship between the social and the economic, where the economic was understood in opposition to, complementary to, or encompassed within the social.[21] Neoliberalism from its inception overturned the "liberal conceit of separate economic, social, and political spheres"; Becker brings this to its apotheosis, forwarding the conviction that all three must be evaluated according to a single logic, that of economics.[22]

One crucial place we see this shift is in Becker's attempt to re-theorize labor. Here we meet the logical outcome of what Karl Polanyi identified as one of the key fictions of classic economics. Becker's work here, along with that of Theodore Schultz and Jacob Mincer, results in the theory of human capital. The notion was first forwarded by Schultz in his 1961 essay "Investment in Human Capital."[23] Here Schultz—who served as chair of the University of Chicago Department of Economics from 1946 to 1961 and was awarded the Nobel Prize in Economics in 1979—proposes that certain objects of consumption should be seen as ways that people invest in their own capital. For example, education, health, and internal migration for better job opportunities ought to be imagined as investments aimed at increasing their own productivity or the rate of return, not of their possessions, but of their very self. People become "a produced means of production."[24] Schultz spends the first section of this essay responding to potential moral concerns about the concept, voiced even by economists. Listing a number of ways in which humans have demeaned human freedom by reducing human actors to inanimate, economic objects—property, slaves, indentured servants—Schultz acknowledges that reducing human actors to capital risks debasing the human. Still, he avers that none other than Adam Smith had advanced a notion of human capital.[25] Laborers who take the initiative to invest in themselves thus are capitalists investing in themselves in order to be more productive workers.[26] In the end, he outlines recommendations for public investment in human capital, despite the caveat that "one proceeds at his own peril in discussing social implications and policy."[27]

Becker was simultaneously developing a similar concept in work sponsored by the National Bureau of Economic Research, culminating in his 1975 monograph *Human Capital: A Theoretical and Methodological Analysis*.[28] Here, Schultz's moral caveats are left behind, and Becker offers a full-fledged analysis of the economic return on investment of various improvements to human persons as capital, for both the individual and society. He focuses primarily on the question of education. For Becker, from a prima facie economic perspective, the time and money spent on education makes little sense unless it produces financial gain.[29] Absent here—and as we will see elsewhere—is any sense of education and knowledge as goods in and of themselves, necessary for the flourishing of persons and communities. Equally absent is any sense of the effects of negative social structures. Instead, he claims blithely in his conclusion that clearly "some persons earn more than others simply because they invest more in themselves [and] 'abler' persons tend to invest more than others."[30]

Under this regime, "capital" is "everything that in one way or another can be a source of future income" including any physical or psychological factors.[31] But what is key here, contra Schultz's caveats, is that human capital—and any improvements that produce a return on investment—is inseparable from the person who possesses it. To this extent, it differs from all other capital: "Ability to work, skill, the ability to do something cannot be separated from the person who is skilled and who can do this particular thing. In other words, the worker's skill really is a machine, but a machine which cannot be separated from the worker himself."[32] In this way, persons are transformed from either laborers or simply rational, preference-maximizing consumers to "a conception of capital-ability ... so that the worker himself appears as a sort of enterprise for himself."[33] As Wendy Brown notes, "all market actors are rendered as little capitals (rather than as owners, workers, and consumers)," who must manage and market the self as a personal enterprise and investment.[34]

Under Becker's economics, the human is not one partner in a process of exchange deploying the principle of utility to satisfy needs and wants; the human person is now an entrepreneur, a producer of the self as a mode of production, an "enterprise-unit" in "a society made up of enterprise-units."[35] What is more, no longer is the human person circumscribed within a space from which he or she can participate in economic activities or make economic choices; now capital has achieved totality, defining both the space and structure of not only of the market and (as we will see with Friedman) the state but human personhood as well.

## The Evacuation of Ethics

At the same time that Becker is birthing this new creature, he also redefines ethics. Just as *Homo capitalus* is the fully economized person, morality also becomes fully economized. This change in ethics, as we shall shortly see, radicalizes Hume's is-ought distinction used by Frank Knight in his drive to make economics a science.

On a prima facie reading, Becker's innovations in ethics might be easy to miss insofar as he deploys traditional moral language drawn from the Aristotelian virtue tradition. But he puts this language to a very different use. Consider, for example, his 2007 article, "Habits, Peers, and Happiness: An Evolutionary Perspective," co-authored with Luis Rayo.[36] The article's opening sentence directly echoes that of *The Nicomachean Ethics*: "The principal motivating factor in our lives is the pursuit of happiness."[37] But happiness here does not consist, as it does for Aristotle, in achieving the multiplicity of goods intrinsic to the full flourishing of individuals and communities. Rather, Rayo and Becker reduce happiness to utility, positing moreover that it can be defined by a mathematical "happiness function" tied to variables of income and social position (circularly defined via income levels) rooted, they suggest, in human biology. As they state unequivocally:

> we presume that maximizing happiness is the fundamental goal of the individual when making decisions. In fact, we believe that happiness *evolved* precisely as a decision-making device. In this sense, we consider that maximizing happiness is closely linked, *if not identical*, to maximizing utility in the standard economic way.[38]

Echoing Haidt, Harris, and Zak, Becker presumes that ideal human behavior lines up with economic activity and that this dynamic is grounded in human biology. Just as Aristotle tied human behavior to his metaphysical biology, Rayo and Becker empirically ground it in an economized biology. *Homo capitalus* is a biological creature.

In addition to happiness and a biological grounding for behavior, they press forward with Aristotelian concepts in advancing their argument. For example, after asserting a conundrum that happiness derived from increased income seems to be fleeting, they note: "We rapidly become accustomed to a more expensive lifestyle. A common name for this feature is *habit formation*."[39] Or later, "as is suggested by common wisdom, income is strongly habit forming."[40] While it seems a truism that most people adjust their lifestyles as their income increases, Rayo and Becker never actually define what they mean by habit formation; it seems to mean little more than "become accustomed to," or, as we shall see, it may mean "become addicted to." In other words, having income creates a feeling of pleasure (a.k.a., happiness) that quickly, like a drug, fades, so that more income is needed to sustain those same sensations of pleasure; so that, in short, "additional income can indeed buy happiness."[41] Thus, habit here is not aimed at any notion of the good; it is simply the need to constantly experience the euphoria of an *increased* income. This notion of happiness is very different than Aristotle's rather complex account of the relationship between character, action, and virtue formation in which habit plays an important role and virtue itself is its own reward.

Yet income alone does not supply happiness; rather, happiness is a function of how one perceives one's social position relative to one's peers. Increase in peer income relative to one's own position is described as a "negative externality," decreasing one's happiness.[42] Deploying their mathematical happiness function, they conclude: (1) an advance in social position has only a short-lived positive effect on happiness; (2) a general increase in income that results in no changes in current income differentials does not affect happiness; (3) those who have recently "received a positive income shock and . . . have advanced recently in the social ranking" are therefore happier; and (4) for the unfortunate person that does not advance in income relative to her peers, she "eventually become(s) habituated to her new, lower social position."[43] Hollingshead's socioeconomic status and Gianaros and Manuck's socioeconomic position turns out to be a major feature of happiness and of habit formation.

We will return to their fourth point shortly, but first let us turn briefly to a second theme that resounds loudly throughout Becker's corpus: namely, that the goods or ends individuals pursue are simply a matter of "taste." This discussion of taste—which also resounds through the work of Haidt and Zak—comes into clearest focus in what Ross Emmett names as one of the two key methodological statements of the Chicago School, namely, Becker and Stigler's article *"De Gustibus Non Est Disputandum."*[44] The historic meaning of this phrase is that a person's personal preferences or tastes are merely subjective opinions, capricious whims that have no basis for their being preferred. They cannot be evaluated as right or wrong. Rational persuasion on the rightness or the wrongness of a taste is not possible. They are irrational and variable, whimsical from one season to the next. Emotivism is fully embraced.

Becker and Stigler take a different tack. As they note:

> Our title seems to us to be capable of another and preferable interpretation: that tastes neither change capriciously nor differ importantly between people. On this interpretation, one does not argue over tastes for the same reason that one does not argue over the Rocky Mountains—both are there, will be there next year, too, and are the same to all men.[45]

The significance of this claim lies in an ongoing dispute within economics. As we will see in the third part of this chapter, Frank Knight—in his endeavor to establish economics as a science in the early part of the century—drew a bright line between human conduct, which can be observed as objective facts, and the subjective desires, tastes, or "values" underlying that conduct. Economics, Knight held, could only deal with the former and then only descriptively.[46] Becker and Stigler overturn this position, with the important closing caveat:

> We are proposing the hypothesis that widespread and/or persistent human behavior can be explained by a generalized calculus of utility-maximizing behavior, without introducing the qualification "tastes remaining the same." It is a thesis that does not permit of direct proof because it is an assertion about the world, not a proposition in logic.[47]

Desires are not subjective and therefore ordered to some good and chosen for reasons according to the understanding of the good by a free actor, as they are for the tradition prior to Becker and Stigler. Rather, they are themselves observable, objective entities, stable across time, biologically grounded and habitually fixed. Free and rational choices are no longer part of the equation. Becker and Stigler support their thesis by developing what they name "stable, well-behaved preference functions," akin to the mathematical happiness function discussed earlier.

In unfolding their argument, Becker and Stigler make two significant interventions at the level of ethics. The first intervention (essentially) equates tastes with addiction. Traditionally, the term "addiction" has carried a negative moral valence, often equated with vice. Yet Stigler and Becker broaden the scope of addiction to include any activity for which a person may experience increased desire combined with increased consumption over time:

> Tastes are frequently said to change as a result of consuming certain "addictive" goods. For example, smoking of cigarettes, drinking of alcohol, injection of heroin, or close contact with some persons over an appreciable period of time, often increases the desire (creates a craving) for these goods or persons, and thereby cause their consumption to grow over time. In utility language, their marginal utility is said to rise over time because tastes shift in their favor.[48]

This framework can be utilized to examine scientifically any activity or good that is consumed.

They employ this framework to evaluate two possible addictions—heroin use and the consumption of "good" music. Within this framing, they purport to demonstrate that, "by definition, [an] addiction is beneficial" not if it motivates a person to pursue an activity traditionally understood as a good or if the object consumed contributes to human flourishing; rather, it is beneficial if it maximizes a utility function. Their conclusion is most striking:

> In the same way, listening to music or playing tennis would be addictive if the demand curves for music or tennis appreciation were sufficiently elastic; the addiction again is the result, not the cause, of the particular elasticity. Put differently, if addiction were surmised (partly because the input of goods or time rose with age), but if it were not clear whether the addiction were harmful or beneficial, the elasticity of demand could be used to distinguish between them: a high elasticity suggests beneficial and a low elasticity suggests harmful addiction.[49]

Put differently, the demand curve can tell you about addictions, which are just tastes and thus not of their own accord moral or immoral; though one could predict whether the addiction was harmful or not by the elasticity of the demand.

They then extend their argument beyond addictive behavior to other customary behaviors as well as advertising and fashion. While admitting that some activities do not evidence a desire-based increase in consumption over time, or increase for only a short period of time and then fade, the math nonetheless remains the same:

Note that this analysis is similar to that used in the previous section to explain addictive behavior: utility maximization with stable preferences, conditioned by the accumulation of specific knowledge and skills. One does not need one kind of theory to explain addictive behavior and another kind to explain habitual or customary behavior. The same theory based on stable preferences can explain both types of behavior, and can accommodate both habitual behavior and the departures therefrom.[50]

Thus, they conclude that any "widespread and/or persistent human behavior can be explained [*and, correlatively evaluated as beneficial or harmful*] by a general calculus of utility-maximizing behavior."[51] In other words, they believe that one can in fact literally "account" for tastes and can do so by searching for the mathematically representable law beneath the behaviors. Addiction is the result, not the cause of the behavior. The general rule of utility maximization functions as a law-like norm for the explanation of any human behavior. In this way, tastes—or values—are no longer per se rationally incommensurable; in fact, the "fact-value" distinction has disappeared, as all values/tastes can be represented mathematically as facts—tastes—and along with actions are subsumed into one scientifically analyzable norm, utility maximization. More importantly, no longer are actions evaluated according to how they impact human skills or health or flourishing or community; moral evaluation (positive/negative, beneficial/harmful) are now solely represented and predicted based on the economic models. Thus, there is an evacuation of the content and substance of morality—substantively: there is no difference between listening to good music, heroin use, growing in love for another person, or shopping. It is simply a matter of elasticity and utility curves.

Consider, for example, another of Becker's signal foci, the economic re-evaluation of crime, as captured in his essay "Crime and Punishment: An Economic Approach," included in his edited volume on this topic.[52] Becker's focus here are the 'normative' economic questions of public policy—that is, "how many resources and how much punishment *should* be used to enforce different kinds of legislation? Put equivalently, although more strangely, how many offenses *should* be permitted and how many offenders *should* go unpunished?"[53] He asserts that answers to these questions can be found by reconceptualizing crime through a grid of economic intelligibility, shifting away from its typical moral or legal connotations and redefining it as "an economically important activity or 'industry.'"

We see this in a series of steps. First, the phenomenon of crime and societal responses and repercussions are appraised simply in market terms. Data on revenues to offenders and expenses to society (of government law enforcement and direct costs laid out by private citizens) generates a calculus of the "net cost or damage to society" for a wide variety of offenses from "felonies—like murder, robbery, and assault . . . but also tax evasion, the so-called white-collar crimes, and traffic and other violations."[54] Again, as with the tastes analyzed earlier, there is a flattening of moral valence, with no difference for evaluative purposes between premeditated murder and running a red light; only costs are considered.[55]

Second, there is a shift from act to agent in two ways. As is clear from the aforesaid, by reframing crime as an economic object, society becomes the agent-consumer and has to assess the return on investment for various approaches to law enforcement. But equally, individual criminal behavior is explained simply through economic utility: "a person commits an offense if the expected utility to him exceeds the utility he could get by using his time and other resources at other activities. Some persons become 'criminals,' therefore, not because their basic motivation differs from that of other persons, but because their benefits and costs differ."[56] No longer is criminal action distinguished from other actions or analyzed on the basis of moral, anthropological, or social valences; it is now evaluated solely from the perspective of the agent, that is to say, society. Offenders are labeled "risk preferers," as criminal activity is transmuted into a matter of tastes.[57] A criminal is no longer a person who pursues vicious ends, but rather is conceptualized "only as anyone whomsoever invests in an action, expects a profit from it, and who accepts the loss of risk."[58] And any particular criminal behavior should be evaluated—individually and societally—by the results of its yield curve.

Most importantly, we see that all behaviors are evaluable under the science of economics, whether those behaviors were thought to be moral or immoral in the past. As Becker himself states clearly in his conclusions: "The theory developed in this essay can be applied to any effort to preclude certain kinds of behavior, regardless of whether the behavior is 'unlawful.'"[59] We see the modern version of this in Freakonomics, the hidden side of everything. Individuals are not the agents that they once were; their behaviors are not their own.

## Biology, Economics, and the Erasure of Freedom

In 1974, Becker stated that "a useful theory of criminal behavior can dispense with special theories of anomie, psychological inadequacies, or inheritance of special traits and simply extend the economist's usual analysis of choice."[60] Contemporaneously, what the emerging neurosciences are beginning to categorize as that proxy for vice, antisocial personality disorder, and looking for in our biology is really in Becker's mind best understood via models of economic choice. Thirty-five years later, in "Habits, Peers, and Happiness: An Evolutionary Perspective," he has begun to develop something quite different—in fact, an "evolutionary" or biological perspective.[61] Here the literature of socio-biology informs his theory about the power of relative social status vis-à-vis his posited "happiness function" discussed earlier. As he notes, interest in SEP had been increasingly of interest to economists on two levels "both applied (i.e., the study of habits and peer influences over behavior and the analysis of happiness surveys) and the theoretical (i.e., a search for biological foundations)."[62] Becker and Rayo bring these two literatures together, showing "how several nontrivial empirical results can be rationalized using existing biological insights."[63]

In light of this, Becker and Rayo assert unequivocally, that their "happiness function" has "a strong biological foundation"[64] and "measures the biological desirability of alternative decisions."[65] Avoiding any shadow of teleology, they aver that "happiness is not the goal of the evolutionary process. Rather, it is merely an instrument implicitly used by an organism's genes to guide his actions, with the ultimate goal of increasing the likelihood that these genes are passed on to future generations."[66] Notably, in this essay, they do not actually correlate biological insights with their happiness function; that work comes in a subsequent essay, "Evolutionary Efficiency and Happiness."[67] Here, they presume their findings from "Habits" but take them one step further: "using economic tools, we argue that the above features can be evolutionarily advantageous in the sense of improving the individual's ability to propagate his genes. Our goal, in other words, is to provide a biological foundation for these traits."[68]

Here they provide a "stylized" account of evolutionary biology, an account redolent of the discourse of selfish genes and "fitness" current as the millennium turned. Asserting that the happiness function (V) posited previously is in fact "innate,"[69] they seek no timid goal; in fact, their aim is "to characterize the theoretical end point of a natural selection process in which, via trial and error, the fitness-maximizing happiness functions have come to replace all the rest."[70] Insofar as the happiness function is simply a mathematized calculus of utility, they therefore are arguing for the biological—in fact, genetic—grounding of utility. Like Zak's Oxytocin Virtue Cycle, happiness is grounded in biology.

Prescinding from the technical, mathematized presentation of their argument, one thing is clear: the selfish gene is at work.[71] This biological-genetic grounding of the happiness function is important because, in the subtlest of moves, happiness/pleasure/utility maximization are taken out of the realm of freedom and reason and become "mere instruments" of deeper biological processes, now confirmed by the mathematical laws of economics. In fact, as they state clearly:

> The theoretical problem of finding the fitness-maximizing happiness functions can be conveniently stated as a metaphorical principal-agent problem. As is customary in the literature, the principal represents the process of natural selection, and the agent represents an individual carrying a set of genes. In the present context, the principal designs the innate happiness function of the agent, with the goal of maximizing the propagation of the agent's genes. Importantly, the happiness function is only a means to this end: the principal does not directly care about the agent's happiness level. The agent, on the other hand, is born with the happiness function designed by the principal and, via his actions, seeks only to maximize his level of happiness. In the process, however, he inadvertently serves the principal's goal.[72]

The principal—nature, the gene—designs, has a goal, maximizes, and does not directly care. The principal—that is, an economized biology—is the main actor; the invisible hand has become biologized. The "agent"—the human person—is one who unknowingly and "inadvertently serves the principal's goal."

Thus, while Becker and Rayo may prima facie describe the actions of persons as voluntary, the person and her actions are no longer free. In fact, throughout Becker's corpus, "freedom"—that concept so sacred within classical economic theory—is largely missing.[73] This turn to the sociobiological grounding of economic theory comes toward the end of Becker's career, but the outlines of a tension between freedom and biological/social control are present from the beginning. When speaking of theft or drug use, Becker suggests that such activity may not be "free," strictly speaking;

addiction (whether to heroin or good music) may compel a person's behavior, as there is always a desire for more. But insofar as an actor makes a choice—"chooses," for example, between taking heroin or not taking it, listening to Yo-Yo Ma or not—the action remains voluntary if not free, a distinction that accords with Sam Harris.

Moreover, even beyond addiction, choices like tastes "are entirely stable and predictable responses, determined (even predestined) by given circumstances and prior behaviors."[74] As Kathryn Blanchard notes, "choice," at least in Becker's work, no longer has a necessary relationship with "freedom." It has become a word that refers merely to the use of individual power. Yet that power is not freely exercised: "The human being is always and everywhere under the power of a single, uncomplicated sovereign master (to replace Bentham's pleasure and pain): rational, [utility-maximizing] self-interest. From such a master, economics offers no escape."[75] Our culture—and particularly those who champion neoliberal economics—retains the rhetoric of freedom. But behind this rhetoric, freedom has been redefined on market terms; society has been replaced by isolated and competitive individuals; and choices are driven by self-interest (perhaps genetic) rather than the common good. True moral autonomy—or free will—is but an illusion.[76] It is the market that is and must remain truly free.

Here is where Becker's social location as a sociologist is not incidental to his insights. The endpoint of all of these analyses, as mentioned earlier, is public policy. Becker believes that economics and public policy go hand-in-hand; but for Becker, the task of the state is not simply to protect negative freedoms. Rather, "economists can [and ought] to advise policy makers on the best ways [using economic mechanisms] to encourage more desirable behavior and discourage the less desirable—in other words, they can enable social control of the sort that free-marketeers fervently disavow."[77] Economics, in other words, becomes "the science of the systematic nature of responses to environmental variables," which can be optimized through behavioral, psychological, and structural manipulation of the conditions of choice.[78]

But as soon as the improvement of social outcomes is paired with the improvement of human capital, we have met a new nexus of governmentality, where, as Foucault notes, "the problem of the control, screening and improvement of the human capital of individuals, as a function of unions and consequent reproduction," is inevitable. By reenvisaging human action and behavior through an economic grid, human behavior becomes subject to control not necessarily through direct oppression or exclusion of those whose behavior lies outside the norm but by using "new techniques of environmental technology or environmental psychology"[79] that operate invisibly on the rules of the game rather than directly subjugating persons.[80]

Neuroscience simply gives the most recent iteration of this vision. With the work of Becker, Stigler, and Rayo, we see the diminishment of rational free actors, the elevation of moral "tastes," and the belief we find in Zak and Harris that we can create conditions to get people to act in certain ways. And we can see that neuroscience supplies the facts about this newly formed figure, evacuated of freedom and choice and determined by an economized biology, whom we have called *Homo capitalus*. *Homo capitalus* is a new being, quite different from Frank Knight's *Homo economicus* with its origins in the thought of John Stuart Mill. But before we tell the story of Frank Knight we must describe how Milton Friedman—the great champion of

*Homo economicus*—set the stage for the artifactual *Homo capitalus*, an artifact of scientific modeling.

## Milton Friedman and the Economizing of the State

In some ways, the story could end here insofar as contemporary neoliberalism provides the social imaginary that has inchoately perfused the neuroscience of morality. But as in epidemiology, identifying the pathogen is only the first step. To stem a pandemic, it is equally important to trace the etiology, to identify mutations in the agent, and to locate the source of the malaise so as to eliminate or contain the microbe and chart a new future. Thus, in our quest to understand this troubling account of morality, we must track its intellectual and social history. Becker was not sui generis. His scientific economics is deeply dependent on the economic theory of his predecessor, Milton Friedman.[81] The alignment between their works was recognized in 2011 when the University of Chicago established the Becker Friedman Institute for Research in Economics, in order to honor both men. Key innovations in classical economic theory introduced by Friedman, as well as by his predecessor, Frank Knight, laid the groundwork for Becker's key moves. Yet, Becker fundamentally altered Friedman's approach. While Becker inherited Friedman's commitment to economics as a tool of social policy, he radically reinterpreted Friedman's commitment to freedom as well as Knight's sacred figure of *Homo economicus*. In order to understand this mutation and the ways that it has shaped the neurosciences, it is essential to review Friedman's main contributions to neoliberal economics.

### Government, Competition, and Carving Out a New "State of Nature"

Friedman is widely considered to be the most influential economist of the twentieth century.[82] He joined the faculty at the University of Chicago in 1946 and is credited as the intellectual force that established the Chicago School of Economics. In 1976, he was awarded the Nobel Prize in Economics "for his achievements in the fields of consumption analysis, monetary history and theory and for his demonstration of the complexity of stabilization policy."[83] Among his many works, key items include *A Theory of the Consumption Function* (1957), *Capitalism and Freedom* (1962), and *A Monetary History of the United States* (with Anna Schwartz, 1963).

Like Becker, Friedman did not limit himself to strictly academic venues. From the beginning of his career, he adopted the neoliberal strategy of spreading his ideas to the masses via popular media. As early as 1946, he penned a popular pamphlet with George Stigler entitled "Roofs or Ceilings: The Current Housing Problem"—critical of postwar attempts at rent control, described by one author as "beautifully and cunningly written," that takes his free-market ideas to their logical and somewhat extreme limits.[84] J. Daniel Hammond notes that for the early part of his life and career, Friedman did not have an active interest in economic and social policy.[85] Rather, it was only during his first year at the University of Chicago, after he attended the first meeting of the

MPS and met Hayek, that he began to shift his focus from economics and statistics to a more robust engagement with "the political and philosophical ideas that undergird policy."[86] This engagement with popular audiences continued throughout his life; in his retirement, he and his wife Rose D. Friedman created a ten-part series for PBS entitled *Free to Choose*, forwarding his economic ideas, as well as a companion book of the same title, which stands as the nonfiction bestseller of 1980.

Friedman identified himself with the nineteenth-century "classical liberal" tradition, a position we will dispute.[87] For him, liberalism "emphasized freedom as the ultimate goal and the individual as the ultimate entity in the society"; laissez-faire, he argued, reduced the role of the state in its interference with *individuals*.[88] Rather than the clunky phrase "19th century liberalism," he coins the phrase the "new liberalism"—thus, neoliberalism[89]—which he maintains is a retrieval of Adam Smith. But he also clearly avowed that this was not a simple retrieval. Demonstrating Foucault's thesis, he notes:

> Neo-liberalism would accept the nineteenth century liberal emphasis on the fundamental importance of the individual, but it would substitute for the nineteenth century goal of laissez-faire as a means to this end, the goal of the competitive order . . . The state would police the system, establish conditions favorable to competition and prevent monopoly, provide a stable monetary framework, and relieve acute misery and distress. The citizens would be protected against the state by the existence of a free private market; and against one another by the preservation of competition.[90]

Thus, where the state had previously protected the individual from the market, now the market stands between the individual and the state, protecting individual freedom. In this way, Friedman claimed that economic liberties were indispensable for political liberties; his foil here was socialism but, as we saw in the Interlude, toward the end of his career, his economic principles became tools of despotism.

Friedman laid the groundwork for Becker in a number of ways. On the one hand, as we will see, following Knight, Friedman played a key role in the twentieth-century effort to establish economics as a science. In one of his seminal articles, "The Methodology of Positive Economics" (1953), he championed the idea of "positive economics." Economist Julian Reiss names this essay as "undoubtedly one of the—or perhaps the—most influential and most widely and hotly debated papers on economic methodology."[91] Positive economics is characterized by three things. First, in keeping with his forebears as well as the philosophical climate of the day, Friedman held that positive economics—as an objective science—was value free; it was firmly premised on the fact/value distinction. As he notes, it "is in principle independent of any particular ethical position or normative judgments . . . [I]t deals with 'what is,' not with 'what ought to be.'"[92]

He takes it one step further, however, by emphasizing the ability of economics to *predict*, which for him was the key mark of a true science. Thus, the distinguishing task of positive economics is to establish the law-like generalization to predict consequences depending on variables "in precisely the same sense as any of the physical sciences."[93] Just as moral philosophy will become "moral science" in the nineteenth century, the economic branch of moral philosophy becomes economic science in the twentieth century.

Third, while he accepted Knight's premise that economics (facts) must be carefully separated from ethics (values), Friedman rejected Knight's position that given the abstract, scientific nature of economics and its inability to determine ends and goods, economics should remain separate from politics and public policy. For him, economics could not be amoral. It was a positive science, but positive economics would be in the service of what he called normative economics (policymaking). Normative economics is "an art . . . a system of rules for the attainment of a given end."[94] While positive economics must distinguish itself from its normative counterpart, the art of normative economics is entirely dependent upon positive economics. Positive economics can tell normative economics at what leverage points to achieve the desired goals.[95]

That he makes the distinction between positive and normative economics so early in his career is notable. For as Krugman notes, one of the things that marks Friedman's career and locates him as "the greatest" economist of the twentieth century was that he was a "policy entrepreneur" who sought from the 1950s forward to bring the findings of economic science to bear on government economic policy, both in the United States and internationally.[96] As much as he was dedicated to the science of economics, he was even more deeply committed to shaping public policy. In other words, for Friedman, a key responsibility of economics was to provide the science to help shape the ends, the goals of public life, which entails normatively selecting the ends he hopes to build into policy. Thus, for Friedman, ethics begins to be subsumed under the purview of economics via policy.

But the "norms" that economics and government seek to implement are of a very specific type. Here public policy was not of the Keynesian variety, which saw government as responsible for achieving certain content outcomes, such as a living wage, adequate health care for all citizens, or full employment. For Friedman, Keynesian thought would place government "planning" in the lead, moving society down the slippery slope toward socialism and collectivism.[97] Instead, the proper role for political economy in shaping public policy was to ensure that the political domain internalized the proper formal economic principle, namely, to facilitate competition. Government's first principle—its main end or norm—is to enable economic competition, as he noted clearly in his 1962 work "Capitalism and Freedom." Economics has priority over politics.

Contrary to popular opinion of his day, Friedman held that economics and politics did not easily meld together. One could not expect that democracy, as a political order, would easily fit any economic system, for example, socialism. "[D]emocratic socialism is a contraction in terms."[98] The new liberalism would understand that the principles of liberalism were both political *and* economic. The idea that economics was one thing and politics was another was a recipe for disaster. Economic freedom was a necessary precondition for political freedom, or democracy.[99] Thus, it is not politics that promotes individual, social, or political freedom—*economics* is the primary engine of political freedom.[100]

In other words, although Friedman vociferously championed the "fact-value" distinction, his quasi-religious dedication to the self-organizing market based on competition dictated the form of the political.[101] His theory required a minimal role for the state in all but a few areas, where he assigned it massive responsibility for intervention, requiring the state to maintain permanent vigilance and active intervention to keep the market free. Economics becomes the formal principle for the internal regulation of the state. Competition becomes key; the state must create, within its domain and control, the Hobbesian state of nature in order for men to be free. Finally, Friedman is credited with expanding classical economic analyses (i.e., persons as rationally calculating utility maximizers) to new questions within macroeconomics, paving the way for Becker's extension of microeconomic analysis to all areas of human life.

What we see here is what Foucault names clearly as a key feature of "economic positivism." As neoliberalism moves into its second phase, it creates an "economic grid" against which the political can be judged.[102] This grid anchors and justifies "a permanent political criticism of political and governmental action."[103] Thus, positive economics after Friedman sees as one of its roles a constant vigilance and critique of government policy. This economic vigilance requires the government to leave a zone of free activity for individual, laisse-faire in some sense, while at the same time asserting governmental vigilance and intervention in a few key areas. Here Friedman again differentiates himself from classical economics by identifying an error made in what he calls "19th century individualist philosophy," by which he means the Bentham-Mill approach to political economy. The state must intervene in some areas but not others. Neoliberal political economy must steer a path between Scylla and Charybdis. Friedman notes:

> *A new faith* must avoid both errors. It must give high place to a severe limitation on the power of the state to interfere in the detailed activities of individuals; at the same time, it must explicitly recognize that there are important positive functions that must be performed by the state. The doctrine sometimes called neo-liberalism which has been developing more or less simultaneously in many parts of the world and which in America is associated particularly with the name of Henry Simons is such a faith. No one can say that this doctrine will triumph.[104]

The goal is to protect individual liberties and to halt state overreach, while at the same time the state must assert its powers in order to create conditions for competition and free markets.

## The Freedom of *Homo Economicus*

Contrary to Becker, who transforms the rational utility maximizer into a being biologically inclined to utility maximization and so governable through inducement and self-investment, here Friedman's avowed commitment to classical liberalism is firm, for behind his adamant antagonism to government intervention stands his deep commitment to the freedom of individuals to pursue their own understanding of the good. As he states clearly, "(F)reedom has nothing to say about what an individual does with his freedom; it isn't an all-embracing ethic by any means." The goal for the believer in freedom is "to leave the ethical problem for the individual to wrestle with."[105]

Here a number of things come into relief. First, in spite of his avowed separation of positive and normative economics, and in spite of his avowal that government policy ought not seek substantive ends, Friedman's rhetoric was shaped by a deep commitment to a substantive good: the freedom of the individual, who is imagined to be at his freest when exercising his power to act vis a vis wealth. It is a *norm*, by which social arrangements can be judged. More than simply a value, Blanchard argues that this commitment shaped Friedman's conceptual apparatus: "Freedom, in Friedman's mind, is not only the pre-condition upon which a *laissez-faire* economy can function; it is also the goal toward which market mechanisms are directed," a goal they will achieve if governments do not interfere, except in the domain where it can enable the most freedom, namely, by enacting policies that enable competition.[106]

Yet, this freedom of persons is the freedom enacted by the state that takes the free market—that is to say, economics—as its principal form aimed at creating the conditions of competition, which enables freedom of the individual. Thus, Friedman holds to a classical liberal understanding of the person as *Homo economicus*.[107] What is more, *Homo economicus* ought not only be free of government; Friedman conceives of *Homo economicus* as free from his fellows. Later in *Capitalism and Freedom*, he returns to what he calls "the economist's favorite abstraction of Robinson Crusoe," where he discusses the dynamics of economic exchange by envisaging now "a number of Robinson Crusoe households on different islands," which have to figure out how to cooperate economically. The metaphor is telling. Although living in proximity to one another, human persons no longer constitute a community; rather, they are "at their core, [imperfect and] disconnected individuals . . . 'a collection of Robinson Crusoes, as it were . . . each of whom lives from himself.'"[108]

In this sense, Friedman is a classical liberal as well. Freedom, for Friedman, is a Kantian transcendental. It is an *a priori* condition for the possibility of human powers to be exercised. Thus, Friedman's anthropology strongly retains a notion of free will and rationality. Politics secures freedom by holding back the power of those who would wield power in order to enable freedom for citizens to determine and pursue their own understanding of the good. Government had always to be on guard, lest it begin to overpower everyone, curbing the freedom of all. Friedman is also Kantian in that he does not think we have access to the good in any metaphysical sense; thus, government should not try to enact the good, just create the right structures so that individuals can enact their own goods. His utilitarianism comes into play within these boundary conditions. Good, for Friedman, is the purview of the individual, not society, nor economic science. The greatest good for the greatest number of people is possible only within the framework of government that secures freedom.[109]

By limiting the scope of government policies designed to create the space of freedom for the individual, the "new liberalism" creates a space for individuals, or what Friedman calls "independent economic units," to exercise their desires. By leaving ownership and economic resources in private hands, maximal freedom and liberty is preserved.¹¹⁰ The free actor must be free of government in order to produce his own goods and his own good.¹¹¹ Although he gestures here to "values" beyond wealth accrual, in practice he effectively envisages persons as "economic units." Friedman's "economic units" are the precursors to Becker's "enterprise units."

Friedman's reduction of human anthropology to "economic units" is the first mutation away from Knight's *Homo economicus* on the way to the human being imagined by Becker as human capital, *Homo capitalus*. *Homo capitalus*, like a piece on a monopoly board, must have the game controlled by rules such that It can "self-create" without intervention from It's fellows, in fact, in competition with them and without intervention from the powers of the state.

## Goods and the Games People Play

Economics, for Friedman, was a science that could monitor the facts of power enabling individuals to enact their own goods. The economist ought not to determine goods for the individual, and government ought only to create the conditions for the possibility for individuals to define and pursue their own goods. Freedom is content-less, value-neutral, a necessary condition for the possibility of the production of individually determined goods. But in the supposedly value neutrality of economic science, goods are only discerned as the fulfilling of desires. Economic science does not recognize what is good, only that people seek to fulfill the desires for those things that they determine to be good. Political economy just sets up the rules according to which everyone must adhere in pursuing the goods that they desire to pursue.

Foucault observes that under neoliberalism, both the economy and the state become understood as a "game." Both are regulated activities with rules that shape the play, the outcome of which is not known by anyone. The individual players are enterprise units in the game framed by the state.¹¹² The economic or enterprise units know what games they want to play, but the rules for all games are the rules that are set out for all individuals such that they can play specific games aimed at specific goods. Thus, it is no accident that "game theory" emerges as a component of economic science, invented by John von Neumann and Oskar Morgenstern in 1944. Game theory "the study of the ways in which *interacting choices* of *economic agents* produce *outcomes* with respect to the *preferences* (or *utilities*) of those agents, where the outcomes in question might have been intended by none of the agents."¹¹³ "Man" is just a piece in a game board enabled by economics as the form of the political that claims to free humans. A number of economists, including Paul Samuelson and John F. Nash, Jr., have been awarded the Nobel Prize in Economics for their work in game theory.¹¹⁴

It is certainly true that Friedman held that government should not tell us what games to play, what goods to aim at. It is the job of government to create the space for multiple games to be played, for different goods to be sought. Government should prohibit those pursuing the goods of baseball from imposing those goods on those who would rather be pursuing the goods of football. Economics just tells us the rules that should govern all the games which various individuals are playing; it cannot tell us what games we ought to be playing. Yet, by the time we get to Becker we see that economics becomes the game of all games, in which the goods of all the games played by *Homo capitalus* are thought to be the highest good, the good of investing in oneself so that one can play the game of games, market economics. It should come as no surprise, then, that economic games have become a staple methodology of the neuroscience of morality.

As Krugman notes, Friedman is "the best spokesman for the virtues of free markets since Adam Smith. But he slipped all too easily into claiming both that markets always work and that only markets work. It is extremely hard to find cases in which Friedman acknowledged the possibility that markets could go wrong, or that government intervention could serve a useful purpose."[115] Again and again, Friedman called for market solutions to every problem—education, health care, the illegal drug trade—deploying free market economic orthodoxy; yet Friedman did not take seriously the way that economics could be gamed by market forces. Government was to be agnostic about which version of the good life would survive market competition, all the while elevating individualistic notions of the good life over shared communal notions of the good life. This means, of course, that government was not to be at all agnostic about what was to be the good life, having elevated competition and individualistic notions of the good life to be the only norms.

In this sense, Friedman is following the path of economic science laid out by his teacher Frank Knight. Knight had championed the strong Humean distinction between facts and values. For Knight, it was the task of other disciplines, such as theology or philosophy, to define the good. Economics sought solely to understand the economic laws by which people enacted their notions of the good. Friedman also adhered to this distinction, noting that economics could only tell us the rules of the game, not whether the game was good. However, Friedman did not heed Knight's warning. Knight had stated that the economic science that understands the laws of "want satisfaction" of the goods desired "may deteriorate the character of its participants: playing a game, even in a sportly fashion, is not the same as seeking the Good. Thus, in market society, we become something less than the people our ethical systems call us to be."[116]

The character of the players may or may not have deteriorated. After all, without a firm commitment to goods, one can never tell about character, except perhaps to say that those with the most wealth—those who generate a positive yield curve and win at the economic game of games that is political economy—would be deemed the most moral, the most prosocial. What we have shown is that Becker's *Homo capitalus* depended upon Friedman's way of imagining political economy as the setting out of political rules that would ensure freedom of players to play the games they want to play, to secure the goods they want to secure. However, we can also say that *Homo capitalus*, enabled by Friedman's robust *Homo economicus*, finds Its progenitor in Frank Knight's somewhat more circumscribed *Homo economicus*.

## Frank Knight and the Severing of Ethics and Economics

As noted earlier, those who tell the story of neoliberalism often locate the first phase as beginning in the 1930s with the ascendance of Ludwig von Mises and Friedrich

Hayek's development of Ordoliberalism. Alongside those developments, the Chicago School was laying its foundations as well. For the notion of human capital and the reconfiguring of the relationship between economics from ethics was not created *ex nihilo* by Becker and Friedman. The groundwork for these innovations was laid by their teacher, Frank H. Knight, who is generally considered to be the founding figure of the Chicago School.[117]

Knight, whose prolific publishing career spanned the fifty-year period from 1917 to 1967, joined the full-time faculty at the University of Chicago in 1928. He is largely regarded as one of the most influential economists in the United States from the early 1920s to the late 1950s, serving as the primary mentor for Friedman, Stigler, Paul Samuelson, and many others more famously associated with the Chicago School.[118] His first and most famous book *Risk, Uncertainty, and Profit* was published in 1921.[119] His work on the distinction between risk and uncertainty would transform economics, risk being an unknown that could be probabilistically calculated and uncertainty being an unknown that cannot be modeled. He is also credited as one of the major figures in establishing price theory as the center of the Chicago School.[120] With his colleague Jacob Viner, Knight taught the foundational "Price Theory" course (Econ 301) from the late 1920s to the mid-1940s, authoring the required text *The Economic Organization* in 1933.[121] With Viner, he also edited *The Journal of Political Economics* for almost twenty years, positioning it as the primary champion in the field of theory and application of a price-theoretic perspective on economics.[122] He helped found the University of Chicago's famous Committee on Social Thought, the subsequent bastion of Hayek from 1950 to 1972, and participated in the founding (and many subsequent) meeting of the Mont Pelerin Society.[123]

Knight stands as an important link between the development of nineteenth-century economic theory and Milton Friedman. Knight's lifelong focus on ethics, and his struggle to articulate the relationship between economics and ethics, place him in continuity with Adam Smith and John Stuart Mill, as we shall see. Given his constant engagement with questions of moral philosophy, as well as differences between his work and where it was taken by Friedman, Becker and others, one might claim, as Ross Emmett does, that "ironically, the Chicago School can be said to owe everything, and nothing, to Knight."[124] Or, as Emmett puts it elsewhere, Knight "remains in a netherworld somewhere between the classical and neo-liberalism."[125]

Yet as we will see in the next chapter, the focus of economic theorizing changes dramatically from the nineteenth to the twentieth centuries, and Knight was a lever making that shift possible.[126] As we move from classical economics to neoliberal economics, the object of study shifts from mechanisms and interconnections of production, exchange, and social structures to ways these can be harnessed to enable (or induce) choices of means for individuals to achieve individually chosen ends. Thus Knight's vision of *Homo economicus* created the conditions for the mutation into *Homo capitalus*.

One clue that anthropology has shifted emerges in a new definition of economics circulating by the 1930s, forwarded by British economist Lionel Robbins: "Economics is the science of human behavior as a relationship between ends and scarce means which have mutually exclusive uses."[127] Traditionally, the "science" of human behavior was the realm of the field long known as moral philosophy. "Science" within philosophy simply meant knowledge, not the restrictive, formal, law-like form of knowledge understood by contemporary empirical science. But critically, as we move into the twentieth century, the nascent field of economics claims human behavior as its specialty.[128] To do so, it needs to make a number of moves. First, it needs to establish itself as a "science." Second, it needs to differentiate itself from other fields traditionally concerned with human behavior, for example, ethics. Third, it needs to posit an account of 'the human' that permits a reproducible—and therefore predictable and controllable—model of behavior. Once economics becomes a science, *Homo economicus* is born, and once the science has separated itself from moral philosophy, the groundwork is laid for *Homo capitalus*. We see all three shifts at play in the work of Frank Knight. To highlight these, let us turn to a close reading of the first of his famous two-part lecture delivered at Harvard in 1922, published as "Ethics and the Economic Interpretation." [129]

## Facts, Values, and the Birth of Economic Science

As a realm of scholarly activity, Knight championed a vision of economics as the science that discovered and described the "laws" that governed human economic behavior. As he states, "The economic man is the individual who obeys economic laws, which is merely to say that he obeys *some* laws of conduct, it being the task of the science to find out what the laws are."[130] Embracing human reason, the rational man "knows what he wants and orders his conduct intelligently with a view to getting it."[131] The economist does not study the ends, but the means to those ends. It is only as the study of the means that economics can be imagined as a science.[132] In positing this definition, Knight is striving to bring economics up to what he perceives to be the gold standard, that of the natural sciences, as in many respects "economics has been far behind the natural sciences."[133]

These "laws" and their related models discovered by economists are, in Knight's view, purely formal. "Economics deals with the form of conduct rather than its substance or content." Wealth stands in for all things that one might desire, whether it be money, prestige, power, or any other good. Wealth is "merely an abstract term covering everything which men do actually (provisionally) want."[134] In other words, economics is for Knight solely a discipline of "instrumental rationality," a deliberation about means to achieve ends that are given and seem to be inscrutable. What ought to be desired is not at stake in the science of economics; only the means are scientifically discoverable and the task of science is to rationally weigh those means.

Knight imagines means in terms of "cause-and-effect relations" of human conduct, delimiting "conduct" in a way very different from his Chicago School heirs:

> Conduct is not co-extensive with human behavior; much of the latter is admittedly capricious, irrational, practically automatic, in its nature. Different actions have in various degrees the character of conduct, which we define with Spencer as "the adaptation of acts to ends," or briefly, deliberative or rational activity. Much that is

at the moment virtually reflex and unconscious is, however, the result of habit or of self-legislation in the past, and hence ultimately rational.[135]

Conduct, or "human acts," are those actions that are directed toward ends via deliberative or rational activity.[136]

Conduct is teleological in that human actors generally reason to ends, but economics must refrain from engaging with ends in any way. Thus, Knight is faced with a conundrum. He wants to very clearly limit economic science to a descriptive rather than a normative project. As a science, "dedicated to the search for truth," economics must eschew the temptation to evaluate the "ends" toward which human conduct is directed, and even to be "purified of all prejudices as to the goodness or badness of its [own] principles and results."[137] For economics to be scientific, any substantive or subjective component of human action—including ends, means to those ends, knowledge of ends and means, or preferences—must all be determined prior to the work of the economist. The economist mimics MacIntyre's description of the manager.

In order to carve out conduct from its ends, Knight draws a bright line between economics and ethics.[138] Are human motives, wants, and desires best treated by the descriptive economic science? Or are they not values, or oughts, which are of a different character, and thus not amenable to scientific investigation?[139] Arguing against fellow economists who he believes fallaciously encompass ends within the purview of economics, Knight affirms Hume's is-ought distinction, limiting the domain of economic science to the analysis of conduct/facts/the "is," relegating ends/values/"oughts" to other branches of human knowing.[140] One reason for this demarcation is, he believes, that wants, desires, and ends are not stable; they are constantly changing. Here Becker differs from his predecessor. Yet in trying to navigate this fine line, Knight plants the seed from which Becker will sprout, claiming:

> For the purpose of defining economics, the correct procedure would appear to be to start from the ordinary meaning of the verb to economize, that is, to use resources wisely in the achievement of *given* ends. In so far as the ends are viewed as given, as data, *then all activity is economic. The question of the effectiveness of the adaptation of means is the only question to be asked regarding conduct, and economics is the one and all-inclusive science of conduct.* From this point of view, the problem of life becomes simply the economic problem, how to employ the existing and available supplies of all sorts of resources . . . in producing the maximum amount of want-satisfaction, including the provision of new resources for increased value production insofar as the present population finds itself actually desiring future progress.[141]

The door is open now for Friedman and Becker. Insofar as the ends are given, all activity is economic. Friedman and Becker run with the idea that "all activity is economic," laying the groundwork for the popularizers of neuroscience. In addition, the job of defining—or rather, as we will see herein, interpreting—ends is the job of other non-scientific disciplines, such as philosophy, theology, and history.[142] Friedman mostly accepts this second point, whereas Becker ignores it. What distinguishes Knight, Friedman, and Becker is what they think the human actor *is*, a point to which we shall now turn.

## Is/Ought, Economics/Ethics

As Aristotle noted, all knowledge is of the general. It is derived in order to cover many instances of a kind of object. If the point is to discover the laws of economic behavior, which is now thought to be the model for all human behavior, then the human, the "economic man," is necessarily an abstraction appropriate to that model. Where Friedman and Becker thought they had captured human behavior in their economic models of behavior, Knight admitted candidly that he was dealing with an abstraction. Put differently, economic science presupposes an anthropology, an account of who or what the human economic actor is. Knight understood that he was engaging in anthropological philosophizing. He unabashedly deployed the term "economic man," presuming the anthropology forwarded by John Stuart Mill of "the human whose sole activity is choice, and who chooses based on a calculation of pure self-interest."[143] But where the phrase *Homo economicus* was coined to criticize Mill's anthropology (as we will see in Chapter 5), this figure as the focal point of a scientific economics becomes for Knight, to a degree, necessary and positive.

Yet while validating *Homo economicus*—the human that obeys economic laws the way that celestial bodies obey the laws of physics—as the model for the science of economics, Knight recognized the limits of this anthropology. He admits the criticism made by some that the economic man does not exist. Human actors do not check the laws of the science of conduct and then act. Human actors "neither know what they want—to say nothing of what is 'good' for them—or act very intelligently to secure the things which they have decided to try to get."[144] Thus, Knight recognizes that *Homo economicus* is necessarily an idealized abstraction useful only for the purposes of scientific analysis: "a science of conduct possible only if its subject-matter is made abstract to the point of telling us little or nothing about actual behavior."[145]

Knight also comes across rather cynical about human reason and character. While economics must treat the ends as givens, he believed human reason to be highly imperfect, "a frail instrument, often corrupted by the baser elements in human nature," utilized to pursue baser human nature—self-interest.[146] This weakness in human nature complicates the study of conduct such that, in relation to the natural sciences, economics still falls short. The data for the science of conduct is disanalogous to natural science. Its data is provisional, shifting, and idiosyncratic to the individual, rendering its generalizations fruitless. People act toward the end in front of them with some vague awareness that the end is not the ultimate end.[147] Human behavior is not wholly rational, either in its end or in its means.

Despite these vagaries that are difficult to render rational, Knight envisages human actors not only as agents seeking to satisfy particular desires or ends; rather, he envisages them as endlessly caught up in the creation of desire itself. People desire not just more, but better ends, or things that they think they ought to want.[148] As we will see with John

Stuart Mill, Knight imagines choice in desires and the ability to give some ranking of goods, with "'higher,' more evolved and enlightened wants."[149] As he notes:

> Life is not fundamentally a striving for ends, for satisfactions, but rather for bases for further striving; desire is more fundamental to conduct than is achievement, or perhaps better, the true achievement is the refinement and elevation of the plane of desire, the cultivation of taste. And let us reiterate that all this is true to the person acting, not simply to the outsider, philosophizing after the event.[150]

Thus, behind all these wants—which are all, always at the same time, completely economic and completely "ideal, conventional, or sentimental"[151]—lies "'the restless spirit of man' who is an aspiring rather than a desiring being."[152]

As we will see in the next chapter, Mill had a higher view of the human, while also acknowledging the rather reductive nature of all sciences of conduct. Yet insofar as aspiration is cast as a form of desire, Knight is left with a bifurcated anthropology—the human person at once the rational utility calculating actor—the abstraction *Homo economicus* that does not really exist—and the being with no basis to act, whose desires "multiply in at least as great a ratio as the heads of the famous hydra."[153] This person must be free to choose, pursue, and negotiate with others in society their own ends; yet this "free" conduct can be mapped (and later predicted) by economic laws that are as "universal as those of mathematics and mechanics."[154]

What is more, in insisting on the formal nature of economic science, its agnosticism regarding ends, and the correlative bifurcation of economics and ethics, Knight renders ends as incommensurable preferences. Blanchard argues that Knight so reduces desire that desire for friendship, beauty, or social approval originates in the same place as desire for water or air. The mechanics behind the deepest and the most frivolous desires are the same. The scientific discovery for the mechanics of shoe buying is not that different from the mechanics of impoverished parents acquiring food for their hungry children. As Knight states it, "If the Good is Satisfaction, there are no qualitative differences, no 'higher' and 'lower' as between wants and that is better which is smaller and most easily appeased."[155] "Put this way," Blanchard notes, "it may seem absurd, and yet this is precisely what economics does."[156] Knight readily acknowledges and laments the logic that his economic science requires. Throughout his corpus, one finds frequent laments of the moral and social failings of laissez-faire.[157] Put differently, Knight conceives of ethics as the pursuit of the good, and that economics as a science can give humankind the tools to achieve those goods. But as we noted earlier, he is less sanguine about the deleterious effects of market dynamics on human character, with self-interest-driven want satisfaction paving a downward social spiral.[158]

He names precisely such a concern immediately following his panegyric account of the person as an aspiring, desiring being. Every actor feels the difference between what one should want, and what one really wants, and he notes the disconnect is more felt by the unthinking actor than the sophisticated actor, who "argues himself into the 'tolerant' (economic) attitude of *de gustibus non disputandum*."[159] Contrary to Becker and Stigler, Knight sees this flight of fanciful ends or tastes not merely as a fact, but as a morally problematic fact, counseling that "[a] sounder culture leads away from this view."[160] He stands slightly horrified at this insight, yet these implications are precisely what are later drawn out to full strength by Friedman, Stigler, and Becker.

## The Limits of Economic Science

Knight not only understands the limits of economic science as an abstraction but also understood that economic science could get very messy if it moved into the realm of ethics and social policy. For Knight, the solution to these problems lies not in economics but rather in ethics and public discourse as nonscientific discourses. As Emmett notes, after the 1930s, Knight began to turn his attention more to questions of social philosophy and ethics, particularly "the role of social scientific inquiry in the defense of free society."[161] George Stigler makes a similar point about human capacity to build a free society with free individuals.[162] As we have already noted, Knight assiduously sought to put limits on the scope of economics, knowing well that "economists' knowledge . . . has almost nothing to do with real human beings or their real-world problems."[163] And, over against the economics mainstream of the time, dominated by American Progressives, Keynesian interventionalists, institutionalists, and social gospellers, he was quite circumspect about the extent to which economics could actually help to solve societal problems. Knight thought government could really do little to help. Knight held that economic analyses could discover knowledge about human economic behavior, but its science was valid only in discovering what the economic laws are, not what they ought to be.

As Robert Nelson notes, Knight "doubted the possibility of the scientific management of society through the manipulation of self-interest in the market or otherwise."[164] The findings of economics—and particularly price theory—were of "limited relevance" to public policy.[165] While they could and should inform the democratic processes of public discourse, the latter was the proper forum for hammering out differences in ethical judgment regarding conflicting values. Here, again, Friedman diverges from Knight. Friedman conceives of the public square as a space of primarily—or perhaps, solely—of competition between isolated, individuated Robinson Crusoes. Knight, however, worked with a deeply communal sense of the human person. He understood that individual wants and "tastes and appreciations" are taught and shaped by one's culture.[166] Social discussion, thus, is not about bargaining from fixed individual preference positions to divide up the economic pie. Rather, the whole point of political discussion is to change minds; as a result of democratic deliberation, individual preferences should be constantly revised, leading to the necessary convergence ("likemindedness") of the values or ends the community should pursue.[167]

In this, as we shall see in Chapter 6, Knight is more aligned with Smith, than he is with Mill and Bentham, believing that economic and other social problems are, ultimately, not structural or political, but religious or moral problems.[168] The dissolution of society is not primarily a problem of the economic order, but a failure in pursuing the correct ends. Like Smith, Knight understood himself to be a moral philosopher, and most of his writings are in social philosophy rather than technical economics. As Robert Nelson notes, it was in his capacity as a moral philosopher "that the key figures in the

Chicago school of economics encountered him and in which he exerted his greatest influence on its future development."[169]

Yet while the real solutions lie in the realm of religion, philosophy, and ethics, in the end, Knight, by reducing ends to wants and preferences, has rendered these disciplines powerless. In claiming for economics the status as *the* science of human behavior, he negates the possibility that any other claimants—religion, philosophy, ethics—could have purchase on the truth. There is no rational, reasonable way to adjudicate between ends. If ends are not "data," if they are instead "values," then they are not amenable to scientific description and therefore not candidates for any sort of science or truth-claims. Ethics is relegated to emotivist preferences.[170] He opens the door for expressive individualism. In so doing, however, he lays the groundwork for Friedman's creation of normative economics about what society should do to begin to displace ethics. With Becker, ends become data, and the discipline of ethics disappears entirely, subsumed within "a 'glorified' economics."[171] What remains in both Becker and the neuroscientific narrative of morality are fragments and simulacra of prior moral traditions, deployed rhetorically to mask the transmogrification of ethics.

In his drive to be scientific, Knight followed his predecessor John Stuart Mill. As we shall show, he embraces the positive economic science, the is-ought distinction, and he understood human freedom, not as something secured by state-enforced competition, but rather as something within the will of humankind, a hardwired capacity to seek and achieve certain goods rooted ultimately in a sort of natural law. Thus, behind his abstraction of *Homo economicus* lies a more robust moral anthropology, a vision that is lost in the work of Milton Friedman. Yet, Emmett argues, "Surprisingly, one could argue that Knight also helped to set the tone for Chicago's move to an applied policy science."[172] No social problem could be viewed as out of bounds for economic investigation, because one could not say in advance what knowledge might be generated. Intelligent social action required, he argued, both education in price theory among the citizenry and the economics profession's commitment to keep their policy discussion open until a fair degree of common agreement within the profession was reached.[173]

## The *Imago Oeconomiae*

In many ways, the cultural allure of Freakonomics is a result of Becker's work to turn all human behavior into predictable events responsive to subtle forces exercised by a different kind of invisible hand. Becker, along with the infrastructure of the neoliberal cultural strategy and the political influence of the Chicago School, helped to move neoliberal thinking from an esoteric economic thought-community of whom many were suspicious into something that now informs the self-identity of most of the contemporary West. As more than one commentator has opined: we are all neoliberals now.[174] He did so by radically transforming what an older utilitarianism—and, indeed, his economic predecessors—had thought to be idiosyncratic tastes, pleasures, pains, values, and preferences into stable, equalized quantities. So stabilized, one could now give a scientific account of human behavior—one mathematically mapped by the laws of economics and grounded in evolutionary biology.

To do so required him to theorize rationality and freedom—and therefore the human actor—very differently. *Homo economicus* was no longer a laissez-faire figure. The human person remains, rhetorically, a rational actor, but rationality here is of a particular variety. Unlike classical economics, where government is challenged to free subjects from political control so that they can rationally deliberate and enact their own goods, human rationality here is reduced to a process of calculation, an instinctive drive to maximize utility. This biologically grounded law-like nature of behavior is what renders tastes stable over time and similar between people. One's taste for buying locally grown produce or serving the poor is governed by the same consumptive law of utility maximization as another's taste for heroin. Once one digs down to the deterministic laws of economics invisibly driving all behavior, actions are the result of choices, which are voluntary, but no longer really free. And those choices, if rational, will seek always to increase investment in the enterprise that is the now capitalized human person so as to endlessly enhance economic outcomes.

The resonances between this most recent phase of neoliberalization and the neurosciences should by now be clear. We will flag a few at this point and return to a more careful analysis in our conclusion. But we note, of course, that like their neuroscientific heirs, economists from Knight to Becker characterize morality no longer as goods but hold to a theory of tastes and preferences. Morality has undergone a thorough going economization, even where traditional virtue language is deployed, with "vice" or harmful behavior being defined as failure to meet certain economic standards and beneficial behavior as that which most fully adheres to the ideal of "prosociality," the market. There is hardly any difference between Sam Harris's understanding of volition over freedom and Becker's. And like Becker and Stigler, he believes that some external control—whether by governmental control or some other social control through medical screening—of behaviors is necessary for the good of the whole of a functional society. There is a shared focus on main features of SES or SEP in the search for proxies for vice—education, income, marriage, addiction, criminality; as well as direct engagement with those biological scientists seeking the formula for prosociality, be it named wisdom or happiness.

By the end of his career, Becker has come to hold that the "invisible hand" of economic science, the "hidden side of everything," is grounded in the biological aspects of human being. The neuroscientists of morality adopt this invisible hand, forwarding a vision of the market grounded in our genes that subsequently shapes our brains and therefore behaviors, with only a modicum of rational agency or control on those behaviors. As such, the task of economics is to inform policies and practices designed to invisibly shape and direct individual behavior; the neurosciences promise to provide an ideal modality for controlling *Homo capitalus*.

For different reasons, their forebears would take umbrage at this vision of the person. Yet behind their work lies Milton Friedman and Frank Knight. Where Becker and Stigler focused on microeconomics, Friedman believed the macro-level work of political policy not only could be used but also should be used to solve all kinds of social problems and to encourage behaviors that would improve human flourishing.

With the positive science of economics, we could know the facts, and once we knew the facts scientists might be able to discover where the problems were, and political and social apparatuses could be deployed in order to solve those scientifically discovered facts. Retaining a tentative hold on the fact/value distinction that he inherited from Knight, the state here loses its freedom, becoming completely governed by the logic and needs of economics. As was made visible in Chile, Friedman's economics enabled a macro biopolitics of state terror. From the economization of the state, it is a short step to the economization of the human person; equally, it is a short step from the loss of the freedom of the state to the loss of the freedom of persons. With Becker, neoliberalism and its methodological individualism redirects its focus to covert, micro-level interventions on embodied individuals. Thus, the arc of biopolitics that begins in the seventeenth century becomes complete.

Haidt and Zak would certainly counter that they explicitly seek to distance themselves from *Homo economicus*, particularly insofar as he stands alone, isolated, rational, and selfish. But such protestations would be disingenuous insofar as the anthropology informing their work is *Homo economicus*' heir. Foucault, speaking here of neoliberalism, could equally be speaking about the neuroscientists of morality insofar as they are:

> extending the economic model of supply and demand and of investment-costs-profit so as to make it a model of social relations and of existence itself, a form of relationship of the individual to himself, time, those around him, the group, and the family . . . [It also] functions in their analysis or program as a support to what they designate as the reconstruction of a set of what could be called "warm" moral and cultural values which are presented precisely as antithetical to the "cold" mechanism of competition. The enterprise schema involves acting so that the individual . . . is not alienated from his work environment, from the time of his life, from his household, his family, and from the natural environment . . . The return to the enterprise is therefore at once an economic policy or a policy of the economization of the entire field, of an extension of the economy to the, the entire social field, but at the same time a policy which presents itself or seeks to be a kind of Vitalpolitik with the function of compensating for what is cold, impassive, calculating, rational, and mechanical in the strictly economic game of competition.[175]

Here Foucault crystallizes the entire oeuvre of Haidt and Zak.

Although more inchoate in the work of the Chicago School, further analysis of neoliberalism would also begin to make sense of the rhetoric that appears throughout the neuroscience and popular literature, correlating poverty with vice. As enterprise-units, whose inscribed purpose is to increase their capital value, each individual is held responsible and accountable for his or her own actions, success, and well-being. As David Harvey notes: "This principle extends into the realms of welfare, education, health care, and even pensions . . . Individual success or failure are interpreted in terms of entrepreneurial virtues or personal failings (such as not investing significantly enough in one's own human capital through education) rather than being attributed to any systemic property (such as the class exclusions usually attributed to capitalism)."[176] This responsibilization, where virtues and vices begin to be defined economically where the whole moral weight rests on the individual, also traces its roots to the seventeenth century. Here the seed of *Homo economicus* was laid, emerging ultimately in the work of John Stuart Mill and his utility maximization principle. In fact, as we shall see, the term was meant to be critical of Mill, who in turn was seeking to correct the work of his godfather, Jeremy Bentham. It is to these two figures—along with their alliances with Thomas Malthus and David Ricardo—that we turn in the next chapter.

# 5

# Springs of Action and the Political Management of the Poor

We have arrived at the birth of *Homo economicus*, that supposedly free agent, who is—or ought to be—unencumbered by government and society and able to make rational decisions for his own good and in his own interest. It is this figure, we argue, that in the late twentieth century mutated into *Homo capitalus*, effectively becoming the anthropology animating the neuroscientific narrative of morality. Stable, static, dead—this docile entity depleted of ontological and moral content, fit for the purpose of modeling human behavior mathematically and scientifically, has minimal rationality and less freedom, being subtly directed by the dictates of biological and social pressures.[1]

But as our narrative of the twentieth century makes clear, *Homo economicus* is not a timeless figure; he has never been static. He has morphed and shifted, mutated and evolved over the past three centuries, constantly reconfigured to fit underlying permutations in political economy, in tandem with—and in service to—the emergence of economics as a science of society. Yet *Homo economicus* was born in a particular place and at a particular time—on an island in the north Atlantic in the late nineteenth century. His progenitors emerged in the mid-eighteenth century, a time when natural and moral philosophy were giving way to the human sciences, at a moment when both poverty (as a concept) and modern capitalism were emerging together, and when the relationships and power between economics, persons, and the state was being decisively reenvisaged. No matter how he morphs, these conditions of his genesis continue to shape fundamental features of his nature. Thus, in order to understand the anthropology animating the neuroscientific narrative of morality, it is crucially important to trace the threads back to their genesis.

Three features of the context within which *Homo economicus* was sculpted are key to understanding his contemporary character. The first is the assumption that economics and moral behavior go hand-in-hand. This assumption only began to emerge in the seventeenth century with the shifting social conditions and rise of the Poor Laws described in the Interlude. But very quickly, it became a given of Western, industrialized culture, framing debates on virtue and vice going forward. As late as 1875, for example, we find American abolitionist, entrepreneur, and early libertarian Lysander Spooner arguing in his treatise entitled *Vices Are Not Crimes* that economic realities play a role in an agent's ability to acquire and/or enact virtue. "[P]overty," he declaimed, "is the natural parent of nearly all the ignorance, vice, crime, and misery there are in the world."[2] For Spooner, poverty caused ignorance and indebtedness, it destroyed self-respect, and drove the poor to despair and drink. With echoes of Dickens, he held that poverty and its effects did not primarily *derive* from individual vice—as clearly his interlocutors held—but rather from social forces outside personal control. Change social circumstances and vice would fade away. Yet both Spooner and his interlocutors presumed a relationship between morality—primarily vice—and economics.

Although eliding the question of poverty, this presumed relationship between economics and ethics was, as we saw, an early target of Knight's work. Knight saw one of his main tasks as separating economics as the science of human behavior from ethics. That he perceived such a need signals a second key feature of this history: that by the turn of the twentieth century, ethics had been reconceptualized no longer as moral philosophy but rather as a kind of moral science inextricably tied to the emerging social science, economics. As *Homo economicus* was a fiction necessary for establishing economics as a science, as we will see in this chapter, he was equally central to reconfiguring ethics as a science.

Thus, the possibility of an endeavor like the *neuroscience* of morality stems from our second theme: the development of the social sciences. Knight unabashedly acknowledges his debt to John Stuart Mill, a key figure in the rise of the positive social sciences. While Mill was accused of imagining the human actor as *Homo economicus*—a name he never embraced—he also championed the science of *ethology* (the science of character), a zeal for which he inherited from his father, James Mill, and godfather, Jeremy Bentham. These figures—along with other theorists like David Ricardo and Thomas Malthus—birthed the social sciences out of a fusion of philosophical beliefs, economic commitments, and political machinations, instilling in these fields largely unexamined assumptions. If, as we have noted, the neurosciences are a fusion of neurobiology with the human sciences, particularly psychology and economics, understanding the rise of the social sciences is critically important for probing the assumptions that underlie this new field—and particularly its claims about morality. As we will show, much of what we have encountered in the neuroscientific narrative of morality—its conceptualization of poverty, its heavy dependence on SES and SEP as stand-ins for community, its reconfiguration of virtue and vice into the proxies anti*social* or pro*social* traits, as well as its core anthropology—all derive from the historical precursors shared by the social sciences.

Third, these architects of the social sciences did more than simply advance novel philosophical ideas. They sought to operationalize these ideas via the organs of the state, with an intriguing focus on social control of the bodies and lives of the poor. Thus, we find Mill warning against the reductive anthropology of political economy and attempting to temper Bentham's fervor for political and social reform. Yet his efforts were largely in vain insofar as political economy as a form of biopolitics—or, as we will call it, a biopolitical economy—had by then been firmly established. As Wendy Brown notes, Foucault charts how in the mid-eighteenth century, the market became the "new site of truth or veridiction," a place from which the organization of society, especially the poor, could find leverage points.[3] Out of the Poor Law Reform of 1834 emerges a new relationship between the state and individual freedom, "establishing interest-driven *homo oeconomicus* as the subject it governs."[4] The social sciences of economics, ethology, and psychology become key tools in the ongoing production of this new regime of truth.

In this chapter, we begin with *Homo economicus* and Mill's anthropology, calling to mind that Mill was also engaged in the systemization of a positivistic social science. We will show that Mill's drive to systematize the social sciences found its origin in Bentham's drive to articulate the natural laws of social ordering for the purpose of engineering society. With Bentham's "springs of action" we see the origins of the *Homo capitalus* already taking shape, but only among the impoverished. We will then explore the way the Poor Law Reform of 1834 was a triumph of Benthamite social engineering. To make this point, we will argue that two other social scientists—Ricardo and Malthus, channeling Joseph Townsend—were pivotal figures in the transformation of economics from the domain of moral philosophy into the domain of social science.

## Mill's Positivist Ethics, Positivist Social Science

John Stuart Mill (1806–73) has been called "the most influential English language philosopher of the nineteenth century."[5] Firmly ensconced within the tradition of British empiricism, Mill articulated key innovations in ethics, the social sciences, and political economy that indelibly shaped these fields as they moved into the twentieth century. Unlike the figures in our previous chapter, Mill was not an academic. Rather, at the age of seventeen, he embarked on a thirty-five-year career with the East India Company, a British joint-stock company that at one point in the nineteenth century accounted for half of the world's trade and oversaw a standing army of over 260,000 men in India.[6] His career culminated in his role as Chief Examiner of Correspondence, a position roughly equivalent to Undersecretary of State for the British Empire.[7] This position provided him the means to write theory and philosophy in the development of classical economics. Toward the end of his life, he served a term as a member of Parliament.

Mill's work stands in the tradition of the British empiricists, from Bacon through Locke and Hume, informed by the work of two key figures in his life—the psychology of his father, James Mill, and the political economy of his godfather, Jeremy Bentham.[8] James Mill (1773–1836) was a Scottish "political philosopher, historian, psychologist, educational theorist, economist, and legal, political and penal reformer," who was educated at the University of Edinburgh and deeply influenced by leading figures of the Scottish Enlightenment.[9] James was also an early collaborator with, and close friend of, Jeremy Bentham and David Ricardo. He labored as a prolific independent writer and journalist for the first half of his career until he secured a position at the East India Company in 1819, as a result of his three-volume *History of British India*.[10] His background, his connections, and the remarkably intense education to which he submitted his eldest son beginning at the age of three (when he began teaching him Greek), profoundly shaped the work of the younger Mill.

## The Possibility of a Moral Science

John Stuart Mill was an early voice in the social science of ethology—the study of human behavior from a biological perspective. It would not be until Darwin's 1872 *The Expression of the Emotions in Man and Animals* that ethology would begin to capture the imagination of the powerful. But Mill's positivism in the area of ethics paved the way for the transformation of moral philosophy into social science, much in the same way that natural philosophy had become natural science in the nineteenth century.[11]

Mill's account of both knowledge and morality is related to his anthropology, which was both informed by and yet different from his fellow social philosopher and interlocutor Auguste Comte. Both Comte and Mill were positivists, holding that every rationally justifiable statement finds its origins in empiricism and thus is scientifically verifiable. Both Comte and Mill sought naturalistic accounts of human behavior, but unlike Comte who grounded his approach in the community, Mill's account began in the psychology of the individual (particularly informed by his father's psychological work).[12] Mill's anthropology is different from Comte's because Comte's was a "Catholic positivism, making little of the individual."[13] Mill's positivism "is English and Protestant, full of the consciousness of the individual, and resolute in the attempt to know human nature on its subjective side."[14] Mill's individual is Locke's individual. On Mill's reading, the phenomenal self was grounded in the material of the brain. However, he held that psychological awareness was ontologically different than brain physiology. He still understood the human animal to be a part of the natural world; thus, the human animal was dependent on the laws of physiology, even while self was the product of its experiences.[15]

As a naturalist and an empiricist, Mill "consider[ed] every human activity as a cause of effects and an effect of causes, and so a part of 'nature' in that wide sense of the word in which it means simply the object of knowledge—the *'facies totius universi.'"*[16] The "face of the whole universe" refers to the surface phenomena to which we have access through our sense impressions. For Mill, echoing his Scottish Enlightenment forbearers, sense impressions are our only source for knowledge or ideas; there can be no *a priori* source for either. Sense impressions of nature and culture produce experiences that are somehow recorded on the physiological body—the physiological body existing prior to experiences. All knowledge begins in sense impressions. We, as humans, read the "face" of nature and culture and are literally stuck in the surface phenomena.

Consistent with his Scottish Enlightenment context, Mill holds that the mind is known to itself phenomenally through its feelings and consciousness.[17] Only in attending to the feelings and phenomenal experiences can one begin to create a science of the self—a psychology. As Charles Douglas notes, "[T]he feelings or consciousnesses which belong or have belonged to it [the self], and its possibilities of having more, are the only facts there are to be asserted of Self—the only positive attributes, except permanence, which we can ascribe to it."[18] Mill's empiricism shines through here. The human only has access to the phenomena, to the original sense impressions, and our sense impression of the memories of consciousness.

To Mill's credit, he avoids reductive science; the self is not exhausted by its mental states. Even while the human animal only has access to these feelings and consciousnesses, he does maintain that there is a subject that stands behind the sense experience of objects (the phenomenal experience, the face of the universe) and who stands further behind the act of observing. As such, the self remains somewhat of a mystery, ultimately enigmatic to itself in terms of its depth. This self, standing behind and reading the surface impressions whether of the inner or outer world, is the source of possibility for freedom in Mill's account, as we shall shortly see.

Nonetheless, science can elucidate this depth of self to some degree. This science of psychology (especially as developed by his father) made it possible to have a science of character (ethology). Thus, just as we can predict the behaviors of planetary movement, but not without some variation in the actual observations or perturbations (as Mill calls them), we can also know the universal laws of character formation without knowing all the particular details of the experiences of a particular person that have formed his particular character.[19] With the combination of the general laws and the particularities of experience, one can know the whole of human action and feeling, and attempt to construct a science of human nature.[20] In addition, as he notes, all of the causes within the internal life of the person—"the facts of each particular case"—contribute to various actions and activities of the person. The psyche is forged not only by its biological predispositions and desires but also in congruence with social engagement and the cultivation of desire.[21]

The human animal, as part of nature, is the animal whose behavior is produced by its psychological constitution (its natural features) and the social environment within which that constitution develops. Human experience gives the content in the form of feelings and consciousnesses, which are particular to each psychological individual. If we know each contributor cause, we can predict behavior. Thus, a positive science of the human is possible. If one knows the motives and the character of the individual's mind as well as the inducements, one can infer unerringly what the person's actions will be as readily as a physical event.[22] This deterministic nature of human activity means that, like the deterministic behavior of celestial bodies, human activity can also be studied scientifically. This idea of philosophical necessity and of controlling inducements animated much of Mill's work in articulating laws for parliament—a tendency he shared with Bentham, as we shall shortly see. For, if we know the kinds of inducements that would animate desired behaviors, society could indeed plan on the behaviors of its people, if not frankly control them.

In spite of his commitment to discovering the scientific structure of morality, this kind of determinism—grounded in the biological constitution of the human animal and the material social structures of society—weighed heavily on Mill, for he was also a strong proponent of freedom. John Milbank suggests that Mill, as a positivist, does not give a robust account of freedom and that it was only the German theorists that appealed to the neo-Kantian subject as a means to preserve freedom—a subject that sits *a priori* above the biological and social structures, standing apart from the political structures and outside history.[23] To a certain extent, Milbank is correct. However, Mill was aware of this problem, and he notes in his *Autobiography* that his despair over the inability to escape his deterministic tendencies persisted until he "gradually saw light through it."[24]

Mill resolves the tension between his commitment to naturalistic determinism—both biological and social determinism—and to freedom, by an appeal to the will and an inner unity to human action. The "will is the child of desire,"[25] biological desire. Yet it is also capable of choosing among desires. In other words, the will is part of the causal mechanism of behavior, but because it chooses among several desires, it is not entirely determined. A person can learn to desire beyond the merely biological, or to curb one desire in order to promote other (higher) desires. In learning to choose higher desires, a person's desire can mold his volition.[26] One could, under the influence of the will, have chosen one action over another, when the other action would have been preferable. Mill preserves personal responsibility as a top-down control mechanism. Where the person is determined from the bottom up by all the natural causes and laterally by experiences that constitute the self, the will can come to exert top-down pressure to adjudicate between a person's various desires. Thus, she can freely control her actions.

Moreover, one's desires can be educated and self-fashioned; cultivated desires are equivalent to character, a position that, as we saw, was taken up by Frank Knight. One can have a habit of willing, which Mill calls purpose.[27] The volitional self can be cultivated, such that she comes to desire certain pleasures over others, like the pleasure of reading over the pleasures of playing parlor games. The cumulative result—the effect—of past volitions he names character. Character then serves as both the source and product of voluntary conduct.[28] Character is formed for a self and this formation:

> is not inconsistent with its being, in part, formed *by* him as one of the intermediate agents. His character is formed by his circumstances (including among these his particular organization); but his own desire to mould it in a particular way, is one of those circumstances, and by no means one of the least influential.[29]

Mill gives a kind of power to the individual's will to self-form. "We are exactly as capable of making our own character, *if we will*, as others are of making it for us."[30] Pressures are not merely bottom up (biological pressures), nor are they merely horizontal pressures (social pressures). Self-cultivation—top-down causation—is possible. Such causes are in fact willed and formed by oneself. We can have a science of human nature, even while the will—if we have been practiced at willing—may exert a greater pressure than that by which nature or society has shaped the person to act. But it will be an imprecise science because the willful self participates in the chosen action.

The science of psychology is to discover the laws of mind; the science of ethology is to discover laws governing the formation of character. "Ethology is the science which corresponds to the art of education in the widest sense of the term, including the formation of national or collective character as well as individual."[31] Ethology is "the exact science of human nature" because it hopes to participate in the formation of willful selves capable of choosing higher-order desires.[32] On the nature of this science, Mill sets out to correct Bacon and his merely inductive method, which (as we will see in Chapter 6) had rejected the deductive method as medieval flights of fancy. For Mill, deductive science is possible and indeed useful, if aided by the inductive method. Via Mill's empiricism, ethology is just such an inductive science.[33] With this science, we can name the general components of the science of ethology—character formation, nature, nurture, and a cultivated sense of what one wills, or prefers, among all the desires one has. With this knowledge, we can educate the citizen.

## From Ethology to a Positive Science of Society

Having discovered this science of ethology, Mill hoped to create the "science of man [sic] in society—of the actions of collective masses of mankind, and the various phenomena which constitute social life."[34] This positive science of society could discover and delineate the natural causes of the human animal including the ways in which the human person came to exert top-down choice on the system. In other words, equipped with the universal laws of the formation of character, society could then set up structural inducements such that the higher desires could be cultivated. These inducements were thought to be the laws of social development, which could themselves be derived scientifically. In other words, for Mill, the logic of the moral sciences made it possible to have a science of society, all while preserving free will.

The legislator is the architect, following the laws of human nature in order to discern the rules for building the ethical society.[35] "Now, the reasons of a maxim of policy, or of any other rule of art, can be no other than the theorems of the corresponding science."[36] And ethics, in this schema, is the art that uses the science of ethology to enact policies conducive to happiness. While Mill's ethics was theoretically inclined, it was aimed at the practical, which is the happiness of humankind, and indeed, "of all sentient beings," which is the ultimate teleological principle.[37] However, the content of the end, the precise telos toward which the science is deployed, is best known by the art.[38] The legislator, like the physician who takes health or absence of disease as a given end, takes the overall happiness of the populace as his end.

Thus, we can arrive at the way that utilitarianism became palatable to Victorian Britain. Rather than the crass mechanical model developed by Bentham, Mill articulates a way to imagine human freedom in the face of governmental policy that imagines men to be rogues in need of being ground into moral beings.[39] Mill also preserves genteel British mores by granting that the pleasures associated with some cultural practices are better and ought to be encouraged over the crasser, bodily pleasures of the masses of the poor. As noted by Alasdair MacIntyre, Mill's moral theory was teleological, not consequentialist, because it still had a robust relationship to the good. Mill's science of ethics still had some content with higher and lower goods and desires from which the will could choose. But this science of ethics would later collapse into what MacIntyre would call emotivism, or expressivism.[40] While Mill never brings the ends under critical scrutiny, only the means to achieve the given ends, there is still some freedom to adjudicate between the various desires and to move toward the higher desires; but just because he does not critically scrutinize the ends does not mean that Mill is not surreptitiously introducing thicker goods.[41] As he notes:

> For the remainder of the practice of life some general principle, or standard, must still be sought; and if that principle be rightly chosen, it will be found, I apprehend,

to serve quite as well for the ultimate principle of Morality, as for that of Prudence, Policy, or Taste.[42]

Nonetheless, despite his desire to want to understand ethics in a thicker sort of way, we see that he is still captive to the Humean position shared by everyone from Knight to Becker to Haidt that reduces moral ends to matters of mere taste.

Thus, we do not have an argument for teleology, but rather an assertion of a given, general end of happiness. In the next generation of thinkers, including for Frank Knight, ends or tastes are further deflated from the thicker Victorian ethic of individual freedom and cultivated (that is to say, "proper") desires. One merely has to perform the moral calculus to discern the approach one should take. Still, Mill understood that there is a gap between a single figure applying the art of living, deploying his freedom in the midst of biological and social realities, and the scientist that can only deal in generalities, and the political engineer that would build the right kind of society with the right kind of inducements. And insofar as one is dealing in generalities, as science must, one is limited to general definitions of the human actor so that one's models for behavior are applicable. And generalities require necessary fictions.

## The Necessary "Fiction" of Economic Man

The term "economic man" (*Homo economicus*) was first coined by critics of Mill's anthropology, which he posited in his account of political economy.[43] For Mill, political economy was the social apparatus that draws on the biological and social sciences to induce human beings to the proper desires that can meet the necessities of the greatest number of people. Following Hume, he embraces the is/ought distinction;[44] and, as we shall shortly see, he follows Bentham in imagining the deployment of the art of political economy.[45] However, he warns that the definition of a science emerges only after enough facts have been generated, and the definition arises at the end, not at the beginning of an investigation.[46] Even in 1859, with the publication of *On the Definition of Political Economy*, he warns against an expansive and vulgar definition of political economy, one that would encompass all aspects of human living. Yet, ironically, he does just that. For Mill, political economy as a science is an abstract science, and its method is *a priori*.[47] Just as geometry posits an arbitrary definition of a line, political economy posits an "arbitrary definition of man [sic]." The human is "a being who inevitably does that by which he may obtain the greatest amount of necessaries, conveniences, and luxuries, with the smallest quantity of labour and physical self-denial with which they can be obtained."[48]

Still, Mill did not use the term "economic man" or "*Homo economicus*." Rather, the term was deployed against Mill in mockery of this necessarily fictious and "arbitrary definition of man."[49] While he offers neither a descriptive nor normative account of this vision of the human person, it begins to gather steam in the work of economists throughout the remainder of the nineteenth century. It appears that it is only shortly after Mill's death (perhaps 1888 or 1906) that the Latinate version of the term "economic man" (*Homo economicus*) emerges to capture this arbitrary—but eventually normative—anthropology.

However, like Knight, Mill himself did not imagine "economic man" to capture a filled-out, complete, or holistic anthropology. Unlike Becker, Mill recognized that political economy does not cover the fullness of human nature formed in society, but only focused on human desires to possess wealth and the means to achieve it.[50] Thus, for Mill, to understand the human person solely as "economic man" would be too reductive and restrictive, making an "entire abstraction of every other human passion or motive." It is, thus, a fiction that makes it possible "to obtain the power of either predicting or controlling the effect [of certain causes]."[51] In order for the science of society to achieve the level of predictability, this fictive being was required as a model to permit explanation. Ironically, as Wendy Brown notes, Mill made it clear that no political economist has ever been so absurd "as to suppose that mankind are really thus constituted, but . . . this is the mode in which science must necessarily proceed."[52] Mill would be surprised to find the unintended consequences of this fiction, where the abstraction of science has come to stand in for the human actor, as it does for Becker.

What is more, his detractors notwithstanding, Mill's human person transcends individual wealth-seeking behavior. In *On Liberty*, Mill wrestles with the question of where to draw the line between state and individual sovereignty. And, as Brown notes, Mill comes down on the side of the individual, "formulat[ing] us as little sovereigns choosing our means and ends."[53] In other words, *contra* Becker, "the subject is not [yet] circulating or fungible human capital instrumentalized by itself, society, economy, or the state."[54] Persons are full-fledged human actors capable of maximizing utility or not. They are not puppets subsumed into the machinery of society. The necessary fiction, which is necessary for political-economic models, must not be conflated with the full-fledged, willful agent making decisions about the art of living.

But as we will see in his forebears, for Mill this only seems to be true for those persons with financial means. For as for Bentham and Hume before him (as we shall shortly see), the poor for Mill were not truly free. He was kinder to the both the industrious poor and the idle poor than they were—he did not accept Malthus's harshness or Bentham's draconian workhouses. But he waffled with regard to state intervention into their sexuality.[55] He endorsed Malthus's principle of population and hoped that the poor could be enticed to moral restraint when it came to sexual activity. His early work promoted separating the sexes in the poor houses so as to prevent sexual activity by and even endorsed state involvement in birth control.[56] While he later tempered his enthusiasm for birth control, he still believed that irresponsible procreation on the part of the poor was an offense against "the higher and middle classes" who "sacrificed" to support them as well as being a crime against said offspring. Thus, state aid in the form of employment or food could legitimately be tied to social, moral, and, failing those, legal restraints against their procreation.[57] Unlike *Homo economicus*, then, the poor are not free.

Thus for Mill, identifying the human agent as a sovereign draws a political boundary; although generally guided by the principle of utility, it is the subject, who participates in cultivating his own desires, and not the state that ultimately weighs costs and benefits in light of a range of possible ends, within his own sphere of action.[58] Yet while Mill held to a thicker and fuller anthropology and did not envisage the moral or economic agent as stick-figure puppet, he nonetheless created the conditions of possibility for what it would become in the twentieth century by theorizing "man" in his political economy. As we shall see, Mill did not entirely accept Bentham's vision of the human person. Here, however, we see something absent from Knight: different relationships to freedom—and therefore different moral frameworks—for the poor and those of means. This, he inherited from his godfather. Mill tried to save Bentham's project from simply being one of crass engineering. Yet in the end, he crystalized the anthropology that lay behind Bentham, who had imagined society as an engineering project, laying the groundwork for the biopolitics of morality.

## Jeremy Bentham, Social Engineer

The inspiration for Mill's science of ethology is, of course, Jeremy Bentham (1748–1832). Bentham was a philosopher and legal theorist who devoted his formidable skills and energy to proposing and forwarding reforms across the sociopolitical spectrum including reform of: parliament, the Poor Laws, policing, juridical administration, political economy, financial questions, and the penal system.[59] His impassioned commitment to political and religious reform gained him recognition as "the foremost philosophical voice of political radicalism" of his era.[60] Yet his work is marked by deep contradictions, captured most iconically in his famous proposal for the architectural structure of the Panopticon, which we will discuss further herein. Even more, economic theorist Dierdre McCloskey, among many others, ranks Bentham as foundational to contemporary understandings of ethics. She opines: "Since 1790, most ethical theory as practiced in departments of philosophy has derived instead from two other books published about the same time, one by Immanuel Kant (1785) and the other by Jeremy Bentham (1789)."[61]

Mill inherits from Bentham the concept of utility that plays such a key role in his creation of an ethical science. However, the concept was in vogue even prior to Bentham, and the history of its use and meaning is not entirely clear. Bentham himself thought he found the principle in the Italian criminologist and jurist Cesare Bonesana-Becarria (1738–1794) and in the British chemist and natural philosopher Joseph Priestly (1730–1804). Leslie Stephen (1832–1904) notes that Pierre-Paul Le Mercier de la Rivière de Saint-Médard (1719–1801) articulates a principle of utility in 1767 and Francis Hutcheson (1694–1746) articulates a version of it in 1725. Hutcheson's version is "that action is best which secures the greatest happiness of the greatest number."[62] Hutcheson, whose influence on David Hume (1711–1776) is profound, inspired Hume's writing on utility. In fact, Hutcheson's positive view of human nature over against that of Thomas Hobbes (1588–1679) would shape both David Hume and Adam Smith (1723–1790), and therefore shaped their way of thinking about the utility of social relations.

Bentham, however, took Hume's more qualitative and vague notion of utility and gave it mathematical heft.[63] He thought he really could enumerate all things, creating laws of economics that would be akin to the laws of physics. Where Hume had a vague understanding of utility, Bentham had a formula. The difference between the two was the same as a vague notion of gravity in relation to the laws of gravitation. "Bentham hoped for no less an achievement than to become the Newton of the moral world."[64] It was Bentham, then, who set out to do what Hutcheson and Hume had failed to do: "to introduce a mathematical calculation on subjects of morality."[65] Bentham's positivism enabled him to posit a mathematical quantity as a representative marker for the vague realities that gave utility/pleasure to the human animal. Bentham therefore rearticulates a "fundamental axiom" of utility: that "the greatest happiness of the greatest number is the *measure* of right and wrong."[66]

In conjunction with his work on utility, Bentham contributes three additional components to our narrative. First, as he mathematizes utility, he likewise begins to quantify or render measurable the fundamental empirical realities of pleasure and pain, thus further laying the groundwork for Mill's project in political economy. Second, just as Newton had introduced both a science of motion and whole set of uses to which that science of motion could be put, Bentham wanted to analogously articulate the scientific principles of a social science. Third, he then hoped to create the rules of legislation and morals that would guide the running of society. In other words, Bentham is more like an engineer, and the utilitarian calculus would give the precision he needed to get the social mechanics to work, laying the foundation for biopolitics. Bentham accepted Hume's idea that only the wealthy had true freedom, where Mill asserted what we will see to be Adam Smith's more nuanced notion of freedom to try to save Bentham from crassly engineering people and society.

## From Metaphysics to Moral Physics

Like Mill, Bentham sought to create a positive science of morality. As Leslie Stephen notes, he thought that all other philosophical systems of morals failed because they were illusory, and they were illusory because they had no external standard to which they could appeal.[67] Science for Bentham rests on facts, which means "[i]t must apply to real things, and to things which have definite relations to a common measure."[68] And the most indisputably real things were for him those realities perceived through the senses. Bentham denied that one could know what was going on in the world beyond our sense impressions, firmly rooting him in the Humean skeptical empiricist tradition, contrary to Jonathan Haidt's misunderstanding noted earlier. For the science of morality, the grounded senses are the senses of pains and pleasures. Here, Bentham argued, was the measure of all of humankind's activities, happiness. Pain and pleasure are the senses that ground a science of morality just as sight and sound are the ground for the natural sciences. All that is left is the quantification of the moral senses.[69] For Bentham, it was mathematics as a system that permitted one to make comparisons among and between sense impressions, and, as noted by Mary Poovey, numbers had the odd quality of being attached particulars and at the same time of being universal.[70]

Pleasure and pain were not only real, for Bentham—more real and readily accessible to awareness than the things that stimulate pleasure or pain; they had the added benefit of shaping conduct.[71] Bentham referred to them as "springs of action." The "springs of action" were inducements to move in a certain direction. He divided these inducements into two categories: the pathological springs of action gave "an account of all the pains and pleasures which are the primary data"; it is not clear why this was called pathological, except that it seems to refer to the actual physical pleasure or pain experienced.[72] The second category, the dynamical springs of action, gave "an account of the various modes of conduct determined by expectations of pain and pleasure," the ability to foresee what will come into being.[73] Just as science had begun classifying all natural beings, Bentham believed he could use these springs as the basis for developing a system of classification of all human actions. As Stephen notes: "To codify is to classify, and Bentham might be defined as a codifying animal."[74]

With the aid of James Mill, in 1817, Bentham published the *Table of the Springs of Action*. The *Table* was a list of all the simple pains and pleasures and the actions correlated therewith. The *Table*, however, does appear rather arbitrary. In fact, John Stuart Mill was critical of the table because it did not refer to any specific psychologist or theory of psychology. In fact, Stephen notes that the table of the springs of action "is simply constructed to meet the requirements of [Bentham's] legislative theories."[75] Even a glance at the *Table* leaves one wondering how Bentham ended up placing something as a pleasure or pain, or how one distinguishes between pleasures, or between pains. The *Table* does not seem obvious or to follow any sort of rules. "Things present themselves to Bentham's mind as already prepared to fit into the pigeon-holes. This is a characteristic point, and it appears in what we must call his metaphysical system."[76] However, the creation of the table reveals something about how Bentham thought, namely, that he saw the human animal as something real that could be motivated to spring into action via fictitious entities like justice and obligation mediated through an intentional legislative and social agenda.

As a nominalist, Bentham held that words and numbers merely represent physical entities; things such as essences, natures, or the usual topics of metaphysics are not in fact real. That did not mean for him that all language names physical things. He speaks of "fictitious" entities—such as space, time, quantity, quality—which themselves have no physical substance. However, they are not non-entities. They cannot be known except in relation to concrete material things, but they are not non-entities.[77] Analogously, moral and political entities are fictitious entities. One such fictitious entity is obligation, or justice, following Hume. Obligation is not a thing, per se, yet, it has a kind of substance to it. Obligation or justice is derived from the principle of utility, which finds its grounding in the physical realities of pleasure and pain. Thus, Bentham redefines the traditional moral concept of obligation, concluding that an obligation is nothing more than a way of saying that one will suffer pain if one does not keep an obligation. Justice is, similarly, an important moral fiction; to identify an action as just is to simply say that it maximizes pleasure and minimizes pain, which is to say that it is useful.

Thus, just as space, time, quantity, and quality have no substance except for the fact that they are relations of physical things, so virtue, vice, justice, duty, and obligation are all fictitious entities that are mere words if they are disassociated from pleasure and pain. The existence of virtue, vice, justice, duty, and obligation is a matter of universal and constant experience. But other various names referring to these: emotion, inclination, vice, virtue, etc., are only "psychological entities." Take away pleasures and pains, not only happiness but justice and duty and obligation and virtue—all of which have been so elaborately held up to view as independent of them—are so many empty sounds.[78]

The metaphysical reality of pleasure and pain serves as the concrete material substance upon which politics and morals become effective in the world. These fictitious entities—virtue, morality, obligation, justice—have relation to the only substantive things we have, the empirical experience of pleasure and pain. Here Bentham joins Hume in claiming that virtues are artificial.[79]

Thus, for Bentham, the science of morals is the measure of right and wrong, which almost immediately coincides with goodness and badness at the moment of pleasure and pain. The substantive goodness of pleasure and badness of pain is the closest Bentham comes to any reality of goodness. On this point, Bentham embraced the anti-metaphysical stance that had become explicit in Kant's *Critique of Pure Reason*.[80] Both Bentham and Kant inherited this anti-metaphysical stance from Hume. Bentham despised what had been traditionally called metaphysics, which he took to be an illusory science of things "transcending what is physical and belonging to Nature."[81] For Bentham, metaphysics is a "sprig," a small offshoot of logic.[82] What was needed instead was a system that used a mathematical standard to determine right and wrong, in relation to pleasure and pain. He believed that his approach avoided the failures of other systems, particularly the confusions of Cartesians and Kantians.[83] Pleasure and pain, as empirical experiences, become the ground for a standard of measurement for morality. A science of morality is not possible without measurement.

Here we see the roots of what MacIntyre has called emotivism or expressivism. Bentham needs no further argument about the nature of the good than that it maximizes pleasure over pain, because it is clear to all what pleasure and pain are.[84] The logic of his reflection on the metaphysical foundation of morals "appeared to Bentham so obvious as to need no demonstration, only an exposition of the emptiness of any verbal contradiction."[85] One seemingly has a standard that can be applied by one and all—a ground to build the science of morality. The act of distinguishing between pleasures and pains so as to differentiate them seems to be simply an act of naming preferences (or tastes), even if Bentham believes pleasure itself to be a substantive good. It seems difficult to adjudicate amongst the pleasures stimulated by "fictitious entities" such as virtue, vice, justice, and obligation. Yet, his position is not mere preference because it has some relation to that which Bentham thinks is substantively good, namely pleasure.

Our point here is that in the empirical experience of pain and pleasure one can begin to elaborate some experiences and actions as better than others, with no clear rational way to distinguish among them either from some "external" or "objective" standard, or through some intersubjective standard, because pleasure and pain are in the eye of the beholder, so to speak. Still, because we know the moral metaphysics is grounded in the sense experience of pleasure and pain, we can move from the *is* of sense experience to the *ought* of moral architecture, from science to artifice.

## From Moral Physics to Social Engineering

Bentham's views about the nature and ground of moral reality—namely, pleasure and pain—enable his constructive project to get off the ground. Rooted in pleasure and pain, and thus securing the basis for mathematical comparison, one can construct a science of morals ordered to the greatest measure of good for the greatest number of people. This *telos* provides the goal for the social engineer. Once we know how the person works—what is the case—we can structure the social world with inducements that make the greatest pleasure for the greatest number of people.

Here Bentham's social engineering becomes clear. He was a Whig and a radical reformer for his own day. Unlike his theological utilitarian predecessors and contemporaries, for example, Hutcheson and Malthus, respectively, he sought social reform along the lines of a secular and scientific method made possible by numbers.[86] His moral project was to build the great society, to relieve the social unease created by rogues and idlers, economically nonproductive men, especially the poor, and he sought to do this through a science of legislative action. He believed that one had simply to get the right sort of measures in place so as to create a world that maximized the sense impressions of pleasure among the populous and that minimized the sense impressions of pain. Correlatively, sanctions should be used by the legislature to increase pain or decrease pleasure, as a means to motivate actors to behave accordingly to the maximize happiness for the greatest numbers of people. Public authorities must induce motives with the "springs of action" in order to get the right kind of action output in order to get the right kind of society. All of Bentham's scientific work aims at knowing which laws to enact in hopes of enacting a society as it ought to be, measured and meted according to the realities of pleasure and pain.

So, while in theory utilitarianism seems to be teleological, about the (greatest) good, Bentham's vision is primarily a philosophy of right by virtue of the calculus that dictates what *should* be done: "the greatest happiness of the greatest number is the measure of right and wrong."[87] His is a philosophy of right and not a philosophy of good, as the good is pre-given in pleasure. The right legislation or social action is the one aimed at pleasure and happiness for the greatest number. While he hoped his system could articulate what *ought* to be on the firm foundation of what *is* the case in the real world, it was oriented to the way the world could and should be made to be. Stephen, quoting from Bentham's *Works*, notes that "'All the statesmen,' so thought the philosopher [Bentham], 'were wanting the great elements of statesmanship': they were always talking about 'what was' and seldom or never about 'what ought to be.'"[88] Knowing the mechanism of action, and knowing what ought to be—the greatest pleasure for the greatest number of people—one could engineer society.

Bentham sought reform not solely through legislation and social policy. In fact, he is best known for his efforts to inculcate reform through actual material culture—specifically, in the deployment of the Panopticon. The Panopticon was an architectural innovation designed to employ the springs of action to induce men and women to proper behaviors. Initially deployed for the creation of workhouses and prisons, this social structure was eventually adopted in modified forms in industry, education, and more.[89] Bentham's advocacy of the Panopticon is crucial for our story.

Bentham's brother Samuel was an engineer and architect, and had spent time in White Russia with Price Potemkin. In 1786, Jeremy visited his brother at the estate of the prince (writing an essay while there, *In Defense of Usury*), where he was introduced to one of Samuel's architectural inventions, the Panopticon.[90] Simon Werrett argues that Samuel drew inspiration for the Panopticon from Russian absolutist culture, especially in relation to work he was doing for Potemkin as he attempted to impress the Empress Catherine the Great.

The Panopticon was to be built on Potemkin's estate in Krichev in 1784, where Bentham drew inspiration form the spatial structure of the Russian estate, with "the family house, the noble at the centre, his peasant workforce surrounding him."[91] The Panopticon put into one building—the Inspection House—the model Russian estate. In conversations in 1786, the Benthams began to imagine how this Russian prototype could solve the problems of unskilled serf labor and the undisciplined English managers that had been brought to White Russia in order to modernize Russian manufacturing. For Samuel, the Panopticon was about increasing economic productivity for nascent Russian manufacturing.

It was around this time that Jeremy began writing letters to friends and imagining a myriad of possibilities for the Panopticon design. Ever the social engineer, he began to see uses for the Panopticon design everywhere. In his 1791 letter, we find Bentham broadening its application in England, imagining its use for "grinding rogues honest, and idle men industrious."[92] Where for Samuel, the Panopticon was envisaged as a means to control workers, Jeremy translated it into the architecture of prisons for the control of criminals. From there, he designed a factory staffed by convicts; it was a short step from there to "using paupers on a large scale to run machinery devised by his even more inventive brother, Samuel, for working of metal and wood" and for its use in Industry Houses.[93]

For example, in his 1797 *Pauper Management*, Bentham proposed establishing a for-profit, joint-stock company that would erect 250 Industry Houses, each five stories in twelve sectors, which in total would employ up to 500,000 inmates.[94] Bentham believed his innovation to be more humane and economical than most of the workhouses that had resulted from the 1601 Poor Laws. Yet this new design treated the poor as criminals in much the same way as they had been treated in the sixteenth century before the reform, limiting their food, freedom, and moral agency.[95] He agreed with those like David Ricardo and Thomas Malthus, as we shall see, that hunger was the best "spring" for scientifically and economically managing the poor. As Polanyi notes, Bentham held that

> "In the highest stage of social prosperity . . . the great mass of citizens will most probably possess few other resources than their daily labor, and consequently will always be near to indigence." . . . [nonetheless] from the utilitarian point of view the task of the government was to increase want in order to make the physical sanction of hunger effective.[96]

Where poverty was not sufficient to spring the idle pauper into action, hunger was a much better taskmaster. After all, hunger aligns with one of the "two sovereign masters" under which nature "has placed mankind":[97] pain.

In addition to his proposal for Industry Houses, Bentham was very involved with other proto-social scientists (Ricardo and Malthus) in working toward the reform of the Poor Laws. As noted in our Interlude, the poor very much occupied the minds of many reformers of the day. Bentham, Ricardo, and Malthus all believed that no prior legislative treatment of paupers and vagabonds was informed by science, and thus all the Poor Laws prior to their proposed reforms were doomed to failure. While the Panopticon was thought to be a humane reform of prisons and care for the poor, it became for Bentham a total vision for liberal government.[98] As a total vision, it became part of his vision for advocacy of Poor Laws Reform. As Foucault notes, "Panopticism is not a regional mechanics limited to certain institutions; for Bentham, panopticism really is a general political formula that characterizes a type of government."[99]

In the last thirty years of his life, Bentham spent a lot of time, not merely on the principles of legislation and morals, but on political organization.[100] Not only would governmentality be the formal mechanism of legislation, but it would also be deployed through the organization of persons, particularly persons who were rogues and were idle. As Foucault points out, the Panopticon was partly about inducing those controlled to internalize the disciplinary power of those who would control through observation. With the assistance of Ricardo and Malthus, from 1795 until their deaths, Poor Law Reform would occupy all three social thinkers. It is to the central role of the Poor Law Reform that we now turn. After all, it is here that governance through political economy focused on a morality defined by labor, work, population, and sex emerges.

## Ricardo, Malthus, and the Engineering of the Poor Law Reform

Jeremy Bentham died before parliament passed the Poor Law Reform Act of 1834. However, his influence on that reform was deep. The reform was written according to Bentham's version of the theories of utility and his understanding of social science, aimed at social engineering. Bentham spent much of his energy on thinking about the Poor Laws since the attempted reform of William Pitt in 1796. However, before the reform of the Poor Laws could be enacted, two other theories needed to be added to Bentham's "springs of action." The two theories taken together—one promulgated by David Ricardo and the other promulgated by Thomas Malthus—took aim at the vices of sloth and lust found in the poor. The Poor Law Reform of 1834 saw the vices of sloth and lust as essential leverage points for Bentham's "springs of action." While Bentham, Malthus, and Ricardo would all die before the Reform was passed, they nonetheless engineered it.

The first theoretical development was David Ricardo's "iron law of wages."[101] Just as Bentham thought he had discovered a fundamental law of human behavior, working toward a pleasant life, and just as Mill thought he had discovered the laws of ethology, Ricardo thought he had discovered a law of economics, namely, that wages tend to gravitate toward a minimum wage necessary to sustain life. The second theoretical development came from Thomas Malthus. He proposed what he framed as a fundamental law of population growth—the idea that the population grows exponentially, while food sources grow arithmetically. This idea, we will show, was rooted in Joseph Townsend's fanciful but world-changing parable of the goats and the dogs.

It should be noted that in the fourteenth century, Dante enumerated the seven deadly sins, ordering them beginning with the worst: pride, envy, wrath, sloth, greed, gluttony, and lust. It is thus that we find Satan—Dante's exemplar of pride against the divine—frozen alone in the bottom most circle of *the Inferno*. By the late Elizabethan period, Herbert Spenser had changed the ordering to Pride, Wrath, Envy, Avarice (greed), Lechery (lust), Gluttony, Idleness (sloth). In the reforms of both Ricardo and Malthus, we see attempts to first theorize two of the seven deadly sins—lust and sloth—and to numericize them. Thus, where Bentham had hoped to find compelling reason to control the reproductive habits of the poor and to control their industry (to reform their lust and idleness), Ricardo and Malthus proposed "scientifically" compelling ways to bring these two vices under control with the Poor Law Reform of 1834. If something was not done to halt the reproductive habits of the poor or to increase their industrial productivity, or both, then the poor themselves would suffer under their own behavior.[102] We shall begin by engaging with Ricardo's modest development; it was Malthus's theoretical insight that was foundational and would capture the imagination of British society, even while they hated it.

## David Ricardo and the Iron Law of Wages

David Ricardo (1772–1823) was a highly successful stockbroker and London financier who retired a wealthy man at the age of forty-one and, under the urging of his good friend James Mill, turned his attention to writing about economics. Authoring the groundbreaking *Essay on the Effects of a Low Price of Corn on the Profits of Stock* (1815) and subsequently the formidable tome *Principles of Political Economy and Taxation* (1817) under James Mill's tutelage, Ricardo is regarded as a "brilliant British economist [who] was one of the most important figures in the development of [Classical] economic theory."[103] Friends with the elder Mill, Bentham, and Malthus, Ricardo was ranked in a recent survey of economists, as the second most important pre-twentieth-century theorist.[104] For our purposes, we will focus on Ricardo's theory of the prices of labor as it helps to make sense of Bentham's influence on the Poor Law Reform.

Ricardo proposes that the price of labor can be divided into two aspects: the natural price and the market price. The natural price of labor is the price that would allow workers "to subsist and to perpetuate their race, without either increase or diminution."[105] It was the minimum wages required by laborers to purchase food for subsistence.[106] Over time, the natural price of labor tends to rise, because food "has a tendency to become dearer, from the greater difficulty of producing it."[107] In other words, as the cost of living rises, those who work seek and need higher wages. Thus, at heart, the natural price of labor is determined by the law of supply and demand (for food), though this aspect of it is ignored by Ricardo and others. Rather, what bedevils them is not the rising cost of food, but the slothful—the "undeserving" poor—who, because they "refuse" to work, have greater problems producing food. As we will more fully show later, when there are large numbers of the poor, the problem will only be made worse.

The market price of labor—the cost to employers—is likewise subject to the law of supply and demand. It tends to decrease when laborers are plentiful. "[L]abour," Ricardo notes, "is dear when it is scarce, and cheap when it is plentiful."[108] As market prices of labor (or the wages offered) increase, more workers begin to gravitate to those jobs, increasing the supply of workers in that locale and thus driving down wages.[109] Thus, market prices tend to decrease relative to the natural price. Ricardo asserts that the market price tends to conform to the natural price, namely, the price of food,[110] but insofar as there is no necessary connection in his theory, the market price can drop below the natural price. When this occurs, the lives of workers become "most wretched."[111] The number of workers decreases (due to mortality) until the economic balance is once again achieved. However, he continues to maintain that "a small supply of labour, or a trifling increase in the population, will soon reduce the market price to the then increased natural price of labour."[112]

For Ricardo, the tension between natural price and market price is founded in two sources: either bad government or an unchecked and increasing population. Bad governments fail to develop and utilize all the fertile land so as to offer an adequate food supply, and they do not educate their poor inhabitants in industry and morals.[113] Poor morals result in more children being born and poor regulation of the passions results in more children born within marriages.[114] Without remedies that increase industry through more efficient and efficacious land usage or without policies that decrease the ranks of the poor, disaster looms.[115]

For Ricardo, writing in 1821, the Poor Laws, which went into effect in 1601, directly conflicted with the iron law of wages. Ricardo conceived the iron law of wages as a natural law of society, akin to the natural laws of physics. The idea was that the natural mechanisms, aided by rational government, could harmonize the relationship between the natural and market prices of labor. The 1601 Poor Law disrupted the favorable harmonization of these laws in relation to workforce, capital, and technological improvements by meeting the poor's need for food and thereby decreasing the external impetus to industry. Malthus, Ricardo claimed, had fully developed the mathematical demonstration of exponential growth in population in relation to the linear growth of food production, and the iron law of wages complemented Malthus's discovery. The Poor Laws, Ricardo avers, must be reformed, but prudently:

> [A]nd every friend to the poor must ardently wish for their abolition. Unfortunately, however, they have been so long established, and the habits of the poor have been so formed upon their operation, that to eradicate them with safety from our political system, requires the most cautious and skilful [sic] management.[116]

The poor have their part to play in restraining their own desires, but bad government has "rendered restraint superfluous, and [has] invited imprudence, by offering it a portion of the wages of prudence and industry."[117] In short, by supporting the poor financially, government has promoted their idleness and has not promoted their industry. By "industry," Ricardo means that the poor must resist the vice of idleness and become more productive for the economy. By "restraint," Ricardo means prudential restraint of the poor in terms of their lust, as suggested by Malthus as well.

In 1796, William Pitt, then–prime minister, proposed reforming the Poor Laws, in part, by increasing gifts to large families so that they could better care for their children. Following the contemporary wisdom that the wealth and power of the state were measured in population, Pitt's proposal was designed to encourage the poor to have large families. Ricardo believed such an intervention would only increase the numbers of mouths to feed and also increase the numbers of laborers, thus driving the market price of labor downward. Ricardo's proposed reform would not be so crass as to penalize large families, but he maintained that the government must enact laws that would incentivize the poor to keep their families small.[118] By gradually removing what he saw as positive incentives to poverty, Ricardo argued that the ranks of the poor would be contracted. By dissuading the poor from dependency to philanthropy and toward their own industry, the state will be more healthful.[119] The systematic charity offered by the state via parish churches as required according to the 1601 Poor Law, and the casual charity given by men and women of means, was the problem.[120] What lies at the heart of Ricardo's concern is not a concern for the well-being of the poor, but a concern for the well-being of the state. A more rational approach to poverty would be an approach that followed Ricardo's "iron law of wages" and Malthus's writing on demography, as we shall see, might result in a better health and wealth for the state.

## Thomas Malthus, Joseph Townsend, and the Heartless Laws of Nature

Ricardo had envisaged a fundamental relationship between food cost and supply, wages, and numbers of workers. One might wonder: why these three quantities? Although they did not meet until 1813, it is clear that Ricardo's thinking on these matters was shaped by the work of Thomas Malthus (1766–1834) that had exploded into popular consciousness before the turn of the century. Standing behind Malthus was the less visible, but critical, figure of Joseph Townsend. Together, Malthus and Townsend gave further theoretical support for the deployment of the proper "springs of action" to increase industry and reduce the population of the poor. It is here that we find the seeds of *bio*politics.

Malthus was an Anglican cleric and demographer who rose to instant prominence— or notoriety—with his first publication entitled *An Essay on the Principle of Population* (1798). It was originally published anonymously, and it saw five more editions by 1826. As one commentator notes, "the uproar it caused among non-economists overshadowed the instant respect it inspired among his fellow economists."[121] Karl Polanyi marks Malthus's *Essay* as the beginning of classical economics.[122] In 1805, Malthus was given a post as Professor of History and Political Economy at the East India Company College at Haileybury. In 1821 with Ricardo and James Mill, he founded the Political Economy Club, the purpose of which was to develop fundamental principles of economics.¹²³ He was also one of the first Fellows of the Statistical Society of London (now the Royal Statistical Society) founded in 1834. His father, notably, was friends with David Hume.

As he notes in the preface to the second edition of his essay, Malthus maintains that "the only authors from whose writings I had deduced the principle, which formed the main argument of the Essay, were Hume, Wallace, Adam Smith, and Dr. Price,"¹²⁴ though he acknowledges that Townsend had recently treated the same subject. Since the mid-1800s, critics and scholars have held, however, that Malthus more simply appropriated Townsend's work. Like Malthus, Joseph Townsend (1739–1816) was an Anglican cleric as well as a medical doctor who studied at the University of Edinburgh. His 1786 treatise *A Dissertation on the Poor Laws,* informed by his own work among the poor in his own parish and abroad, inspired the work of both Malthus and Darwin's theory of natural selection.¹²⁵

We begin with Malthus. With an eye toward the problem of the explosive increase in the number of poor people over the prior century, the *Essay on the Principle of Population* proposed a relationship between population growth and the economy. The *Essay* in its various editions took aim at the age of marriage and the customs and practices that supported the poor.¹²⁶ His basic thesis was stated simply: "It may safely be pronounced, therefore, that population, when unchecked, goes on doubling itself every twenty-five years, or increases in a geometrical ratio."¹²⁷ However, food sources do not increase exponentially, and thus hardships arise on the population as it grows.¹²⁸ Food, thus, is the limitation on population and the diseases that accompany scarcity.¹²⁹

The *Essay* sets out to prove three propositions:

1. Population is necessarily limited by the means of subsistence.
2. Population invariably increases where the means of subsistence increases, unless prevented by some very powerful and obvious checks.
3. These checks, and the checks which repress the superior power of population, and keep its effects on a level with the means of subsistence, are all resolvable into moral restraint, vice, and misery.¹³⁰

The first premise, Malthus says, does not really need to be proven as it is obvious. The other two need proof and he sets out to provide that proof.

In the sixth edition of the *Essay,* he describes how various checks on the population have played themselves out in various societies in various parts of the world.¹³¹ He divides these checks into two categories: positive checks and preventive checks. Positive checks on population-increases arise either from misery or from vice, or from a combination of the two, all of which shortens the natural duration of life.¹³² Under the heading of misery:

> may be enumerated all unwholesome occupations, severe labour and exposure to the seasons, extreme poverty, bad nursing of children, great towns, excesses of all kinds, the whole train of common diseases and epidemics, wars, plague, and famine.¹³³

These positive checks arise "unavoidably from the laws of nature."[134] Other positive checks on the increases of population arise from vice, like promiscuity and "violations of the marriage bed."[135] All of these positive checks curb population growth, because debauchery leads to disease, misery, and death.

Preventive checks on population growth, according to Malthus, are voluntary, but these are tenuously effective at best. If a poor, educated person has a "distinctive superiority in his reasoning faculties," it will enable him "to calculate distant consequences" and curb population.[136] Innate drives must be curbed, by moral reason. "Of the preventive checks, the restraint from marriage which is not followed by irregular gratifications may properly be termed moral restraint."[137] He notes that "[t]hese considerations are calculated to prevent, and certainly do prevent, a great number of persons in all civilized nations from pursuing the dictate of nature in an early attachment to one woman."[138] Early marriage, which seems to keep one from sexual immorality, produces too many children. What is needed is a reasoned curbing of sexual desire, and through proper moral restraint, delayed marriage can prevent population overgrowth. Continuing, Malthus states:

> If this restraint does not produce vice, it is undoubtedly the least evil that can arise from the principle of population. Considered as a restraint on a strong natural inclination, it must be allowed to produce a certain degree of temporary unhappiness; but evidently slight, compared with the evils which result from any of the other checks to population; and merely of the same nature as many other sacrifices of temporary to permanent gratification, which it is the business of a moral agent continually to make.[139]

Moral (sexual) restraint of the poor will be a much better check on population than the positive checks of starvation, disease, and death. The implicit utilitarian reasoning of "calculating distant consequences" is clearly at work.

Gertrude Himmelfarb charts a transition between Malthus's first and subsequent editions of the *Essay*. In the first edition, Malthus was enamored of naturalism and the laws of nature. Here Townsend's influence is undeniable. Clearly vexed by his clerical responsibility for caring for the poor within his parish, Townsend's short *A Dissertation on the Poor Laws* decries the growing ranks of the poor, the growing tax burden on those with means, and the epidemic of recalcitrant idleness and vice, debauchery and drunkenness, especially among those supported by public means.[140] In words dripping with disdain, he notes:

> Now it is evident that by raising the price of labour you must directly check the progress of the manufactures . . . for in proportion as you advance the wages of the poor, you diminish the quantity of their work. All manufacturers complain of this, and universally agree, that the poor are seldom diligent, except when labour is cheap, and corn is dear. It must be confessed that too many of them have some little resemblance to the animal described by travellers [sic] under the name of Nimble Peter; a creature so inactive, that, when he has cleared one tree, he will be reduced to skin and bones before he climbs another, and so slow in all his motions, that even stripes will not make him mend his pace.[141]

Townsend barely recognizes the poor as fellow human beings. Not only does he also presage here Ricardo's iron law of wages, he signals here what for Polanyi was his key innovation: namely, Townsend grounds the cause of poverty, and all economics, in nature. Not only does he opine that "it seems to be a law of nature that the poor should be to a certain degree improvident," so that there will always be bodies to join the military and do "the most servile, the most sordid, and the most ignoble offices in the community."[142]

His treatise centers on a story he reports as fact—the naturalistic fable of the goats and dogs. This story displays in narrative terms the basic premises of Malthus's theory. The fable is set on one of the Juan Fernandez islands off the coast of Chile—the island that, perhaps not coincidentally, provided the setting for Daniel Defoe's story of Robinson Crusoe. Townsend tells how a pair of goats, set loose on the island, populated the island prolifically, until their numbers were naturally checked by food supply, eventually reaching a "degree of aequipose." This process then continued to cycle naturally in a somewhat idyllic fashion. Discovering that English privateers were provisioning themselves via the goats, wily Spaniards "put on shore a greyhound dog and bitch," who likewise multiplied, they and their offspring feeding off of the goats.

> Had [the goats] been totally destroyed, the dogs likewise must have perished. But as many of the goats retired to the craggy rocks, where the dogs could never follow them, descending only for short intervals to feed with fear and circumspection . . . few of these, besides the careless and the rash, became a prey; and none but the most watchful, strong, and active of the dogs could get a sufficiency of food. Thus, a new kind of balance was established. The weakest of both species were among the first to pay the debt of nature; the most active and vigorous preserved their lives. It is the quantity of food which regulates the numbers of the human species.[143]

No breath is required for Townsend to move from his fable to his conclusion: human population growth is food-dependent. No proof is required for the fundamental claim here: competition is a law of nature.[144]

But his readers need no further argument. His fable is framed throughout the *Dissertation* by his repeated assertion that it is hunger—and basically hunger alone—which is the most crucial motivator. The Poor Laws of 1601 removed that natural spring of action, and replaced it with a legal one, which only had effects to increase the numbers of the poor. "Hunger will tame the fiercest animals, it will teach decency and civility, obedience and subjection, to the most perverse," the implication being that humans are best treated according to their animal nature.[145] As Polanyi notes, Townsend's parable and his claims provided an entirely new starting point for politics and social engineering, appearing to avoid philosophical claims about the foundation of society and grounding his claims about the poor in biological laws of Nature in a new way. As Polanyi notes, Hobbes had claimed despots were necessary because men were *like* beasts, but for Townsend, they were *actually* beasts. He continues, "From this novel point of view, a free society could be regarded as consisting of two races: property-owners and laborers." The latter were limited by food. "No magistrate was necessary, for hunger was a better disciplinarian than the magistrate."[146] Townsend sets the stage for a biopolitical economy of hunger, the coercion of the human beasts for the betterment of the propertied persons.

It is with Malthus, however, that Townsend's vision gains momentum. Following Townsend, Malthus clearly conceived of the poor as subject to the deterministic laws of nature; the natural laws of population—the fact that arithmetic growth of food sources and the exponential growth of population—dictate how society goes. As with Townsend, the poor, for Malthus, lack any sort of capacity for moral agency. Like his older contemporary Bentham, Malthus sought to develop a naturalist science of society. His highly mechanical checks on the problems presented by the poor had a kind of heartless mechanical solution to a seemingly insoluble problem. Nature is a heartless mechanism. Just as the natural laws of physics were not concerned with human desires or needs, the natural laws of society, the social physics as Adolph Quetelet would come to call it, would crunch the poor under the mechanics of society.[147]

However, in the second edition of the *Essay* (published now under his own name in 1803), Himmelfarb notes that Malthus introduced the notion of *prudent* restraint, which gave to the poor some dimension of agency, some way out of the throes of the machine of the natural laws of society. However, prudential judgment was not enough to assure that society would avoid the catastrophe of the principle of population. The poor needed moral direction. So, in subsequent editions, Malthus introduced a stronger notion of *moral* restraint. Moral restraint shifts the burden of moral agency, giving the poor the sense that they could prevent their own vice and misery—or, more precisely, laying the blame for the condition at their own feet. "All that was necessary," Himmelfarb notes, "was that the poor understand that 'they are themselves the cause of their poverty; that the means of redress are in their own hands and in the hands of not other persons whatever.' The 'moral agent' was a free and responsible individual, the master of his own fate."[148] The desire for improvement and the moral agency of the poor, as Himmelfarb notes, was the novel element that would alleviate the plight of the poor from being crushed under the mechanics of society. In short, Malthus would introduce a moral intervention in order to lighten the darkness of the first edition.[149] The poor were victims of the harsh laws of nature in the first edition; there was no hope. In the second edition, the poor were given hope in that they are imagined to have some agency. But if they failed, it was their own moral failing.

So, in the first edition, the poor were to be pitied because they were victims of the harsh laws of nature; in later editions, the poor were themselves the source of their own poverty. It was this intersection of the natural laws of population and the granting of moral agency to the poor that the idea of the deserving poor was redefined from its sixteenth-century concept; this class of poor persons deserved help from the political establishment, because they had curbed their sexual appetites and put their bodies to industrious work.

Moral restraint did two things. First, it granted agency to the poor, such that the poor themselves could avoid the harsh "positive checks" against over population. Second, it gave political economists a basis from which to engineer the future of society. Just as Newton's laws of motion had given a new understanding of forces in nature[150] and permitted novel engineering feats through the manipulation of those laws of nature, Bentham's laws of society would permit social engineering. Bentham's laws, complemented by Ricardo's "iron law" of wages, and Malthus's principle of population inspired by Townsend's hunger thesis, gave government leverage points for intervening for the reform of the poor law. Malthus—like the reformed minded Bentham—was introducing a kinder and gentler biopolitical control lever into society through his notion of moral restraint.

Despite the fact that Malthus believed that his subsequent editions of the *Essay* were less dark and presented a morally reasoned approach to the problem of the poor, Malthus received much abuse even for the latter editions. The vehemence of the critique against Malthus, especially by those in the literary community, makes evident that his detractors could not gain traction against the actual popularity that Malthus enjoyed from the economic and the political classes of Britain.[151] In fact, many of his opponents conceded that Malthus's plan did grant moral agency to the deserving poor, even while the literary classes did not like the moralizing attitude toward the poor. Despite much abuse, Malthus was tremendously influential. He was described as "a sort of 'darling in the public eye,' whom it was unsafe to meddle with."[152] As Himmelfarb notes, the vehement critiques leveled against Malthus were in fact critiques against the morally insensitive melancholia of the first edition, which depicts the seemingly deterministic dimensions of the natural laws of society.

Himmelfarb notes that Malthus's work had proven to be a major source for shaping how British society conceived the poor.

> The point is not simply that Malthus made converts in high places among politicians . . ., philosophers. . ., historians . . ., and nameless and numerous journalists . . . More important were the untold number of people who accepted his thesis without making a public profession of it, sometimes without being consciously aware of it.[153]

Thus, he captured the imagination of society, even the members of society that hated Malthusianism, as Malthus's position would later be called. Himmelfarb goes on to point out that even the most vehement opponents of Malthusianism and Benthamism "and the rest of the materialistic, mechanistic, 'pig philosophy'" of that era, still loved one aspect of Malthus's philosophy, namely, that there was a deserving poor class that worked, and an undeserving poor class that did not.[154]

With Malthus, we get the key to engineering: society could now place numbers on these two sins—sloth and lust. Lust could be quantified by counting the numbers of children born in a system where birth control was ineffective. Sloth could be quantified by counting the numbers of non-working, and therefore undeserving, poor. What differentiated the two classes of poor was whether the poor person asserted his or her moral agency and embraced Malthus's new formulation of moral restraint: delay marriage (curb your lust) and work hard (avoid sloth); that is what is good for society. As Himmelfarb notes, Malthus not only helped to find a "solution" to the problem of the poor, he actually set the terms for society to understand the poor as a problem in need of a solution.[155] His framing of the question would shape the way that the Poor Laws Reform of 1834 would shake out,[156] and, as we have argued, the way that moral thinking would go on to shape political economy of the next generation.

## Social Machinations and the Bodies of the Poor

Though Bentham, Ricardo, and Malthus would not survive to see the Poor Law Reform of 1834—Bentham dying in 1832, Ricardo in 1823, and Malthus in 1834—their fingerprints were all over the law, and their spirit would animate the development of economic, social, and moral thinking rippling down the ages to today. Taken together, they, along with Townsend, give us the puzzle pieces that will provide the social milieu out of which the biopolitical economy of neoliberalism is born and from which the neuroscience of morality emerges.

Townsend would inspire Malthus, providing the biological restraint that hunger puts onto the poor, the first fruit of pain, one of the twin taskmasters of humankind. Ricardo's iron law of wages and Malthus's *Essay on Population* would give Bentham the much-needed scientific grounding for understanding the best ways to leverage the poor for industry and to turn rogues to honesty. Thus, the Poor Law Reform of 1834 found its inspiration in the reformers and helped to further moralize poverty. Where the 1601 Poor Law—designed to solve the problems of the poor created by the closure of the commons—set the trajectory for moralizing of the poor, the radical reformers completed that task. While the radical reformers were hoping for a more humane treatment of the poor, they had to first imagine them to be beasts along with Townsend. Malthus would then humanize them, by granting them a modicum of moral agency. The Poor Law Reform of 1834 helped to shape the cultural sentiment that, with their new-found agency, if the poor remained poor, it was their own moral failing. The poor were supposedly free to change their own plight, but all the while they were caught up in the Panoptic vision of Jeremy Bentham. The poor were now split into two separate camps: the deserving (those that might achieve wealth and thus actual freedom) and the undeserving poor (those that have theoretical freedom, but rejected Bentham's social mechanics).

Mill would find his godfather's systematic and mechanical thinking too crass and would work to reform it. In his attempts to be more careful with a system of logic, Mill would articulate his own positivist social theory, born of his father's work in psychology, and his own work in the science of ethology (character), a precursor to economic science and the neuroscience of morality. By doing so, Mill put himself in a position to articulate a more nuanced understanding of the science of society and political economy. In addition, theoretically, he developed the idea of the self as emergent from both its biology and its social formation, something we see in both the economic science and the neuroscience of morality. Yet Mill's notion of the self is a being that, while constituted from *bios* and *polis*, rises above and chooses from among a myriad of desires. Mill had a space for freedom that seemed to escape the social mechanics of Bentham and his neoliberal and neuroscientific heirs. However, it is probably better to say that his understanding of freedom was not reductive, which is to say that his anthropology was more sophisticated than the one imagined by Bentham, Ricardo, Malthus, and Townsend.

However much Mill might have worked to salvage political economy from the lower anthropology of Townsend's impoverished beasts, his heirs would latch onto

*Homo economicus*, the being that is the artifact of the positivist science of economics. Thus, there are two beings here, one capable of making free and rational self-interested choices, and those lesser beings whose capacity for agency and choice is erased by poverty. The former would become *Homo economicus*, which we have argued is an artifact of economic models and the laissez-faire state, which safeguards their inherent freedom. The latter are undeserving beings whose morality keeps them in chains; they are the vicious antisocial beings, deserving of our pity as long as they conform to the biopolitical economy of the burgeoning neoliberalism, and should be set outside the system, as suggested by Sam Harris and others that would promote genetic virtue. What we see, then, are two beings one that rises to the level of "man," the prosocial economic man of Mill and the other, the antisocial, that roams among the beasts.

The radical reformers of the nineteenth century gave these beasts one possible path toward humanization: they could choose to submit to a biopolitical-economic regime that required them to negate their animalistic sexual desires and accept dehumanizing working conditions in order to become human. On this model, the social mechanics of the state promulgated in scientifically grounded legislation open a door for the poor to exit from their beastly poverty and to enter the society. Thus, ironically by giving up their freedom, they might gain entry into the ranks of the human. For by lifting oneself out of poverty and no longer burdening the state, the state must leave one alone.

This promised freedom, though, is merely theoretical, for under the biopolitical economy of Industry Houses and wage labor, it is unlikely that the poor would achieve the wealth required for true freedom. In this system, we see the fingerprints of the philosophical predecessor of the empiricists, namely, David Hume. Here we find the seeds of the entrepreneurial and industrious souls who are the progenitors to *Homo economicus*. As we will show, these entrepreneurial souls are conceived, not in the mind of Adam Smith, but in the mind of David Hume, to whom we now turn our attention.

# 6

# Bacon, Smith, and the End of Virtue

As we have shown in the previous chapter, Mill's positivist science and the birth of *Homo economicus* were intimately linked. The same is true for the early modern thinkers from Bacon to Hume to Smith. It is not surprising that these figures of the early modern period, who shaped our political and economic philosophies, are the same figures that shaped the new moral and human sciences. Science and politics, knowledge and power seem inseparable in the work of these philosophers. As we outlined in Part I, both the Chicago School and key figures in the neuroscience claim Adam Smith and David Hume as their twin inspirations. In this chapter, we complicate this lineage, granting the influence of Hume on the neurobiological narrative of morality, but arguing that their true progenitor is that towering figure who stands behind Hume: Francis Bacon.

There can be little doubt that Bentham, Malthus, and Ricardo grounded their principles of politics and economy in the empirical philosophy and the metaphysical claims of the premier philosopher of the Scottish Enlightenment, David Hume. As we have seen, Bentham accepts whole-cloth Hume's metaphysical thesis about the human inability to know causes. For Bentham, that did not mean that we are caught in a morass of not knowing, as much as we must ground our knowledge in the one thing of which we can be certain—human experience. The legislator must begin where all empiricists begin, namely, in the ground of sense experience. From the very beginning of *An Introduction to the Principles of Morals and Legislation*, Bentham notes:

> Nature has placed mankind [sic] under the governance of two sovereign masters, *pain* and *pleasure*. It is for them alone to point out what we ought to do, as well as to determine what we shall do. On the one hand, the standard of right and wrong, on the other the chain of causes and effects, are fastened to their throne. They govern us in all we do, in all we say, in all we think.[1]

Pleasure and pain govern Bentham's project of legislating morals. As with all knowledge, Bentham would have us begin not in speculation or in final causes, and not in virtue or in sympathy (where Adam Smith begins); rather, he begins exactly where Hume begins, namely, in sense experience, in pleasure and pain, the 'moral senses.' Just as sense experience is the beginning of all knowledge, moral knowledge—moral science—too must begin in the moral senses of pleasure and pain.

David Hume is best known for two related works, his *A Treatise of Human Nature* (1739-1740) and his *An Enquiry Concerning Human Understanding* (1748), the latter serving as a mature distillation of his youthful insights in the much earlier work.[2] In these works, Hume examines the epistemological foundation of human knowledge working in a manner consonant with Francis Bacon's *New Organon*. While Hume himself was not a political operative, he wrote a massive six-volume political history of England. He wrote on every topic from morals, to politics, to economics, to the empirical sciences. His thesis in the *Treatise* is that all human inquiry, including moral inquiry, must begin in sense experience, which should ground political, scientific, and economic enterprise.

Hume was not the only early modern thinker to write on the relationship of science and politics. It is as true of the rationalists as it is of the empiricists. In the second part of the *Discourse on Method*, the rationalist Rene Descartes (1596–1650) begins with a metaphor for the mind by appeal to architecture of the city. The buildings and cities are designed by a single rational architect, which holds the city together.[3] Catherine Pickstock depicts how, for Descartes, the ordering of human knowledge mimics a well-governed city, appealing as he does to analogies "of architecture, city-planning, and governmental structure to describe his method for the composition and organization of knowledge."[4] As with a city, the mind must be rationally ordered and thus defended from chaos. This citadel of one person, alone, ordering knowledge *is* the paradigm of knowing for Descartes. Formal consistency is more important than embodied and communal goods. Formal consistency permits mastery and control, rather than dependency on the vicissitudes of organic emergence. Matthew Jones, among others, has drawn our attention to the univocity of language and homogeneity of method used by Cartesian science.[5] The universally applicable *mathesis*—both in natural science and in political governance—allows one not only to know geometry but to order all knowledges and goods—including political and moral goods—according to the same measure.

Overlapping with Descartes, Thomas Hobbes (1588–1679) attempts to deploy this univocal Cartesian mathesis in order to actually build the new city, the great polis. Hobbes—an acquaintance of Descartes—was also a geometrician. He also participated in political life and was the secretary to the Lord Chancellor, Francis Bacon (1561–1626). The geometer King, according to Hobbes, would create the space of the city to cohere in a manner similar to the axioms of geometry. Within the geometric mathesis of the city, a plebe might be protected from violence and chaos of the State of Nature, where life "is solitary, poor, nasty, brutish, and short."[6]

The physician John Locke (1632–1704) thought of himself as a natural philosopher—that is to say, a scientist; yet, we know him as a political philosopher. As a natural philosopher, we find Locke speaking in *An Essay Concerning Human Understanding* about primary qualities that are properties or powers inherent in objects. Reason and liberty are powers—properties—of human being.[7] And in the *Second Treatise on Government*, he states that men band together in society "for the mutual Preservation of their Lives, Liberties and Estates," which he calls "by the general Name, Property."[8] In both his natural philosophy and his political philosophy, much hangs on the ideas of properties and powers. Properties adhere closely to the essence of things, including humankind. As he notes, "man ... hath by Nature a Power ... to preserve his Property, that is, his Life, Liberty and Estate."[9] Life is a property of human being; liberty is a property of human being; estate is his property.

Still, as we shall see, the figure who cast the most influence on British empiricism in general, and on David Hume in particular, was Francis Bacon, the father of modern empiricism. Bacon, a political operative his entire life, is important not only because he gives us a new inductive science, a new empirical science, though surely that is also true. He is important because of the stance he strikes to nature, transforming early modern philosophy into techno-science even before robust technological innovation had begun.[10] In other words, in addition to developing a new, inductive method for the acquisition of new knowledge, it was Bacon's stance regarding nature that transformed both science and politics. For Bacon, knowledge, particularly knowledge of nature, was useful for manipulating things.

As we have seen, this form of techno-science has come to shape contemporary research into things like moral formation, all with an eye to controlling human virtue and vice. We shall conclude that modern science is really a Baconian techno-science, knowledge that does technical work according to a mechanical model of work. What is more, modern economic theory is also a techno-science, aimed at understanding human behavior such that it can be manipulated. Human beings have become the raw material for a better, more productive polis, and thus a more moral polis. As we will show, in contrast to a previous way of imagining behavior, Bacon is the founder of the entire project to know and to master the powers in order to create the new Atlantis.

But in order to build this new Atlantis, human anthropology would have to be evacuated of its moral content, its nature, its relationality, and its telos. Rather than Adam Smith, who retained a robust moral anthropology, we find Hume's self-interested, utility-maximizing person of property, which seeds both Malthus's and Bentham's bifurcated anthropology of the beastly poor and the free person-of-industry, which morphs into Mill's *Homo economicus*, which in turn gives way to the person reduced to capital of the Chicago School and of schematic being of neuroscience. Rather than the noble creatures of Bacon's utopian new Atlantis, we find a pale and pathetic creature, caught in the throes of political economy. While we are not arguing that Smith is the right option for a more human science, there can be little doubt that his anthropology is much more humane and not nearly as thin or reductive as Hume's and that of subsequent Humeans.

## Hume and the Origins of Political Economic Morality

David Hume (1711–1776) is widely regarded as one of the most influential philosophers of the modern period:

> Kant reported that Hume's work woke him from his "dogmatic slumbers," and Jeremy Bentham remarked that reading Hume "caused the scales to fall" from his eyes. Charles Darwin regarded his work as a central influence on the theory of evolution. The diverse directions in which these writers took what they gleaned from reading him reflect both the richness of their sources and the wide range of his empiricism.[11]

As we saw in Chapter 5, Hume exerted enormous influence over every theorist standing at the dawn of modern economics, political economy, morality, and social science. As we saw in Part I, it is almost as if Hume is still alive, being widely and frequently cited by contemporary economists and neuroscientists.

Hailing from a strict Calvinist background in Edinburgh, Hume began his studies at the University of Edinburgh at the age of ten or eleven, but left university early and embarked on a program of self-education, discarding along the way any adherence to religion.[12] As a second son, his inheritance was meager, setting him up for an itinerant life of occasional employment, in France, England, and Scotland. Publishing the first edition of the *Treatise* anonymously at age twenty-three, he twice tried to enter the professorate, but was turned down both times, in large part due to his emerging reputation as an atheist and a skeptic; thus, he never held an academic post. MacIntyre argues that Hume lived a sort of double-life—retaining warm personal ties with family and friends in Scotland, while working hard in his professional life to "Anglicize" himself and distance himself from his Scottish identity, changing the spelling of his name from "Home" to "Hume" so the English could pronounce it correctly, writing his works to give the impression that he was English, and living a scholarly and professional life that "was by design to a large degree an English life."[13]

As we have seen, Hume was a radical empiricist, locating the only ground for knowledge in sense experiences, and when it came to matters political, economic, and moral, particularly in the experiences of pleasure and pain. As a radical skeptic, he abjured any possibility for knowing formal and final causes, as they do not simply appear to sense experience. Thus, metaphysical knowledge of God or natures, including human nature, is prone to wild speculation. Upon these fundamental commitments, Hume builds his position on moral knowledge and the virtues. Hume claims that humans denote those objects that induce pleasure as good and those that induce pain as evil. While we cannot say anything about the nature of good or evil, we can say things about pleasure and pain. As we will see, Hume is the intellectual power behind the rise of empiricism, positivism in social science, utilitarianism in moral thought, and is the key person influencing the thought of the popularizers of neuroscience. Hume is key to the social imaginary out of which the neuroscience of morality is born.

Frederick Rosen traces Hume's thinking on the origin of moral knowledge to Pierre Gassendi (1592–1655), a French priest, philosopher, astronomer, and mathematician. Gassendi offered a seventeenth-century reading of the Epicureans in order to argue against Aristotelianism.[14] At the heart of Epicurean philosophy is pleasure and pain, the chief drive being the avoidance of pain. Gassendi put it this way:

> Therefore to speak properly, Right or natural Equity is nothing else but what is mark'd out by Utility or Profit, or that Utility which, by common Agreement, hath been appointed that Men might not injure one another, nor receive any wrong, but live in security, which is a real Good, and therefore naturally desired of everyone.[15]

Justice, for Gassendi, is not found in the facts of nature as Aristotle argued.[16] Justice is simply the securing of order through inflicting pain on those who did not respect the rule against creating harm/pain for others.[17] We see at work here the central feature of empirically based ethics—namely, the avoidance of pain, and the position that the chief advantage that one can give to others is to establish law that prevents pain and promotes pleasure. The advantage, when this position is broadened to all, is called utility. Thus, more broadly for Gassendi, as Rosen notes, it is utility and not justice (or benevolence or sympathy) as we shall see in Smith's critique of Hume, that establishes all of morality. Utility—in its act of reducing pain and increasing pleasure—is that which gives advantage.[18]

Hume took this lesson to heart, speaking of two virtues—justice and benevolence—and their fruit—property. First, neither nature nor God establishes the virtues, for these depend on metaphysical speculation about formal or final causes. While Hume takes his more positive view of human nature from Hutcheson, for whom morality was grounded in the goodness of nature, he rejects "natures" as the source of moral science. In a letter to Hutcheson, he notes:

> I cannot agree to your Sense of *Natural*. Tis founded on final Causes; which is a Consideration, that appears to me pretty uncertain & unphilosophical. For pray, what is the End of Man? Is he created for Happiness or for Virtue? For this Life or for the next? For himself or for his Maker? Your Definition of Natural depends upon solving these Questions, which are endless & quite wide of my Purpose. I have never call'd Justice unnatural, but only artificial.[19]

Justice, a virtue, is not a product of nature, but of artifice. Justice is artificial, in that it is established or constructed out of the best source of human knowledge, the empirically derived moral sense experience of pleasure and pain.

More pointedly, the need for justice arises out of a particular source of pain—the fact of scarcity. Hume's consideration of justice in the *Enquiry Concerning the Principles of Morals* begins with a reflection on abundance. In abundance, there is no need for justice, because in abundance all that is needed is readily available to people. Things like air and water, for example, are readily available, and there is "No laborious occupation required: No tillage: No navigation."[20] In a state of abundance, "the cautious, jealous virtue of justice would never once have been dreamed of."[21] But we do not, of course, live in a state of abundance. Resources are scarce, and, as a result, we must find useful ways of relieving the pain of scarcity.

What is the essence of reducing the pain of scarcity and enhancing the pleasure of abundance? Utility. Utility, grounded firstly in the sense experience of pain and pleasure, aims at increasing pleasure or reducing pain. These two sovereigns induce happiness. Insofar as humans prescind from harming one another, so that they do not inflict pain upon each other, justice is established. Thus, utility demands the creation of that cautious and jealous virtue, justice, which might reduce the pain of scarcity.

Benevolence is justice's counterpoint. While Hume does not articulate the distinction between artificial and natural virtues in the *Enquiry Concerning Human Understanding*, as he did in the *Treatise*, benevolence also qualifies as an artificial virtue. Constructed to bind people together, it too is grounded in utility, this time in the service of securing pleasures. Benevolence functions in concert with sympathy and approbation. Fellow-feeling or sympathy is the capacity of people to feel what others feel. It is something that we have by nature, for Hume, even while we cannot say more about human nature than that humans have this capacity. Sympathy does not solely give pleasure; it is the capacity to feel what the other feels, whether pleasure or pain. Sympathy moves us to act, to relieve that pain or to give another pleasure. In doing so, we receive approbation from others, which generates within us a sense of pleasure. Pleasure derives from giving advantage or being useful to the other. As Rosen notes,

> connected with this link between utility, approbation, and pleasure is a sympathy with the pain and pleasure of others that we share as part of our humanity. Our sympathy with humanity, however, is not the source pleasure; our feelings of pleasure through approbation of utility is the source of our humanity.[22]

Thus, it is utility that motivates benevolence.[23] Benevolence is the virtue that aims at utility by giving advantage to one's fellows. Via sympathy we sense the feelings of pleasure or pain of another and are moved from mere perception toward benevolent motivations aimed at creating more pleasure or reducing pain for others. We thereby receive approbation or praise for one's actions, which increases our own pleasure. Thus, the virtue of benevolence is driven by our own pleasure, the master of all moral behavior.

The skepticism that shaped Hume's metaphysical views also shaped his ethical views; we need only pay attention to sense experience, and, if we go beyond that, we move into the problematic speculation about natures, including human nature. In Part II of section V of the *Enquiry Concerning the Principles of Morals*, which asks the question, why does utility please? he states that the principle of utility is the origin of morality, and he does not need any "abstruse and remote system." In an explanatory footnote, we see Hume's anti-metaphysical stripe:

> It is needless to push our researches so far as to ask, why we have humanity or a fellow-feeling with others. It is sufficient, that this is experienced to be a principle in human nature. We must stop somewhere in our examination of causes; and there are, in every science, some general principles, beyond which we cannot hope to find any principle more general.[24]

The search for causes stops at the level of sense impression; any search for metaphysical causes, especially final causes or the search for natures, leaves one with wild speculation. Pleasure and pain in others cause a sense impression of pleasure or pain in oneself, no speculation necessary. In seeking to give the other advantage, one gets the pleasure of approbation. Utility, while seemingly grounded in sympathy, actually reverts to one's own sense of pleasure; a kind of self-interest seems to be at the heart of Hume's morality.

Thus, the virtues of justice and benevolence—and indeed all the virtues—are derived from utility, which is tethered to the sense experience of pleasure and pain. Contrary to popular opinion, it is not benevolence, not the seeking of a good, that establishes justice. According to Hume, people most often get it backward. Benevolence might seem to mean that you give alms to the poor, either as a command from scripture or according to nature. But benevolence is not properly grounded in experience. For Hume giving to the poor does not lead to goodness, but—as we saw with Hume's heirs in Chapter 5—ultimately to laziness and debauchery. It only results in good for a few people—the one who gives (and thus receives the pleasure of approbation) and the one who receives the gift (and thus has a momentary alleviation of the pain of his poverty). Only the giver and receiver experience pleasure, and that pleasure is experienced for only a short period of time. If one pays attention to experience and to the reasons emergent out of experience, one will see that benevolence, improperly grounded, leads to the exact opposite of happiness because it encourages laziness. For Hume, we must look beyond the immediate experience of pleasure of giving alms and seek to build justice, which is best grounded in utility.

Benevolence grounded in utility, thus, does away with alms-giving. It was this Humean way of thinking that drove the Poor Law reform efforts of Malthus, Ricardo, and Bentham. Rosen notes, utility is intensely social through the artifice of benevolence. But by placing benevolence before utility, the poor felt good in receiving and the rich felt good in giving, but it was harmful because it made the poor lazy. With utility as the originary principle, "beggars might become industrious, hard-working members of society and alms-givers might invest their money in productive enterprises which would provide opportunities for employment for former beggars."[25] Benevolence, alms giving, was a practice not grounded in empirically derived knowledge, and, like the radical reformers at the transition from the eighteenth to the nineteenth centuries, we see that Hume thought the practice was detrimental to the *polis* as a whole.

It is no accident that the upshot of Hume's revision of benevolence is the permission to forgo charity toward the poor. For while the search for causes must forgo any wild metaphysical speculation about final causes or human nature, the move to delimit the search to sense impressions enables the emerging moral scientist to forestall the search for any other causes—for example, the influence of the broader thought-community. This becomes clear, however, when we probe his notion of justice more deeply. For justice for Hume is not simply management of the sense experiences of pain caused by scarce resources via the principle of utility. That it is centered on resources and scarcity is important.

To make this point clearer, let's return to the artificial virtue of justice. An essential virtue for establishing a properly functioning society, Hume's justice is "conceived as the stability of possessions and property" for the industrious.[26] He notes that the hand of nature gives few enjoyments, and it is only by art and industry that "we can extract [enjoyments] in great abundance."[27] Justice arises from utility, and gives him a justification for property and inheritance.[28] Property can only be taken by consent of the owner which creates commerce, which again is useful to society. So, pleasure and pain give rise to utility, which gives rise to justice, which gives rise to property and inheritance, all in service to utility. Whereas for Locke property was grounded in nature, for Hume property is born out of utility, and like justice and benevolence it is the result of artifice.

As with justice, there would be no place for property in a world of abundance.[29] Only in scarcity is property necessary; otherwise, there would be no need to partition goods where there is enough. In a land of plenty, "why give rise to property, where there cannot possibly be an injury?"[30] However, as noted by George Panichas, Hume sees property as a mean between two extremes. In extreme abundance, "there is no need for property because it would serve no purpose," and in the extreme of scarcity, property laws would be "useless to implement, because they would not be followed."[31] The fact that we live under neither extreme means that human desires outrun the supply of desired goods. Thus, like justice, private property is essential for social functioning.[32]

Yet as a product of human artifice, it is a necessary fiction. MacIntyre notes in *Ethics in the Conflict of Modernity* that Hume believed in this useful fiction.[33] This did not preclude Hume from maintaining that property was the proper and philosophically obvious choice in the matter. By grounding private property in the human desire for pleasure and the desire to avoid pain, Hume creates the illusion that it is grounded in nature.[34] MacIntyre makes an even more astute point; even those that disagreed with Hume on nature and human nature still accepted his argument about the necessity of private property. The empirical grounding of his argument virtually sealed acceptance in empirically minded Britain of the eighteenth and nineteenth centuries.

So a picture begins to emerge. Justice is not about right relationships between persons. It is not about mediating relationships or harmonizing the work of the whole of the polis for the good of all. It is an artificial virtue, derivative of utility, made necessary by scarcity, and related to the *stable possession* of property. Justice is in the service of property; property is not in the service of justice. MacIntyre adds one more component to Hume's novel account of justice by unveiling Hume's implicit bias toward wealth. Hume, in his essay "Of the Rise and Progress of the Arts and Sciences," asserts a correlation between pleasure or positive desires and riches, stating: "Avarice, or the desire of gain, is a universal passion, which operates at all times, in all places, and upon all persons."[35] Similarly, he notes that, in the *Treatise*, "Nothing has a greater tendency to give us an esteem for any person than his power and riches."[36] We even take satisfaction "in the riches of others, and the esteem we have for the possessors."[37] As MacIntyre notes, Hume reveals his own esteem for the wealthy:

> [B]y referring first to the possessions of the rich "such as houses, gardens, equipages" and the like, which "being agreeable in themselves, necessarily produce a sentiment of pleasure in everyone, that considers or surveys them," secondly to our "expectation of advantage from the rich and powerful by our sharing of their possessions," and thirdly to "sympathy which makes us partake of the satisfaction of everyone, that approaches us."[38]

Hume clearly was bedazzled by the possessions of the rich and the powerful. What is more, whenever Hume comments on economic questions, it appears that "there is rarely a hint that the continuing and growing prosperity of the rich and powerful has invited anything other than the applause and approbation of the less prosperous."[39]

Elsewhere, MacIntyre makes clear how extensively Hume's moral theory is grounded in economic commitments. Not only does he reduce justice to the protection of property; in Hume's moral psychology, the foundational virtues and vices are radically shaped—and in fact inverted—by possession-based social standing. As MacIntyre notes:

> *Pleonexia* has at last made a social world for itself to be at home in, acquiring for itself that esteem that *timē* once conferred. Hume's values and the values of that English and anglicizing society for which Hume speaks represent a striking reversal of what as recently as the latter part of the seventeenth century has been inculcated in Scottish universities through the reading of the *Nichomachean Ethics* and the *Politics*. And that reversal could not have occurred without the social and economic changes of Karl Polanyi's "great transformation." But it could not have been presented in an intellectually cogent manner without Hume's elaboration of a radically new way of conceiving both the relationship of reason to the passions [reason being now the slave of the passions] and the nature of the passions.[40]

It is precisely this inverted relationship between reason and the passions that reverberates in the modern moral psychology and social science of Jonathan Haidt, Sam Harris, and Paul Zak.

MacIntyre traces the same patterns in Smith noting that the sentiments they lauded were shared by the cultivated eighteenth-century commercial and mercantile class, but not necessarily shared by all human kind.[41] As we will argue in the final section of this chapter, however, while Smith was certainly a man of his time, he held to a different anthropology than Hume, and his account of economic activity has a deeply communal dimension aiming at common goods, as Aristotle and Aquinas understood them. As a result, Smith has been called by some the "last of the virtue ethicists."[42]

Not only are pleasure/good and pain/evil at the foundation of Hume's moral philosophy; he also asserts that the desire to gain more pleasure is a natural desire—a natural cause which is immune to further philosophical scrutiny. In addition, he likewise asserts that wealth is universally perceived as a source of positive sentiments, and it is through wealth that benevolence becomes a possibility. Thus, Hume subtly embeds economics at the very heart of his moral system. As MacIntyre shows, Hume takes the political-economic status quo of mid-eighteenth-century British society and assumes it is the natural state of affairs universally. The emerging British political economy is naturalized and assumed to be the state of nature. Hume disguises "from his readers the importance of certain facts about the condition of their social and economic order." By doing so, Hume "sustained the workings of the agricultural, commercial, and mercantile economy to the profit of some and to the detriment of others, others who are for the most part invisible to Hume."[43]

Thus, it was the propertied, the wealthy, who could be seen as the most moral of all. They had the material conditions of happiness and were indeed happy. They practiced justice by protecting the stability of their property. They were envied, and, if we are to believe Hume, they brought happiness to the poor through their benevolence. Even in the absence of their benevolence, the poor still gain pleasure just by being associated with their wealthy compatriots. Moreover, the wealthy had pleasure from approbation for their philanthropy. Hume, here sounds very much like he would agree with Zak's virtuous cycle, mediated by oxytocin all generated by market economics, as well as Becker and Rayo's account of the happiness function.

Yet this brings us to another subtle problem for Humean thought: how could utility work for the poor? The great mass of the poor had less pleasure and more pain than their landed, propertied compatriots. The artifice of justice and the force of law would have to create means of inducing utility in the poor. Although concern regarding the poor laws had not yet reached the fevered pitch as it would at the close of the century, scathing critiques of the poor and charity were already part of Hume's milieu. Within the social imaginary of his time, there were fables and beliefs about the poor, not least Bernard Mandeville's *Fable of the Bees, or Private Vices, Publick Benefits*. Mandeville's *Fable* was a formative influence on Hume, as well as Hutcheson and Smith, and much of the British scene from the time of its anonymous publication in 1705 and reissue in 1714 and 1729. In this volume, social philosopher Mandeville included his satirical poem, *The Grumbling Hive, or Knaves Turn'd Honest*, where he recounts the fortunes of a colony of bees that was thriving as long as each pursued private gain. At one point, the bees decided to live by honesty and virtue, and the economy of their hive collapses. The moral of the story was that prosperity and social benefit were actually the product of individual vices, and that most accounts of reason or virtue were simply fictions.[44]

In the *Fable*, Mandeville attacked not only traditional understandings of virtue, he also displays the same contempt of the poor—as well as unpropertied laborers—that we saw in Townsend. Gertrude Himmelfarb calls out a particularly pernicious statement:

> Everybody knows that there is a vast number of journeymen weavers, tailors, clothworkers, and twenty other handicrafts, who, if by four days labour in a week they can maintain themselves, will hardly be persuaded to work the fifth; and that there are thousands of labouring men of all sorts, who will, though they can hardly subsist, put themselves to fifty inconveniences, disoblige their master, pinch their bellies, and run in debt, to make holidays. When men show such an extraordinary proclivity to idleness and pleasure, what reason have we to think that they would ever work, unless they were obliged to it by immediate necessity?[45]

He likewise criticized what had become at that time a large network of charity schools for pauper children and orphans that educated them for a life in service and virtue insofar as institutions "inspired . . . by pity or compassion . . . had the effect of encouraging the children in their proclivity to sloth and vice and incapacitating them for a life of poverty and hard work."[46]

Without stating it in such harsh terms, Hume's account of utility reached the same conclusion about the poor as Mandeville. Was there a way, however, that utility might redeem them? For Hume, the solution lies in his argument for free will, which goes like this: We see a person's past pleasure-inducing and harm-minimizing actions, and we infer a good character. We see a person's good character, and we infer that his future actions will be pleasure-inducing and harm-minimizing. Vice versa, we see a person's past harm-inflicting behaviors and we infer an evil character; we see an evil character, and we infer future harm-inflicting behaviors. Yet, we do not have access to the causal relation between the goodness or evil of the action and the goodness or evil of the character. We only have empirical access to one billiard ball moving and then the second billiard ball moving; we do not have access to the cause. In the same manner, we see one pleasure-inducing action (the first billiard ball) and then we see the good effects (the second billiard ball). We cannot reason to a causal free will from observing the results of the actions.

Yet without seeing the cause, we do have a sense impression of pleasure when we see the conjunction of a person's pleasure-inducing/good actions and the good things flowing from those actions. We give praise to the conjunction of good actions and good effects, and we place blame to the conjunction of evil actions and evil effects. But people could only be blameworthy or praiseworthy, if they are free. Thus, we can *infer* that there is freedom of the will. The actors are deemed praiseworthy or blameworthy because the conjunction of their actions and the results flowing from the actions are experienced as pleasurable or painful in the observer, who can mete out praise or blame. Thus, Hume posited the reality of free will based on an argument rising out of his empiricism, his skepticism on causation, and the centrality of pleasure and pain as the moral sense.

We can now return to the question of whether the poor had full agency. Hume would have never agreed that the poor lacked free will, but his system still sets up the poor as lacking robust agency. As we noted earlier, the poor were dependent upon the wealthy at two levels—for their livelihoods and for the sense of pleasure they got from being associated with the wealthy. Hume does not address what ought to be done for the poor. He did, however, believe that the poor ought not to be valorized as virtuous. As we already saw, alms giving by the rich to the poor would result only in momentary pleasure for the giver and the receiver of alms, and induce laziness in the poor receiver. Actually, dealing with the problem of the poor was a little too close to the ground for the philosopher.

But in the end, he did not need to. All he needed to do was to set the wheels in motion for the next generation of thinkers—Bentham, Malthus, and Ricardo—to engineer poverty (or at least the poor) out of existence by grinding "rogues honest, and idle men industrious"—in other words, to turn immoral and unfree men into moral and prosperous figures, who would have a more robust free will. As we saw, Bentham, Malthus, and Ricardo, deployed the emerging "sciences" to abstract from poor individuals and to focus on poverty as the condition. Yet the seeds for imagining the poor to be without agency were sowed by Hume. In a theory where wealth defined freedom and the good (pleasure), Hume created a philosophical framework that naturalized the moral superiority of the rich and cast the poor into an abyss of moral turpitude defined by the unremitting pain of their existence. Hypothetically free, within Hume's framework, the poor could not be fully free because they were caught up in their condition and in need of inducement to exit their state of uselessness. They needed the wealthy—or the state—to elevate them out of the condition of poverty.

Thus, Bentham deployed a Humean metaphysics through the springs of action—those various social mechanisms that would spring the poor past their laziness and their overly active libido. Bentham, ever the engineer, would seek to solve the problem, not ponder the meaning of the problem for something so obscure as "free will." But it was also Humean philosophy that inspired Mill, even while he attempted to correct

Bentham's excesses, and it was Mill who inspired Knight and the economic imaginary of the twentieth and twenty-first centuries. Of course, most contemporary economists as well as those forwarding the neuroscientific narrative of morality would happily acknowledge Hume as their starting point.

But we seem to be missing a piece. After all, it is the question of causation that science attempts to explicate. Hume knew that knowing causes was nearly impossible, and he was wise enough to be careful with attributing causes, even while he reduced all rational and moral behaviors to utility maximization. What is at stake, then, is the ontology of causes, the ontology of power. Morals are the behaviors one sees at end of biological powers/causes and following techno-scientific powers over biology, as well as the deployment and execution of biopolitical-economic powers. Or so, our Humean economists and neuroscientists have led us to believe. Once one knows the truths of reality, one can intervene. While this attitude is certainly true of Hume, it was the same for Hume's predecessor, the progenitor not only of Hume's empiricism and skepticism, but also the father of techno-science: Francis Bacon. To him we now turn.

## Bacon's Power Ontology: From the New Work to the New *Polis*

As many of the figures we have studied thus far, Francis Bacon (1561–1626) stood at the nexus of philosophy, science, and political intrigue. Born into the penumbra of the Elizabethan court, his life charted a rugged forty-seven-year course of positions in the English government, parliament, and service to Elizabeth I and James I, eventually becoming a member of the Privy Council in 1616, Lord Keeper of the Great Seal in 1617, and Lord Chancellor and Baron of Verulam in 1618.[47] But political fortunes can be fleeting; in 1621, he fell from the halls of power, impeached for twenty-three charges of corruption, and was briefly imprisoned in the Tower of London due to unpaid debts. He spent the last five years of his life finalizing his philosophical and scholarly work.

Bacon sits at the origin of our story of economics—living and working at the end of the sixteenth century amid the changes caused by the enclosures and the birth pangs of the new economy. As a member of Parliament and political operative, he was deeply involved in the social and legislative questions surrounding the poor. In 1597, he introduced two bills against enclosure and depopulation, over against the interests of the powerful landlord class.[48] As noted earlier, he was a key member of the committee who wrote the precursor of the 1601 Act for Relief of the Poor.[49]

Bacon's *Novum Organum* sets out new directions for the interpretation of nature.[50] It establishes a new epistemological agenda for science while also setting science on a new practical orientation. Fundamentally, it helps to establish a new metaphysical order, shifting the social imaginary away from the premodern lifeworld in which the human had a place within the movement of the whole of reality, to our modern landscape in which human beings are set apart as unimportant spectators.[51] Bacon's new science was not just knowledge for knowledge's sake; it is meant to be put to work, to relieve the human estate, to relieve the human of its frailties. His optimism regarding the possibilities of such a science led him to write a second, fantasy book, *New Atlantis*. Here he imagines a utopian society—a new *polis*—built according to his new science.

Bacon focuses on building because it is work, the new work, the *novum organum*, that will transform the world. Bacon was most interested how natural, causal forces could be studied and mastered through knowledge. The use of force—power—is the means by which one controls the world—both natural and social. Knowledge of power enables one to know what to do, in both the natural and social realms, in order to efficiently cause new things to come into being. Bacon states:

> [W]e want all and everyone to be advised to reflect on the true ends of knowledge (*scientia*): not to seek it for amusement or for dispute, or to look down on others, or for profit or for face or for power or any such inferior ends, but for the uses and benefits of life, and to improve and conduct it in charity. For the angels fell because of an appetite for power; and men fell because of an appetite for knowledge.[52]

Just two sentences later, Bacon continues by noting that his *New Organon* is a work not for the laying down of dogma "but for human progress, and empowerment."[53] Knowledge is not to be sought for power, but it is nonetheless sought for empowerment. Knowledge is power; but it ought to be a power to bring effects into the world for good, not for self-aggrandizement. At the level of human action, the end/purpose of power over nature is human progress.

Yet the relationship of knowledge to power is very complex and bidirectional. Humans seek knowledge for empowerment, but first power must be exercised over nature so that nature will reveal her secrets. Knowledge, in other words, originates in nature rather than in the human mind. Knowledge derived in this inductive manner originates closer to the source and is more trustworthy than that putatively derived from speculative deduction. In opposing the inductive method to the deductive method, Bacon states: "They [the deductive reasoners] defeat and conquer their adversary by disputation; we conquer nature by work."[54] Inductive science is work done on and to nature. Inductive science is born in the "bowels of nature" and not in the minds of men.[55]

Knowledge—science—is work. Bacon, in explicating the relationship of knowledge to its object, notes that the inductive method both describes and interrogates nature. He refers to these two aspects of induction as the two parts of knowledge. Description of nature—the first part of knowledge—freely follows the contours of its object. However, much more can be learned when nature is "confined and harassed, when it is forced from its own condition by art and human agency, and pressured and moulded . . . since nature reveals herself more through the harassment of art than in her own proper freedom."[56] The work of the new scientists requires the vexation of nature; it must be harassed so that she gives up her secrets. For Bacon, then it is not mere induction, observation, or experience that grounds his empiricism; rather, it is the activity of manipulating and controlling reality so that observations can be made against the controlled condition. Bacon is an advocate of experimental, not merely experiential, science.[57]

This inductive nature of the new science likewise requires a radical rethinking of knowledge as it relates to causes. Bacon notes:

> The sorry state of current human knowledge is clear even from common expressions. It is right to lay down: "to know truly is to know by causes." It is also not bad to distinguish four causes: Material, Formal, Efficient, and Final. But of these the Final is a long way from being useful; in fact, it actually distorts the sciences except in the case of human actions. Discovery of Form is almost hopeless. And the Efficient and Material causes (as commonly sought and accepted, i.e., in themselves and apart from the latent process which leads to the Form) are perfunctory, superficial things, of almost no value for true, active knowledge.[58]

By latent process and latent structure, he means something akin to the hidden mechanism and hidden structure, which requires work to attain. Without such work, Bacon fears that a simplistic reading of cause and effect will lead to deception and not to true knowledge. He is skeptical, then, that knowing the causes is possible without inductive, empirical work, a skepticism he bequeathed to Hume. Only careful attention to efficient and material causes, which point to the deeper, more latent structure and processes, will get us closer to true knowledge. One may start with empirical experience of material causes and work one's way back to the efficient cause. But these themselves tend toward superficial and unstable claims. He continues noting that we creep along by investigating material and efficient causes, with hopes of constructing perfect knowledge, which is knowledge of the laws of nature, which he takes to be the forms of nature—the formal causes. But arriving at formal causes is very difficult.

Thus, Bacon emphasizes different aspects of the four Aristotelian causes; he balances them differently than does Aristotle. Final causes are precluded because we only know the final cause if the motion is the result of human action. To seek knowledge of final causes in nature would be to bias one's observations and thus to confuse the seeker of knowledge. Formal causes are truly laws of nature, and to know them is to know truly. But knowledge of formal causes is difficult, and must be derived from a process that works backward from material and efficient causes, toward the latent structures and processes.[59] So, in his division of the sciences, metaphysics is "inquiry after forms";[60] physics is the examination of material and efficient causes, along with the latent process and latent structure, which point to the forms.

It is these forms that are the prize; it is here that knowledge becomes power: "[H]e who knows forms comprehends the unity of nature," and so he can "bring forth things which have never been achieved."[61] Knowledge of formal causes, which takes inductive, empirical work, gives one power—to "bring forth things" never before produced. Productivity, utility is the aim of human knowing. For Bacon, this power that emerges from science results in two practical arts. One art is subsidiary to physics and the other to metaphysics: mechanics and magic, respectively. Each art gives "command over nature," magic the more so because it uses the forms—the laws of nature—to give command over nature. Perfect knowledge, true knowledge is the power to control nature.

Paolo Rossi reads Bacon in light of the Renaissance Magus, the master, who seeks the secrets of nature, through astrology, alchemy, and necromancy, a form of Gnosticism that arose in the Renaissance. There were those who studied black magic, which sought to reverse the laws of nature, while those who sought the secrets of white magic sought to align their own purposes with laws of nature. According to Rossi, Bacon—Puritan that he was—sought the latter, but he purified his intentions by making the project one that was aimed at relief of the human condition.[62] Sophie Weeks, however, claims that Bacon's project should be read as "an instauration of magic, rather than as an institutional and methodological preparative to the emergence of modern science."[63] Whether one agrees with Rossi or Weeks, it still seems that, as Rossi shows, the alchemical appeal to sacred texts rather than induction is the primary criticism that Bacon levels against magic. Insofar, as the alchemist was experimenting, Bacon approved. The goal, as hard as it is to achieve, was mastery over nature, whether the results be achieved through mechanics or magic. In this sense, Bacon was primarily trying to rehabilitate magic through the new work of knowledge.

With Bacon, then, we see in embryonic form the Newtonian understanding of causes, of forces acting on bodies in locomotion. This understanding of locomotion and of the forces that make movement possible achieves fruition in Newtonian physics and would in time come to influence physiology in the nineteenth century. Claude Bernard—eulogized as the Newton of physiological science—would analogously understand the human body as a series of forces moving the material of the body. What must have been magic to Bacon became for us merely what follows from knowledge of efficient and formal causes, namely, technological control. Here then, we find the inspiration of neuroscientists like Viding and Frith, Persson and Savulescu, Walker and Douglas, as well as Sam Harris. The new method in science must vex or harass nature in order for her to give up her secrets, the latent structures and processes of efficient and material causation. In order to have control over it, one must first instrument nature in order to know it. What Bacon calls forms of nature, or laws of nature, became for us the forces behind the mechanisms—one thing falling on another in the latent, mechanical process. Moreover, what was once the lofty metaphysical structures of Aristotle and the occult magic of Bacon's time would in time fall from its elevated perch and become for us mere physics and mechanics.[64]

So, what of Aristotle's fourth cause—the final cause, the *telos*? As we saw, Bacon precludes the possibility of final causes except in the case of human action. In the rest of the sciences, final causes only confuse if they are imagined to be at work from the beginning of the investigation. Bacon only allows final causation back into his schema of knowledge after severely limiting its scope and bringing it into the realm of human control. Final causes make sense only if deployed in human activity, as a name for the end that a human actor wants to enact. Thus, within Bacon's schema, the final cause provides the justification for the instrumentation of nature, that for the sake of which knowledge is justified politically. The new science exists "to relieve the human estate."[65]

In other words, in Bacon's new empirical science, the pursuit of knowledge is morally, politically, and epistemologically justified by its ability to bring about effects in the world. How do we know that we know something? We know that we know something when we can manipulate the beings of the world through the deployment of knowledge and get them to act for our purposes. In fact, the definition of knowledge under patent law today is precisely this; it can be patented as knowledge if we can do something with the information.[66] True science seeks to understand the power of nature, of the laws of nature, of formal causation. True knowledge, patentable knowledge, is that which can be deployed to control nature and bring about effects in the world. This is power to be used for human empowerment.

Thus, it was not just Bacon's method—induction—that caused a great shift in science; it was equally his understanding of the laws of nature, the metaphysics of formal causes—the power behind efficient causes. As early as Bacon, more than pure observational science of inductive reasoners was at work. Indeed, we see the ordering of knowledge directed at human ends. In other words, Bacon's new work of science was already on the hunt for mechanical manipulation of nature, to relieve the human estate.[67] Already at the time of Bacon, we find the diminution of robustly teleological world, ordered by the hand of God. We find that all purposes of knowing, and thus all purposes for that which is known, are subservient to human ends, subservient to a post hoc political purpose added onto the true metaphysics of the laws of a mechanical nature. According to Bacon, the justification for going forward on the quest for knowledge is empowerment over nature in the crassest of all ways. The justification for instrumenting nature is to harass her to give up her secrets so that she might be coerced and ordered to human production. In other words, science is techno-logical, in much the way that Heidegger means it; we must harness the power in nature in order to control it for human purposes.[68]

The goal of all this knowledge is to achieve a new order, a new Atlantis, if you will. Jacqueline L. Cowan has argued that the function of Bacon's work, *New Atlantis*, is to put into Old World terms what Bacon's New World might look like.[69] Following the familiar genre of a travel saga, the sailors happen upon Bensalem, a perfect society with harmony between religion and science, organized according to natural philosophical knowledge, and put to perfect use for the peace and harmony of men. Bacon's utopian *New Atlantis* valorizes the way that knowledge should be achieved and deployed—its final cause, the relief of the human estate. Peter Lucas has argued that *New Atlantis* was a work of science fiction that influenced how science should go, with wonders achieved by organized and methodical state-funded natural philosophy.[70]

The human mind, for Bacon, should be organized by work to uncover the hidden mysteries of nature, not simply for the power one can wield over nature *qua* power, but for the purposes of relieving the human estate, in order to build a great, peaceful, and harmonious society, a new Atlantis that is no longer fictional. Like Hume, Bacon was skeptical about the mind's ability to unlock nature's secrets, but, unlike Hume, Bacon held that causes could be known through careful work. Where Bacon was skeptical of final causes, Hume is skeptical of knowledge of formal causes. Both remained far removed from the source of all knowledge, sense experience. If one cannot know final causes or formal causes in nature, one certainly cannot know final and formal causes in human nature. Thus, the skepticism of Bacon and Hume, taken together, denatures the human. It is between Bacon and Hume in their skeptical empiricism that anthropology begins to falter.

However, what is revealed through skeptical empiricism is a knowledge of a power ontology, the means to control, to build toward relieving the human estate, according to Bacon, and to protect the estate of powerful, propertied men. In other words, skeptical empiricism gave birth to a kind of optimism that one could actually build Bensalem. For Hume that meant the building of society according to the principle of utility, grounded in pleasure and pain aimed at a society that protected the estate of propertied men, those who are capable of pleasure and whose treasures, in their mere perception, delight the poor who hope to be associated with such men.

Through the more careful empirical science of Ricardo and Malthus, and inspired by Townsend's parable of the goats and dogs and Mandeville's parable of the bees, we see the old world of Christian care for the poor, giving way to the *New Atlantis*, where there would be no poor at all. *Bios*, hunger, is the chief experience of pain that is should prompt the poor into industry. *Bios* is aimed at *polis*, and if one could only build a proper social apparatus—call it a Panopticon—of control, those impoverished, idle rogues that can be ground honest and industrious could enter into the class of propertied mean of wealth, and those that cannot be ground, be cast among the beasts. Some humans, after all, are prosocial and belong in Bensalem; others are antisocial—thrown about by their biology and uncontrollable even by the Panopticon—and thus should not be entitled to the protections of the state, as imagined by Sam Harris. By the time we get to Paul Zak, Bensalem is the market.

Our thesis has been that at the heart of the popularizers of neuroscience, and at the heart of the neuroscience of morality, is a problematic anthropology. The thin, pathetic anthropology at the heart of neuroscience imagines humans as thrown about by *bios*—genes, brains, moral tastes—which can be controlled through the proper political economy, a biopolitical economy bent to grind the antisocial, and idle and vicious rogues into honest, virtuous, and industrious prosocial producers. Thus, it is this Baconian-Humean anthropology that is at the heart of the newest Atlantis, the neoliberal political economy. But must it be that way?

## Adam Smith: An Unlikely Hero

In Part 1 of this book, we traced the anthropology of the emerging neuroscience of morality, suggesting that it adheres to the anthropology of the broader economic imaginary, crystallized in neoliberalism. In Part II of this book, we have shown how that this economic imaginary draws its inspiration from David Hume. But although our contemporary popularizers of neuroscience tip their hat to Hume, they also, along with their neoliberal counterparts, largely cite Adam Smith as their forefather. However, it is not Smith who is the origin of their highly determined capitalized person; rather, that figure filtered through Bentham, Mill, Knight, Friedman, and Becker is the offspring of Hume and Bacon. Despite their homage, our neuroscientists and neoliberals are not the heirs of Smith.

Here at the end of our study, we are going to make this case by sketching the fuller anthropology that animated the work of Adam Smith. In fact, theologian Christina McRorie argues that economics qua science needs a richer anthropology.[71] We are by no means claiming that Smith's anthropology is the correct moral anthropology, nor are we by any means saying that Smith's anthropology is the best among several options. Smith's anthropology is more communal. Even while beginning in affectation, he does not collapse into emotivism, because his understanding of human behavior is tempered by reason. It is altogether more aspirational. We agree with MacIntyre's point that Smith and Hume are the products of their mid-eighteenth-century British context, assuming it to be the natural state of affairs universally. However, there is a stark difference between Smith and Hume that even prompted Smith to revise his *Theory of Moral Sentiments* in order to better counter Hume.[72] If there is to be a possible alternative to the biopolitical power ontology of Bacon in our contemporary techno-neuro-science, might Adam Smith—of all people—point the way?

Adam Smith (1723–1790) was a Scottish philosopher variously referred to as the Father of Economics, the Father of Capitalism, and certainly one of the founders of political economy. His first book, *A Theory of Moral Sentiments*, was published in 1759, during his thirteen-year term on faculty at the University of Glasgow. Generally characterized as a work of moral philosophy, the book met with great acclaim, leading him to eventually leave the university and spend the rest of his life traveling through Europe as a tutor (with much better remuneration) or as an independent scholar. His second major work, *An Inquiry into the Nature and Causes of the Wealth of Nations*, was published in 1776 to equal acclaim as his first book. It is generally characterized as a work of political economy.

How to understand the relationship between these two texts has been referred to classically as "the Adam Smith Problem."[73] On its face, the *Wealth of Nations* appears to be detachable from *Theory of Moral Sentiments*. The differences in genre and focus between the two volumes have led many to read the *Wealth of Nations* as a stand-alone volume or to claim that in the intervening twenty years, Smith changed his mind. Others read them in continuity, noting that he finished the revisions for the sixth edition of *Theory of Moral Sentiments* shortly before his death in 1790, well after the publication of *Wealth of Nations*.[74] Economist Dierdre McCloskey argues that the books are the first two components of an interrelated trilogy, one on temperance (*Theory of Moral Sentiments*), one on prudence (*The Wealth of Nations*), and a third on justice, which was to be a work of jurisprudence and was never completed.[75]

While studying at Oxford, Smith read Hume's *Treatise*. Upon meeting him in 1750, they became lifelong friends. Although Hume had essentially completed his major philosophical works before Smith began writing, as Dennis Rasmussen notes, "almost everything Smith wrote shows unmistakable signs of Hume's influence." Importantly for our purposes, however, what we find is that "Smith almost never simply adopted Hume's views wholesale. On the contrary, he modified almost everything he touched . . . when it comes to moral philosophy Smith's views are generally more nuanced and sophisticated than Hume's."[76]

Space precludes a thorough presentation of Smith's work on economics. We turn to him here primarily due to the frequency with which his name is invoked within both neoliberalism and within the neuroscientific narrative of morality. In these places, scholars and popularizers primarily pay homage to his moral philosophy, and so this is what we will engage here. As we will see, Smith's anthropology is more holistic and thicker than Hume's, such that it seems odd that so many of the positivist economists would try to link themselves to Smith when it is Hume that they mimic. His understanding of morality and virtue is likewise so much more robust than Hume's.

We will say more on Smith's position on the poor, particularly their relationship to his wider anthropology, at the end of this section, but we do want to note here that where the Poor Laws animated our figures in Chapter 5, Polanyi marks the absence of this topic from Smith's work: "In Adam Smith's great work, poor relief was no problem as yet; only a decade later it was raised as a broad issue in Townsend's *Dissertation on the Poor Laws* and never ceased to occupy men's minds for another century and a half."[77] Yet it was not absent from his mind. Smith was deeply critical of the Settlement Act of 1662, which, as part of the Poor Laws, had tied the poor to their local parishes, restricting their mobility and their freedom to choose their occupations, those of their children, where they could live, and where they could work.[78] He was also greatly concerned about wealth inequality, insisting that "no society can flourish, the members of which, in their great majority, are poor and miserable . . . [For Smith] it was impossible that society should get wealthier and wealthier and the people poorer and poorer."[79]

For Polanyi, Smith marks the end of an era; in his era, indeed, the state was invented, but he differed from the generation of Malthus and Ricardo, who held that economics was a sphere of nature and not of community. Wealth for Smith was "an aspect of the life of the community, to the purposes of which it remained subordinate . . . The economic sphere, with him, [was] not yet subject to laws of its own that provide us with a standard of good and evil."[80] In other words, unlike for Hume, Malthus, and Ricardo, the economic sphere did not serve for Smith as a source of the moral law and political obligation. He also explicitly excludes biological and geographic factors as causal economic factors from the very beginning of *The Wealth of Nations*.[81] Rather, for Smith, the source of morality—and, indeed, the moral life—lies elsewhere.

Human nature was denatured by Hume. As outlined earlier, for Hume utility—the advantage one creates for oneself (or an advantage that is created for another) by reducing pain and increasing pleasure—is the ground of all morality. As we saw with Hume, justice and benevolence are artificial virtues—not found in nature or in God—constructed for the sake of utility. Sympathy was the ability of one human to feel the pains and pleasures of another that prompted one to put oneself in the other's place, to imagine how the other feels and, by feeling the displeasure of the other's displeasure, was induced to act to the other's advantage. Doing so elicits the moral approbation—the moral approval—of others, which is pleasurable to oneself. Thus, Hume's moral scheme was primarily about one's own pleasures. It is in being useful that one feels the moral approval of others. This basis grounds moral judgment.

Paul Sagar argues that Smith's account of the human in *Theory of Moral Sentiments* was a direct response to Hume's moral anthropology.[82] Where Smith likewise begins with sympathy, his account of sympathy is radically different from Hume's. In fact, for Smith, sympathy—not utility—is the ground of both his morality and his anthropology. Kathryn Blanchard even names his vision of the human person, *Homo sympatheticus*.[83] It provides a much thicker grounding for moral judgment, specifically via two sets of virtues—propriety and "merit or demerit." These virtues structure Parts I and II of the

*Theory of Moral Sentiments*, respectively.[84] The virtue of propriety is born out of the "sentiment or affection of the heart."[85] As McRorie notes, for Smith a person evaluates "the propriety of her actions by imaginatively identifying with her fellow and deciding whether we should act and feel the same in her shoes."[86] The virtues of merit or demerit are essentially the judgment of praiseworthiness or blameworthiness, or what in his time was referred to as approbation. One moves from being moved by others to creating a new order that creates approbation, which creates cohesiveness with society.

In Part III of the *Theory of Moral Sentiments*, Smith brings these virtues of propriety and merit/demerit together to provide the basis for moral judgment, an activity exercised by the impartial spectator. The impartial spectator is a work of the human imagination that stands above one's own interests to make judgments. The impartial spectator must adjudicate between what one imagines the other feels and what the other actually feels, between perception and reality. One can do this because one has the ability to step back, to abstract from one's own sentiments and the imagined sentiments of the other. This sounds a lot like Aristotelian phronesis. One has to set aside one's own interests and like a judge make a moral judgment. Like all the virtues, this activity of impartial observation is an activity that requires practice. Moral judgment—like propriety and merit/demerit—is gained and honed by practice in social settings. In making these points, Smith counters Hume's claim that the virtues are artificial by showing that, while they are of social origin, it is natural for the human to gain them through practice.

The ground of these three virtues, and therefore moral judgment, is sympathy. As McRorie notes, sympathy for Smith is not simply an emotion but rather a faculty, "a design," as she calls it, "akin to humanity's operating system: it describes the instinctual cognitive and affective ability to understand another's motivations and feelings, through imaginative identification with the other."[87] For Smith, sympathy is far more complex and wide-ranging than Hume's concentration on pleasure and pain. For one thing, it is much more interactional—it is not merely putting oneself in the position of the other and imagining what it might feel like. Sympathy for Hume is much more of an I-It relation; for Smith it is more of an I-Thou relation.[88] The being of the "I" is intimately tied up with the "Thous" of a community. Moreover, it is not merely about imagining what the person is feeling, but about imaginatively climbing into the other's skin, with careful attention to the situation, the other's history and social location, and then imagining how it feels. "Sympathy, therefore, does not arise so much from the view of the passion, as from that of the situation which excites it."[89] Much more is engaged than mere impression—it is to feel another's emotion "in your own breast."[90] Sympathy is natural to the human; reason deployed by the impartial spectator is natural to the human. And unlike the individualism of Hume's system, sociality is likewise natural to the human. Smith clearly has an understanding of the whole of human being taken up in human activity—feeling, rational moral judgment, all contextualized in the social relations of a human community.

This understanding of sympathy provides a more accurate lens for interpreting the oft-quoted and oft-misinterpreted passage from *The Wealth of Nations*—the vignette of the butcher and the baker. Coming right near the beginning of the *Wealth of Nations* (book one, chapter two), Smith opines:

> It is not from the benevolence of the butcher, the brewer or the baker that we expect our dinner, but from their regard to their own interest. We address ourselves not to their humanity but to their self-love, and never talk to them of our own necessities but of their advantages.[91]

This passage is ordinarily interpreted to suggest that Smith reduced all of economics and morality to self-interest. Robert Black, however, reminds us that, first, this passage must be read in light of its immediate context (the first two chapters of *The Wealth of Nations*) and in light of Smith's corpus as a whole (particularly his notion of sympathy in *Theory of Moral Sentiments*).[92] What Smith is describing here is an instance of the practice of the faculty of sympathy—the first step in the engagement between ourselves and the baker is an act of sympathy, an act of imaginatively identifying with the baker, understanding her motivations and feelings, and approving (if appropriate) her price and actions. The impartial spectator has not yet been fully engaged in the deployment of judgment. For in such situations, we must also view our own conduct through the baker's eyes, allowing judgment on the self. Thus, the first step in exchange is not self-interest. Rather, it is putting oneself in the other's place and identifying with her or his interests. The ground of exchange is first and foremost social cohesion.[93]

But sympathy does involve a judgement to be made. As Sagar notes, for Hume:

> When we enter imaginatively into the situation of others, if we find a correspondence between the way that we imagine we would feel were we them, and the way we believe that they actually feel, then this correspondence automatically pleases. By contrast if we find that there is a lack of congruence between how we imagine we would feel, and how we think that they do feel, then we are pained (as in both cases is the other party).[94]

Thus, for Hume, sympathy cannot move beyond utility and one's own pleasure. But for Smith, it is much more complex. For one thing, sympathy also allows judgment of the self, as we reverse the vector, "plac[ing] ourselves in the situation of another man, and view[ing] [our conduct and motives], as it were, with his eyes."[95] Based on the feedback of his peers, who may come to see *him* as blameworthy or praiseworthy in his judgments, the impartial spectator might modify his judgment.

As such, sympathy is integrally connected to justice. "There must, Smith contended, be some pre-conventional internal corrective to the pursuit of self-interest, upon which the conventional structure of operative justice was ultimately built."[96] For Smith:

> Nature has implanted in the human breast that consciousness of ill-desert, those terrors of merited punishment which attend upon its violation, as the great safeguard of the association of mankind, to protect the weak, to curb the violent, and to chastise the guilty.[97]

Thus, justice is the practice that nurtures a capacity that one already has for self-judgment. It is born in the potency of a human nature developmentally and socially nurtured. Justice, then, is not merely the protection of private property, nor is it merely the curbing of one's self-interest from without. Rather, it is the capacity to learn how to curb self-interest from within, to allow the experience of one's community—grounded in the sociality of the human actor—to place limits on the self-interestedness. The justice of the impartial spectator wells up from within as a practice between oneself in congress with the other and with the larger group of others.

This faculty also allows judgment of the self, as we "place ourselves in the situation of another man, and view [our conduct and motives], as it were, with his eyes."[98] In Smith's words about sympathy:

> It is not the soft power of humanity, it is not that feeble spark of benevolence which Nature has lighted up in the human heart, that is thus capable of counteracting the strongest impulses of self-love. It is a stronger power, a more forcible motive, which exerts itself upon such occasions. It is reason, principle, conscience, the inhabitant of the breast, the man within, the great judge and arbiter of our conduct. It is he who, whenever we are about to act so as to affect the happiness of others, calls to us, with a voice capable of astonishing the most presumptuous of our passions, that we are but one of the multitude, in no respect better than any other in it.[99]

As Sagar notes, Smith directly addresses Hume's "soft power of humanity" and "feeble spark of benevolence." Sympathy is not mere sentiment, mere preference, mere moral taste. It is, along with the virtues it engages, partly moral and partly intellectual. One has to imaginatively switch between what one imagines one would feel if one were the other person, the way one believes the other person actually feels. Thus, the faculty of sympathy in concert with the impartial spectator establishes and maintains our connectedness with other persons, while also allowing us to judge ourselves. Reason for Smith is not simply the capacity to calculate utility maximization; nor is reason concerned solely with individual utility maximization. Rather, reason in the form of a disinterested spectator "can counter the excesses of self-love, should one choose to heed its voice."[100] There is no divide between emotion and reason, but a thicker integration of the human person who perceives and acts as unified whole.

Freedom lies in our ability to heed—or not—this voice of the internal spectator. For Smith, "God has put this into our design as part of the overall plan. This is a design with which humans can cooperate in varying degrees; it facilitates moral action, without commanding it."[101] As Blanchard notes, freedom for Smith is

> freedom *from* the unbearable human experience of loneliness and lack of sympathy; and freedom *for* the happiness that comes from flourishing human social relationships that arise from mutual sympathy. Smith's vision of humane freedom can best be summed up as integrity—the wholeness that comes from aligning one's passions with one's intellectual opinions about what is good and appropriate.[102]

Thus, because of Smith's thicker anthropology—the faculty of sympathy, which binds persons to one another, always measured by the impartial spectator—freedom is more robust for him and not something generated by those with industry to rise to the level of the propertied classes. Freedom is never quite the freedom as imagined by Friedman, a self-interested freedom; it is always a freedom (and a self-interest) tempered by sociality.

Given this thicker anthropology, where the faculty of sympathy unites affect and reason, permitting a self-reflexive critical ability to sit in judgment of oneself, and balanced by sociality, virtue plays a critical role throughout Smith's corpus. In fact, Dierdre McCloskey has claimed that Smith is the last virtue theorist in economics. Whereas traditionally, there were four cardinal virtues and three theological virtues, McCloskey points out that for Smith five virtues were critical to the fully moral person—love (or benevolence), courage, temperance, justice, and self-interested prudence.[103] McCloskey notes that while the 1759 edition of TMS has a virtue ethic, his addition of Part VI in 1790 made that clear. "I have inserted," he wrote on February 2, 1789, to his publisher, apologizing for delays, "a complete new sixth part containing a practical system of morality, under the title of the Character of Virtue."[104] The virtue of love—that is to say, benevolence—acted to adjudicate between the competing four cardinal virtues. Smith developed this in conversation with the Christian philosophy of Hutcheson, rejecting Hutcheson's move to set aside self-love as anything but base. For Smith, proper self-love, or proper self-regard, became an essential feature of his moral philosophy. Fellow-feeling was grounded empirically in the observation that the actor took pleasure in seeing others happy and in bringing about the happiness of others.

It is thus that Smith can claim, at the end of *A Theory of Moral Sentiments*, that his system corresponds "pretty exactly" with Aristotle's.[105] Samuel Fleischacker also pronounces Smith a virtue ethicist, with propriety as the mean between excess and defect, or when he points to temperance, or his emphasis on habit, or virtuous friendships.[106] While we are not claiming that Smith is an Aristotelian, even if his view aligns with Aristotle's in many regards, we are claiming that his moral anthropology is more robust and that what he offers has a virtue-based understanding of the practice of moral judgment—both of which have been lost in contemporary economics and neuroscience.[107]

These differences in his anthropology and moral philosophy inflect his economics. Polanyi cites Smith's very strong sense of community founded in the faculty of sympathy as that to which both wealth and self-interest are to be subordinated. Thus, he was not, as Stigler, Becker, and Friedman suggest, someone bent on maximization of human self-interest, which required independence and isolation, resulting in utility for society. He is not a utility-maximizing radical individual. Concerns for the well-being of the community underlie the *Wealth of Nations*. As Blanchard notes, Smith was disturbed by the economic trends of his day and the self-interestedness of the business class. Smith objected to the use of governmental powers to enrich the mercantilists or the monarch himself at the expense of the common good.[108]

Paul Mueller also suggests that Smith also has a much more nuanced account of wealth and economic activity than we find in the Chicago School. Smith did not promote the accumulation of wealth, so much as the production of goods and services.[109] His account of consumption did not promote consumption for its own sake. Rather, for Smith, consumption is teleological—it can either contribute to a person's well-being or "be wasteful, extravagant, ill-conceived, and socially-damaging."[110]

The *telos* of wealth had to do with the qualia of flourishing. Happiness consists in tranquility and enjoyment, the latter foundational for the former.[111] His praise or criticism of wealth or consumption hangs on the tranquility produced. Consumption is natural, insofar as it meets basic bodily and physical needs given to us by nature.[112] As for Aristotle, consumption is titrated to natural needs. Smith is critical of any consumption that is not directed to moral ends. Thus, it is not just consumption *qua* consumption, but consumption within a teleological framework, that leads Smith to conclude "that 'every prodigal appears to be a publick enemy, and every frugal man a publick benefactor.'"[113]

Unlike those economists who root modern economics in preference satisfaction, Smith is rather more frugal and temperate. Smith splits the difference between the utility-maximizing preference-satisfying spender, and, rather more like the Stoics, separates happiness and consumption completely. Rather, frugality permits one to consume within the teleological framework, which gives more happiness. One is not frugal in order to accumulate; one is frugal in order to contribute to the good of the community.[114] Thus, for Smith, the human person is defined neither by economic activity nor by self-interest.

These positions on the relationships between economics and human identity also shape his understanding of the poor. Amartya Sen, in his Introduction to a recent edition of *Theory of Moral Sentiments*, makes clear how Smith differed from his counterparts that we have engaged thus far both in his concern for the poor and workers, and in his egalitarian understanding of humanity. As noted earlier, Smith was deeply concerned about poverty and inequality, and the punitive measures in the Poor Laws, such as the Settlement Act. He advocated for public interventions on behalf of the poor such as free education and poverty relief, and was always attuned to the ways in which economic practices worked against the underdog and the workingman, noting, for example, "When the regulation, therefore, is in favor of the workmen, it is always just and equitable, but it is sometimes otherwise when in favor of the masters."[115]

More strikingly, Smith voices repeatedly a strong sense of the equality of persons regardless of class or nationality (and perhaps even gender), tracing inequalities to social rather than natural causes, what Sen refers to as his "strong epistemic inclination to see people everywhere as being essentially similar."[116] Rather than seeing nature as contributing between differences in the status of persons, *Wealth of Nations* suggests that the difference "between a philosopher and a common street porter . . . seems to arise not so much from nature as from habit, custom, and education."[117] Elsewhere he elaborates on the stark differences in the living and working conditions between "persons of rank and fortune," who have leisure for educating and improving themselves, and "the common people." The latter have no time or resources for leisure, and must start working "as soon as they are able to work" and therefore are bereft of any opportunity for self-improvement "or even to think of anything else."[118]

This egalitarian sensibility extends for Smith globally. He was deeply critical of the oppressive actions of the East India Company in India, especially with regard to the devastating famine of 1770; and he defended the Irish against British derision.[119] As Sen notes:

Smith is also incensed by the presumption of superior racial endowments of the white man, and at one stage even bursts into unconcealed wrath: "There is not a negro from the coast of Africa who does not, in this respect, possess a degree of magnanimity which the soul of his sordid master is too often scarce capable of conceiving."[120]

Thus, Smith differs in many ways from his contemporaneous counterparts. He remains altogether more teleologically oriented, where persons are integrated into communities, ordered not merely to self-interest, but to the happiness that comes from being integral parts of larger communities. He is not just a virtue ethicist because he draws on virtues as concepts, but because he champions—over against Hume and the Modern Moral theorists—a number of crucial components of the virtue tradition. Where Hume and Kant are primarily concerned with finding the ground of moral knowledge—Hume grounding it in the senses of pleasure and pain, Kant in the reasoned categorical imperative—Smith seems to have grounded moral knowledge in self-knowledge, namely, temperance, cultivated by the reasoning of the impartial spectator. He does not propose a test of right or wrong by appealing to some categorical imperative, or to a moral calculus of the greatest good for the greatest number of people. He is concerned with the one who would judge the goods possible on practical considerations over against a scientifically derived set of rules, with an eye to communal flourishing for others and self-flourishing in the midst of community.[121] He would do so using the habits of the virtues cultivated in community that at the same time move one toward that the telos of friendship and community. In this, he is rather more like Aristotle at the end of book 9 of the Nicomachean ethics, or Hannah Arendt in *The Human Condition*. Humans only truly flourish as social animals.

If all these scholars are correct in their readings of Smith's corpus an important question arises: how has he become identified with the modern *Homo economicus*? Here we turn to his relationship with David Hume. As Fleischacker notes, "Smith's thought circles around Hume's: there is virtually nothing in either TMS or WN without some sort of source or anticipation in Hume, although there is also almost no respect in which Smith agrees entirely with Hume."[122] Marie Martin concurs: "For anyone familiar with Hume's moral theory, Smith's *Theory of Moral Sentiments* reveals unmistakable signs of the profound influence of Hume, not only in the views expressed, but in the examples used, the descriptions of sentiments and in the criticisms of rival theories."[123]

Where does he agree with Hume? First, Smith follows Hume in general in tracing moral judgment, ultimately, to feelings. As Fleischacker notes:

> The impartial spectator is supposed to be free of partial feelings—feelings that depend on a stake it might have in a dispute, or on blind favoritism or dislike for one party or the other—but it is not supposed to be free of feelings altogether, nor to reach for a principle it might derive from reason alone, independent of feeling.[124]

Thus, according to Fleischacker, sentiment is the first step in a process of moral deliberation. Sentiment is the glue that one has that binds a community, one to another. Smith and Hume are in agreement here.

But at the same time, Hume and Smith diverge in two ways, particularly on the role of utility and relatedly on the teleological nature of human being. As Fleischacker notes: "none of Smith's predecessors had developed such an essentially social conception of the self. Hutcheson and Hume both see human beings as having a natural disposition to care about the good of their society, but for Smith, all our feelings, whether self-interested or benevolent, are constituted by a process of socialization."[125] Sentiment can be cultivated; it is not merely a fact of human feeling as it is for Hume, or merely biological in origin, the way that sentiment, moral intuition, or moral tastes are for Zak or Haidt. In short, Smith's anthropology is much more balanced between the faculties of sympathy and reason, while also participating in and ordered to the social.

Thus, even though feelings or sentiments are starting points for moral judgment, they are not merely instincts, originating in some amoral observable fact without moral import, nor are moral feelings unmediated by the impartial spectator. For Smith, over against Hume, there is no is-ought distinction in human nature. Some sentiments are better than others (oughts—we should have them) and we must "learn to acquire new sentiments or alter the ones we have."[126] Thus, sentiment—whether positive (as in feelings of love) or negative as in feelings of repulsion—can be deceptive, and must be refined through deliberation—a top-down control. One must judge the feelings in order to know whether one ought to act on those feelings, for surely an initial sentiment of love toward another is not sufficient to make an action morally legitimate; nor is repulsion sufficient to know whether one ought to overcome repulsion in order to act morally. Thus, we learn when to trust sentiment and when not to trust it. We are not bandied about, thrown to and fro by sentiment. Sentiment can be educated toward some good for Smith. Therefore, Smith and Hume diverge most significantly on the question of utility, for utility is derived from sentiment in Hume in a very different way than in Smith.[127]

Marie Martin outlines these differences in detail, noting that their positions are diametrically opposed. For Hume, utility was not only the "foundation of the chief part of morals," but because sense impressions are disconnected from reason, the calculative work of utility is more disjointed.[128] Yet for Smith, utility is never the source of virtue and rarely the source of moral approbation. Insofar as the faculty of sympathy works in concert with the faculty of reason and the impartial spectator, his account is more holistic, nuanced, and textured.[129]

Moreover, it is teleological as well. Hume following Bacon eschews teleology. Yet for Smith, as Martin notes, "the natural world is ordered into a system of final causes by a benevolent Providence." All of nature, including human nature, has "some end or purpose."

> Nature's "economy" is such that we are endowed with no principles of thought or action with any tendency to conflict with our welfare unless the same principle has an even greater tendency to promote it. "This benevolent and all-wise Being can admit into the system of his government no partial evil which is not necessary for the universal good." Smith's famous economic doctrine of the hidden hand, the beneficial but unintended consequences of individuals pursuing their private interests, is merely one instance of his more general theory of final causes.[130]

The invisible hand, however, is not so much the invisible force of economic law, as it is the hand of Providence. In fact, Lisa Hill argues that the logic of *Wealth of Nations* makes no sense without an appeal to a divine being.[131] Blanchard notes that although Smith did not write as a theologian, his work is deeply influenced by his Scottish Calvinist tradition. He uses the terms "God" and "Nature" interchangeably, but he is no Deist; instead, behind his language "he has a particular being in mind who works to orchestrate human happiness."[132] Thus, human economic activity—as well as human life as a whole—is ordered to some good, a good that exceeds the individual good being pursued, and not merely the communal/social good. It is gratuitous in its excess and gives rise to common goods. Smith's world is an ordered world, a world ordered and accompanied by God, a world order to goods and the flourishing of humans and creation.

This returns us to McCloskey's earlier comments about the centrality of love or benevolence in Smith's corpus. There can be little doubt that Part VI of the *Theory of Moral Sentiments* is a celebration of the virtues of propriety, prudence, and benevolence.[133] Added to the final edition in 1790, scholars understand Part VI to be a direct rejoinder to Hume; in Part VII, he argues that all systems of morality can be reduced to one of these three virtues. Though he does not state it outright, he presents his system of morality—born in sympathy and in the judgment of the impartial spectator—as grounded in the virtue of benevolence, a form of the theological virtue of charity.

Might it be, thus, that at heart, Smith's anthropology is a theological anthropology—an understanding of the human person based on the benevolent, charitable, imaginative Creator, who always stands in sympathetic relationship with creation? That is a longer argument to be made at another time. What seems clear is that Smith's economics are animated by his vision of the human, his anthropology. While Smith begins in the affectation of sympathy, something that emerges in sense experience, the reasonableness of the impartial spectator sits in judgment. Moreover, the affectation of sympathy is what binds one to one's community, which grows ever-wider from family, friends, neighbors, outward to the whole cosmos. As he notes in *Theory of Moral Sentiments*, one has for his own desire some feeling and hope for the flourishing of all of the beings of creation. Smith's anthropology is fuller, richer, and very different from Hume's, which, as we have shown, animates modern economic theory and the moral anthropological models of the neuroscience of morality.

## From Bacon to Becker: The Artifactual Being of a Social Imaginary

Our narrative has now found its genesis. Part II has traced how the three intertwined "sciences" at the heart of the neuroscience of morality—economics, the social sciences, and ethics—emerged like dendrites from one animating center, Bacon's empiricist power ontology. Having cut natural philosophy off from final causes, Bacon supplied a post hoc *telos* for the work of all modern quests after knowledge, a *telos* which appeared anthropologically centered—the noble project of relieving the human estate—but which in fact aimed at the welfare of the social body, the new Atlantis. Redescribing power as the final common denominator for all motion, including moral and political motion needed to build this new *polis* free of suffering and misery, Bacon tethered the modern sciences to power, worked visibly upon the bodies of the poor from Mandeville forward and then, in the twentieth century, invisibly upon all human bodies.

Where Bacon failed to ground the human in his natural philosophy of the new Atlantis, Hume stepped in. Hume would supply what we might call the "scientific" ground of anthropology in "empirical" moral senses. Yet, one would need to be careful; just as formal and efficient causes in natural philosophy were now mere inferences, so also would be appeals to utility and virtue, the latter of which we discover is simply artifice. For Hume, we can say what is the case, but inferring the good beyond senses of pleasure and pain is a bridge too far. One cannot derive an "ought" from an "is." Deploying Bacon's power ontology, for Hume, wealth was the power—the agent of moral and political motion—that transformed theoretical freedom into actual freedom, a theme that the Chicago School in its various mutations will take up. Such freedom—and therefore, moral agency—is only available to those in possession of this means of power.

Bentham—armed with Hume's empiricism, Malthus and Ricardo's empirically derived theories, and Bacon's vision for engineering a political economy that could free the human from the bondage of misery to become self-directed moral agency—synthesizes all the pieces and movements that give rise to the positive social sciences. The result is psychology, economics, and the ethology or moral theory critiqued by MacIntyre. Mill, while furthering the positivist arm of science, warns that his model for the human actor is too reductive. Yet his warning is brushed aside. Knight, picking up Hume's "is" and "ought" distinction, drives a further wedge between empirical economics and any moral reality that cannot be reduced to his economized model of human action. Friedman employs this fully economized anthropology to subtly invert the interrelationship of economics and politics, championing a vision in which society serves the economy, with capital as the "spring" or driver of both human freedom and human moral activity. The poor—so visibly animating Bacon through Mill—have been more aggressively marginalized, siloed off under the aegis of psychology and other sciences aimed at controlling the antisocial. Becker and company, accepting the economic model as exhaustive of human action and accepting the Humean sentiments as foundational for human action, completes the circuit: the freedom previously stripped from the poor is now, likewise, stripped from those with means, who have become mere animals who act under the sway of inducements. Thus, we arrived at *Homo capitalus*—the neuroscientific model of the human actor, which animates the neuroscience of morality.

# Concluding Un(neuro)scientific Postlude

## Between Beasts and Angels

*There is no doubt that science is becoming a servant of politics and industry, to the great detriment of its cultural mission.*[1]

We return once again to Ludwik Fleck. No more can scientific "cognition be comprehended as a function of two components only, as a relation between the individual subject and the object."[2] Indeed there are three components: "Between the subject and the object there exists a third thing, the community. It is creative like the subject, refractory like the object, and dangerous like an elemental power."[3]

We began this study by unveiling the neuroscientific narrative of morality, probing what its questions really are about, what motivates and shapes its quests to know the nature of human moral action. Specifically, we asked this emerging thought-community about its "discovery" of the neuroscience of morality. We have excavated and attempted to articulate what would have to be believed such that the claims of neuroscience about morality could be true. We have found that these claims presume certain beliefs about the essence of morality, about the nature of the human animal, about what matters in its surroundings, and about the role of science and the state in actualizing this vision of the human person and its actions (moral anthropology). And we have shown how it is that the sciences—biological, human, social, moral—have from the beginning of the modern era worked together with the state in order to establish these beliefs as "true."

Throughout this process, we have watched as these various philosophical-cum-scientific thought-communities enabled society at large to imagine itself along the lines of the abstract being proposed in their scientific models. We have also watched as this social imaginary has reciprocated, seeding the thought-community of the sciences with particular assumptions about morality, the human person, the community, and the role of the state that have inchoately yet ineluctably shaped their quests. Indeed, science generally and the neuroscience of morality particularly do not so much discover a world independent of human thinking, as much as they enable particular aspects of the world to come into relief. Thus, the most recent mutation *Homo capitalus*—an artifact of scientific models of human behavior—has not been discovered by the neuroscience of morality. Rather, this figment of the social imaginary that is neoliberal biopolitical economy is so deeply interwoven into our culture that it inevitably shapes the neuroscientific imagination. Unsurprisingly, then, the neuroscience of morality subsequently "discovers" in the human brain and genome what it had already imagined the human animal to be, as if looking in a mirror. Merging science with the desire to relieve the human estate, the neuroscience of morality becomes an engineering project—a bio-political-economic project of molding real, living human animals into its image.

But this is not simply a twenty-first-century aberration. Rather, we have ended our study showing how the seeds for this image of the human were planted at the beginning of the modern project. Early modern philosophy set us off on a trajectory of scientific questions—a scientific quest—that has arrived at this abstract being, this figment of our imagination, this artifact of economic models. Due to the way in which these thinkers were embedded in their own social imaginaries, the source of modern notions of moral behavior has long been assumptions about economic behavior. Once posited as "the hidden side of everything," the economization of morality was complete. And through biopolitical economy, these forebears of the neuroscience of morality engaged politics and economics to alter the *bios* of real, living human persons to fit the *polis* that they desired.

To this point, we have told the story in reverse, as we have traced the genealogy of this mutant person naturalized by the neuroscientific narrative of morality. In this postlude, we bring the strands of the story together, reprising it in brief and highlighting the key conceptual moves and questions that catalyzed the various mutations of this artifactual being. For it is those moves that will help us identify the central questions that remain for us all going forward: what might be required for a different—and more human—science? Where might we find a thicker moral anthropology that grounds an account of morality that truly promotes human flourishing? And what sort of community—and economics— might be sufficiently creative and refractory without being dangerous to the well-being of real people?

In short, how might a more philosophically sophisticated science—that understands itself as a product of a social history—reimagine its cultural mission? Is a more human science possible, a science that understands human thinking to be entangled both with communities and with the objects of its inquiry? Would not such a science understand that one of its limitations is human thinking itself? Surely the scientist—the subject that seeks to know the object of an enquiry—is entangled at various levels of his or her thought-community; there is no god's-eye view of the object, no view from nowhere, among a thought-community. How might scientists become more conscious of their thought-communities and how these both enable and constrict their thinking? After all, our thought-communities not only enable us to see our objects of inquiry better; they also blind us to other dimensions of our investigations. In short, only by understanding how we are entangled with particular social histories will we be able to see how deeply we are already committed to a wide variety of beliefs, especially to a specific anthropology emergent from particular thought-communities. Should this anthropology not be critically engaged? What if scientists refused a reductive, economized anthropology? Would their science then not only be more human and more humane, but more honest? Science, which aspires to know and understand the world, must first know and understand itself. In turning the critical lens on itself, we end by reflecting on the possibilities for a more human science, one that admits upfront that we are always engaged in a moral anthropology and that our practice of science is always enmeshed in a thick nexus of social imagination.

## Naturalizing an Artifactual Being

Thus, we asked at the outset: what would have to be believed about the nature of morality in order for morality to be studied scientifically? The account emerging from the neuroscientific literature barely resembled more traditional understandings of morality. Gone are rules and principles, obligations and practices, means and ends, and goods and evils. Occasionally, the neuroscientific narrative of morality retained the language of virtue from the tradition, but in the end, it preserved only a vestige of it, a simulacrum. Rather, we found that vice was no longer a category of behavior but had instead been subtly embedded in lists of clinical symptoms, which coalesced into a diagnosis, namely, antisocial personality disorder. We found a similar mélange of clinical and traditional language in the neuroscience of wisdom, discovering not surprisingly that virtue was simply the flipside of the diagnostics of vice—reduced to prosocial attitudes and behaviors. Yet here, there was freer play with language of wisdom, happiness, gratitude, and comprehensive lists of traditional virtues weaving through the literature. The neuroscientific popularizers suggest that they had "discovered" the sources of traits deemed prosocial—care, harm, fairness, loyalty, love, and more—while also deploying language of psychopathy and antisocial behaviors, with heavy emphasis on the importance of prosocial behaviors that create social cohesion, exemplified par excellence in capitalist markets. Beyond this simple slippage between traditional virtue language and clinical proxies, we also saw a puzzling moral inversion where a few manifesting sociopathic tendencies were esteemed, admired, and valued—as long as they were economically successful.

This led us to a series of questions: who is the person engaged in these actions? How did "economics"—a domain that did not exist in its own right prior to the early twentieth century—come to be so central to the neuroscience of morality? How was it that this facet of social life came to define what matters in the surroundings or environment of human actors? And whence the broadly held assumption that those whose biology is defective must come under some sort of control, be it social, political, economic, or biological?

The easy answer was that the neuroscientific narrative of morality is the heir of David Hume—a debt that the field transparently and gladly acknowledges. But as we dug deeper, we discovered that the roots of this narrative encompass far more than Hume. We now see how the story we have recounted—from Bacon to Becker—has shaped the ways that our broader social imaginary and, therefore, the neurosciences understand the work of science, the human person, what is most important about human behavior (morality), and its own role in collaborating with political agents in fitting persons into this imaginary.

Thus we saw that the story begins not with Hume, but rather with Francis Bacon and the particulars of his social context. Bacon reframed the scientific endeavor, introducing a mutation into what was then "moral philosophy," positing an empiricism that bracketed final causes in order to obtain better knowledge about the nature of reality. True knowledge could now only be known through empirical observation, particularly through the work of experiments. In bracketing formal causes because they bias observation, Bacon unmoored material, efficient, and formal causes from a moral order. Connections between his new work of knowledge and the moral order had to be re-established and linked to human purposes. The human will filled the vacuum, with knowledge now directed to a single end: relieving the human condition of all hardship. Captured in his vision of Bensalem, moral philosophers—who will variously become natural, social, and ethical scientists over the next three hundred years—were recast as those charged to collaborate with political processes to build the new Atlantis.

Whence this new *telos*? It cannot be entirely incidental that as Bacon reimagined the pursuit of scientific knowledge, a burgeoning social problem was roiling his milieu—growing masses of impoverished people, dislocated, starving, living in misery. From his position as chancellor to Elizabeth I, he sought to bring some relief to this crisis. Consolidating a century-long attempt to address this symptom of emergent capitalism, the 1601 Act for the Relief of the Poor lessened more overt, public, bodily punishments and continued certain medieval commitments—for example, that caring for the poor was an obligation of Christian charity and that the center of such charity should be the local parish. Yet by codifying such efforts into law, the Act embodied and empowered new and emerging "truths" about the poor—that some were "deserving" of public assistance because they could not work; that those who were able to work did not deserve public support; that whether deserving or not, their sexuality had to be controlled and that the most appropriate place for the poor was an institutional setting—an almshouse for the deserving, a workhouse for the undeserving, and a house of correction for those who refused to work. For a primary impetus of the Act was not simply charity; it was to remove the threat posed by the poor to the civil order.

Forthwith, moral philosophy, the natural sciences, and the social sciences are all heirs to Bacon and the Baconian context. Mandeville, too, sees the *telos* of moral philosophy as building the new Atlantis, in his case "Publick Benefit." This end is not achieved by empirically harassing knowledge from nature nor by the charitable relief of human misery. The poor, in fact, vex Mandeville, not only the undeserving poor who resist being commodified into the abstraction of labor, but equally poor orphans and hardworking craftspeople who, regardless of their efforts, are conceptualized and castigated as—in their very essence—creatures of sloth and vice. Standing at the birth of capitalism, Mandeville has no place for pity or compassion, and traditional virtues—such as even honesty and thrift—will run an enterprise into the ground. The public good will be achieved, in Mandeville's myth, only by self-interested pursuit of prosperity. Where Bacon severed knowledge from the moral order and tethered it to a new *telos*, Mandeville takes the next step—using that *telos* to invert the moral order itself. In his new regime, what were formerly considered virtues are now vices, and former vices—especially envy, greed, and self-interest—mutate into virtues, a morality that for all practical purposes is available only to those with means.

Mandeville's inversion was operationalized by Hume, who radicalized Baconian empiricism. Where Bacon had bracketed final causes, now even formal causes are suspect, far removed as they are from sense impression and derived by speculation on material and efficient causes. Thus, for Hume, Bacon's post hoc moral justification of knowledge was unmoored from sense experience. Following empiricism to its logical conclusion, morality would need to be grounded in sense impression, in the experiences of pleasure and pain. The only moral principle derived from sense impression and the calculus of pain and pleasure is utility. Utility, thus, becomes the sum total of morality. In a deft sleight of hand, the conventional virtues are now simply those habits that have been artificially fabricated post hoc in order to advance utility. They do not themselves derive from a natural order.

But if not rooted in the materiality of nature, they are for Hume rooted in a materiality—that of property. Hume's account of justice, benevolence, utility, and ethics is predicated on an economic vision—one of a fear-inducing scarcity which is the primal source of pain and the right to property which provides a bulwark, against that pain—at least for "the industrious." Justice is reduced to the protection of property; benevolence toward the poor is, ultimately, socially harmful. In fact, charity enslaves the poor; freedom is only theoretical for those without money, the means of enacting their own freedom, and charity makes it worse. In the end, as with Mandeville, in Hume's moral psychology, the traditional virtues and vices are inverted by possession-based social standing. Thus, Hume—that forebear of twenty-first-century ethics, economics, and neuroscience—subtly embedded the emergent economics of eighteenth-century Britain at the very heart of his moral system.

The plight of the poor did not go unnoticed after Hume's death, as Adam Smith continued to reflect in his *Theory of Moral Sentiments*. In fact, new legislation for the care of the poor was introduced in 1795, but it did not pass. It set off a conversation between those with a more traditional notion of charity and the empiricism of the radical reformers Joseph Townsend, Thomas Malthus, David Ricardo, and Jeremy Bentham. Industry, not charity, becomes the chief virtue. But as Malthus "discovered," overpopulation of the poor meant they would outrun their food source and increase their own and the public woe. Thus, they must learn to control their lust, delay their marriage and childbearing; they must be motivated to work, to curb their propensity to sloth—then, they too could rise to the level of the truly free, and therefore, potentially the truly virtuous person. From this point forward, a bifurcated human agent emerges— with some persons reimagined as labor and others as free—abstracted beings whose moral and ontological status is defined relative to their access to wealth. What was needed was a political economics, one that could control the vices of the poor and at the same time transform them into prosocial producers for the wealth of the state. If the poor cannot control their *bios*, the result is disastrous for the state; if their moral tastes can be shaped appropriately by the Panopticon of the political economy, the *polis* wins. Thus is born a biopolitical economy.

This agent is industrialized by Bentham. Intoxicated with Hume's skeptical empiricism, Bentham truly believed that all government prior to Hume was making decisions in the absence of true, empirical knowledge. Accepting Hume's claim that the twin sovereigns of human behavior were pleasure and pain, he believed that these levers could be operationalized to advance human industry and morality. He adds to the Hume–Malthus foundation the belief that the poor could be lifted out of the un-freedom of their poverty with the assistance of his principles of legislation and morals, reshaping existing government institutions with the utility-based springs of action that could, at last, grind rogues honest and idle men industrious. Equipped with the right scientific facts, via Ricardo (the iron law of wages) and Malthus (the law of population), he envisaged building the great society that would elevate people from the enslavement of poverty to the true freedom of wealth.

Thus, Hume's empiricism reshaped moral, political, and social philosophy—with the emerging subfield of economics—grounding them in a new positivism. After the momentum created by Bentham's radical reform movement, each is transformed into a science. Just as physics and chemistry emerge from natural philosophy in this period, psychology, sociology, and economics emerge from moral and political philosophy. Yet they all remain deeply intertwined. The bifurcated, economized anthropology shaped, for example, the emerging natural science (or was it a social science) of phrenology, finding in skull bumps the vices of the poor and the virtues of the rich. Moreover, from Bacon to Bentham, wealth became deeply enmeshed with the emerging understanding—the imaginary—of the state. It equally shaped the imagination of ethics. Continuing, but again mutating, the long-standing connection between ethics and the *polis*, the emerging moral/social/economic scientists allied themselves with political processes in order to ensure that individual human behavior serves the ends of "the wealth of nations."

John Stuart Mill softened Bentham's mechanical science of society and brought a form of rationality back to his forebears' pleasure-seeking actor. Yet in attempting to extend his father's psychology to the science of character—ethology—he cemented Hume's radically empiricized, economized philosophy into the twin paradigms of utilitarianism and what others would mockingly call *Homo economicus*. A towering intellect, Mill knew that the models he was generating in ethology and in economic science were inadequate to the reality of human agents and human action. Yet the freedom Mill championed was for those with the economic means to rationally maximize their utility; the poor—though to be assisted by the state—remained unfree, so unfree, in fact, that the government should control their reproduction. Hume's bifurcated anthropology, intertwined with utility, grounded in property, advances. And despite his misgivings, in giving shape to this scientific artifact "economic man," Mill inadvertently set the trajectory for the twentieth century.

Mill's *Homo economicus* provided Frank Knight with the scientific model, par excellence, for establishing economics as an empirical science once and for all. Like Mill, Knight seemed to truly wish to avoid reducing persons to economics; but instead, he completed the process by intentionally severing the science of economics from the moral philosophy he deeply knew still needed to be present. Economics could only discover the "is" of human action; the "ought" must be derived elsewhere. Knight, who would never have wanted to unmoor the facts of economics from the values of morality, nonetheless facilitated the process.

Yet Knight stands as an outlier from both his forebears and heirs in one key respect: he has no use for the springs of actions. In severing economics from ethics, he equally sought to disconnect it from social policy. Here Knight forwards half of the Baconian vision, forging an economics devoted to unearthing the laws, the formal causes, of economic reality. Scientific economic knowledge ought not, for Knight, be re-tethered to an imported, post hoc final cause. Indeed, the human condition must be relieved, but for Knight, this is the work of other disciplines.

This distance from social policy might be one reason that, for Knight, the poor are suddenly absent from our narrative. Of course, Knight is working in a different context—no wrangling over the Poor Laws in the United States. And as wealthy and poor alike are devastated in the Great Depression, long-standing canards about the "deserving" and "undeserving" poor are momentarily sidelined until after the Korean War, neoliberals standing as a minority voice. But equally, Knight stands at a moment—and facilitates—the descent of ethics into emotivism. For insofar as anthropology is now fully economized, to unmoor ethics from economics is to cut any last threads between ethics and reason, a loose-end Mill valiantly tried to hold onto. Morality, now wholly and solely circumscribed by bodily experiences of pain and pleasure, ironically becomes, at once, utterly subjective but also now only discoverable by the new fields with jurisdiction over the human—the biological and social sciences. Where economics can discover the "is" of human action (i.e., what humans *do*) it will be for psychology, sociology, and biology to harass nature more thoroughly to discover the internal causes of human action, the ultimate substrate upon which the springs of action can be worked. And the poor, sequestered in the successors of Bentham's institutions—mental hospitals, prisons, or racially segregated communities (of low SES)—become the subjects of such research.

And so, *Homo economicus* won the day—only one half of Hume's bifurcated anthropology advances through twentieth-century European and US neoliberalism. From this point forward, economics and ethics alike presume a vision of the human person who has the material capacity to choose between goods. Now, armed with only pleasure and pain, Knight's heirs would derive a full political economy. Milton Friedman completed it. For Friedman, *Homo economicus* was not simply a reductive scientific model—he was the true nature of the rational, utility-maximizing being, advanced as part of a larger project to subtly—or invisibly?—allow economics to become the dominant form of political reason. Freedom is founded in economic success; one's own moral good is secured in economic success. Economic success both enabled one's moral vision to be exercised and was the sign that one had achieved full moral agency. For Friedman, economic rationality is where the individual actor would assert, not merely his tastes, but his full moral vision.

As for Mill and Knight, Friedman believed *Homo economicus* retained some freedom and agency in economic success/moral action. With Gary Becker, however, the un-freedom of the bifurcated other half of human nature now subsumes the whole. Becker simply elevates the animality of Mandeville's bees and Hume's moral sentiments over any form of rationality, reimagining the traditional *telos* of virtue—happiness—as a mathematical utility function and vices (such as crime and addiction) as virtues as long as they generate a sufficiently elastic demand curve. As for Hume, virtues and vices here are artificial names for different aspects of utility. Becker's engagement with moral concepts evolves over his career, culminating in the claim that the happiness function and other "moral" (economic) behaviors are rooted in human biology. But Becker shifts the location of the invisible hand, now embedding it in human biology, enabling economics to become the new form of reason *simpliciter* and to become the ontological category for the human person. Biological forces, biological desires, intuitions, and tastes are what drive the human animal. And knowing the bio-psycho-social levers of these drives, the role of economics is to guide public policy to enable society to encourage behaviors conducive to the endless furthering of the market, endless profit for those with property. The economization of the person is complete. Human actors are now subject to the hidden side of everything—biological and social powers and forces—of which they are simply voluntary but unfree conduits. Thus, with Becker, the trajectory begun with Bacon is complete: *Homo economicus* has reached its terminal mutation: it has become *Homo capitalus*.

Becker and his lineage lie at the core of the neuroscientific thought-community. The popularizers of the neuroscience of morality are correct in demurring that their systems have left *Homo economicus* behind, for what the narrative offers is an *apologia* for Becker's even more abstract, less rational, and less free, artifact. Put differently, in the neurosciences, one finds an anthropological mutation, where capital—a force in the power ontology—has become the ontological category with human as its modifier. This completes the trajectory Polanyi names, where now not only those who "labor" but the human *in toto* has been transformed into a commodity. It is an artifact most recently mutated by neoliberalism but bequeathed to us by early modern thinkers in their quest to develop scientific models that then set in motion a cascade of transformations in how we think about the nature of human persons and the nature of their actions. This imagined abstract being stands-in for the real human being. But via the rhetoric of the popularizers with the backing of neuroscience, many believe it to be true and allow themselves to be reshaped in its image.

Zak, who identifies as a neuroeconomist, marries neuroscience and economics. The invisible hand of the market is the moral molecule oxytocin. Oxytocin provides not only an evolutionary basis for markets, but also a defense of markets as necessary for the promotion of group happiness—the overarching goal of utility. Via oxytocin, which binds people together, Zak envisions a world in which all are wealthy and happy in the market milieu. Like Becker, Zak has little space for rational choice, but instead finds humans act on things that they find pleasurable. Thus, Zak has a biological basis—that is to say, a bottom-up basis—on which to describe the "up" of human behavior and to narrate the neuroscientific basis of social organization. By increasing that "spring of action" oxytocin, which biologically promotes the greatest pleasure for the greatest number of people, the neuroeconomics can help engineer society while relieving the human estate.

We see this equally within the esoteric thought-community of the neuroscience of morality, where those like Gianaros and Manuck, Caspi, Sadeh, and others seek to correlate antisocial traits and low socio*economic* status. Low SES/poverty affects genes, which confer maladaptive brain states, which leads to bad or antisocial behaviors—again, a bottom-up causality in which poverty via biology makes antisocial persons. And in what does SES consist? Hollingshead's measure, as with most of its analogs, assays essentially two variables: marital status and employment—or sex and idleness, the twin vices of Malthusian theory and the Benthamite Panopticon. Thus, the neuroscientific narrative of morality clinically operationalizes and measures what Townsend and

Malthus imagine as determinative in the human environment, a trajectory which sprang from Hume's fragmented anthropology—in which the poor remained locked in their beastial un-freedom and only the achievement of wealth gave one actual freedom. Alongside Hollingshead, and catalyzed by the methodological individualism of emerging neoliberalism, the catecholamine hypothesis of behavioral disorders met with SES to provide further scientific backing for the Malthusian naturalization of the connection between poverty and vice.

But not only do politics, economics, and morality emerge from the (socio)biological. Behind these studies an assumption reigns: antisocial (anti-economic) persons disrupt the social fabric, diminishing the flourishing of all. Although correlating biology and SES, our neuroscientists repeatedly aver that their quest is motivated by a desire to get to the root of violent or criminal behaviors. They share a conviction that those whose biology is defective must come under some sort of social control (Meyer and Lindenberg, Viding and Frith, Raines, Walker's Genetic Virtue Project), political control (Harris, Gianaros, and Manuck), or economic control (Zak). Bios produces the right polis—the market. If one cannot flourish or be happy in the naturalized market, then there must be some biological problem.

Thus, the neuroscientific narrative of morality is an exercise in biopolitics. Harris is very much like Bentham. Harris holds that society should apply social controls in order to help those with antisocial behaviors to reform, and if they cannot be reformed, they should be removed from—though not punished by—society. After all, they are victims of defective biology. In fact, good political systems do just that; they create horizontal social controls that override the failings of biology. For Harris, insofar as there is no such thing as free will and since his proposed interventions aim at alleviating harms and promoting pleasures of society as a whole, social control cannot be a violation of human freedom. Yet, unlike Bentham and Hume, Harris believes that *oughts* are scientifically discoverable. He has a modicum of a teleology that bucks the trends of all is empiricist predecessors. Yet, Harris's position does not mean that he departs from that of Becker. For like them, he has no significant notion of free will, and any behavior that is pleasure-inducing can be found in brain states. And while Harris does not call pleasures addictions the way that Becker does, he does not propose a society built toward pleasures, but rather a society regulated by government that might prevent harms. Thus, government can promote certain behaviors over others, but the limit for what gets one kicked out of society are behaviors that result in harm to others. Thus, the regulative function of society is just to prevent people from causing unpleasurable or painful experiences.

Haidt has a slightly more willful *Homo capitalus*. Armed with the knowledge of moral foundations, Haidt believes we can tweak riders so they can better learn how to control the elephantine emotions. His current projects are aimed at better cooperation, and for this he notes that markets are miraculous, that corporations are example of hives (Mandeville's bees) united into one mind. Groups and group cohesion are a product of our biology, and we would do well to have the proper political economy to get humans to behave. Because serotonin levels or feelings of moral disgust/moral anger/loyalty/love emerge automatically from the emotional centers of the brain, and because the elephant is only marginally under the control of the rider, little of moral behavior is under rational constraint or rational control. If causation in behavior is mostly bottom up, and if there are errors in bottom-up control, then one can only conclude that we must put into place social controls that will encourage certain behaviors or eliminate others. As slaves to their passions and to precognizant factors that shape behavior, humans thus must be ruled if they are to flourish. Some sort of external political intervention from the *polis* is necessary if markets cannot provide happiness in order to bring defective *bios* under control. Social mechanisms ought to be put into place to control those biological mediated behaviors, either through a market that promotes prosociality or through a politics that restrains the elephantine human.

For Zak, control of behavior is through markets, which increase oxytocin, which induces pleasure. In fact, market economics is the means to shape moral communities without the drastic visible hand that Harris proposes. Once we understand how oxytocin works individually and socially, we will know how to create a society that is more prosperous and prosocial. Zak also has an evolutionary story of society that supports his biologizing of economics. In a story that echoes Comte, the human animal has successively transcended mother, family, clan, and religion, all of which are limited by their ideologies and thus do not secure care for the whole of humanity, and has now reached an apex where market economic relations created by neoliberal political economy—because of the way that they increase oxytocin levels—provides the best organization of society. He very much seeks to harness the power of the market. There is a balance between the biological oxytocin-mediated factors that drive our behaviors and the social organizational factors that markets produce. Oxytocin binds us together, and market trade and fellow-feeling spur behaviors that will produce stable and growing economies. Thus, capitalism is a biologically grounded social practice that provides the (morally) best route to human flourishing, or so the story goes. Zak and Haidt have translated their putatively descriptive programs into business schools, promoting ventures that promise a monetary return on investment.

As the popularizers tell it, this vision settles a long-standing problem in evolutionary biology, the putative anomaly of cooperative behavior aimed at group rather than individual survival. Moreover, since the antisocial human cannot control the biologically determined behavior, some sort of biopolitical control becomes necessary. But whether overt or subtle, the political and economic order acts as the regulative condition for the possibility of moral control of the animal emotions that govern human behavior. What the neuroscience of morality has putatively discovered is that moral behavior is really a species of political economy.

Thus, we have ended our study claiming that early modern philosophy set us off on a trajectory of scientific questions—a scientific quest—that has arrived at this abstract being, this figment of an economized imagination. This neoliberal lifeworld of WEIRD countries is the social imaginary in which the thought-community of the neurosciences finds a home. It is no wonder that their ideas about the nature of the human actor and its morality resonate so deeply with the contemporary thought-community of mainstream society. They share a common history, and common assumptions about the nature that the scientists are on the quest to find. They understand each other because they share a common imaginary.

Shaped by their own socioeconomic imaginary, the early modern thinkers we have engaged likewise reimagined the human actor in order to alter the *bios* of real, living human persons to fit the *polis* that was desired. The project to improve the human condition came at great cost to the well-being of many. And today, as we have argued, the offspring of this biopolitical-economic imaginary has built a city where antisocial venture capitalists can flourish, while human persons, human nature, and nature are consumed and destroyed. Does any hope remain for a more human or humane science?

## Toward a More Human Science

The human is the animal that by nature is cultured. As Bernard Stiegler has pointed out, the individual human stands in a mutually co-constituting relationship with its culture.[4] Neuroscientists are likewise cultured, standing in a mutually co-constituting relationship with their culture. And the culture that makes neuroscience a possibility is a culture tethered to neoliberalism. Shaping our social milieu, neoliberalism and the neurosciences together are the most recent chapter in the longer story of the social sciences, including economics and neuroscientific precursors, that has shaped how moral behavior is imagined. Neuroscience—the fusion of neurobiology with the social and psychological sciences—now stands as the human science, par excellence. Or, as Amy Guttmann has claimed, it is the science that "strikes at the very core of who we are."[5]

But the neuroscience of morality is not alone in this. In fact, we would venture that a similar story to the foregoing could be told about almost any contemporary scientific endeavor. Given the nature of neoliberalism, it is unlikely that any contemporary scientific domain is not likewise enmeshed in the neoliberal imaginary and does not, therefore, participate in and further the biopolitical economy. Still, there is something significantly different about neuroscience, because it claims knowledge of what it is to be human. As such, the science-biopolitical complex as a whole "strikes at the core of who we are"—it strikes out on a quest to discover who we are while simultaneously striking into "nature" a particular image of the human, forging *Homo capitalus* into our psyches and onto our bodies via the machinery of biopolitics.

What would it take for science to become un-enmeshed, to free itself from economization and the politico-philosophical commitments of the neoliberal age? What would it take to reorient it and to begin to move toward a more human science? That this problem has been 400 years in the making renders the solution to our situation extraordinarily complex. It is, after all, difficult to think outside of the regnant social imaginary. But every quest begins with a first step, a first question. We propose here that the first step is for those who seek knowledge—as individuals and as collectives—to begin to reflect seriously on the activity of knowing in general and of doing science in particular, to become more cognizant of what is required or makes it possible for any one scientist to perceive or think about reality and the objects of her or his inquiry, and for any particular scientific community to understand the deep ways in which it is enmeshed with our contemporary culture on so many levels. And since we do not limit our understanding of the word *sciencia* to those working in the "hard" sciences, we direct this conversation equally to those in all fields on quests to elucidate any knowledge related to the nature and identity of the human person—particularly knowledge of morality. As such, we direct this conversation to philosophers, ethicists, medical practitioners, social workers—all who engage in this quest on a theoretical or practical level.

Our inquiry has been informed deeply by the work of Ludwik Fleck. Whereas Fleck emphasized the communal dimensions that sustain these bodies of knowledge, Ernst Cassirer (1874–1945), the neo-Kantian philosopher, adds another facet. He notes the human animal is not like a bacterium or a slug or a lizard, merely responding to signals of a glucose source or a threat source. Rather, the human animal is *animalum symbolicum*, the symbolic animal. Reality is mediated to the human animal not merely by physical signals, but rather by symbolic forms that exist within human culture. Cassirer names five symbolic forms: mythology/religion, art, history, language, and science. Every culture has something of each of these symbolic forms. Each form serves a purpose. Every culture has its founding mythology, which creates its fundamental beliefs about nature. For the ancient Greeks, it was the raw power of nature that is represented by the gods. For the early moderns like Thomas Hobbes, it was the state of nature, where human life is "solitary, poor, nasty, brutish, and short." Mythology, according to Cassirer, becomes religion when the moral dimension is added: life is this way, but it ought to be another way. An example might be the founding myth of John Rawls, who imagines human life as selfish, brutish, and prone to chance, and for whom the founding morality (religion) is the mythology of the original position, where one imagines that one is set behind the veil of ignorance, thus in a position to define the forms of justice (morality) based on what would seem fair if one was in the lottery of life. Science is a symbolic form that mediates reality through mathematics. One cannot merely see a quark, but its existence is "observed" indirectly, and is mediated in (and to) the human mind by mathematical symbols. Each symbolic form has work to do in a culture, and it has a scope of activity that is appropriate to it. Tyranny emerges when one symbolic form becomes *the* symbolic form by which all other symbolic forms must be understood. Science has become *the* symbolic form par excellence for contemporary WEIRD cultures, with modern neuroscience assuming pretensions of explaining the very being of the human animal.

As we have argued, the quest of science is a human quest to know. The first step toward a more human science, then, requires science to acknowledge that human knowing is a social activity embedded in a cultural context. The activity of the scientist who seeks to know is grounded and instantiated in not only their primary scientific thought-community but a multitude of scientific and cultural communities—and, indeed, within a social imaginary, which is itself inchoate and dynamic. So, for any one scientist, all of these dimensions are brought to bear in both active and passive elements that stand in the background but are yet in play to some degree. Some of these elements will be recognized as biases, and there may be an attempt to control or to mitigate them. Some of these elements will go unnoticed, shaping the questions asked and the answers found, sometimes for the better, and sometimes for the worse. When shared by a number of scientists, these elements constitute a thought-style that binds them together and shapes the work they do, particularly their desire for knowledge and the questions they pursue. Thus, what is possible for any one person within a science to perceive and to think about reality is always in relation to some thought-community.

As particular scientists venture forward into the unknown, they not only draw on the thought-style of their community but also engage their own creativity. Catalyzed by both of these sources, they desire to know the unknown. This desire to know is aspirational in two senses. First, it is particular—it asks particular questions made possible by virtue of their thought-community. Second, it is teleological, which is to say that the desire to know aims not only at what is but also at what ought to be. There is a sense that we ought to know the truth. The scientist herself desires to move from the place of what-is-known to bring what-is-unknown into being-known. The act of venturing out beyond the limits of a thought-community, while always tethered to it, is the act of imagination.

Scientists desire to know reality as it exists in itself, independent of any one individual's perception or knowledge of it. Yet, knowledge of reality is limited. Moreover, scientists want to index their findings to a reality that exists independent of any human observation—the "mind-independent object." Yet, the object has its own integrity, its own being. This unknown can emerge into the realm of what is known only through symbolic mediation. Just as a scientist synthesizes a particular scientific thought-style and her own creative aspirational desires to know, the knowledge of the object of an investigation is a synthesis of the object's integrity as a separate being and the thought-style deployed. A particular scientists' thinking is enabled by and at the same time is limited by his or her community's shared style of knowing. That style both enables and disables perception, enabling us to see some aspects of an object, but blinding us to others. So, knowing is the synthesis of a particular scientist asking her particular questions about particular objects. As importantly, however, insofar as some aspect of an object can be known, knowledge is possible because the mind-independent being lends itself to the synthetic work of the scientist. Put differently, what appears to be the case to any sociohistorical thought-community is provisional at every level. It is provisional by virtue of the limitations of the thought-community, by the limitations of the creativity and aspirations of the scientists, and by the fact that the object may not lend itself to the particular kind of activity of a thought-community and its scientist (or the scientist and her thought-community).

As discussed in the Prelude, findings of an individual scientist—new pieces of knowledge—are then taken back for assessment by the thought-community, to see if they confirm or resist settled opinions. If the findings do not conform to previously held knowledge, the scientists have to ask, should the prior knowledge trump the new evidence, or does the new evidence call into question what the thought-community holds to be true? As we have seen, scientific thought-communities have been oriented toward the practical, pursuing knowledge not only as a good in itself, but in order to change reality. In other words, science has been more like engineering projects than mere knowledge-projects. Thus, not only is a scientific thought-community aimed at discovery, it is aimed at both the good of knowledge and the possible instrumental goods that might flow forth from our having gained the knowledge. Thus, in some sense, science is not only about constructing knowledge in conversation with a thought-community, but it is often also about constructing social realities.

Thus, we can conclude a few things. As we have shown, not only is a thought-community a moving and fluid thing as it seeks what is and what ought to be, but it also both makes possible and delimits its members' access to any object of inquiry. Moreover, these objects are also fluid and dynamic, ever-changing not only in terms of the individuality of the particular being that is observed but also in the evolutionary sense of the fact that the object-being is itself moving along some historical trajectory—it is becoming and/or unbecoming. Thus, the sociohistorical drive to take up with reality is fluid and the being with which it takes up is fluid. Knowledge, then, is unstable and is itself in motion.

In the case of knowledge, the truth of the matter is that we are ignorant, however much we may know. All knowledge opens onto other knowledge. All scientific findings open spaces for new scientific findings. We desire to no longer be in the state of ignorance, because not being ignorant is good. But knowing is provisional and can never fully sate the desire; thus, acknowledging this provisional nature of our own knowledge is also good. To realize that the thing known is itself in a state of becoming (and/or unbecoming), and thus that our state of knowledge is itself temporal, is also good. To know is a good; to know that one does not and can never fully know is an essential good.

The scientific impulse then is a metaphysical moral enterprise. The human act of knowing is teleological, aiming both at our best imagination of real goods and at what we imagine ought to be. Yet once we are aiming at goods, at a *telos*, we have slipped into the realm of the moral—for it is in relation to goods that virtues and vices are defined. It is only once one knows the *telos* (and knowing the *telos* is itself imperfect) that one can say what a virtue or vice is. Both are always aimed at goods, with the vices tending to miss the goods at which one aims. Beyond this general character of science, the neuroscience of morality explicitly seeks to discover the virtue of the human animal, that feature that makes her unique among the animals. As best we can tell, the human animal is the only animal that can say "it is good" or "it is good to know the reality of my own being." But no being can exhaustively know its own being, for she would have to be outside herself in order to know herself.

But if we follow Bacon and sever the relationship between science—as the pursuit of knowledge—and the *telos* of knowing (after all a *telos* is not known in the same way as a rock), what follows is a trajectory that, given the particular history we have described, has culminated in the biopolitical economy of neoliberalism. We have pointed to the danger that comes with the social engineering project that is the biopolitical economy. This imaginary has produced a worldwide system that has led to the destruction, not only of other cultural imaginings, but of vast numbers of people and the very ecological reality that produces all beings. The neuroscience of morality aims to be the science *par excellence*, the scientific standard to which all other sciences and forms of knowledge should bow. But it is simply channeling a grounding produced by the regnant social imaginary. Between the scientist and the object of her investigation, "there exists a third thing, the community." As Fleck notes, and as we have argued, the neuroscientific thought-community is "creative like the subject, refractory like the object, and dangerous like an elemental power."

The empiricist mantra, "there is nothing in the mind that is not first in the senses," is true in one sense.[6] Inspired by Fleck, we have challenged the neuroscientific version of this mantra. Wojciech Sady suggests that "Fleck reversed this maxim: there is nothing in the senses that is not first in the mind."[7] In other words, the content of a culture—the languages, ideas, and concepts—makes perception possible; it is that through which all sense experience is interpreted. Thus, we receive our thought-styles, which mediate reality through symbolic forms. In other words, our truth claims are a synthetic and a participatory event. They are a synthesis between culture, which has particular symbolic forms and are manifest in thought-communities, and the objects of inquiry. Teasing apart what the researcher as an individual brings to the table, what culture contributes in terms of its symbolic forms, and what reality brings to the table, is a difficult, if not impossible, task. It is the cultural task of science to mediate reality to the human mind in just this way. But because science—in the main—has forgotten its social ground, it thinks it observes reality unmediated by the senses and unmediated by the thought-styles existing in thought-communities. When science forgets this cultural dimension of its project, it errs.

This then is the end of our story: the neuroscientist does not discover the mind-independent nature of her nature, but she aesthetically and ethically must create it. Because it has not recognized that human science is a cultural endeavor, and that the culture itself must be rigorously interrogated, the result of the late modern, neoliberal biopolitical economy has been aimed at control. If we hope to shift science away from its biopolitical captivity, we must come to understand that it is a creative and imaginative project that must always work from the unstable ground between knowing and not knowing, recognizing that our knowing can never exhaust the remainder of reality that escapes our findings. The objects we encounter are free; they can only be ensnared so much; something of their being always slips between the cracks of our attempts to know. As scientists, our attitude should be that of the artist, who attempts to paint the light, but whose canvas only captures something of the light, never the light itself. In fact, in our humility, we should come to recognize that the net by which we know is not only constructed by our thought-community, but that the net itself is constantly changing. And that which we seek to ensnare with our nets is itself quite independent of the net and ever-changing. We must become poets and mystics, humble and unsure, lest we harm that which we think we have fully captured. We should proceed knowing that our projects are marginal projects—beginning at the margins of a very particular, and in our case WEIRD, thought-community—especially as we seek to claim some sort of power over those beings that live at the margins of our world. The neoliberal biopolitical economy is the moral landscape in which we now live; but it is possible to imagine human nature differently.

## *Acedia* or Joy: *Fuga finis* or the Freedom of Humility

In an essay on the context of medicine (another practically oriented science), Robert Spaemann, a Catholic theologian said that without a good end, we become spiritually lethargic. Spiritual lethargy was, in the history of the tradition of virtues, a vice—acedia.

> To keep the ultimate end of the human being in mind requires the exercise of the deeper powers of the human being. Without this exercise, hence, as a consequence of the *fuga finis*, the human being aimlessly roams around, so to speak, in the infinite quantity of what can be known.[8]

There is a kind of spiritual lethargy that emerges if there is no sense of the ultimate end of the human, aspirational as it may be. How could one—how could a thought-community—choose among so many possible ends? The flight of ends, the *fuga finis*, means that we are doomed to wander about, directionless, pulled hither and yon by any number of ends. With regard to knowledge, Spaemann means that we can be correct provisionally about some domain of reality, one of "the infinite quantity of what can be known," without having discovered something that is true. In the spiritual malaise of our time, we take one approach to knowledge—the modern scientific approach, one approach in the infinite quantity of what is possibly known—to be the whole of what can be known.

Given that knowledge as sociohistorically instantiated is provisional, and given that the knower herself is creative and driving to sate her desire to know more, and given that objects of knowledge are in fact in motion and ever becoming, there are an infinite number of correct ways that one can take up with reality. That one can be correct about various domains or through various strategies taken toward "the infinite quantity of what can be known" does not mean that anything goes. Put differently, while the economic sciences in some reductionistic circular way may occasionally stumble upon a mathematical curve that appears to have predictive value if enough variables and "externalities" are ignored, in our spiritual *acedia*, our culture takes this sociohistorically derived economic theory as if it represents the totality of knowledge of human behavior. We believe that this science has discovered our true nature, our true being. And, to make matters worse, that totalizing vision is implemented via policy to engineer a globalized WEIRD biopolitical economy that overruns nature, including human nature, destroying it. In the spiritual lethargy of our time, we cannot imagine our being otherwise. *Acedia* overwhelms imagination.

In the philosophical narrative we have told, Hume won the sociohistorical day in that his thinking, grounded in the industrializing culture of his day, both produced and conformed to the way that property, wealth, and freedom were linked together. Yet, even in his own day, Adam Smith—whose name is invoked by the Humean culture of biopolitical economy—took aim directly at Hume and proposed a very different anthropology, consisting of a very different notion of community. Certainly, the human is animal. Yet, its being stands out from its animality. Hume and the Humeans—of yesterday and today—fail to recognize that this being exceeds both their thinking about it and the sum of her parts. Desire, grounded in biological need, leaps beyond the limitations of the body for congress with other beings.

Reality is mediated to human knowledge through intermediaries in the give and take of thought. It finds its origin in the give and take of community. The poetic imagination, which is also the scientific imagination, is not something that arises simply in a brain, but also emerges from these mediations in the give and take of individuality and community, combined with the give and take of symbolic forms—

morality and/or science, for example—emerges from communities of thinkers. This poetic imagination engages in poeisis with the object of her questioning, and represents it in the artifactual productions, say, pieces of art or journal science. This poetic imagining is a god-like gift that exists well in excess of the body, the brain, necessitating culture, language, community, in order for it to achieve a modicum of knowledge. Knowledge exists, most certainly, but the being of our knowledge does not exist in the same way that the being of the object exists. Thus, the human is outside herself in knowing, which participates not only in her knowledge, but in the being of the thing in reality. For an older social imaginary, this ability to be outside one's body in consciousness of the world outside made the human not merely animal, but angelic or god-like.

While this language of "god-like" or "angelic" hails from an older social imaginary, the imaginary of our day elevates one symbolic form—that of science—setting it apart, making it sacred. At the dawn of the early modern period, the new social imaginary bracketed that older social imaginary, where the human was not merely animal, but closer to the angels, and creatively, imaginatively, and communally took up a different way that we stand outside our own being, namely, the scientific attitude. Yet that scientific attitude is no less a product of animality, community, symbolic form— science. And by elevating that symbolic form above all others, by allowing it to establish its mythologies and its moralities, that is to say, its religions, it has become scientistic. In doing so, it has said, there can be no angels, ignoring the very angelic ground of its own origins in human consciousness. Consciousness, which is always emergent from culture and symbolic form, always emergent from community and aimed outside itself desirous for food, for comfort, for flourishing, for more community, is also emergent from brains, surely. Consciousness—emergent from brains and culture (community and symbolic form)—turns to engage, top-down, its animality and its way of being community. Consciousness makes us like the angels.

The power of imagination, which is a power of brain, body, culture, community, society, and history, is what is most needed now. Smith recognized a problem in Hume's skepticism; he challenged Hume, claiming that the human was and must needs be more than animal desire, lest he perish. This challenge was leveled at Hume's belief that the only thing of which one can be certain is pleasure and pain. In his focus on its animality, Hume let the communion that precedes it in language, society, and history, sit idly by, bracketed from thinking, in service to some fanciful notion of truth. And thus, the particular eighteenth-century, British form of social organization lays hidden—and is taken to be the natural—in the history of our culture, which naturalizes a particular form of social organization. *Polis* emerges from *bios*, we are told, in a kind of linear way. Had nineteenth-century and early-twentieth-century thinkers paid closer attention to Smith, neoliberalism and its attendant biopolitical economy might never have been. Yet, that is not to say that Smith is our hero. But he provides one example, standing at the moment this particular trajectory took a different route, pointing to the priority of communion as productive of a form of being human.

Yet, there are other exemplars, both recent and ancient, to which we can turn. In the West, thinkers like Thomas Aquinas or Augustine had a different way of imagining desire and will, ordered to communion with the whole of being, which is the highest good. Yet, the human does not know the highest good. The emptiness of not knowing results in the desire to know and to be known. But to know and to be known is both distinct from and in communion with the whole. At the same time, the whole is already known within the depths of one being—in one's desire, one has some knowledge of what is not known. The human even knows that she can have no being worth having without city or culture or the community. For how else could she put words to that emptiness and that desire? She desires communion with the community of the cosmos, and beyond cosmos she desires communion with the highest good that is ontologically other than all there is.

Aquinas and Augustine also knew that our thinking about the whole of the cosmos, and our thinking about the *summum bonum* that is outside cosmos, can lead to tyranny, selfishness, and evil. Building the city into whatever one takes the *summum bonum* to be is very likely to build the wrong city, a city that takes one's own community to be the community *par excellence*. Building the city out of one symbolic form—say the positivistic scientific one that emerged in a small little culture in the midst of the north Atlantic somewhere between the eighteenth and twenty-first centuries—is to build a city of devils, where human nature and nature are consumed and destroyed; or so we have argued.

What is needed then is, as Spaemann suggests, a sense of the ultimate being of the human, what we could be if we realized our own being, which is communal, symbolic, embodied, desirous of being at one with the whole of what is. We must have a vision of our own being, acknowledging that our knowledge of ourselves will always be limited. There is no way of imagining ourselves exhaustive of our being. We must understand that any vision—including an individual's own vision—is itself sociohistorical, and thus a provisional vision of the city, falling short of what is true of the reality of one's own being, and the being of the whole. Thus, we must have other intellectual virtues (understanding and wisdom), which must themselves be understood as the virtues of a particular sociohistorical moment, that will keep our knowledge (Scientia) from making claims that purport to be exhaustive of *the* fundamental truth about *the* fundamental reality. For who can claim to possess the whole of being in one's own mind, including the being of knowing of the whole?

After all, in human congress with all that is, we will come upon those who have different sociohistorical thought-communities that take up with reality in very different symbolic forms, with different languages, arts, histories, mythologies, religions, and sciences. They will find different meanings to flourishing and they will have different visions of the *summum bonum*. If we understand our own vision of the good life to be provisional, even while it can also be good and beautiful, we will bracket our own way of being, to entertain others, to eat with them and commune with them. We will hope to see what others see and to know what they know to be good and true and beautiful. After all, other ways of being-in-the-world are part of the community of the cosmos.

Thus, we will need the virtue of prudence (practical wisdom), so as to enact the provisional vision that we imagine is the best for our own thriving and the thriving of our communities. We must know how to integrate our animality (through the practice of temperance) and to assert that others in our community must also flourish for oneself to flourish (justice), and when that is not possible, we must work courageously in the face of threats to our own being to enact that vision of the city in which all can flourish, and where flourishing is aimed at the *telos* of communion of the whole with the whole of being.

Thus, following Spaemann, we can say that what is most needful is a perspective of the true nature and *telos* of the human, an anthropology. Only with an anthropology—with all of its contingencies—standing in the background, can we know what practices are necessary to begin to flourish in our time, to recreate economies and communities and science and knowledge that will protect and promote human well-being, despite the biopolitical economy of our own sociohistorical moment. After all, we have argued that the biopolitical economy of neoliberalism has an evacuated anthropology that, in replacing the imago Dei with the image of Mammon, has done great harm to untold persons and creation. Yet, even in having a more robust and adequate anthropology, we will only have *an* anthropology, not *the* anthropology. Under the biopolitical-economic regime of neoliberalism, we are told that it has *the* true anthropology, that the figment of its imaginary is the whole truth about human being and that we must conform to and implement its form of being-in-the-world for the entirety of the world. This has led to despair, leaving us wandering aimlessly in the great quantity of what can be known, overwhelmed by the city that is being built by neoliberal regimes of truth and power.

The only remedy to the destructive arrogance of neoliberalism, and to the subsequent spiritual lethargy that it engenders, is an aspirational vision of what it means to be fully human. What is most needed is the virtue of wisdom, not as imagined by neuroscientists. True human wisdom is a violation of the great principle of non-contradiction. To know oneself, one has to know that one does not know, even oneself. For the human, to know is, at the same time, to know there is a great quantity that one does not know. After all, the desire that we have to know not only reveals something true about the objects to be known, but it also reveals inchoately what is not known. To know is to not know. In every instance of our knowing, we must have wisdom to see that we do not know fully, and that we will never know fully. In this interplay of knowing and not knowing, all that is left for us to do is to seek justice cautiously for all beings, for one does not know with certainty; to do so mercifully, because excessive harm can flow from what we know and do not know; and to walk humbly, head bowed, with the mystery of it all.

Fin

# Notes

## Introduction

1. Barbara Oakley, *Evil Genes: Why Rome Fell, Hitler Rose, Enron Failed, and My Sister Stole My Mother's Boyfriend* (Amherst, NY: Prometheus Books, 2008).
2. Dean A. Haycock, *Murderous Minds: Exploring the Criminal Psychopathic Brain* (New York: Pegasus Books, 2014).
3. Kent A. Kiehl, *The Psychopath Whisperer: The Science of Those Without Conscience* (New York: Crown Publishers, 2014).
4. See Adrian Raine, *The Psychopathology of Crime: Criminal Behavior as a Clinical Disorder* (Cambridge: Academic Press, 1997); Adrian Raine, *The Anatomy of Violence: The Biological Roots of Crime* (New York: Vintage Books, 2014); James Fallon, *The Psychopath Inside: A Neuroscientist's Personal Journey into the Dark Side of the Brain* (New York: Current, 2013); Simon Baron-Cohen, *The Science of Evil: On Empathy and the Origins of Cruelty* (New York: Basic Books, 2012); Michael Stone, *The Anatomy of Evil* (Amherst, NY: Prometheus Books, 2009); Peter DiDomenica and Thomas G. Robbins, *Journey from Genesis to Genocide: Hate, Empathy, and the Plight of Humanity* (Pittsburgh, PA: Dorrance Publishing, 2013); Michael Shermer, *The Science of Good and Evil* (New York: Henry Holt, 2004); Barbara Sahakian and Julia Gottwald, *Sex, Lies, and Brain Scans: How fMRI Reveals What Really Goes on in Our Minds* (Oxford: Oxford University Press, 2017).
5. Walter Sinnott-Armstrong and Christian B. Miller, eds., *Moral Psychology: The Evolution of Morality: Adaptations and Innateness*, vol. 1 (Cambridge, MA: MIT Press, 2007); *Moral Psychology: The Cognitive Science of Morality: Intuition and Diversity*, vol. 2 (Cambridge, MA: Bradford Books, 2007); and *Moral Psychology: The Neuroscience of Morality: Emotion, Brain Disorders, and Development*, vol. 3 (Cambridge, MA: Bradford Books, 2007).
6. Patricia Churchland, *Braintrust: What Neuroscience Tells Us about Morality* (Princeton, NJ: Princeton University Press, 2012).
7. Ralph D. Mecklenburger, *Our Religious Brains: What Cognitive Science Reveals about Belief, Morality, Community and Our Relationship with God* (Nashville, TN: Jewish Lights Press, 2012).
8. Matthew Liao, *Moral Brains: The Neuroscience of Morality* (Oxford: Oxford University Press: 2016); J. D. Trout, *Why Empathy Matters: The Science and Psychology of Better Judgement* (New York: Penguin Group, 2010); Walter Sinnott-Armstrong, *Moral Psychology: The Neuroscience of Morality: Emotion, Brain Disorders, and Development* (Cambridge, MA: MIT Press, 2007); Darcia Narvaez and Allan Schore, *Neurobiology and the Development of Human Morality: Evolution, Culture, and Wisdom* (New York: W.W. Norton & Company, 2014).
9. See "The BRAIN Initiative," *Obama White House Archives*, https://obamawhitehouse.archives.gov/BRAIN. The BRAIN Initiative website can be found at https://braininitiative.nih.gov/. See also the next generation of NIH BRAIN Initiative

embodied in the public–private partnership: "the Brain Initiative" at https://www.braininitiative.org/.
10. A. Paul Alivisatos et al., "The Brain Activity Map Project and the Challenge of Functional Connectomics," *Neuron* 74, no. 6 (June 2012): 970–4.
11. Emily Underwood, "A $4.5 Billion Price Tag for the Brain Initiative?," *Science Insider*, June 5, 2014.
12. See Maria Popova, "'Brain Culture': How Neuroscience Became a Pop Culture Fixation," *The Atlantic*, August 18, 2011, a review of Davi Johnson Thornton, *Brain Culture: Neuroscience and Popular Media*.
13. Rafael Yuste and Cori Bargmann, "Toward a Global BRAIN Initiative," *Cell* 168, no. 6 (2017): 956–9; Suparna Choudhury et al., "Big Data, Open Science and the Brain: Lessons Learned From Genomics," *Frontiers in Human Neuroscience* 8 (2014): 239; A. Paul Alivisatos et al., "A National Network of Neurotechnology Centers for the BRAIN Initiative," *Neuron* 88, no. 3 (2015): 445–8.
14. "The BRAIN Initiative."
15. The therapeutic promises of the BI are at the forefront: NIH, "BRAIN Priority Areas," https://braininitiative.nih.gov/strategic-planning/brain-priority-areas; Thomas Insel, Story Landis, and Francis Collins, "The NIH BRAIN Initiative," *Science* 340, no. 6133 (May 10, 2013): 687–8. However, the therapeutic applications of the HGP were less than expected: Nicholas Wade, "A Decade Later, Genetic Map Yields Few New Cures," *The New York Times*, June 12, 2010.
16. Barack Obama, "Remarks by the President on the BRAIN Initiative and American Innovation," *White House Archives*, https://obamawhitehouse.archives.gov/photos-and-video/video/2013/04/02/president-obama-speaks-brain-initiative-and-american-innovation#transcript.
17. Ibid.
18. PBS Newshour, "President Obama Announces BRAIN Initiative," *News Broadcast*, YouTube, April 2, 2013, https://www.youtube.com/watch?v=Ol4SUlpXxXc.
19. Obama, "Remarks by the President."
20. Ibid.
21. Ibid.
22. Ibid.
23. For a detailed version of this history see: M. Therese Lysaught, "Love Your Enemies: Life Sciences in the Ecclesially-Based University," in *The Ecclesially-Based University in a Liberal Democratic Society*, ed. John Wright and Michael Budde (Grand Rapids, MI: Brazos Press, 2004). See also: see John Beatty, "Origins of the U.S. Human Genome Project: Changing Relationships between Genetics and National Security," in *Controlling Our Destinies*, ed. Phillip Reid Sloan (Notre Dame, IN: Notre Dame Press, 2000), 132; Robert Cook-Deegan, *The Gene Wars: Science, Politics, and the Human Genome* (New York: Norton, 1994); Diana B. Dutton, *Worse than the Disease: Pitfalls of Medical Progress* (New York: Cambridge University Press, 1988), 9; Timothy Lenoir and Marguerite Hays, "The Manhattan Project for Biomedicine," in *Controlling Our Destinies*, ed. Phillip Reid Sloan (Notre Dame, IN: Notre Dame Press, 2000), 30; Lily E. Kay, "A Book of Life? How a Genetic Code Became a Language," in *Controlling Our Destinies*, ed. Phillip Reid Sloan (Notre Dame, IN: Notre Dame Press, 2000).
24. PBS Newshour, "President Obama Announces BRAIN Initiative," at 5:37.
25. Ibid.

26  Presidential Commission for the Study of Bioethical Issues, "Gray Matters: Topics at the Intersection of Neuroscience, Ethics, and Society," https://bioethicsarchive.georgetown.edu/pcsbi/node/4704.html; Misti Ault Anderson, "Bioethics Commission Releases Final Neuroscience Report as Part of BI: Focuses on Controversial Topics That Must Be Addressed If Neuroscience Is to Progress and Be Applied Ethically," https://bioethicsarchive.georgetown.edu/pcsbi/blog/2015/03/26/bioethics-commission-releases-final-neuroscienc/index.html.
27  Emily Underwood, "US BRAIN Initiative Gets Ethical Advice," *Science Magazine*, May 14, 2014.
28  Anderson, "Bioethics Commission Releases Final Neuroscience."
29  NIH, "The Human Genome Project," https://www.genome.gov/human-genome-project.
30  See Charles Taylor, *Modern Social Imaginaries* (Durham, NC: Duke University Press, 2003), 30.
31  At its most basic, the term "political economy" refers to the intersection of political life and economic life. More specifically, it refers to a movement that arose in the eighteenth century, as Europe and, specifically, the emerging British empire, were transitioning from mercantilism to capitalism in order to facilitate, as Wendy Brown notes, the "economical governing of the polity, rather than to the politics or powers of economic life"; see Brown, *Undoing the Demos: Neoliberalism's Stealth Revolution* (Cambridge, MA: MIT Press, 2015) Kindle location 1320. See also Michel Foucault, *Birth of Biopolitics* (New York: Palgrave, 2008), 15–16: "[P]olitical economy introduces a new and particular regime of truth into governmental rationality," transforming the market from a site of justice to a site of veridiction.
32  Robert W. Doty tells this story in "Neuroscience," in *The History of the American Physiological Society: The First Century, 1887–1987*, ed. John R. Brobeck, Orr E. Reynolds, and Toby A. Appel (New York: Oxford University Press, 1988).
33  See the website "Milestones in Neuroscience Research," https://faculty.washington.edu/chudler/hist.html. This same framing is reproduced in the Wikipedia page on the "History of Neuroscience," https://en.wikipedia.org/wiki/History_of_neuroscience (Accessed October 15, 2021).
34  "Scimago Journal Rankings," https://www.scimagojr.com/journalrank.php?category=2801.
35  See also Popova, "'Brain Culture': How Neuroscience Became a Pop Culture Fixation."
36  See, for example, Thomas Douglas, "Moral Enhancement," *Journal of Applied Philosophy* 25, no. 3 (2008): 228–45; Ingmar Persson and Julian Savulescu, "The Perils of Cognitive Enhancement and the Urgent Imperative to Enhance the Moral Character of Humanity," *Journal of Applied Philosophy* 25, no. 3 (2008): 162–77; Ingmar Persson and Julian Savulescu, "Getting Moral Enhancement Right: The Desirability of Moral Bioenhancement," *Bioethics* (2011): 124–31; Mark Walker, "Enhancing Genetic Virtue: A Project for Twenty-First Century Humanity," *Politics and the Life Sciences* 28, no. 2 (2009): 27–47.
37  John Z. Sadler, *Values and Psychiatric Diagnosis, International Perspectives in Philosophy and Psychiatry* (New York: Oxford University Press, 2005).
38  Eddy Nahmias, "Is Neuroscience the Death of Free Will?" *New York Times*, Opinion Pages, November 13, 2011, https://opinionator.blogs.nytimes.com/2011/11/13/is-neuroscience-the-death-of-free-will/.
39  Sam Harris, *Free Will* (New York: Free Press, 2011).
40  Daniel Wegner, *The Illusion of Conscious Will* (Cambridge, MA: MIT Press, 2002).

41 Jerry Coyne, "You Don't Have Free Will," *The Chronicle of Higher Education*, March 18, 2012, https://www.chronicle.com/article/Jerry-A-Coyne-You-Dont-Have/131165.
42 Jeffrey Rosen, "The Brain on the Stand," *The New York Times Magazine*, March 11, 2007, https://www.nytimes.com/2007/03/11/magazine/11Neurolaw.t.html.
43 Tom Chivers, "Neuroscience, Free Will and Determinism," *The Telegraph*, October 12, 2010, https://www.telegraph.co.uk/news/science/8058541/Neuroscience-free-will-and-determinism-Im-just-a-machine.html.
44 Kathleen Vohs and Jonathan Schooler, "The Value of Believing in Free Will," *Psychological Science* 19, no. 1 (2008): 49–54.
45 Bruce Rogers-Vaughn identifies this same trope, noting:

> "I began to notice how much blaming was occurring in our society, particularly toward those who were not succeeding in the 'land of opportunity.'
>
> On cable and online news outlets, pundits could be heard villainizing the less fortunate. Apparently if people were poor, or were struggling in some way, it was their own damned fault. Even those in the shrinking middle class were often portrayed as less than sufficiently successful, as deficient in some fundamental way" (*Caring for Souls in a Neoliberal Age* [London: Palgrave-Macmillan, 2016], 3).

46 See "The Big Show with Bill Cunningham" (January 4, 2009) at Lauryn Bruck, "Cunningham on the Poor: 'They're Poor Because They Lack Values, Ethics, and Morals,'" *Media Matters for America*, January 15, 2009, https://www.mediamatters.org/bill-cunningham/cunningham-poor-theyre-poor-because-they-lack-values-ethics-and-morals. The "law of unintended consequences" originates in Adam Smith's *Wealth of Nations* and was cited as the reason that laissez-faire markets are necessary. See also: Chuck Colson, "Credit Where It's Due: Morality, Poverty, and Evangelicals," March 18, 2010, https://www.christianpost.com/news/morality-poverty-and-evangelicals.html; Bill O'Reilly, "The O'Reilly Factor," June 11, 2004, cited in Gabe Wildau, "O'Reilly: '[I]rresponsible and Lazy . . . That's What Poverty Is,'" *Media Matters for America*, June 18, 2004, https://www.mediamatters.org/bill-oreilly/oreilly-irresponsible-and-lazy-thats-what-poverty; Teddy Goodson, "Does Charity Breed Poverty?" *Blue Virginia*, May 23, 2010, https://bluevirginia.us/2010/05/does-charity-breed-poverty; Larry Elder, a conservative black talk-radio personality, offers an extended version of these sorts of remarks in his 2008 book *Stupid Black Men: How to Play the Race Card and Lose* (New York: St. Martin's Press, 2008).
47 See, e.g., "Talk Poverty," https://talkpoverty.org/basics/.
48 See, e.g., Clancy Blair and C. Cybele Raver, "Poverty, Stress, and Brain Development: New Directions for Prevention and Intervention," *Academy of Pediatrics* 16, no. 3 (April 2016): S30–S36; and Bessel van der Kolk, *The Body Keeps the Score: Brain, Mind, and Body in the Healing of Trauma* (London: Penguin Books, 2015).
49 See for example, Paul Zak, *The Moral Molecule* (New York: Dutton, 2013).
50 American Psychiatric Association, *Diagnostic and Statistical Manual of Mental Disorders*, 5th ed. (Washington, DC: American Psychiatric Association, 2013), 301.7.
51 Alasdair MacIntyre, *After Virtue: A Study of Moral Theory* (Notre Dame, IN: University of Notre Dame Press, 1984), 23.
52 Ibid. On his presentation of the choice between Nietzsche or Aristotle, see chapter 9, 109–20; on his understanding of emotivism, see 11–35. Recently, MacIntyre has shifted his language from emotivism to expressivism. See Alasdair MacIntyre, *Ethics in the Conflict of Modernity: An Essay on Desire, Practical Reasoning, and Narrative* (New York: Cambridge University Press, 2016), 17–19.

53 MacIntyre, *Ethics in the Conflict of Modernity*, 92.
54 Due to its prominent role in popular discourse about morality, we embarked on this study expecting race to be a central focus of our research. Yet although race is undoubtedly one of the dominant social imaginaries in US and Western culture, literature on the neuroscience of morality is eerily silent on this topic. Despite the centrality of "urban populations" and socioeconomic status mapped by zip codes in the studies we will cite, despite observations regarding high rates of antisocial personality disorder within prison populations and so forth, the racial demographics of study subjects or the differential implications for people of color of findings from these neuroscientific studies was—in our reading—never mentioned. The only place the neurosciences seem engaged with the question of race is in the search for neuroscientific bases for prejudice, social segregation, and how people perceive and respond to race. See, for example, Bradley D. Mattan, Kevin Y. Wei, Jasmin Cloutier, and Jennifer T. Kubota, "The Social Neuroscience of Race-Based and Status-Based Prejudice," *Current Opinion in Psychology* 24 (December 2018): 27–34. These studies map, of course, onto our larger thesis, locating the "cause" of racism in our biology— our brains, usually the amygdala—providing a "natural" explanation for it and thereby absolving agents from their behavior.

We have found only one article in which the neurosciences have begun to address its racial context. In an incisive 2019 article in *Frontiers of Human Neuroscience* entitled "'Seeing Color,' A Discussion of the Implications and Applications of Race in the Field of Neuroscience," Sade J. Abiodun takes her thought-community to task, asking "whether the Neuroscience community has successfully been held accountable for its actions, or whether the attempt to remain 'objective' has, in essence, resulted in harmful complicity in the perpetuation of scientific racism."
55 David Stedman Jones, *Masters of the Universe: Hayek, Friedman, and the Birth of Neoliberal Politics* (Princeton, NJ: Princeton University Press, 2013), 2, 8.
56 For this history, see Jim Yong Kim et al., *Dying for Growth: Global Inequality and the Health of the Poor* (Monroe, ME: Common Courage Press, 2002).
57 See Rogers-Vaughn, *Caring for Souls*, 116 and 54–5. Rogers-Vaughn is joined in this insight by French philosopher Bernard Stiegler, in his book, *The Age of Disruption: Technology and Madness in Computational Capitalism* (Cambridge, UK: Polity Press, 2019).
58 Rogers-Vaughn, *Caring for Souls*, 36. See also Brown, *Undoing the Demos*.
59 Brown, *Undoing the Demos*, Kindle location 59, 172–9.
60 David Harvey, *A Brief History of Neoliberalism* (Oxford: Oxford University Press, 2008), 23.
61 Brown, *Undoing the Demos*, Kindle location 332–40.
62 Harvey, *A Brief History of Neoliberalism*, 41.
63 Rogers-Vaughn, *Caring for Souls*, 19–20.
64 Brown provides a complex and nuanced critique of the gender of *Homo economicus*, making clear that it remains not only normatively male but that under neoliberalism, "gender subordination is both intensified and fundamentally altered" (Brown, *Undoing the Demos*, Kindle location 1520). We will therefore in this book refer to *Homo economicus* and his offspring using the male pronoun. We also find *Homo capitalus* to be so completely objectified that personal pronouns no longer apply; we will therefore refer to *Homo capitalus* as "It."
65 Foucault, *Birth of Biopolitics*, 1–2.

66 Rogers-Vaughn, *Caring for Souls*, 42. See also Brown as noting that neoliberalism "structure[es] markets it claims to liberate from structure, intensely governing subjects it claims to free from government, strengthening and retasking states it claims to abjure" (48–9).

67 Paul J. Zak, *The Moral Molecule: The Source of Love and Prosperity* (New York: Dutton, 2012).

68 Andreas Meyer-Lindenberg, et al., "Neural Mechanisms of Genetic Risk for Impulsivity and Violence in Humans," *Proceedings of the National Academy of Sciences USA* 103, no. 6 (April 18, 2006): 6269–74; Adrian Raine, "From Genes to Brain to Antisocial Behavior," *Current Directions in Psychological Science* 17, no. 5 (October 1, 2008): 323–8; Adrian Raine, "Schizotypal Personality: Neurodevelopmental and Psychosocial Trajectories," *Annual Review of Clinical Psychology* 2 (2006): 291–326; Essi Viding and Uta Frith, "Genes for Susceptibility to Violence Lurk in the Brain," *Proceedings of the National Academy of Sciences* 103, no. 16 (April 2006): 6085–6.

69 Suzanne Meeks, Shruti N. Shah and Sarah K. Ramsey, "The Pleasant Events Schedule—Nursing Home Version: A Useful Tool for Behavioral Interventions in Long-term Care," *Aging & Mental Health* 13, no. 3 (2009): 445–55; Martin Seligman, *Authentic Happiness* (New York: Atria Books, 2004).

70 Persson and Savulescu, "The Perils of Cognitive Enhancement," 162–77; Raine, "From Genes to Brain to Antisocial Behavior."

71 Thomas W. Meeks and Dilip V. Jeste, "Neurobiology of Wisdom: A Literature Overview," *Archives of General Psychiatry* 66, no. 4 (2009): 355–65.

72 Douglas, "Moral Enhancement"; Persson and Savulescu, "The Perils of Cognitive Enhancement"; Persson and Savulescu, "Getting Moral Enhancement Right"; Walker, "Enhancing Genetic Virtue."

73 See Richard Joyce and Richard Garner, eds., *The End of Morality: Taking Moral Abolitionism Seriously* (New York: Routledge, 2019). In pronouncing the demise of morality, Joyce and Garner do not seem to recognize the etiology of the malaise that, in their opinion, has led to the abolition of morality.

74 Taylor, *Modern Social Imaginaries*, 2.

75 Ludwik Fleck, *Genesis and Development of a Scientific Fact*, ed. T. J. Trenn and R. K. Merton (Chicago: University of Chicago Press, 1979), 112.

76 Ibid.

77 Ludwik Fleck, "Crisis in Science," in *Cognition and Fact: Materials on Ludwik Fleck*, ed. Robert S. Cohen and Thomas Schnelle (Dordrecht: D. Reidel Publishing, 1986), 156.

78 Meeks and Jeste, "Neurobiology of Wisdom."

79 Raine, "From Genes to Brain to Antisocial Behavior"; Raine, "Schizotypal Personality."

80 William Bennett, John DiIulio, and John P. Walters, *Body Count: Moral Poverty . . . and How to Win America's War against Crime and Drugs* (New York: Simon & Schuster, 1996). In this book, DiIulio coined the term "superpredators" to refer to urban youth as "'radically impulsive, [and] brutally remorseless youngsters . . .'" and used it elsewhere to forecast a massive increase in juvenile violence and incarceration over the coming decade. Now widely understood as racially coded scare tactic, this term and DiIulio's work in criminology helped to fuel the shift to mass incarceration of Black youths and men that we discuss later in the Interlude.

81 Jonathan Haidt, *The Righteous Mind: Why Good People are Divided by Politics and Religion* (New York: Pantheon Books, 2012); Meeks and Jeste, "Neurobiology of Wisdom"; Seligman, *Authentic Happiness*.

82 Avshalom Caspi et al., "Role of Genotype in the Cycle of Violence in Maltreated Children," *Science* 297, no. 5582 (2002): 851–4; Avshalom Caspi et al., "Influence of Life Stress on Depression: Moderation by a Polymorphism in the 5-HTT Gene," *Science* 301, no. 5631 (2003): 386–9; Naomi Sadeh et al., "Serotonin Transporter Gene Associations with Psychopathics Traits in Youth Vary as a Function of Socioeconomic Resources," *Journal of Abnormal Psychology* 119, no. 3 (2010): 604–9.

83 Taylor, *Modern Social Imaginaries*, 23.

84 Jeremy Bentham, "An Introduction to the Principles of Morals and Legislation," in *The Works of Jeremy Bentham*, ed. John Bowring (Edinburgh: William Tait, 1838–1843; reprinted New York, 1962).

85 Jeremy Bentham, Table of the Springs of Action, https://www.laits.utexas.edu/poltheory/bentham/springs/index.html.

86 Jeremy Bentham, "To Jaques Pierre Brissot de Warville, November 25, 1791," in *The Correspondence of Jeremy Bentham*, vol. 4: October 1788 to December 1793, ed. A. T. Milne, in *The Collected Works of Jeremy Bentham*, gen. ed. J. R. Dinwiddy (London: UCL Press, 2017), letter 821, 341–2.

## Prelude to a Neuroscience of Morality

1 Wojciech Sady, "Ludwik Fleck," *Stanford Encyclopedia of Philosophy* (Winter 2021 Edition), ed. Edward N. Zalta. Fleck was a survivor of the concentration camps at both Auschwitz and Buchenwald, his life spared perhaps because of his ability to provide medical services, eventually helping to develop an anti-typhus vaccine. He testified in the Nuremburg Trials against German physicians who conducted experiments on concentration camp prisoners.

2 Fleck, *The Genesis and Development of a Scientific Fact*. Originally published as *Entstehung und Entwicklung einer wissenschaftlichen Tatsache. Einführung in die Lehre vom Denkstil und Denkkollektiv* (Schwabe und Co., Verlagsbuchhandlung, Basel, 1935).

3 As Fleck notes, the carnal scourge was an umbrella diagnosis capturing all venereal diseases that would be "crystallized during the following centuries into various entities [including] what we now call leprosy; scabies; tuberculosis of the skin, bone, and glands; small pox (variola); mycoses of the skin; gonorrhea, soft chancre, probably also lymphogranuloma inguinale, and many skin diseases still regarded as nonspecific today, as well as general constitutional illnesses such as gout" (*Genesis and Development of a Scientific Fact*, 1).

4 As Sady notes, "Traditionally—and today some still think so—facts were considered to be what is given and accessible through the senses. Modern empiricists claimed that there is nothing in the mind that was not first in the senses. Fleck reversed this maxim: there is nothing in the senses that was not first in the mind" (Sady, "Ludwik Fleck").

5 Fleck's project would be helpfully extended by analyzing how the racist exoteric community in the United States and Europe imagined syphilis differently in Black and African-American bodies, providing the conceptual apparatus for the infamous "Tuskegee Study of Untreated Syphilis in the African American Male" conducted by the US Public Health Service between 1932 and 1972. For more on this case see James H. Jones, *Bad Blood: The Tuskegee Syphilis Experiment*, revised ed. (New York: Free

Press, 1993). For more on the relationship between racism as a social imaginary and medical science see Harriet A. Washington, *Medical Apartheid: The Dark History of Medical Experimentation on Black Americans from Colonial Times to the Present* (New York: Anchor, 2008); and Rebeca Skloot, *The Immortal Life of Henrietta Lacks* (New York: Broadway Books, 2011).

6   Fleck, *Genesis and Development of a Scientific Fact*, 42.
7   Ibid.
8   Ibid., 46.
9   Ibid., 5, quoting Josef Hermann, *Es gibt keine constitutionelle Syphilis: Ein Trostwort für die gesamte Menschheit* (Westphalia: Hagen, 1891; 4th ed., Leipzig: Otto, 1903).
10  Ibid., 27.
11  Ibid. If this process sounds like Thomas Kuhn's *The Structure of Scientific Revolutions*, it is because Kuhn was familiar with Fleck's work. It should be noted that Kuhn read Fleck's book well before he wrote *The Structure of Scientific Revolutions*.
12  Sady, "Ludwik Fleck."
13  Ibid.
14  Ibid.
15  See chapter three, "The Nature of Normal Science," in Thomas S. Kuhn, *The Structure of Scientific Revolutions*, 3rd ed. (Chicago, IL: University of Chicago Press, 1996).
16  Ibid.
17  Sady, "Ludwik Fleck." As he further notes: "In contemporary society, almost everybody belongs to many thought-collectives; e.g., a scientist may also be a member of a certain church, political party, mountain climbing club. An individual usually belongs to distant thought-collectives, so that conflicts between thought-styles coexisting in him/her do not arise. Most people belong only to exoteric circles; only few become members of any esoteric circle, sporadically belonging to more than one."
18  Fleck, *Genesis and Development of a Scientific Fact*, 2.
19  As he also notes, astrological interpretations likewise shaped the conceptual space, with many believing scientifically that "the conjunction of Saturn and Jupiter under the sign of Scorpio and the House of Mars on 25. XI 1484 was the cause of the carnal scourge [Lustseuche]. Benign Jupiter was vanquished by the evil planets Saturn and Mars. The sign of Scorpio, which rules the genitals, explains why the genitals were the first place to be attacked by the new disease" (ibid., 2).
20  Sady, "Ludwik Fleck."
21  Sady continues: "Fleck also stresses that there is no spontaneous creation of concepts (1935a, II.1). This is why a new research starts usually—although not always—from proto-ideas which often are of a religious or philosophical character, which had existed centuries before they acquired a scientific character. For example, long before Copernicus there was a proto-idea of a heliocentric system, before Lavoisier—a proto-idea of chemical elements, before Dalton—a proto-idea of atom, and before Leeuwenhoek—a proto-idea of microbe (1935a, II.2). Proto-ideas are vague, and therefore in the scientific understanding they cannot be considered as true or false. (Even though they were true for the members of corresponding thought-collectives). But they can become a point of departure for investigation" (ibid.).
22  J. B. Thompson, *Studies in the Theory of Ideology* (Berkeley, CA: University of California Press, 1984), 6.
23  Charles Taylor, *Modern Social Imaginaries* (Durham, NC: Duke University Press, 2007), 23.

24 Ibid.
25 Ibid.
26 Ibid., 24.
27 Foucault, *Birth of Biopolitics*, 20.
28 As Larry Squire notes in the Preface to his multivolume *The History of Neuroscience in Autobiography*, vol. 1, "Neuroscience is quintessentially interdisciplinary, and careers in neuroscience come from several different cultures including biology, psychology, and medicine" (Cambridge: Academic Press, 1998), ix. In light of our claim that contemporary neuroscience is characterized by multiple thought-communities, we find it notable that Squire, the president of the Society for Neuroscience from 1993 to 1994, uses the term "cultures" to characterize the different interlocutors captured under the neuroscience umbrella.
29 See Taylor, *Modern Social Imaginaries*, 30.

# Chapter 1

1 Baron-Cohen, *The Science of Evil*; Michael H. Stone and Gary Brucato, *The New Evil: Understanding the Emergence of Violent Crime* (Amherst, : Prometheus Books, 2019).
2 Viding and Frith, "Genes for Susceptibility to Violence Lurk in the Brain."
3 Meyer-Lindenberg et al., "Neural Mechanisms of Genetic Risk for Impulsivity and Violence in Humans." It should be remembered that a functional polymorphic gene is a gene that is capable of being transcribed into a functional protein, though the protein product is functions differently than the "normal" gene, where normal simply means the gene form that the majority of the population possesses.
4 Viding and Frith, "Genes for Susceptibility to Violence Lurk in the Brain," 6085.
5 Ibid.
6 We first noticed this use of the word "make" in Laurence Tancredi, *Hardwired Behavior: What Neuroscience Reveals about Morality* (Cambridge: Cambridge University Press, 2005).
7 Sadler, *Values and Psychiatric Diagnosis, International Perspectives in Philosophy and Psychiatry*.
8 By human sciences we mean those social and psychological sciences, including things like anthropology, sociology, psychology, psychiatry, social work, and public health, each having its separate theories, models, approaches, and methodologies. Rather than listing these sciences at each juncture, we will refer to them as the human sciences. These are the sciences that attempt to understand human behavior for the purposes of being able to intervene in human behavior. We will use human sciences and social sciences interchangeably.
9 Joseph J. Schildkraut, "The Catecholamine Hypothesis of Affective Disorders: A Review of Supporting Evidence," *American Journal of Psychiatry* 122, no. 5 (1965): 509–22.
10 David Lester, "The Concentration of Neurotransmitter Metabolites in the Cerebrospinal Fluid of Suicidal Individuals: A Meta-Analysis," *Pharmacopsychiatry* 28, no. 2 (1995): 45–50; Marie Åsberg, "Neurotransmitters and Suicidal Behavior: The Evidence from Cerebrospinal Fluid Studies," *Annals of New York Academy of Sciences* 836 (1997): 158–81. For example, persons with histories of attempted or completed

suicide show low cerebrospinal fluid (CSF) concentrations of 5-hydroxyindoleacetic acid (5-HIAA), a metabolite of serotonin, when compared to control subjects.

11 Emil F. Coccaro, "Central Neurotransmitter Function in Human Aggression and Impulsivity," in *Neurobiology and Clinical Views on Aggression and Impulsivity*, ed. Michael Maes and Emil F. Coccaro (New York: Wiley, 1998), 143–68; Åsberg, "Neurotransmitters and Suicidal Behavior."

12 Emil F. Coccaro et al., "Diminished Prolactin Responses to Repeated Fenfluramine Challenge in Man," *Psychiatry Research* 22 (1987): 257–9; David Stoff et al., "Test-retest Reliability of the Prolactin and Cortisol Responses to d,l-Fenfluramine Challenge in Disruptive Behavior Disorders," *Psychiatry Research* 42 (1992): 65–72.

13 Kevin M. Malone et al., "Prolactin Response to Fenfluramine and Suicide Attempt Lethality in Major Depression," *British Journal of Psychiatry* 168 (1996): 324–8.

14 Stephen B. Manuck et al., "Socio-economic Status Covaries with Central Nervous System Serotonergic Responsivity as a Function of Allelic Variation in the Serotonin Transporter Gene-linked Polymorphic Region," *Psychoneuroendocrinology* 29 (2004): 651–68.

15 See Stephen Manuck et al., "The Socioeconomic Status of Communities Predicts Variation in Brain Serotonergic Responsivity," *Psychological Medicine* 35 (2005): 519–28; Stephen Manuck et al., "Aggression, Impulsivity, and Central Nervous System Serotonergic Responsivity in a Nonpatient Sample," *Neuropsychopharmacology* 19 (1998): 287–99; Janine Flory, Stephen Manuck, and Matthew Muldoon, "Retest Reliability of Prolactin Response to dl-Fenfluramine Challenge in Adults," *Neuropsychopharmacology* 26 (2002): 269–72; Janine Flory et al., "A Comparison of d, l-Fenfluramine and Citalopram Challenges in Healthy Adults," *Psychopharmacology* 174 (2004): 376–80; Karen Matthews et al., "Does Socioeconomic Status Relate to Central Serotonergic Responsivity in Healthy Adults?" *Psychosomatic Medicine* 62 (2000): 231–7.

16 Manuck et al., "The Socioeconomic Status of Communities." It should be noted that a variation is not an abnormality. A variation is a functional difference in anatomy or physiology.

17 Manuck et al., "Socio-economic Status Covaries," 652. The length and diversity of this list of correlate conditions is worth noting.

18 Ibid., 520.

19 Manuck et al., "The Socioeconomic Status of Communities."

20 These authors see the use of census tract data as an improvement over prior measures, without mentioning the racial profile of this data. As is widely known, especially in urban areas, race is correlated with census track, with "four times as many Blacks and three times as many Hispanics" living in census tracts that have been designated as "poverty areas" in 1990 (U.S. Bureau of the Census, *Statistical Brief: Poverty Areas*, 1995, https://www.census.gov/prod/1/statbrief/sb95_13.pdf.) For the implications of racialized data, see Sade J. Abiodun, "'Seeing Color': A Discussion of the Implications and Applications of Race in the Field of Neuroscience," *Front Hum Neurosci* 13 (August 13, 2019): 280. Thus, there is an unspoken correlation between their findings and race. See especially Peter Gianaros and Stephen Manuck, "Neurobiological Pathways Linking Socioeconomic Position and Health," *Psychosomatic Medicine* 72, no. 5 (2010): 455.

21 Manuck et al., "The Socioeconomic Status of Communities." Note that although this is supposed to be a more complex variable, the components remain economic.

22 Ibid., 526.

23 Ibid.
24 Ibid.
25 Peter Gianaros et al., "Perigenual Anterior Cingulate Morphology Covaries with Perceived Social Standing," *Social Cognitive and Affective Neuroscience* 2 (2007): 161–73.
26 This scale asks subjects to rank their own perception of their social status by marking a rung on a ladder.
27 Gianaros et al., "Perigenual Anterior Cingulate Morphology."
28 Ibid., 170. Emphasis added. pACC refers to the perigenual area of the anterior cingulate cortex, a region of the brain involved in emotional and behavioral regulation.
29 Gianaros and Manuck, "Neurobiological Pathways Linking Socioeconomic Position and Health."
30 As we will see in Part II, Gary Becker likewise adopts the construct of socio-economic positioning (SEP) in his analyses.
31 Gianaros and Manuck, "Neurobiological Pathways Linking Socioeconomic Position and Health."
32 Peter Gianaros et al., "Potential Neural Embedding of Parental Social Standing," *Social Cognitive and Affective Neuroscience* 3 (2008): 91–6.
33 Gianaros and Manuck, "Neurobiological Pathways Linking Socioeconomic Position and Health," 452. Emphasis added.
34 Ibid., 457.
35 John Ashburner and Karl Friston, "Voxel-Based Morphometry—The Methods," *Neuroimage* 11 (2000): 805–21.
36 Earl Babbie, *The Practice of Social Research*, 10th ed. (Belmont, CA: Wadsworth, 2004), 119.
37 Catherine Marshall and Gretchen B. Rossman, *Designing Qualitative Research*, 5th ed. (Thousand Oaks, CA: Sage, 2011), 63–4.
38 Babbie, *The Practice of Social Research*, 128. Note that common sense is also part of a social construct. See Antonio Gramsci, *Selections from the Prison Notebooks*, trans. Q. Hoare and G. Nowell Smith (London: Lawrence & Wishart, 1971), 321–43.
39 Ibid., 132.
40 Ibid., 131; Fisher, "The Importance of Variable Names," in Babbie, *The Practice of Social Research*, 130–1.
41 Babbie, *The Practice of Social Research*, 128.
42 Gertrude Himmelfarb, *The Idea of Poverty* (New York: Alfred A. Knopf, 1983). Economist Martin Ravallion in his historical study of references to "poverty" in literature confirms Himmelfarb's thesis, naming the period of roughly 1740–90 as the first of two "Poverty Enlightenments." See Martin Ravallion, "The Two Poverty Enlightenments: Historical Insights from Digitized Books Spanning Three Centuries" (The World Bank Development Research Group, Director's Office, January 2011). For a more in-depth study of this thesis, see Martin Ravallion, *The Economics of Poverty* (Washington, DC: Georgetown University Press, 2016).
43 Mary Poovey, *A History of the Modern Fact: Problems of Knowledge in the Sciences of Wealth and Society* (Chicago: University of Chicago Press, 1998).
44 See Karl Polanyi, *The Great Transformation: The Political and Economic Origins of Our Time* (Boston, MA: Beacon Press, 2001). We discuss this further in Chapter 5.
45 Ravallion, "The Two Poverty Enlightenments," 3.

46 Bernard Beck, "Bedbugs, Stench, Dampness, and Immorality: A Review Essay on Recent Literature about Poverty," *Social Problems* 15, no. 1 (1967): 101–14.
47 Ravallion, "The Two Poverty Enlightenments," 3. Ravallion notes that this was "followed by a resurgence starting in the mid-1980s, with the overall peak just a couple of years before the turn of the 21st century." Ravallion's survey spans 1700–2000; given the reinvigorated attention to global health since 2000, the shock of the Great Recession of 2008, and increased consciousness of income and wealth inequalities, we may well be in what Ravallion would term a third Poverty Enlightenment.
48 Michael Harrington, *The Other America: Poverty in the United States* (New York: Scribner's, 1962; Reprint Edition 1997).
49 Hubert H. Humphrey, *War on Poverty* (New York: McGraw-Hill, 1964); Arthur B. Shostak and William Gomberg, eds., *New Perspectives on Poverty* (Englewood Cliffs, NJ: Prentice-Hall, 1965); Louis A. Freeman, Joyce L. Kornbluh, and Alan Haber, eds., *Poverty in America* (Ann Arbor, MI: University of Michigan Press, 1965); Robert E. Will and Harold G. Vatter, eds., *Poverty in Affluence* (New York: Harcourt, Brace, and World, 1965); Hannah H. Meissener, ed., *Poverty in the Affluent Society* (New York: Harper and Row, 1966); Margaret S. Gordon, ed., *Poverty in America* (San Francisco, CA: Chandler, 1965); Leo Fishman, ed., *Poverty Amid Affluence* (New Haven: Yale University Press, 1966); Florence Heller Graduate School for Advanced Studies in Social Welfare, *Colloquia: 1963–1964, Poverty and Dependency* (Waltham, MA: Brandeis University, 1965); Harold L. Wilensky and Charles N. Lebeaux, *Social Welfare and Industrial Society* (New York: Free Press, 1965).
50 Daniel Patrick Moynihan, *The Negro Family: A Case for National Action* (Washington, DC: US Government Printing Office, 1965). For an annotated edition of this report with historical commentary, see Daniel Gleary, "The Moynihan Report: An Annotated Edition," *The Atlantic Monthly*, September 14, 2015, https://www.theatlantic.com/politics/archive/2015/09/the-moynihan-report-an-annotated-edition/404632/.
51 The long unpublished paper can now be found at: August B. Hollingshead, "Four Factor Index of Social Status," *Yale Journal of Sociology* 8 (2011): 21–52, https://sociology.yale.edu/sites/default/files/files/yjs_fall_2011.pdf. See also Julia Adams and David L. Weakliem, "August B. Hollingshead's 'Four Factor Index of Social Status': From Unpublished Paper to Citation Classic," *Yale Journal of Sociology* 8 (Fall 2011): 11.
52 August B. Hollingshead and Frederick C. Redlich, *Social Class and Mental Illness: A Community Study* (New York: John Wiley & Sons, 1958). This study is, like that of Gianaros and Manuck, notable for the way it elides the issue of race. To contextualize their study, the authors narrate the social history of New Haven and how it contributed to the class stratifications that define their study; in this history, African Americans are mentioned a handful of times, but then they essentially disappear from the remaining analysis, but for one mention (see chapter 7 on "Class and Prevalence of Disorders"). Glossing over the statistical anomalies in the racial composition of their patient population, they draw important class-based conclusions. For example, they find that mental disorders of the higher classes (I–II) tend to be of the "neurotic" variety, whereas the disorders of Classes IV–V tended to be of the psychotic variety. They also find that "the lower the class, the greater proportion of patients in the population" (216). Finally, people from Classes IV and V were less likely to categorize their own behavior or that of others as "psychopathological," whereas there was a much great readiness to do so in Classes I–II (see, e.g., 173).

53 August B. Hollingshead, "Commentary on 'The Indiscriminate State of Social Class Measurement,'" *Social Forces* 49 (1971): 565.
54 According to Adams and Weakliem, Hollingshead's "Two Factor Index of Social Position" was also not published—he had it "privately printed [as a pamphlet] and sold for 1 dollar per copy. The Two Factor Index offered a procedure which combined the occupation and education of the head of the household to generate a single measure of social status" (12). This too was received enthusiastically by the social scientific community.
55 Adams and Weakliem, "August B. Hollingshead's 'Four Factor Index of Social Status,'" 12–13.
56 Ibid., 11.
57 Cirino and his colleagues specifically examine six instruments developed between 1971 and 1994 to test how well they correlate in terms of their findings (see Paul T. Cirino et al., "Measuring Socioeconomic Status: Reliability and Preliminary Validity for Different Approaches," *Assessment* 9 (2002): 145–55). The instruments they cite and/or assess include: the Hollingshead Four Factor Index of Social Status (1975); Blishen, Carroll, and Moore (1987); Entwisel and Astone (1994); Nakao and Treas (1992); the Revised Duncan Socioeconomic Index (1981); and the Siegel Prestige Scale (1971).
58 Babbie, *The Practice of Social Research*, 128.
59 See David Hilfiker, *Urban Injustice: How Ghettos Happen* (New York: Seven Stories Press, 2003).
60 Gianaros and Manuck, "Neurobiological Pathways Linking Socioeconomic Position and Health," 2.
61 Ibid., 5.
62 Maurice M. Rapport, Arda Alden Green, and Irvie H. Page, "Serum Vasoconstrictor, Serotonin; Isolation and Characterization," *Journal of Biological Chemistry* 176, no. 3 (1948): 961–9.
63 Irving J. Selikoff and Edward H. Robitzek, "Tuberculosis Chemotherapy with Hydrazine Derivatives of Isonicotinic Acid," *Dis Chest* 21, no. 4 (1952): 385–38.
64 Ibid., 401.
65 David Healy, *The Creation of Psychopharmacology* (Cambridge: Harvard University Press, 2002).
66 Michael Rosenbloom, "Chlorpromazine and the Psychopharmacologic Revolution," *JAMA* 287, no. 14 (2002): 1860–1.
67 Schildkraut, "The Catecholamine Hypothesis of Affective Disorders."
68 Bruce Rogers-Vaughn, "Blessed are Those Who Mourn: Depression as Political Resistance," *Pastoral Psychol* 63 (2014): 506.
69 Dan German Blazer, *The Age of Melancholy: "Major Depression" and Its Social Origin* (New York: Routledge, 2005).
70 Rogers-Vaughn, "Blessed are Those Who Mourn," 506.
71 Rogers-Vaughn, *Caring for Souls*. See also M. Therese Lysaught, "That Jagged Little Pill and the Counter-Politics of the Community of the Expelled Sacramentality and Psychiatric Medications," *Christian Bioethics* 24, no. 3 (2018): 246–64.
72 Rogers-Vaughn, "Blessed are Those Who Mourn," 507.
73 Ibid., 507.
74 In the words of Peter Kramer, "Depression is the Opposite of Freedom" (*Against Depression* [New York: Viking, 2004], 14).

75 See A. V. Horwitz, "How an Age of Anxiety Became an Age of Depression," *The Milbank Quarterly* 88, no. 1 (2010): 112–38. The World Health Organization recently declared that "By 2020, depression will be the second leading cause of world disability" (Rogers-Vaughn, "Blessed are Those Who Mourn," 509; World Federation for Mental Health, "Depression: A Global Crisis," October 10, 2012, https://www.who.int/mental_health/management/depression/wfmh_paper_depression_wmhd_2012.pdf). Rogers-Vaughn also argues convincingly that the neoliberal cultural paradigm *produces* mental illness by the ways that the changes it has wrought in material, social, and political conditions "dismember the soul" (510, passim).

76 Randy A. Sansone and Lori A. Sansone, "Personality Disorders: A Nation-Based Perspective on Prevalence," *Innov Clin Neurosci* 8, no. 4 (April 2011): 13–18. As noted, ASPD was only defined as a disorder in 1980 with the DSM-III. The literature notes that the prevalence of ASPD "can reach 80% in correctional settings" (Donald W. Black, "The Natural History of Antisocial Personality Disorder," *Canadian Journal of Psychiatry* 60, no. 7 (July 2015): 309–14). Black and others fail to elaborate on further facts behind this statistic, namely that in the United States, 34 percent of the population in correctional settings are African-American, that African Americans and Hispanics who make up approximately 32 percent of the US population comprised 56 percent of all incarcerated people in 2015; and that African Americans are incarcerated at more than five times the rate of whites (NAACP, "Criminal Fact Sheet," https://www.naacp.org/criminal-justice-fact-sheet/ [Accessed October 15, 2021]).

77 Hervey M. Cleckley, *The Mask of Sanity: An Attempt to Re-Interpret Some Issues About the So-Called Psychopathic Personality*, 5th ed. (St. Louis, MO: Mosby, 1976).

78 American Psychiatric Association, *Diagnostic and Statistical Manual of Mental Disorders*.

79 John M. Oldham, "The Alternative DSM-5 Model for Personality Disorders," *World Psychiatry* 14, no. 2 (June 2015): 234–6.

80 American Psychiatric Association, *Diagnostic and Statistical Manual of Mental Disorders*.

81 National Institute of Mental Health, "RDoC Frequently Asked Questions (FAQ)," https://www.nimh.nih.gov/research/research-funded-by-nimh/rdoc/resources/rdoc-frequently-asked-questions-faq.

82 Note Adrian Raine's article of the same title, "From Genes to Brains to Antisocial Behavior," 323–8.

83 Viding and Frith, "Genes for Susceptibility to Violence Lurk in the Brain"; Meyer-Lindenberg et al., "Neural Mechanisms of Genetic Risk for Impulsivity and Violence in Humans."

84 It should be noted again that a polymorphism is a functional gene, though its function is different—either more or less efficient—than the gene possessed by the majority of a population. J. W. Buckholtz et al., "Genetic Variation in MAOA Modulates Ventromedial Prefrontal Circuitry Mediating Individual Differences in Human Personality," *Molecular Psychiatry* 13, no. 3 (2008): 313–24; Luca Passamonti et al., "Monoamine Oxidase-A Genetic Variations Influence Brain Activity Associated with Inhibitory Control: New Insight into the Neural Correlates of Impulsivity," *Biological Psychiatry* 59, no. 4 (2006): 334–40; Leanne M. Williams et al., "Polymorphism of the MAOA Gene is Associated with Emotional Brain Markers and Personality Traits on an Antisocial Index," *Neuropsychopharmacology* 34 (2009): 1797–809.

85 Viding and Frith, "Genes for Susceptibility to Violence Lurk in the Brain," 6085–6.

86 Meyer-Lindenberg et al., "Neural Mechanisms of Genetic Risk for Impulsivity and Violence in Humans," 6269–74.
87 Low-efficiency means less MAOA-I, which means less degradation of major neurotransmitters; high efficiency means more MAOA-I, which means more degradation of major neurotransmitters.
88 It should be noted that Meyer-Lidenberg et al. were not interested in behavior, just neural structure and function.
89 Meyer-Lindenberg et al., "Neural Mechanisms of Genetic Risk for Impulsivity and Violence in Humans," 6269 (emphasis added). Note that they are correlating here genetic variation, neurobiological activity, *and* neurobiological structure.
90 Caspi et al., "Role of Genotype in the Cycle of Violence in Maltreated Children," 851–4, cited in Meyer-Lindenberg et al., "Neural Mechanisms of Genetic Risk for Impulsivity and Violence in Humans," 6269. Note that this study did not explore the connection between this genetic polymorphism and behavior; researchers instead extrapolate from other studies to associate these changes with presumed behavioral outcomes.
91 Lester, "The Concentration of Neurotransmitter Metabolites in the Cerebrospinal Fluid of Suicidal Individuals: a Meta-Analysis"; Asberg, "Neurotransmitters and Suicidal Behavior."
92 Viding and Frith, "Genes for Susceptibility to Violence Lurk in the Brain," 6085.
93 Ibid., emphasis added.
94 Caspi et al., "Role of Genotype in the Cycle of Violence in Maltreated Children."
95 Supplementary material for Caspi et al., "Role of Genotype in the Cycle of Violence in Maltreated Children," 3.
96 Ibid.
97 Ibid., 853, emphasis added.
98 Sadeh et al., "Serotonin Transporter Gene Associations."
99 Ibid., 606.
100 Lukas Pezawas et al., "5-HTTLPR Polymorphism Impacts Human Cingulate-Amygdala Interactions: A Genetic Susceptibility Mechanism for Depression," *Nature Neuroscience* 8 (2005): 828–34.
101 Meyer-Lindenberg et al., "Neural Mechanisms of Genetic Risk for Impulsivity and Violence in Humans," 6269.
102 Viding and Frith, "Genes for Susceptibility to Violence Lurk in the Brain," 6085.
103 Meyer-Lindenberg et al., "Neural Mechanisms of Genetic Risk for Impulsivity and Violence in Humans," 6269.
104 Baron-Cohen, *The Science of Evil*; Raine, "From Genes to Brains to Antisocial Behavior."
105 Terrie Moffitt and Avshalom Caspi, "Evidence from Behavioral Genetics for Environmental Contributions to Antisocial Conduct," in *The Explanation of Crime: Context, Mechanisms, and Development*, ed. Per-Olof H. Wikström and Robert J. Sampson (Cambridge: Cambridge University Press, 2006), 108.
106 Adrian Raine, *The Anatomy of Violence: The Biological Roots of Crime* (New York: Vintage, 2013).
107 For an interesting take on the importance of a moral anthropology of another social science—namely the science of economics—see Christina McRorie, "The Emptiness of Modern Economics: Why the Dismal Science Needs a Richer Moral Anthropology," *The Hedgehog Review* 16, no. 2 (Fall 2014): 120–9.
108 Raine, *The Anatomy of Violence*.

109 Gianaros and Manuck, "Neurobiological Pathways Linking Socioeconomic Position and Health," 450.

## Chapter 2

1. "Milestones in Neuroscience Research," https://faculty.washington.edu/chudler/hist.html. This page is curated by Eric Chudler, UW's Executive Director of the Center for Neurotechnology.
2. Lorenzo Livianos-Aldana, Luis Rojo-Moreno, and Pilar Sierra-SanMiguel, "Gall and the Phrenological Movement," *The American Journal of Psychiatry* 164, no. 3 (2007): 414.
3. Donald Simpson, "Phrenology and the Neurosciences: Contributions of F. J. Gall and J. G. Spurzheim," *ANZ Journal of Surgery* 75 (2005): 475.
4. Ibid., 475–6.
5. John van Wyhe, "The History of Phrenology," *The Victorian Web*, http://www.victorianweb.org/science/phrenology/intro.html. See also John van Wyhe, "The Authority of Human Nature: The *Schädellehre* of Franz Joseph Gall," *BJHS* 35 (2002): 17–42, http://www.historyofphrenology.org.uk/texts/2002van_wyhe.htm.
6. Livianos-Aldana et al., "Gall and the Phrenological Movement," 414; Martin S. Staum, *Labeling People: French Scholars on Society, Race and Empire, 1815–1848* (Montreal: McGill-Queen's University Press, 2003). Per van Wyhe, the British Phrenological Society was only disbanded in 1967, right around the time of the founding of the Society of Neuroscience.
7. John van Wyhe, "Reading Phrenology," *The History of Phrenology on the Web*, http://www.historyofphrenology.org.uk/literature.html.
8. Ibid.
9. Staum, *Labeling People*; see also George Combe, "On the Coincidence Between the Natural Talents and Dispositions of Nations, and the Development of Their Brains," in *A System of Phrenology*, 5th ed. (Edinburgh: MacLachlan and Stewart, 1853), 327–61, http://www.historyofphrenology.org.uk/system/national_character.htm; and Dan van Ness, "Applying Restorative Justice to the Genocide in Rwanda," *Restorative Justice International*, March 30, 2012, http://www.restorativejusticeinternational.com/2012/applying-restorative-justice-to-the-genocide-in-rwanda/. See also Abiodun, "'Seeing Color.'"
10. Staum, *Labeling People*; and Sherrie L. Lyons, *Species, Serpents, Spirits, and Skulls: Science at the Margins in the Victorian Age* (Albany, NY: New York Press, 2009), 141–3.
11. Simpson, "Phrenology and the Neurosciences," 476.
12. Ibid.
13. Meeks and Jeste, "Neurobiology of Wisdom," 357.
14. Though Meeks and Jeste associate conditions such as dementia with a corollary lack or absence of wisdom, it is unclear how this direct link is actually made in their reasoning. They seem to suggest that if wisdom could somehow be ingrained, strengthened, or rehabilitated, then those who suffer with neurocognitive disorders might remain or become wise, though this association is never fully spelled out.
15. Martin Seligman and Christopher Peterson, *Character, Strengths, and Virtues: A Handbook in Classification* (Oxford: Oxford University Press, 2004).
16. Meeks and Jeste, "Neurobiology of Wisdom," 356.
17. Van Wyhe opines: "Rather than portraying phrenology as having succumbed to an inexorable progress of 'science' or representing the Victorians as having become less

'gullible,' phrenology can be understood to have been diffused and absorbed into a host of other practices and traditions—as such many of its components live on" (van Wyhe, "The History of Phrenology"). That phrenology is not entirely a thing of the past, see Harriet Dempsey-Jones's account of University of Oxford research group that tested Gall's theory using modified MRI techniques in "Neuroscientists Put the Dubious Theory of 'Phrenology' Through Rigorous Testing for the First Time," *The Conversation*, January 22, 2018, http://theconversation.com/neuroscientists-put-the-dubious-theory-of-phrenology-through-rigorous-testing-for-the-first-time-88291.

18  Meeks and Jeste, "Neurobiology of Wisdom," 355.
19  Meeks and Jeste state that they chose ten definitions. However, full citations of only six studies can be found in their article. These include: Richard J. Sternberg, *Wisdom, Intelligence, and Creativity Synthesized* (New York: Cambridge University Press, 2003); Paul B. Baltes, Jacqui Smith, and Ursula M. Staudinger, "Wisdom and Successful Aging," *Nebraska Symposium on Motivation* 39 (1991): 123–67; Scott C. Brown and Jeffrey A. Greene, "The Wisdom Development Scale: Translating the Conceptual to the Concrete," *Journal of College Student Development* 47, no. 1 (2008): 1–19; Monika Ardelt, "Wisdom as Expert Knowledge System: A Critical Review of a Contemporary Operationalization of an Ancient Concept," *Human Development* 47, no. 5 (2004): 275; Leonard A. Jason, Arne Reichler, Caroline King, Derryk Madsen, Jennifer Camacho, Wendy Marchese, "The Measurement of Wisdom: A Preliminary Report," *Journal of Community Psychology* 29, no. 5 (2001): 585–98; Gerard M. Brugman, "Wisdom and Aging," in *Handbook of the Psychology of Aging*, ed. J. E. Birren and K. Warner Schaie, 6th ed. (Burlington, MA: Elsevier Academic Press, 2005), 445–69. Three other "articles" are cited in a table by Kitchener, Meacham, Wink, and Helson; however, full bibliographic information is not supplied in the references. This, however, would only bring the total to nine definitions.
20  Meeks and Jeste, "Neurobiology of Wisdom," 356.
21  Ibid.
22  Ibid., 357. On altruism, see John Milbank, *Being Reconciled: Ontology and Pardon* (London: Routledge, 2003), 139.
23  Sternberg, *Wisdom, Intelligence, and Creativity Synthesized*, 152.
24  Meeks and Jeste, "Neurobiology of Wisdom," 356.
25  Ibid.
26  Ibid.
27  Ibid.
28  Sternberg, *Wisdom, Intelligence, and Creativity Synthesized*, 152.
29  Paul B. Baltes, "The Aging Mind: Potential and Limits," *The Gerontologist* 33 (1993): 580–94. Paul B. Baltes and Ursula M. Staudinger, "The Search for a Psychology of Wisdom," *Current Directions in Psychological Science* 2, no. 3 (1993): 75–81.
30  Paul B. Baltes and Ursula M. Staudinger, "Wisdom: A Metaheuristic (Pragmatic) to Orchestrate Mind and Virtue Toward Excellence," *American Psychologist* 55, no. 1 (2000): 123.
31  Ibid., 124.
32  Ibid.
33  Ibid.
34  Ardelt, "Wisdom as Expert Knowledge System," 275–6.
35  Ibid., 263.
36  Scott C. Brown, "Learning Across the Campus: How College Facilitates the Development of Wisdom," *Journal of College Student Development* 45, no. 2 (2004): 134–48.

37　Brown and Greene, "The Wisdom Development Scale."
38　Jason et al., "The Measurement of Wisdom," 590.
39　Ibid., 591.
40　Ibid., 591–2.
41　Ibid., 591.
42　Equally, as Viding and Frith point to impulsivity that tends toward aggression as a central antisocial trait, Meeks and Jeste consider its opposite, namely, "emotional homeostasis," to be a subcomponent of wisdom. They draw on three studies (Brugman, "Wisdom and Aging"; Ardelt, "Wisdom as Expert Knowledge System"; and Brown and Green, "The Wisdom Development Scale") but again, their umbrella term elides and ignores important nuances and differences in these studies.
43　As already noted, one article cited by Meeks and Jeste is a review article by Monika Ardelt, which challenges other definitions they use. Yet we could critique both Ardelt's work and Meeks and Jeste's appropriation of it a la our analysis of prosocial attitudes and behaviors above. Ardelt's article cites two of her own articles (Monika Ardelt, "Wisdom and Life Satisfaction in Old Age," *The Journals of Gerontology Series B: Psychological Sciences and Social Sciences* 52, no. 1 (1997): P15–P27; and Monika Ardelt, "Empirical Assessment of a Three-Dimensional Wisdom Scale," *Research on Aging* 25, no. 3 (2003): 275–324) in which she attempts to operationalize a definition of wisdom. The more important of these two papers is the development of what Ardelt calls a three-dimensional wisdom scale (3D-WS). Wisdom here is operationalized as a latent variable of cognitive, reflective, and affective indicators. That is, wisdom is not directly measured but is a construct of three other psychological constructs, each of which already has established measures. Ardelt complied 114 items from several existing scales and 18 additional items to assess the cognitive, reflective, and affective dimensions of wisdom. By the cognitive dimension of wisdom, Ardelt means the ability of a person to understand and comprehend the deeper meaning and significance of "phenomena and events, particularly with regard to intrapersonal and interpersonal matters" (Ardelt, "Empirical Assessment," 278). The reflective dimension, Ardelt notes, is "a prerequisite to the development of the cognitive dimension of wisdom" (Ibid.). The affective dimension refers to the emotional state one has when engaging the world, reflecting on oneself, or engaging with others. By affective, Ardelt means both "feelings and acts of sympathy and compassion, and the absence of indifferent or negative emotions and behavior toward others" (ibid., 278–9).

From Ardelt's description, it is easy to see the relationship between emotional homeostasis and prosocial attitudes and behaviors. In Ardelt's version, emotional stability seems necessary to see clearly into the deep reality of the world, and emotional attunement to the other also is required, not just in terms of feelings for others or attitudes, but in action, behavior toward others. But again, much is lost in reducing her account to these two concepts. Lastly, as noted by Ardelt herself, the conceptual definition and the operationalized 3D-WS is being designed for large, standardized surveys, but she does not indicate to what end and purposes such surveys will be used.

44　Udo Dannlowski et al., "Reduced Amygdala–Prefrontal Coupling in Major Depression: Association with MAOA Genotype and Illness Severity," *International Journal of Neuropsychopharmacology* 12, no. 1 (2009): 11–22; Andreas Heinz et al., "Amygdala-Prefrontal Coupling Depends on a Genetic Variation of the Serotonin Transporter," *Nature Neuroscience* 8, no. 1 (2005): 20–1; Pezawas et al.,

"5-HTTLPR Polymorphism Impacts Human Cingulate-Amygdala Interactions," 828–34.
45  Meeks and Jeste, "Neurobiology of Wisdom," 360.
46  Ibid., 359.
47  Heinz et al., "Amygdala-Prefrontal Coupling Depends on a Genetic Variation of the Serotonin Transporter."
48  Meeks and Jeste, "Neurobiology of Wisdom," 360.
49  Ibid., 359.
50  Ibid., 357.
51  Ibid. Meeks and Jeste here refer to Jean Decety and Philip Jackson, "The Functional Architecture of Human Empathy," *Behavioral and Cognitive Neuroscience Reviews* 3, no. 2 (2004): 71–100.
52  Rüdiger Seitz, Janpeter Nickel, and Nina Azari, "Functional Modularity of the Medial Prefrontal Cortex: Involvement in Human Empathy," *Neuropsychology* 20, no. 6 (2006): 743–51. This work draws on the work of Josef Perner and Birgit Lang, "Development of Theory of Mind and Executive Control," *Trends in Cognitive Sciences* 3, no. 9 (1999): 337–44. The theory behind the "theory of mind" is that the average person carries with them a theory of mind that allows them to "theorize" about what the person is thinking. It is a shorthand for being able to intuit the thoughts of another person. Some thinkers at times refer it as "mind-reading."
53  Jean Decety et al., "The Neural Bases of Cooperation and Competition: An fMRI Investigation," *Neuroimage* 23, no. 2 (2004): 744–51.
54  Ibid.
55  Ibid., 749.
56  Ibid., 750.
57  James K. Rilling et al., "Neural Correlates of Social Cooperation and Non-Cooperation as a Function of Psychopathy," *Biological Psychiatry* 61, no. 11 (2007): 1260–71, quoted by Meeks and Jeste, "Neurobiology of Wisdom," 358.
58  Jorge Moll et al., "Human Fronto-Mesolimbic Networks Guide Decisions About Charitable Donation," *Proceedings of the National Academy of Sciences of the United States of America* 103, no. 42 (2006): 15623–8.
59  Rachel Bachner-Melman et al., "Dopaminergic Polymorphisms Associated with Self-Report Measures of Human Altruism: A Fresh Phenotype for the Dopamine D4 Receptor," *Molecular Psychiatry* 10, no. 4 (2005): 333.
60  Bachner-Melman et al. here cite Stephen V. Faraone et al., "Meta-Analysis of the Association between the 7-Repeat Allele of the Dopamine D(4) Receptor Gene and Attention Deficit Hyperactivity Disorder," *American Journal of Psychiatry* 158, no. 7 (2001): 1052–7; and Naomi Lowe et al., "Joint Analysis of the Drd5 Marker Concludes Association with Attention-Deficit/Hyperactivity Disorder Confined to the Predominantly Inattentive and Combined Subtypes," *American Journal of Human Genetics* 74, no. 2 (2004): 348–56.
61  Bachner-Melman et al., "Dopaminergic Polymorphisms," 333–5.
62  Bachner-Melman et al., cite Eric Wang et al., "The Genetic Architecture of Selection at the Human Dopamine Receptor D4 (Drd4) Gene Locus," *American Journal of Human Genetics* 74, no. 5 (2004): 931–44.
63  Bachner-Melman, "Dopaminergic Polymorphisms," 335.
64  One further point that Meeks and Jeste seem to miss that is in Bachner-Melman both the prosocial genetic signature and the antisocial genetic signature seem important for herd survival. In terms of inclusive fitness, the terms "antisocial" and "prosocial" seem

inappropriate. As we will see in Chapter 3, these ideas align conveniently with the work of Paul Zak.
65  As we will see in Chapter 3, Jonathan Haidt reinforces our claim.
66  An entire issue of the *Journal of Applied Philosophy* (25, no. 3 [2008]) was devoted to the question of human enhancement, including moral enhancement, as was the October 2018 issue of the *Journal of Medicine and Philosophy* (43, no. 5). One indication that this is not a marginal conversation, a search on "moral enhancement" in just *AJOB Neuroscience* yielded (in 2019) 178 citations. For a more developed argument, see Ingmar Persson and Julian Savulescu, *Unfit for the Future* (Oxford: Oxford University Press, 2012).
67  Douglas, "Moral Enhancement."
68  Persson and Savulescu, "Getting Moral Enhancement Right"; Persson and Savulescu, "The Perils of Cognitive Enhancement," 162–77.
69  Persson and Savulescu, *Unfit for the Future*.
70  Walker, "Enhancing Genetic Virtue."
71  Walker cites several authorities for his claim: Robert Plomin et al., *Behavioural Genetics*, 4th ed. (New York: Freeman, 2001); Raymond Cattell, *The Inheritance of Personality and Ability* (New York: Academic Press, 1982); Lindon Eaves, Hans Eysenck, and Nicholas Martin, *Genes, Culture, and Personality: An Empirical Approach* (London: Academic Press, 1989); Kerry Jang et al., "Heritability of the Big Five Dimensions and Their Facets: A Twin Study," *Journal of Personality* 64, no. 3 (1996): 577–91; Kerry Jang et al., "Heritability of Facet-Level Traits in a Cross-Cultural Twin Sample: Support for the Hierarchy Model of Personality," *Journal of Personality and Social Psychology* 74 (1998): 1556–65; John Loehlin, *Genes and Environment in Personality Development* (Newbury Park, CA: Sage, 1992); and John Loehlin, Lee Willerman, and Joseph Horn, "Personality Resemblances in Adoptive Families: A 10-Year Follow-Up," *Journal of Personality and Social Psychology* 42 (1987): 1089–99.
72  Walker, "Enhancing Genetic Virtue," 33.
73  Walker's selection of evidence notwithstanding, there may well be genes that contribute to some degree to various personality traits, though it seems doubtful that these traits will be so narrowly defined as truthfulness, justice, or caring. That is, there will not be one gene for truthfulness, but a constellation of genes working together, likely in response to and alongside certain environmental features, such as class, socioeconomic status, nutritional, educational, and political features. Walker's theory minimizes the social/environmental factors that might contribute to personality traits, including virtue.
74  Walker, "Enhancing Genetic Virtue," 3. Clearly a "third" route of enhancement not mentioned here is the disposal or "non-implantation" of those embryos with the problematic genetic profiles.
75  Oddly enough, Walker at points refers to the state's neutrality on the good, but in the entire section called "Making the World Better," he uses better as a noun, as in the idea that we can arrive at some "univocal conception of better," and "what if better is different for every individual." Walker, "Enhancing Genetic Virtue," 36. It seems he does this in order to avoid any claim that he wants to deploy a particular conception of the good.
76  Walker, "Enhancing Genetic Virtue," 41.
77  Sam Harris, as we shall see in Chapter 3, is not far behind.

78 Gerald McKenny, *To Relieve the Human Condition: Bioethics, Technology, and the Body* (New York: SUNY Press, 1997).
79 David Simpson, "Francis Bacon (1561–1626)," *Internet Encyclopedia of Philosophy*, https://www.iep.utm.edu/bacon/. See also Francis Bacon, *The New Organon*, ed. Lisa Jardine and Michael Silverthorne (Cambridge: Cambridge University Press, 2000).
80 As we noted in Chapter 1. See also Jorge Moll, Ricardo de Oliveira-Souza, and P. J. Eslinger, "Morals and the Human Brain: A Working Model," *Neuroreport* 14, no. 3 (2003): 299–305.
81 Insofar as our account makes clear the ways that the development of antisocial personality disorder has been shaped by a deeply racialized and socioeconomic history, this use of Hare's test is a case in point of the biopolitical impact of neuroscience. See Alix Spiegel, "Creator of Psychopathy Test Worries About Its Use," *NPR*, May 27, 2011, https://www.npr.org/2011/05/27/136723357/creator-of-psychopathy-test-worries-about-its-use; and Christa McLeod, "Why California Got it Right: Assessing Psychopaths Before Release," *Rutgers Law Record* 45 (2017–2018): 145–69, https://lawrecord.com/files/45_Rutgers_L_Rec_145.pdf.
82 Warren Kinghorn, "Combat Trauma and Moral Fragmentation: A Theological Account of Moral Injury," *Journal of the Society of Christian Ethics* 32, no. 2 (2012): 57–74; William P. Mahedy, *Out of the Night: The Spiritual Journey of Vietnam Vets* (New York: Ballantine Books, 1988).
83 Maureen Dowd, "Virtuous Bankers? Really?" *New York Times*, November 11, 2009, https://www.nytimes.com/2009/11/11/opinion/11dowd.html.
84 Ibid.
85 David Linden, "Addictive Personality? You Might Be a Leader," *New York Times*, July 23, 2011, https://www.nytimes.com/2011/07/24/opinion/sunday/24addicts.html.
86 David Segal, "Just Manic Enough: Seeking Perfect Entrepreneurs," *New York Times*, September 18, 2010, https://www.nytimes.com/2010/09/19/business/19entre.html.
87 Ibid.
88 Alexander Eichler, "Stockbrokers More Competitive, Willing To Take Risks Than Psychopaths: Study," *The Huffington Post*, September 26, 2011, https://www.huffingtonpost.com/2011/09/26/stockbroker-psychopath_n_981950.html.
89 Daisy Grewal, "Rich People Have Less Compassion, Psychology Research Suggests," *The Huffington Post*, April 11, 2012, https://www.huffpost.com/entry/rich-people-compassion-mean-money_n_1416091.
90 Ibid.
91 Daniel M. Bartels and David A. Pizzaro, "The Mismeasure of Morals: Antisocial Personality Traits Predict Utilitarian Responses to Moral Dilemmas," *Cognition* 121, no. 1 (2011): 154–61.
92 Jeffrey Sachs, "The Global Economy's Corporate Crime Wave," *Project Syndicate*, May 8, 2011, https://www.project-syndicate.org/commentary/the-global-economy-s-corporate-crime-wave.
93 Quotation from Decety et al., "The Neural Bases of Cooperation and Competition: An fMRI Investigation," 745. Emphasis added. See also S. J. Blakemore and C. Frith, "Self-Awareness and Action," *Current Opinion in Neurobiology* 13, no. 2 (2003): 219–24; Decety and Jackson, "The Functional Architecture of Human Empathy." This way of understanding agency is also the way that agency is imagined by Sam Harris as we shall see in Chapter 3.

## Chapter 3

1. See SJR, *Scimago Journal and Country Rank*, https://www.scimagojr.com/journalrank.php?category=2801&year=2018.
2. "Jonathan Haidt's Home Page," *NYU Stern*, http://people.stern.nyu.edu/jhaidt/.
3. "Jonathan Haidt," *NYU Leonard N. Stern School of Business*, https://www.stern.nyu.edu/faculty/bio/jonathan-haidt.
4. Jonathan Haidt, *The Happiness Hypothesis: Find Modern True in Ancient Wisdom* (New York: Basic Books, 2006); Haidt, *The Righteous Mind*. Other titles include Jonathan Haidt and Greg Lukianoff, *The Coddling of the American Mind: How Good Intentions and Bad Ideas are Setting up a Generation for Failure* (New York: Penguin, 2018); Jonathan Haidt, *All Minus One: John Stuart Mill's Ideas on Free Speech* (New York: Heterodox Academy, 2018); and Corey L. M. Keyes and Jonathan Haidt, eds., *Flourishing: Positive Psychology and the Life Well-Lived* (Washington, DC: American Psychological Association, 2002).
5. "Jonathan Haidt," *TED.com*, https://www.ted.com/speakers/jonathan_haidt. See also: Jonathan Haidt, "Of Freedom and Fairness," *Democracy Journal* 28 (Spring 2013), https://democracyjournal.org/magazine/28/of-freedom-and-fairness; Jonathan Haidt, "We Need a Little Fear," *The New York Times*, November 7, 2012, https://www.nytimes.com/2012/11/07/opinion/after-the-election-fear-is-our-only-chance-at-unity.html; Jonathan Haidt and Marc Hetherington, "Look How Far We've Come Apart," *The New York Times*, September 17, 2012, https://campaignstops.blogs.nytimes.com/2012/09/17/look-how-far-weve-come-apart/; Jonathan Haidt, "Forget the Money, Follow the Sacredness," *The New York Times*, March 17, 2012, https://campaignstops.blogs.nytimes.com/2012/03/17/forget-the-money-follow-the-sacredness/; Jonathan Haidt, "How to Get the Rich to Share the Marbles," *The New York Times*, February 20, 2012, https://campaignstops.blogs.nytimes.com/2012/02/20/how-to-get-the-rich-to-share-the-marbles/. For a complete list, see: Jonathan Haidt, "Essays: Featured Essays/Talks by Jonathan Haidt," *The Righteous Mind*, https://righteousmind.com/about-the-author/essays/.
6. Haidt has helpfully posted a PDF of his bibliography to his website: https://www.righteousmind.com/wp-content/uploads/2012/08/RighteousMind.References.pdf.
7. Haidt, *The Righteous Mind*, xiv–xv.
8. Ibid., xv.
9. Western thought has been caught between two approaches to knowledge: Rationalism and Empiricism. Kant certainly was steeped in the more rationalist camp; however, it was Hume—the empiricist—that awoke him from his dogmatic slumber. Yet, Haidt seems to misunderstand Jeremy Bentham. Bentham was not a rationalist; he comes out of the tradition of empiricism—directly from Hume, as we show in Chapter 5. Although Haidt is correct that Bentham created a moral calculus, like other British empiricists, he grounded morality in the moral sentiments.
10. Haidt, *The Righteous Mind*, 26.
11. For some of his articles on disgust see: Paul Rozin, Jonathan Haidt, and Clark McCauley, "Disgust," in *Handbook of Emotions*, ed. Michael Lewis, Jeannette Haviland-Jones, and Lisa Barrett, 3rd ed. (New York: The Guilford Press, 2008); Thalia Wheatley and Jonathan Haidt, "Hypnotic Disgust Makes Moral Judgments More Severe," *Psychological Science* 16, no. 10 (October 2005): 780–4; Simone Schnall, Jonathan Haidt, Gerald L. Clore, and Alexander H. Jordan, "Disgust as

Embodied Moral Judgment," *Personality and Social Psychology Bulletin* 34, no. 8 (2008): 1096–109; Jonathan Haidt, Clark McCauley, and Paul Rozin, "Individual Differences in Sensitivity to Disgust: A Scale Sampling Seven Domains of Disgust Elicitors," *Personality and Individual Differences* 16, no. 5 (1994): 701–13; Yoel Inbar, David Pizarro, Ravi Iyer, and Jonathan Haidt, "Disgust Sensitivity, Political Conservatism, and Voting," *Social Psychological and Personality Science* 3, no. 5 (2012): 537–44; Paul Rozin, Laura Lowery, Sumio Imada, and Jonathan Haidt, "The CAD Triad Hypothesis: A Mapping Between Three Moral Emotions (Contempt, Anger, Disgust) and Three Moral Codes (Community, Autonomy, Divinity)," *Journal of Personality and Social Psychology* 76, no. 4 (1999): 574–86.

12 See Haidt, *The Righteous Mind*, 3–31.
13 Ibid., 3–4.
14 Ibid.
15 Ibid., xiv. Italics in original.
16 Ibid., 70.
17 Haidt cites here studies similar to those we analyzed in chapter one: Kevin M. Beaver, Meghan W. Rowland, Joseph A. Schwartz, and Joseph L. Nedelec, "The Genetic Origins of Psychopathic Personality Traits in Adult Males and Females: Results from an Adoption-Based Study," *Journal of Criminal Justice* 39 (2011): 426–32; Daniel M. Blonigen, Brian M. Hicks, Robert F. Krueger, William G. Iacono, and Christopher J. Patrick, "Psychopathic Personality Traits: Heritability and Genetic Overlap with Internalizing and Externalizing Psychopathology," *Psychological Medicine* 35 (2005): 637–48; and Essi Viding, James R. Blair, Terrie E. Moffitt, and Robert Plomin, "Evidence for Substantial Genetic Risk for Psychopathy in 7-Year-Olds," *Journal of Child Psychology and Psychiatry* 46 (2005): 592–7.
18 Again, Haidt cites neurobiological studies: "Brain scanning studies confirm that many emotional areas, including the amygdala and the vmPFC, are much less reactive in psychopaths than in normal people," referencing James R. Blair, "The Amygdala and Ventromedial Prefrontal Cortex in Morality and Psychopathy," *Trends in Cognitive Sciences* 22 (2007): 387–92; Kent A. Kiehl, "A Cognitive Neuroscience Perspective on Psychopathy: Evidence for Paralimbic System Dysfunction," *Psychiatry Research* 147 (2006): 107–28; and James R. Blair, "Responsiveness to Distress Cues in the Child with Psychopathic Tendencies," *Personality and Individual Differences* 27 (1999): 135–45. He closes by citing Hervey M. Cleckley's *The Mask of Sanity*: "For the best clinical portraits of psychopaths and their indifference to others, including their parents, see Cleckley."
19 Haidt, *The Righteous Mind*, 62–3.
20 Ibid., xiv and 114.
21 He adopts this now meme-like acronym from Joseph Henrich, Steven J. Heine, and Ara Norenzayan's 2010 article "The Weirdest People in the World?" *Behavioral and Brain Sciences* 33, nos. 2–3 (2010): 61–83. Abiodun calls out the racial profile of the cohort that Haidt engages: "Discrepancies in inclusivity can be examined in the everyday practices of research labs, as exemplified by the 'representative sample' conundrum: Oftentimes, participant samples recruited for studies fall into the category of being W.E.I.R.D (White, Educated, Industrialized, Rich, and Democratic)," in Abiodun, "Seeing Color." The same critique applies to Harris and Zak.
22 Haidt, *The Righteous Mind*, 125.

23 For two critiques of Lawrence Kohlberg's six-stage theory of moral development see John R. Snarey, "Cross-Cultural Universality of Social-Moral Development: A Critical Review of Kohlbergian Research," *Psychological Bulletin* 97, no. 2 (1985): 202–32; and Joan G. Miller, David M. Bersoff, and Robin L. Harwood, "Perceptions of Social Responsibilities in India and in the United States: Moral Imperatives or Personal Decisions?" *Journal of Personality and Social Psychology* 58, no. 1 (1990): 33–47.
24 Haidt, *The Righteous Mind*, 131–4.
25 Ibid., 159.
26 Ibid., 134–8.
27 Ibid., 138–41.
28 Ibid., 142–6.
29 Ibid., 170, recounts the story of Bernd Brandes, who agreed to allow Armin Meiwes to eat him in a psychosexual murder fantasy. Meiwes was convicted only of manslaughter since the murder was consensual.
30 Ibid., 185.
31 Ibid., 218.
32 Ibid., 219–20, 314, 350. That morality and virtue are equated with prosociality is captured when Haidt finally defines the term "morality" in his last chapter: "Moral systems are interlocking sets of values, virtues, norms, practices, identities, institutions, technologies, and evolved psychological mechanisms that work together to suppress or regulate self-interest and make cooperative societies possible" (314). See also 335.
33 Ibid., 283.
34 Ibid., 272.
35 Ibid., 317.
36 Ibid., 270.
37 Ibid., 285.
38 Ibid., 273.
39 Ibid., 313.
40 Ibid., 214.
41 Ibid., 212.
42 Ibid., 322, 324, and 328.
43 Disclaimers notwithstanding, in his visual display of the alignment between various political positions and the six "moral foundations" (Figures 12.2, 12.3, and 12.3), only social conservatism is displayed as balanced. He also avers that due its "blindspot" regarding moral capital, "liberalism . . . is not sufficient as a governing philosophy" (Haidt, *The Righteous Mind*, 342) and that he believes "that libertarians are right on many points" (Haidt, *The Righteous Mind*, 353). Since Haidt has made these figures publicly available through *The Righteous Mind* website, we have not reproduced them here, but we encourage readers to consult them: https://www.righteousmind.com/wp-content/uploads/2012/08/Figures-for-The-Righteous-Mind.pdf.
44 Throughout his book, Haidt criticizes *Homo economicus* as a strictly rationalist model. We will see, however, in Chapter 4, how closely Haidt's theory aligns with recent developments in economic theory.
45 Haidt, *The Righteous Mind*, 274–9. It is hard to miss here the resonance between his final metaphor of the hive and Bernard Mandeville's classic 1705 poem *The Fable of the Bees, or, Private Vices, Publick Benefits*, which is regarded as a classic prototype of many of the economic ideas developed by Adam Smith. See Chapter 6.
46 Haidt, *The Righteous Mind*, 335.

47 Ibid., 353–6.
48 See "The Righteous Mind" website: https://righteousmind.com/capitalism-and-morality/.
49 See Jonathan Haidt and Melvin Konner, "Capitalism and Moral Evolution: A Civil Provocation," *On Being with Krista Tippett*, June 2, 2016, https://onbeing.org/programs/jonathan-haidt-melvin-konner-capitalism-and-moral-evolution-a-civil-provocation/; and Jonathan Haidt, "How Capitalism Changes Conscience," *Center for Humans and Nature*, September 28, 2015, https://www.humansandnature.org/culture-how-capitalism-changes-conscience.
50 Haidt, *The Righteous Mind*, 135, emphasis added.
51 Ibid., 29.
52 Ibid., 33, italics in original; see also 103.
53 Ibid., 58.
54 In a section excised from *The Righteous Mind* before publication, Haidt notes: "If any ethical theory can claim to be the natural, normal, default way in which human beings think about morality, it is virtue ethics . . . [I]t fits so well with what we now know about moral psychology. First, if the mind is like a rider (conscious controlled processes) on an elephant (unconscious automatic processes), then only virtue ethics addresses the whole mind." (https://www.righteousmind.com/wp-content/uploads/2012/08/Righteous-Mind-outtake.virtue-ethics.pdf). In other words, virtue theory is the one approach to ethics that could challenge Haidt's position—but he does not engage it.
55 The archived website for Project Reason can be found at: https://web.archive.org/web/20100306140031/http://www.project-reason.org/.
56 Sam Harris, "Science Can Answer Moral Questions," *TED.com*, https://www.ted.com/talks/sam_harris_science_can_answer_moral_questions; and Sam Harris, "Can We Build AI Without Losing Control Over It?" *TED.com*, https://www.ted.com/talks/sam_harris_can_we_build_ai_without_losing_control_over_it.
57 Some examples include: Sam Harris and Mark S. Cohen, "The Functional Neuroanatomy of the Belief," *Society for Neuroscience Annual Meeting*, San Diego, CA, October 25, 2004; Sam Harris, Sameer A. Sheth, and Mark S. Cohen, "Functional Neuroimaging of Belief, Disbelief, and Uncertainty," *Annals of Neurology* 63, no. 2 (2008): 141–7; and Sam Harris et al., "The Neural Correlates of Religious and Nonreligious Belief," *PLoS ONE* 4, no. 10 (2009): e7272.
58 Sam Harris, *The End of Faith: Religion, Terror, and the Future of Reason* (New York: W.W. Norton, 2004); Sam Harris, *Waking Up: A Guide to Spirituality without Religion* (New York: Simon and Schuster, 2014). His most recent book *The Four Horsemen: Conversations that Sparked an Atheist Revolution* (New York: Random House, 2019), is co-authored with Christopher Hitchens, Richard Dawkins, and Daniel Dennett.
59 Glenn Greenwald, "Sam Harris, the New Atheists, and Anti-Muslim Animus," *The Guardian*, April 3, 2013, https://www.theguardian.com/commentisfree/2013/apr/03/sam-harris-muslim-animus. See Harris's *Islam and the Future of Tolerance: A Dialogue*, co-authored with Maajid Nawaz (Cambridge, MA: Harvard University Press, 2015).
60 Sam Harris, *The Moral Landscape: How Science Can Determine Human Values* (New York: Free Press, 2010). See also Sam Harris, *Free Will* (New York: Free Press, 2012).
61 While his work is mostly work of public philosophy, it is rather thin on argumentation and highly simplistic its dismissal of criticisms. Space here precludes a comprehensive critique of his philosophical positions. Instead, our aim in this

section is to present his work and illustrate some of the problems with his overall philosophical stance.
62 Harris, *The Moral Landscape*, 2.
63 Ibid., 21.
64 Ibid., 28. Emphasis in original.
65 Harris, *End of Faith*, 61–2.
66 Ibid., 63.
67 Ibid., 30.
68 Ibid., 170–1.
69 Ibid., 190.
70 Harris, *Moral Landscape*, 62.
71 Ibid., 104.
72 Ibid., 65.
73 Harris, *End of Faith*, 104.
74 Ibid., 107–8.
75 Ibid., 108.
76 Ibid., 108–9.
77 Harris, *Moral Landscape*, 109.
78 Ibid.
79 Ibid.
80 Ibid., 2–3.
81 Ibid., 191.
82 Zak, *The Moral Molecule*.
83 See Zak's website: https://pauljzak.com/; Paul Zak, "Trust, Morality – And Oxytocin?" TED.com, https://www.ted.com/talks/paul_zak_trust_morality_and _oxytocin.
84 Zak, *The Moral Molecule*.
85 Zak's first book, *Moral Markets: The Critical Role of Values in the Economy* (Princeton: Princeton University Press, 2008) brought together an array of natural and social scientists, as well as scholars of law, philosophy, and management; it draws on evidence from neuroscience and these other domains to argue that modern economic markets only work because most people act virtuously most of the time.
86 Zak's most recent book *Trust Factor: The Science of Creating High-Performance Companies* (New York: AMACOM, 2017) seeks to operationalize his neuroscience. His consulting firm, Ofactor, works with companies to do so, see: https://ofactor.com.
87 "Paul Zak," Claremont Graduate University, Department of Social Science, Policy, and Evaluation, https://www.cgu.edu/people/paul-zak/.
88 As is noted on his Claremont webpage: "Zak was one of the first scientists to integrate neuroscience and economics into a new discipline: neuroeconomics. His research has identified the brain processes that support such virtuous behaviors as trustworthiness, generosity, and sacrifice, as well as those whose absence leads to evil, vice, and conflict. He uses these results to increase flourishing by individuals, organizations, and societies" (ibid.).
89 Zak, *The Moral Molecule*, 5–9.
90 Ibid., 8.
91 Paul J. Zak, Angela A. Stanton, and Sheila Ahmadi, "Oxytocin Increases Generosity in Humans," *PloS ONE* 2, no. 11 (2007): e1128. In a similar vein, see also Jorge A. Barraza, Michael E. McCullough, Sheila Ahmadi, and Paul J. Zak, "Oxytocin Infusion

Increases Charitable Donations Regardless of Monetary Resources," *Hormones and Behavior* 60, no. 2 (2011): 148–51.
92 These pathways are not strictly biochemical or physiological pathways, but his use of the term and the way he describes them give them an air of scientific validity.
93 Zak, *The Moral Molecule*, 63.
94 Ibid.
95 Ibid., 64.
96 Ibid.
97 Ibid., 75.
98 Ibid., 140–5.
99 Ibid., 138–40.
100 Ibid., 140–5, 49–51.
101 Ibid., 159. Italics in the original.
102 Ibid., 160.
103 Ibid.
104 Ibid., 164.
105 Ibid.
106 Ibid., 169.
107 Ibid.
108 Thomas B. Edsall, "How Could Human Nature Have Become This Politicized?" *New York Times*, July 8, 2020, https://www.nytimes.com/2020/07/08/opinion/trump-politics-psychology.html.
109 Zak, *The Moral Molecule*, 75.

# Interlude between Neuroscience and the Economic Imaginary

1 Steven Levitt and Stephen Dubner, *Freakonomics: A Rogue Economist Explores the Hidden Side of Everything* (New York: William Morrow and Company, 2005, revised 2007); Steven Levitt and Stephen Dubner, *Superfreakonomics: Global Cooling, Patriotic Prostitutes, and Why Suicide Bombers Should Buy Life Insurance* (New York: William Morrow, 2011); Steven Levitt and Stephen Dubner, *Think Like a Freak: The Authors of Freakonomics Offer to Retrain Your Brain* (New York: William Morrow, 2014); and Steven Levitt and Stephen Dubner, *When to Rob a Bank: . . . and 131 More Warped Suggestions and Well-Intended Rants* (New York: William Morrow, 2015).
2 See "Steven D. Leavitt," http://pricetheory.uchicago.edu/levitt/.
3 See the Center for Radical Innovation for Social Change, https://centerforrisc.org/.
4 The TGG Group, http://www.tgggroup.com/index.php.
5 Stephen J. Dubner, "The Probability that a Real-Estate Agent is Cheating You (and Other Riddles of Modern Life)," *The New York Times Magazine*, August 3, 2003, https://www.nytimes.com/2003/08/03/magazine/probability-that-real-estate-agent-cheating-you-other-riddles-modern-life.html.
6 http://freakonomics.com/about/.
7 Rogers-Vaughn, *Caring for Souls*, 36.
8 Foucault, *Birth of Biopolitics*, 111, 116, on Nazism and state power.
9 Ibid., 116.
10 Paul Krugman, "Who Was Milton Friedman?" *The New York Review of Books*, February 15, 2007. In 1976 Friedman was quoted in *Newsweek* magazine saying

that "the elementary truth is that Great Depression was produced by government mismanagement." The irony, Krugman notes, is that here Friedman was faulting the government for not intervening more directly.

11  Foucault, *Birth of Biopolitics*, 116.
12  Ibid.
13  Brown, *Undoing the Demos*, Kindle location 1121. See also Timothy Mitchell, *Rule of Experts: Egypt, Techno-Politics, Modernity* (London: University of California Press, 2002).
14  Brown, *Undoing the Demos*, 1121, 1136.
15  Peter Harrison, *The Territories of Science and Religion* (Oxford: Oxford University Press, 2015), 119.
16  Jones, *Masters of the Universe*, 98.
17  Ibid., 31.
18  Foucault, *Birth of Biopolitics*, 160.
19  Ibid., 218–19, citing F. A. Hayek, "The Intellectuals and Socialism," *The University of Chicago Law Review* (Spring 1949): 417–20, 421–3, 425–33.
20  Hayek, "The Intellectuals and Socialism," 417–18. See also Lawrence J. McQuillan, "The Courage to be Utopian," *Mises Institute*, https://mises.org/library/courage-be-utopian.
21  Rogers-Vaughn, *Caring for Souls*, 171, citing Jamie Peck, *Constructions of Neoliberal Reason* (Oxford: Oxford University Press, 2010).
22  Foucault, *Birth of Biopolitics*, 244.
23  Orlando Letelier, "The 'Chicago Boys' in Chile: Economic Freedom's Awful Toll," *The Nation*, September 21, 2016, originally published August 1976, available at: https://www.thenation.com/article/archive/the-chicago-boys-in-chile-economic-freedoms-awful-toll/. See also Naomi Klein, *Shock Doctrine: The Arise of Disaster Capitalism* (New York: Picador, 2008); and Jean Drèze and Amartya Sen, *Hunger and Public Action* (New York: Oxford University Press, 1991).
24  For detailed analyses of the effects on most Chileans, see: Peter Winn, ed., *Victims of the Chilean Miracle: Workers and Neoliberalism in the Pinochet Era, 1973–2002* (Durham, NC: Duke University Press, 2004); and Warwick Murray, Lida Kousary, and Jonathan Barton, "Land of Miracles? A Critical Analysis of Poverty Reduction Strategies in Chile, 1975–2005," *International Development Planning Review* 31, no. 2 (June 2009): 127–63.
25  Rogers-Vaughn, *Caring for Souls*, 110–12.
26  Ibid., 111. See also Anne Case and Angus Deaton, *Deaths of Despair and the Future of Capitalism* (Princeton, NJ: Princeton University Press, 2020).
27  Rogers-Vaughn, *Caring for Souls*, 112, citing Sakia Sassen, *Expulsions: Brutality and Complexity in the Global Economy* (Boston, MA: Harvard University Press, 2014); and Zygmunt Bauman, *Wasted Lives: Modernity and Its Outcasts* (Cambridge, UK: Polity Press, 2004).
28  Rogers-Vaughn, *Caring for Souls*, 113.
29  Peck, *Constructions of Neoliberal Reason*, 26.
30  Rogers-Vaughn, *Caring for Souls*, 113.
31  Peck, *Constructions of Neoliberal Reason*, 26. See also Rogers-Vaughn, *Caring for Souls*, 116, citing Slavoj Žižek, *Violence: Six Sideways Reflections* (New York: Picador, 2008), 12–13; and https://thedisorderofthings.com/2015/06/18/capitalism-a-history-of-violence/.

32  See: ACLU, "Mass Incarceration," https://www.aclu.org/issues/smart-justice/mass-incarceration.
33  See Michelle Alexander, *The New Jim Crow: Mass Incarceration in the Age of Colorblindness* (New York: The New Press, 2010); Kara Gotsch and Vinay Basti, "Capitalizing on Mass Incarceration: U.S. Growth in Private Prisons," August 2, 2018, https://www.sentencingproject.org/publications/capitalizing-on-mass-incarceration-u-s-growth-in-private-prisons; The Federal Bureau of Prisons, "Inmate Race," updated October 16, 2021, https://www.bop.gov/about/statistics/statistics_inmate_race.jsp. See also Ava DuVernay's 2016 film, 13th.
34  Polanyi, *The Great Transformation*, 88, 89. [First edition 1944].
35  See Ravallion, "The Two Poverty Enlightenments," 2011.
36  Polanyi, *The Great Transformation*, 91.
37  Robert Bucholz and Newton Key, *Early Modern England, 1485–1714: A Narrative History* (Hoboken, NJ: John Wiley & Sons, 2009), 176. As Ava DuVernay makes clear in her film *13th*, the first way that southern Whites moved to police freed Blacks after the Civil War was to charge them with crimes of movement (loitering) and idleness (vagrancy). Parallel to our account in Chapter 6, this removed them from a state of freedom and returned them to a state of confinement by the state.
38  Intriguingly, Francis Bacon was a major drafter of the 1601 Poor Laws. See Gladys Boone, *The Poor Law of 1601, with Some Consideration of Modern Developments of the Poor Law Problem*, unpublished MA Thesis, University of Birmingham, United Kingdom, 1917, 81, https://etheses.bham.ac.uk/id/eprint/6134/.
39  Polanyi, *The Great Transformation*, 90.
40  Ibid., 82. Polanyi notes that Speenhamland set the rates based on an assumption that "bread" cost one-third of a family's income—the same metric that was used to establish the poverty thresholds in the 1960s (where "bread" had been replaced with "food"). That metric is still in place today.
41  Polanyi opines that if the poor/workers had not been prevented from organizing, it might have worked.
42  Polanyi, *The Great Transformation*, 100–4; and Richard H. Tawney, *Religion and the Rise of Capitalism: An Historical Study* (London: John Murray, 1922), 263.
43  Polanyi, *The Great Transformation*, 109.
44  R. H. Tawney, *The Agrarian Problem in the Sixteenth Century*. Introduction by Lawrence Stone (New York: Harper Torchbooks, 1967), 260.
45  Ibid., 268.
46  Ibid., 269.
47  Eamon Duffy, *The Stripping of the Altars: Traditional Religion in England 1400–1580* (New Haven, CT: Yale University Press, 2005); see also Kelly Johnson, *Fear of Beggars: Stewardship and Poverty in Christian Ethics* (Grand Rapids, MI: William B. Eerdmans Publishers, 2007), 79. According to the National Archives of the United Kingdom, £136,00 in 1540 has the purchasing power of £57,304,579.20 in 2017.
48  Without a note of irony, sixteenth-century Anglican cleric Joseph Townsend—who we will meet further in Chapter 5—notes the role of the dispossession of the Catholic Church in the creation of the problem of the poor, but in the same breath, due to his clear anti-Catholic sentiments, seems to blame the church for the poor for sustaining lazy, indigent people in the first place (Townsend, *A Dissertation on the Poor Laws, By a Well-Wisher to Mankind* (1786), Section III, https://socialsciences.mcmaster.ca/econ/ugcm/3ll3/townsend/poorlaw.html).

49 Michael Perelman, *The Invention of Capitalism: Classical Political Economy and the Secret History of Primitive Accumulation* (Durham, NC: Duke University Press, 2000).
50 Polanyi, *The Great Transformation*, 81.
51 Ibid., 72.
52 Ibid., 74.
53 Ibid.
54 Ibid., 75.
55 Ibid., 75–6.
56 Ibid., 79.
57 This is concurrent, of course, with the commodification of Africans in the development of chattel slavery. Although these two streams emerge around the same time point (late 1400s), the reconfiguration of English citizens as commodities takes almost three centuries. Notably, the same moral configurations are applied to both Africans and the English "undeserving" poor, although the violent consequences for Africans were generally more severe. Similar parallels could be traced with regard to the commodification of land in Africa and other colonial locations and the enclosure of the commons.
58 Ibid., 79, 81, 82.
59 Ibid., 76.
60 Ted Bergstrom and Robert F. Schoeni, "Income Prospects and Age-at-Marriage," *Journal of Population Economics* 9, no. 2 (1996): 115–30.
61 Tawney, *The Agrarian Problem*, 105–6.

# Chapter 4

1 Haidt, *The Righteous Mind*, 150.
2 Brown, *Undoing the Demos*, Kindle location 52–65.
3 Ibid.
4 Foucault, *Birth of Biopolitics*, 161.
5 Kathryn Blanchard, *The Protestant Ethic or the Spirit of Capitalism: Christians, Freedom, and Free Markets* (Eugene, OR: Wipf and Stock, 2010), 162. Blanchard notes, "neoliberal economics is a particular school of ethics." David Harvey notes: "In so far as neoliberalism values market exchange as 'an ethic in itself, capable of acting as a guide to all human action, and substituting for all previously held ethical beliefs,' it emphasizes the significance of contractual relations in the marketplace" (Harvey, *A Brief History of Neoliberalism*, 3).
6 Brown, drawing on the work of Ronen Shamir ("The Age of Responsibilization: On Market-Embedded Morality," *Economy and Society* 37, no. 1 (February 2008): 1), defines "responsibilization" as the deployment of sole responsibility for one's condition upon the worker, the indigent person, or the "entity at the end of the pipeline." See Brown, *Undoing the Demos*, Kindle location 1903.
7 Foucault, *Birth of Biopolitics*, 270–1.
8 Press release, NobelPrize.org, Nobel Media AB 2019, October 13, 1992, https://www.nobelprize.org/prizes/economic-sciences/1992/press-release/.
9 The Becker-Posner Blog is now archived at the University of Chicago. See: https://www.becker-posner-blog.com/.

10 See "George J. Stigler, 1911-1991," The Library of Economics and Liberty, https://www.econlib.org/library/Enc/bios/Stigler.html.
11 Foucault, *Birth of Biopolitics*, 222.
12 Brown, *Undoing the Demos*, Kindle location 326-32. See also Foucault, *Birth of Biopolitics*, 219; Ross Emmett, "Did the Chicago School Reject Frank Knight? Assessing Frank Knight's Place in the Chicago School of Economics Tradition," in *Frank Knight and the Chicago School in American Economics* (London: Routledge, 2009). As Emmett notes: "Chicago's training of students is designed to inculcate a price-theoretic way of seeing the world" (ibid., 147).
13 Foucault, *Birth of Biopolitics*, 270.
14 Ibid., 268-9.
15 Gary Becker, *The Economics of Discrimination*, 2nd ed. (Chicago: University of Chicago Press, 1957).
16 Gary Becker, "Crime and Punishment: An Economic Approach," *The Journal of Political Economy* 76 (1968): 169-217.
17 Gary Becker, *A Treatise on the Family* (Cambridge, MA: Harvard University Press, 1998); Gary Becker and H. Gregg Lewis, "On the Interaction between the Quantity and Quality of Children," *The Journal of Political Economy* 81 (1973): S279-S288; Gary S. Becker, Elizabeth Landes, and Robert T. Michael, "An Economic Analysis of Marital Instability," *Journal of Political Economy* 85 (1977): 1141-88.
18 Gary Becker and Kevin M. Murphy, "A Theory of Rational Addiction," *Journal of Political Economy* 96, no. 4 (August 1988): 657-700.
19 Gary S. Becker, "The Economic Way of Looking at Life," Nobel Prize Lecture, 1992. See also: Gary S. Becker and Guity Nashat Becker, *The Economics of Life: From Baseball to Affirmative Action to Immigration, How Real-World Issues Affect Our Everyday Life* (London: McGraw-Hill, 1998).
20 Blanchard, *The Protestant Ethic*, 146-7.
21 Foucault, *Birth of Biopolitics*, 240.
22 Rogers-Vaughn, *Caring for Souls*, 43, quoting William Davies, *The Limits of Neoliberalism: Authority, Sovereignty and the Logic of Competition* (London: SAGE Publications, 2014), 20.
23 Theodore W. Schultz, "Investment in Human Capital," *The American Economic Review* 51, no. 1 (1961): 1-17.
24 Ibid., 3.
25 Ibid., 2.
26 Per Foucault, prior to American neoliberalism, labor was only analyzed as a factor of time or in terms of numbers, that is, "the possibility of employing more hours of labor thus made available to capital. Consequently, there is a neutralization of the nature itself of labor, to the advantage of this single quantitative variable of hours of work and time" (*Birth of Biopolitics*, 220).
27 Schultz, "Investment in Human Capital," 13.
28 Gary S. Becker, *Human Capital: A Theoretical and Empirical Analysis, with Special Reference to Education*, 2nd ed. (New York: National Bureau of Economic Research, 1975).
29 Becker opens Part I of the book with an epigraph from Alfred Marshall: "The most valuable of all capital is that invested in human beings." Notice, however, how Becker elides the terms—Marshall is referring to *external* capital invested in human beings; for Becker, persons are only referred to as human capital. In his second footnote, he also

credits Adam Smith and J. S. Mill as pioneers of this concept as well as "the brilliant work which greatly influenced" his own thinking by Milton Friedman (ibid., 15).

30  Ibid., 245.
31  Foucault, *Birth of Biopolitics*, 224.
32  Ibid.
33  Ibid., 225.
34  Brown, *Undoing the Demos*, Kindle location 418. See also Rogers-Vaughn, *Caring for Souls*, 44 and 2; and Christopher Bollas, *The Shadow of the Object* (New York: Columbia University Press, 1987).
35  Foucault, *Birth of Biopolitics*, 225.
36  Luis Rayo and Gary Becker, "Habits, Peers, and Happiness: An Evolutionary Perspective," *American Economic Review* 97, no. 2 (2008): 487–91. Becker does this throughout his corpus. For example, describing the desires that underlie preferences he again employs traditional language of virtues and vices, such as "health, prestige, sensual pleasure, benevolence, or envy" (Don Browning, "Egos without Selves: A Theological-Ethical Critique of the Family Theory of the Chicago School of Economics," *Annual of the Society of Christian Ethics* 14 [Autumn 1994]: 130, citing Gary Becker, *The Economic Approach to Human Behavior* [Chicago: University of Chicago Press, 2008], 5).
37  Rayo and Becker, "Habits, Peers, and Happiness," 487.
38  Ibid., emphasis added. As a mathematical equation, the "happiness function" continues, as we will see, "Knight's belief that economists study the *form* of human behavior, not its content" (Blanchard, *The Protestant Ethic*, 145).
39  Rayo and Becker, "Habits, Peers, and Happiness," 487.
40  Ibid., 487–8.
41  Ibid., 488.
42  Ibid., 490.
43  Ibid., 489–90.
44  Translation: "There's No Disputing or Accounting for Taste." Becker and Stigler, "*De Gustibus non est Disputandum*," *The American Economic Review* 67, no. 2 (March 1977), 76–90. This essay was later expanded into Becker's book, *Accounting for Tastes* (Cambridge, MA: Harvard University Press, 1996). See Ross B. Emmett, "Frank Knight and the Chicago School," paper presented at the Becker Friedman Institute for Economic Research, The University of Chicago "The Legacy of Chicago Economics" (October 5, 2015), 4, footnote 8; the other key statement is Milton Friedman's "The Methodology of Positive Economics," discussed below.
45  Ibid., 76.
46  Ross Emmett holds that Frank Knight would have strongly opposed Becker and Stigler's position. He has penned a riposte, in the voice of Knight, in "*De Gustibus Est Disputandum*: Frank H. Knight's Reply to George Stigler and Gary Becker's '*De Gustibus Non Est Disputandum*' With an Introductory Essay," *Journal of Economic Methodology* 13, no. 1 (2006): 97–111.
47  Becker and Stigler, "*De Gustibus*," 76.
48  Ibid., 77–8.
49  Ibid., 81. Or, as he states clearly: "We should state explicitly, to avoid any misunderstanding, that 'harmful' means only that the derivatives in [equation 9] are negative, and not that the addiction harms others, nor, as we have just indicated, that it is unwise for addicts to consume such commodities" (81, footnote 9). In economics, elasticity refers to the degree to which patterns in consumption change

according to a change in price. For elastic demands, consumption changes greatly according to price. For inelastic demands, on the other hand, consumption does not vary as much according to price.
50  Ibid., 83.
51  Ibid., 76, emphasis added.
52  See Gary S. Becker, "Crime and Punishment: An Economic Approach," in *Essays in the Economics of Crime and Punishment*, ed. Gary S. Becker and William M. Landes (Cambridge, MA: National Bureau of Economic Research, 1974).
53  Ibid., 2.
54  Ibid., 3, 6. As should come as no surprise, his calculus suggests that fines—or economic penalties—are the most optimal form of punishment or deterrent.
55  See also Foucault, *Birth of Biopolitics*, 253.
56  Becker, "Crime and Punishment," 6.
57  Ibid., 11, 12, 17, et passim.
58  See Foucault, *Birth of Biopolitics*, 252–9.
59  Ibid., 41.
60  Becker, "Crime and Punishment," 2.
61  Ibid.
62  Rayo and Becker, "Habits, Peers, and Happiness," 487.
63  Ibid., Becker and Rayo appear to be drawing on the following articles for their biological information: Shane Frederick and George Loewenstein, "Hedonic Adaptation," in *Well-Being: The Foundations of Hedonic Psychology*, ed. Daniel Kahneman, Ed Diener, and Norbert Schwarz (New York: Russell Sage Foundation), 351–401; Eric R. Kandel, James H. Schwartz, and Thomas M. Jessell, *Principles of Neural Science* (New York: McGraw-Hill, 2000); and Arthur J. Robson, "The Biological Basis of Economic Behavior," *Journal of Economic Literature* 39, no. 1 (2001): 11–33.
64  Rayo and Becker, "Habits, Peers, and Happiness," 487.
65  Ibid., 488. Relative to our account of the neurobiological narrative of virtue in Chapter 2, they state importantly, "The theoretical work on happiness is far less abundant, but has been expanding in recent years. *A central goal of this literature is to provide a biological foundation for the observed empirical patterns*" (488, emphasis added).
66  Ibid., 488.
67  Luis Rayo and Gary S. Becker, "Evolutionary Efficiency and Happiness," *Journal of Political Economy* 115, no. 2 (2007): 302–37.
68  Ibid., 303.
69  Ibid.
70  Ibid., 304.
71  Rogers-Vaughn highlights the Darwinian character of neoliberalism, pointing to the violence inherit in a construct of "survival of the fittest" (*Caring for Souls*, 45). As we will see in Chapter 5, Darwin inherits this metaphor from Townsend. Rogers-Vaughn cites Susan Searls Giroux on the Sadean (a la Marquis de Sade) character of neoliberalism: "The essential plot ingredients of Sade's malevolent, imaginary universe are uncannily recapitulated in the hard realities of a racially driven neoliberalized society that I have already sketched above: ruthless, efficient instrumentalization; the severing of all social bonds; compulsory amoralism; violence transvalued as pleasure, luxury, indulgence, spectacle; icy, emotionless judgement duly capable of producing endless corpses; erotic excess that hardens into indifference and apathy; relentless social fragmentation and violent isolation;

the dissolution of thought; the exercise of force and domination that quickly betrays itself as masochistic self-destruction. A tale of two sovereignties—the sadistic and the neoliberalized—both predicated on absolute negation" (*Caring for Souls*, 45, citing Giroux, "Sade's Revenge: Racial Neoliberalism and the Sovereignty of Negation," *Patterns of Prejudice* 44, no. 1 (2010): 1–26 at 17).

72  Rayo and Becker, "Evolutionary Efficiency and Happiness," 304.
73  The single reference to freedom found in the essays cited in this chapter comes on the final page of "*De Gustibus*": "Addiction, advertising, etc., affect not tastes with the endless degrees of freedom they provide, but prices and incomes, and are subject therefore to the constraints imposed by the theorem on negatively inclined demand curves, and other results" (89). Similarly, Stigler notes that "Things like justice and freedom require ethical evaluation and judgement, whereas economic principles should be straightforward and unencumbered by morality" (Blanchard, *The Protestant Ethic*, 153). It thus seems no small irony that in 2007, Becker was awarded the National Medal of Freedom.
74  Blanchard, *The Protestant Ethic*, 154.
75  Ibid., 161.
76  Brown, *Undoing the Demos*, 1086; As we will see, Friedman posits economic freedom as the necessary precondition for political freedom.
77  Blanchard, *The Protestant Ethic*, 146–7.
78  Foucault, *Birth of Biopolitics*, 270.
79  Ibid., 259–60.
80  Foucault sees Becker's focus on crime as an instance of the intersection of the "economization of everything" and the restructuring of political reason in market terms. He first connects it to the longer history of capitalism, noting that prima facie, the neoliberal analysis of crime "at first appears to be the simplest possible return to the eighteenth-century reformers like Beccaria and especially Bentham" (ibid., 248). Yet he marks important intertwinings of *Homo penalis*, *Homo criminalis*, and *Homo economicus* (ibid., 250–3). It seems the coincidence of the neoliberal reconfiguration of crime and policing is less than coincidental with the extraordinary rise in incarceration and shift to private, for-profit prisons in the United States beginning in the 1980s, a shift also connected with the neuroscientific narrative of vice.
81  Daniel B. Klein and Ryan Daza, "Gary Becker," *Econ Journal Watch* 10, no. 3 (September 2013): 286. Becker cites Milton Friedman as one of the most significant influences on his work: "He was by far the greatest living teacher I have ever had."
82  Krugman, "Who Was Milton Friedman?"; "Milton Friedman, a Giant Among Economists," *The Economist*, November 23, 2006; and William L. Davis, Bob Figgins, David Hedengren, and Daniel B. Klein, "Economic Professors' Favorite Economic Thinkers, Journals, and Blogs," *Econ Journal Watch* 8, no. 2 (2011): 126–46.
83  "Milton Friedman—Facts," *Nobelprize.org, Nobel Media AB 2019*, https://www.nobelprize.org/prizes/economic-sciences/1976/friedman/facts/.
84  Krugman, "Who was Milton Friedman," 7. Krugman notes that the pamphlet was originally a publication of the Foundation for Economic Education, an organization with the founder of the John Birch Society on its board and which "spread a libertarian gospel so uncompromising it bordered on anarchism."
85  J. Daniel Hammond, "Milton Friedman [Ideological Profiles of the Economics Laureates]," *Econ Journal Watch* 10, no. 4 (September 2013): 330.
86  Ibid., 327.

87 Milton Friedman, *Capitalism and Freedom* (Chicago: University of Chicago Press, 2002, Kindle edition), Kindle location 14.
88 Ibid., 33.
89 Ibid., 51.
90 Milton Friedman, "Neoliberalism and Its Prospects," originally published in *Farmand* 2 (1951): 89–93. It is interesting to note, however, that in *Capitalism and Freedom*, he uses the example of exchange between the islands of Robinson Crusoe households—model of cooperation and peaceableness (Kindle location 172). Not only is this echoed later in the work of Zak and Haidt; it echoes Daniel Defoe, as we will see in Chapter 6.
91 Julian Reiss, "Review of *The Methodology of Positive Economics: Reflections on the Milton Friedman Legacy*, ed. Uskali Mäki," *Erasmus Journal for Philosophy and Economics* 3, no. 2 (Autumn 2010): 103–10.
92 Milton Friedman, "The Methodology of Positive Economics," in *Essays in Positive Economics* (Chicago: University of Chicago Press, 1966), 3–16, 30–43.
93 Ibid., 4. See also Reiss, "Review of *The Methodology of Positive Economics*," 104.
94 Friedman, "The Methodology of Positive Economics," 3.
95 Ibid., 5.
96 Krugman, "Who Was Milton Friedman?" As outlined in the Interlude, Friedman is (in)famous for advising Chilean dictator Augusto Pinochet. See: Andre Gunder Frank, "Economic Genocide in Chile: Open Letter to Milton Friedman and Arnold Harberger," *Economic and Political Weekly* 11, no. 24 (1976): 880–8.
97 Friedman, "Neoliberalism and Its Prospects," 2.
98 Friedman, *Capitalism and Freedom*, Kindle location 63–70.
99 Ibid.
100 Friedman, "Neoliberalism and Its Prospects," 8.
101 Friedman, *Capitalism as Freedom*, Kindle location 95–6, 100. See also Milton Friedman and Rose Friedman, *Free to Choose: A Personal Statement* (New York: Houghton Mifflin Harcourt, 1980), ix–x; and Hammond, "Milton Friedman," 330.
102 Foucault, *Birth of Biopolitics*, 246–7.
103 Ibid.
104 Friedman, "Neoliberalism and Its Prospects," 2.
105 Friedman, *Capitalism and Freedom*, Kindle location 140–9.
106 Blanchard, *The Protestant Ethic*, 125. See also Friedman, *Capitalism and Freedom*, 8.
107 Defending this thin and often counterfactual anthropology is the gist of "The Methodology of Positive Economics."
108 Blanchard, *The Protestant Ethic*, 128.
109 Ibid., 131.
110 Friedman, "Neoliberalism and Its Prospects," 4. See also Blanchard, *The Protestant Ethic*, 128.
111 See especially Foucault, *Birth of Biopolitics*, 270–1.
112 Ibid., 173, 176.
113 Don Ross, "Game Theory," *The Stanford Encyclopedia of Philosophy* (Fall 2021 Edition), ed. Edward N. Zalta.
114 "Game Theorists Who Have Received the Nobel Prize," http://lcm.csa.iisc.ernet.in/gametheory/nobel.html.
115 Krugman, "Who Was Milton Friedman."
116 Frank Knight, "The Ethics of Competition," in *Selected Essays by Frank H. Knight*, ed. R. B. Emmett, 61–93 (Chicago: University of Chicago Press, [1923] 1999); see also Emmett, "Did the Chicago School Reject Frank Knight," 5.

117 Foucault names Henry Calvert Simons as "the father of the Chicago School" citing his 1934 article "A Positive Program for Laissez-Faire" as "the first, fundamental text of this American neoliberalism" (Foucault, *Birth of Biopolitics*, 216). Others name Knight. Some analysts trace more discontinuity within the Chicago School than continuity. Dierdre McCloskey, for example, differentiates what she calls "the Good Old Chicago School" of Frank Knight, Jacob Viner and Ronald Coase from the "new" Chicago School of Milton Friedman, George Stigler, and Gary Becker (Steven G. Medema, "Adam Smith and the Chicago School," in *The Elgar Companion to Adam Smith*, ed. Jeffery Young [Cheltenham: Edward Elgar Publishers, 2010]). As we will see in Chapter 6, these two camps interpret Adam Smith very differently. For a critical assessment of both sides of this claim, see Ross Emmett, "Did the Chicago School Reject Frank Knight?"

118 Chris Leitner, "Frank Knight's Economic and Social Theology," *Le Québécois Libre* 326 (November 15, 2014), http://www.quebecoislibre.org/14/141115-8.html.

119 Frank H. Knight, *Risk, Uncertainty, and Profit* (Boston and New York: Houghton Mifflin Co., The Riverside Press, 1921).

120 Emmett, "Did the Chicago School Reject Frank Knight," 4. Interestingly, like Hollingshood's original study, *The Economic Organization* was not formally published until 1951 by August Kelley, Inc., but rather was circulated in "typed and mimeographed editions" for two decades (Ross Emmett, "Frank H. Knight and *The Economic Organization*," James Madison College, Michigan State University Working Papers Series, Working Paper No.: 0405-01, [April 2005]: 1). Unlike Hollingswood, by the time *The Economic Organization* was published, Knight no longer held some of the views expressed in the book (ibid., 3). It was Knight's opinion some years later that he had not authorized Kelley to publish it and that any copyright it held "was a pure invention" (ibid., 4).

121 Frank Knight, *The Economic Organization* (New York: Augustus M. Kelley, 1951). Emmett notes that "Knight's role as creator of the Chicago price theory tradition is symbolized today by the fact that the first chapter of *The Economic Organization* ('Social Economic Organization') remains on the reading list for Gary Becker's and Kevin Murphy's Econ 301 class at Chicago today" ("Did Frank Knight," 4). Precursor chapters and materials that eventually ended up in the 1933 volume trace back to at least 1921, and perhaps earlier (Emmett, "Frank H. Knight and *the Economic Organization*," 6).

122 Emmett, "Did the Chicago School Reject Frank Knight?" 4.

123 Ross Emmett, "The Passage from Classical to Neo-Liberalism: Frank H. Knight's Role Re-Considered," March 6, 2011, https://papers.ssrn.com/sol3/papers.cfm?abstract_id=1779102.

124 Emmett, "Did the Chicago School Reject Frank Knight?" 10.

125 Emmett, "The Passage from Classical to Neo-Liberalism," 6.

126 Blanchard, *The Protestant Ethic*, 91.

127 Lionel Robbins, *Essay on the Nature and Significance of Economic Science* (London: Macmillan, 1932), 21. Here Robbins is rejecting a definition of "economics as the study of the causes of material welfare," 9.

128 While certain economists in the 1930s–1960s might have thought they were restricting analyses to traditionally "economic" choices, with Becker, this "economic science of human behavior" is then extended to everything.

129 Frank Knight, "Ethics and the Economic Interpretation," *The Quarterly Journal of Economics* 36, no. 3 (1922): 454–81. Although a prolific scholar, after the mid-1930s,

Knight only published a handful of articles on economic theory (Emmett, "Frank Knight and the Chicago School," 3).
130  Knight, "Ethics and the Economic Interpretation," 474.
131  Ibid.
132  Ibid., 473.
133  Ibid., 455.
134  Ibid., 475.
135  Ibid., 473, fn. 1.
136  Interestingly, Knight's distinction here between "conduct" and general human action mirrors Thomas Aquinas's fundamental distinction between "human acts" and "acts of man." See Thomas Aquinas, *Summa Theologica* I-I, q. 1. Oddly, while Knight holds to such vestiges of classical understandings of moral theory, he rejects others, in particular the fundamental premise of both Aristotelian and later utilitarian or, in his phrase, "hedonistic" moralities, that the goal of human behavior and the moral life is happiness (see Knight, "Ethics and the Economic Interpretation," 469). What is more, "in regard to 'real ends,' we should note the futile quest of a Summum Bonum by ethical thinkers" (ibid., 472, footnote 8).
137  Ibid., 455. Presaging Robbins by a decade, Knight notes that the fundamental debate in economics is "whether the science is properly concerned with facts and cause-and-effect relations, or with 'welfare.' In other provinces of science such controversies would seem absurd" (ibid., 456).
138  Ibid., 454.
139  Ibid., 456. Clearly, Knight presumes the givenness of the "fact-value" distinction, the genesis of which (as we will see in Chapter 6) lies over a century before him.
140  Ibid., 467. Throughout the essay, he takes issue with various forms of biological warrants.
141  Ibid., 472–3, emphasis added. Here we see the beginnings of Becker's "economization of everything."
142  Blanchard, *The Protestant Ethic*, 95.
143  Ibid., 92.
144  Knight, "Ethics and the Economic Interpretation," 474.
145  Ibid., 475.
146  Robert Nelson, "Frank Knight and Original Sin," *The Independent Review* 6, no. 1 (Summer 2001): 7.
147  Knight, "Ethics and the Economic Interpretation," 475.
148  Ibid., 459.
149  Ibid.
150  Ibid.
151  Ibid., 472, 473.
152  Ibid., 473.
153  Ibid., 470.
154  Frank Knight, *Selected Essays by Frank H. Knight*, vol. 1, ed. Ross Emmett (Chicago: University of Chicago Press, 1999), 28–9. See also Knight, "Ethics and the Economic Interpretation," 474.
155  Knight, "Ethics and the Economic Interpretation," 457.
156  Blanchard, *The Protestant Ethic*, 112.
157  Emmett, "Frank Knight and the Economic Organization," 5, 11–12.
158  Frank Knight, *The Ethics of Competition* (New York: Routledge, 2017), 5.
159  Knight, "Ethics and the Economic Interpretation," 459.

160 Ibid.
161 Emmett, "Frank Knight and the Chicago School," 3.
162 George J. Stigler, "Frank Hyneman Knight," Working Paper 37. Working Papers Chicago, IL: Center for the Study of the Economy and the State, The University of Chicago, 1985; cited in Emmett, "Frank Knight and the Chicago School," 3.
163 Blanchard, *The Protestant Ethic*, 92.
164 Nelson, "Frank Knight and Original Sin," 7. Nelson notes that Knight labeled such thinking as mere rationalist and "scientistic propaganda": "The plain fact is that a fully rational 'science' of human behavior, in the literal sense, is impossible." Or again, a "natural or positive science of human conduct" is "an absurdity" (Knight, *The Economic Organization*, 258, 260, 261).
165 Emmett, "Did the Chicago School Reject Frank Knight?" 5.
166 Nelson, "Frank Knight and Original Sin," 20.
167 Ibid., 20–1. See also Knight, *The Economic Organization*, 265, 258.
168 Ibid., 7.
169 Ibid.
170 As he tellingly states:

> Economics has always treated desires or motives as facts, of a character susceptible to statement in propositions, and sufficiently stable during the period of the activity which they prompt to be treated as causes of that activity in a scientific sense. It has thus viewed life as a process of satisfying desires. If this is true then life is a matter of economics; only if it is untrue, or a very inadequate view of the truth, only if the "creation of value" is distinctly more than the satisfaction of desire, is there room for ethics in a sense logically separable from economics. (Knight, "Ethics and the Economic Interpretation," 456–7)

171 Knight, "Ethics and the Economic Interpretation," 456.
172 Emmett, "Frank Knight and the Chicago School," 6.
173 Ibid.
174 Tim Robertson, "We Are All Neoliberals Now," *Eureka Street*, April 20, 2017, https://www.eurekastreet.com.au/article/we-are-all-neoliberals-now.
175 Foucault, *Birth of Biopolitics*, 242.
176 Harvey, *A Brief History of Neoliberalism*, 65–6.

# Chapter 5

1 Irene C. L. Ng and Lu-Ming Tseng, "Learning to be Sociable: The Evolution of Homo Economicus," *The American Journal of Economics and Society* 67, no. 2 (2008): 265–86.
2 Lysander Spooner, *Vices are Not Crimes*, 1875, https://static1.squarespace.com/static/55a3c833e4b07c31913e6eae/t/55a52368e4b0994cd9068873/1436885864688/Vices+Are+Not+Crimes.pdf.
3 Brown, *Undoing the Demos*, Kindle location 721, 735–43.
4 Ibid.
5 Christopher Macleod, "John Stuart Mill," *The Stanford Encyclopedia of Philosophy* (Summer 2020 Edition), ed. Edward N. Zalta, https://plato.stanford.edu/archives/sum2020/entries/mill/. Oddly, in this essay, Macleod does not discuss Mill's work on political economy.

6 See Nicholas Capaldi, *John Stuart Mill: A Biography* (Cambridge: Cambridge University Press, 2004). See also Richard Reeves, *John Stuart Mill: Victorian Firebrand* (London: Atlantic Books, 2008).
7 Macleod, "John Stuart Mill."
8 See John Stuart Mill, *A System of Logic, Ratiocinative and Inductive: Being a Connected View of the Principles of Evidence and the Methods of Scientific Investigation*, 8th ed. (New York: Harper and Brothers, 1882), 592.
9 Terence Ball, "James Mill," *The Stanford Encyclopedia of Philosophy* (Winter 2018 Edition), ed. Edward N. Zalta, https://plato.stanford.edu/archives/win2018/entries/james-mill.
10 As Ball notes, from 1802 to 1819, Mill authored "some 1,400 editorials [as well as] hundreds of substantial articles and reviews."
11 For the transition of natural theology and natural philosophy into science, see especially Harrison, *The Territories of Science and Religion*. Chapter three, "Signs and Causes," is of particular note as it details the transition as it begins to take form in the early modern period. Also relevant is Ian G. Barbour, *Religion and Science: Historical and Contemporary Issues* (San Francisco, CA: Harper Collins, 1997), 49–75.
12 Mill, *A System of Logic*, 592.
13 Charles Douglas, *John Stuart Mill: A Study of His Philosophy* (Edinburgh: William Blackwood and Sons, 1895), 119.
14 Ibid.
15 Ibid., 122–30.
16 Ibid., 114.
17 Ibid., 152.
18 John Stuart Mill, *An Examination of Sir William Hamilton's Philosophy and of the Principal Philosophical Questions Discussed in His Writings*, ed. J. M. Robson (Toronto: University of Toronto Press, 1979), 208. It is interesting that Mill mentions permanence, which suggests that the self perceives itself as enduring through time. However, the permanence seems not to be a "positive attribute," but rather seems to be more akin to what Kant means in the schematism as a kind of a priori of "interior" experience.
19 Mill, *A System of Logic*, 598–9.
20 Ibid., 599.
21 Ibid., 582–3.
22 Ibid., 582.
23 See John Milbank, *Theology and Social Theory: Beyond Secular Reason*, 2nd ed. (Oxford: Blackwell, 2006), 75.
24 John Stuart Mill, *The Autobiography of John Stuart Mill* (Rockville, MD: Arc Manor, 2008), 168–9.
25 John Stuart Mill, *Utilitarianism*, 2nd ed., ed. George Sher (Indianapolis, IN: Hackett Publishing, 2001), end of ch. 4.
26 Douglas, *John Stuart Mill*, 134; Mill, *A System of Logic*, 550.
27 Douglas, *John Stuart Mill*, 136.
28 Ibid.
29 Mill, *A System of Logic*, 584.
30 Ibid.
31 Ibid., 602.
32 Ibid., 543.
33 Ibid., 604.

34 Ibid., 607.
35 Ibid., 653–4.
36 Ibid., 653.
37 Ibid., ch. 7, section 7, 658. As with Becker, Mill employs the language of the virtue tradition, locating happiness as the goal of even the science of ethology. Though Mill similarly changes the content of the terms in deploying the language, he is much closer to the virtue tradition than Becker.
38 Ibid., 656–7.
39 Jeremy Bentham referred to his panopticon as "a mill for grinding rogues honest, and idle men industrious," in a letter to a French correspondent. See Bentham, "To Jaques Pierre Brissot." 342.
40 MacIntyre, *After Virtue*, 11–35. Recently, MacIntyre has shifted his language from emotivism to expressivism. See MacIntyre, *Ethics in the Conflict of Modernity*.
41 MacIntyre, *After Virtue*, 63–5.
42 Mill, *A System of Logic*, 658.
43 Joseph Persky, "Retrospectives: The Ethology of *Homo Economicus*," *The Journal of Economic Perspectives* 9, no. 2 (Spring 1995): 221–31.
44 Mill, *A System of Logic*, 657. For Hume, "a proposition of which the predicate is expressed by the words *ought* or *should be*, is generically different from one which is expressed by *is* or *will be*."
45 John Stuart Mill, "On the Definition of Political Economy, and on the Method of Investigation Proper to It," *London and Westminster Review* October 1836. *Essays on Some Unsettled Questions of Political Economy*, 2nd ed. (London: Longmans, Green, Reader & Dyer, 1874), 312–13.
46 Mill, "On the Definition of Political Economy," 310–11.
47 Ibid., 325–6.
48 Ibid., 326.
49 Persky, "Retrospectives: The Ethology of *Homo Economicus*," 21.
50 Mill, "On the Definition of Political Economy," 321.
51 Mill, *A System of Logic*, 624.
52 Mill, "On the Definition of Political Economy," 322. See Brown, *Undoing the Demos*, Kindle location 1388–95.
53 Brown, *Undoing the Demos*, Kindle location 1367.
54 Ibid., 1367–82.
55 Michael Quinn, "Mill on Poverty, Population, and Poor Relief: Out of Bentham and Malthus?" *Revue d'études benthamiennes* (2008): 4. As we noted earlier, Mill's person is Locke's person, and here again they align. See, e.g., Christian Sonk, "John Locke Publishes His Plan to Reform the Poor Laws," *Bringing the Past to Virtual Life* blog, https://hist235.hist.sites.carleton.edu/timeline/john-locke-publishes-his-plan-to-reform-the-poor-laws//.
56 Ibid.
57 Ibid.
58 Brown, *Undoing the Demos*, Kindle location 1367–82.
59 James E. Crimmins, "Jeremy Bentham," *The Stanford Encyclopedia of Philosophy* (Summer 2019 Edition), ed. Edward N. Zalta, https://plato.stanford.edu/archives/sum2019/entries/bentham.
60 Ibid.
61 Deirdre McCloskey, "Adam Smith, the Last of the Former Virtue Ethicists," *History of Political Economy* 40, no. 1 (2008): 43–4.

62 Douglas, *John Stuart Mill*, 178.
63 Mary Poovey notes that even toward the end of the eighteenth century, Bentham had already wanted to move away from the more theological utilitarianism of Hutcheson and Malthus and to a more secular utilitarianism by giving numerical value to the various pleasures to stand in as markers of utility. See Poovey, *A History of the Modern Fact*, 279, 282–4.
64 Douglas, *John Stuart Mill*, 179.
65 This is a quote that Bentham may have used, but it comes from a very lengthy title from Hutcheson, "An Inquiry into the Original of our Ideas of Beauty and Virtue in Two Treatises, in which the Principles of the late Earl of Shaftesbury are Explained and Defended against the Fable of the Bee: And the Ideas of Moral Good and Evil are Established, according to the Sentiments of the Ancient Moralists, with an Attempt to Introduce a Mathematical Calculation on Subjects of Morality," in Leslie Stephen, *The English Utilitarians*, vol. 1 (London: Duckworth and Co., 1902), 178.
66 Quoted in Stephen, *The English Utilitarians*, 178. Emphasis added.
67 Ibid., 240.
68 Ibid., 241–2.
69 Ibid., 243.
70 Poovey, *A History of the Modern Fact*.
71 Stephen, *The English Utilitarians*, 241–2.
72 See "Table of the Springs of Action," Explanation no. 14, https://www.laits.utexas.edu/poltheory/bentham/springs/index.html.
73 Stephen, *The English Utilitarians*, 250.
74 Ibid., 247.
75 Ibid., 252. The Table of the Springs of Action is complicated to understand, even with Bentham's elaborate explication of the table. It appears the Table was mostly just a way for Bentham to imagine leverage points for his principles of legislation and morals.
76 Ibid., 247.
77 Ibid., 247–8.
78 Ibid., 249. See "Table of the Springs of Action" Explanation no. 14.
79 We will explicate Hume on this point in the next chapter.
80 Immanuel Kant, *The Critique of Pure Reason*, trans. Paul Guyer (Cambridge: Cambridge University Press, 2009).
81 James E. Crimmins, "Bentham's Metaphysics and the Science of Divinity," *Harvard Theological Review* 79, no. 4 (1986): 387–411, 388.
82 Stephen, *The English Utilitarians*, 247–24.
83 Bentham believed his approach was superior insofar as it avoided both Cartesian innate ideas of a moral sense and the Kantian *a priori*. He did remain somewhat Kantian insofar as he saw pleasure as a kind of measure of the good (pleasure immediately coinciding with the good for the human being). Thus, where for Kant goodness is a noumenal reality that cannot be known in itself, Bentham avoids anything metaphysical by focusing on its phenomenal instantiation in human sensory experience.
84 MacIntyre, *After Virtue*, 11–35; MacIntyre, *Ethics in the Conflict of Modernity*, 17–19.
85 Stephen, *The English Utilitarians*, 249.
86 See Ibid., 196–7.
87 Jeremy Bentham, *The Works of Jeremy Bentham* (Edinburgh: William Tait, 1838–1843), 227, quoted in Stephen, *The English Utilitarians*, 178.

88 Bentham, *The Works of Jeremy Bentham*, 122, quoted in Stephen, *The English Utilitarians*, 184.
89 It is with zero irony that a current e-learning tool, widely used in universities and other settings, has named itself Panopto.
90 Simon Werrett, "Potemkin and the Panopticon: Samuel Bentham and the Architecture of Absolutism in Eighteenth Century Russia," *Journal of Bentham Studies* 2 (1999): 1–25.
91 Ibid., 13.
92 Bentham, "To Jaques Pierre Brissot."
93 Polanyi, *The Great Transformation*, 111–12.
94 Ibid., 112.
95 According to Michael Quinn, Bentham proposed indenturing all minors to the Industry Houses until the age of twenty-one as a way of reducing and eventually eliminating the need to collect taxes for poor relief. "Explicitly, the basis of Bentham's plan lay in the transformation of the economic value of a child, from negative to positive. Crudely, children ate less and, especially as they approached the age of liberation, produced more than adults" (Michael Quinn, "Mill on Poverty," 31, available at: https://journals.openedition.org/etudes-benthamiennes/185#tocto2n8). In order to increase the number of indentured children, Bentham advocated early marriage between poor children and apparently took great steps to "facilitate marital sex in the pauper panopticons" (Quinn, "Mill on Poverty," 33).
96 Polanyi, *The Great Transformation*, 123, quoting Bentham in *Principles of Civil Code*, ch. 14, section 1. See the digitized version of the Browning edition of Bentham's works, vol. 1 at https://www.laits.utexas.edu/poltheory/bentham/pcc/.
97 Bentham, *Principles of Legislation and Morals*, ch. 1.
98 See especially Janet Simple's critique of Foucault's reading of the Panopticon. Janet Semple, *Bentham's Prison: A Study of the Panopticon Penitentiary* (Oxford: Oxford, 1993), 322.
99 Foucault, *Birth of Biopolitics*, 67.
100 Stephen, *The English Utilitarians*, 213.
101 David Ricardo, *On the Principles of Political Economy and Taxation* (London: John Murray, 1821), http://www.econlib.org/library/Ricardo/ricP2.html. Unless otherwise specified, all references to Ricardo's *Principles* are cited by chapter.paragraph.
102 Thomas Robert Malthus, *Essay on the Principle of Population*. The 1826 edition is the expanded edition. The first edition was published anonymously in 1798, http://www.econlib.org/library/Malthus/malPlongCover.html. All citations to Malthus's *Essay* are cited by book.chapter.paragraph in this electronic version unless otherwise noted.
103 "David Ricardo," The History of Economic Thought, Institute for New Economic Thinking, https://www.hetwebsite.net/het/profiles/ricardo.htm.
104 Daniel B. Klein et al., "Characteristics of the Members of Twelve Economic Associations: Voting, Policy Views, and Favorite Economists," *Econ Journal Watch* 9, no. 2 (May 2012): 149–62.
105 Ricardo, *On the Principles of Political Economy and Taxation*, 5.1.
106 Ibid., 5.2. It is significant that Ricardo's theory of price focuses on reproduction and hunger.
107 Ibid., 5.3.
108 Ibid., 5.5.
109 Ibid., 5.6.
110 Ibid., 5.5. This is clearly just an assertion.

111 Ibid., 5.7.
112 Ibid., 5.13.
113 Ibid., 5.22.
114 See Tawney's discussion of the enclosures and the age of marriage in the Interlude.
115 Ricardo, *On the Principles of Political Economy and Taxation*, 5.23.
116 Ibid., 5.36 and 5.37.
117 Ibid.
118 Ibid., 5.37.
119 Ibid., 5.38.
120 For an explication of the perversity thesis—that aid to the poor is actually harmful—see Stephen Monroe Tomczak, "From Townsend to Malthus to the Poor Law Report: An Examination of the Ideas Concerning the Relationship of Public Aid and Reproduction on Policy Development, 1786–1834," *Journal of Sociology and Social Work* 3, no. 2 (December 2015): 27.
121 Lauren F. Landsburg, "Thomas Robert Malthus," *The Library of Economics and Liberty*, https://www.econlib.org/library/Enc/bios/Malthus.html.
122 Polanyi, *The Great Transformation*, 127.
123 "The Political Economy Club," The History of Economic Thought, Institute for New Economic Thinking, https://www.hetwebsite.net/het/schools/peclub.htm.
124 Malthus adds this statement in the Preface to the second edition. See *An Essay on the Principle of Population: Or a View of Its Past and Present on Human Happiness*, 7th ed. (London: Reeves and Turner, 1872).
125 Townsend, *A Dissertation on the Poor Laws*. For the influence of Townsend on Malthus and Darwin, see Polanyi, *The Great Transformation*, 119; and Tomczak, "From Townsend to Malthus to the Poor Law Report". All citations to Townsend's *Dissertation* are cited by section.paragraph in this electronic unless otherwise noted.
126 Malthus, *Essay on the Principle of Population*, I.I.9. Notably, no attention was paid to reigning in the lusts or increasing the industry of the wealthy.
127 Ibid., I.I.16.
128 Ibid., I.I.17.
129 Ibid., I.II.1–2.
130 Ibid., I.II.22.
131 As Himmelfarb has noted, Malthus thought he was describing the problem in the first edition, but many people seemed to think that because he took pains to enumerate the various "natural" checks on population growth, he was promoting the checks (Himmelfarb, *The Idea of Poverty*, 122–6).
132 Malthus, *Essay on the Principle of Population*, I.II.9.
133 Ibid., I.II.9.
134 Ibid., I.II.13.
135 Ibid., I.II.12.
136 Ibid., I.II.4.
137 Ibid., I.II.11.
138 Ibid., I.II.5. Jenise DePinto cites Patrick Brantlinger's observation that "although Malthus does not emphasize race ... [he] has, for good reason, been called 'the founding father of scientific racism'" (Jenise Ruth DePinto, "Re-Imagining Empire and Nation in Early Victorian Britain: Race, Class, and Gender in the Condition of England Question" [Dissertation, Stony Brook University, 2005], 32, citing Brantlinger, *Dark Vanishings: Discourse on the Extinction of Primitive Races, 1800–1930* [Ithaca: Cornell University Press, 2003], 17).

139  Malthus, *Essay on the Principle of Population*, I.II.6.
140  Biographers describe Townsend as one who cared deeply for the poor; see, e.g., A. D. Morris, "The Reverend Joseph Townsend MA MGS (1739–1816) Physician and Geologist—'Colossus of Roads,'" *Proceedings of the Royal Society of Medicine* 62, no. 5 (May 1969): 471–7. However, his language about toward the poor in his *Dissertation* is deeply disdainful and tinged with anti-Catholic rhetoric.
141  Townsend, *Dissertation on the Poor Laws*, V:2.
142  Ibid., VII:1.
143  Ibid., VIII:2.
144  Philipp H. Lepenies argues that the originality of Townsend's *Dissertation* "lies in the fact that the notion of competitive markets was defined as a 'natural law'" (Philipp H. Lepenies, "Of Goats and Dogs: Joseph Townsend and the Idealisation of Markets—A Decisive Episode in the History of Economics," *Cambridge Journal of Economics* 38, no. 2 [March 2014]: 447). He further argues that Townsend and Malthus "share a revolutionary methodology that removed the market mechanism from any cultural and social context in the name of science."
145  Townsend, *Dissertation on the Poor Laws*, III:1, continuing to IV:1. See also Polanyi, *The Great Transformation*, 119.
146  Polanyi, *The Great Transformation*, 119–20.
147  Porter, *Rise of Statistical Thinking*, 47–8.
148  Himmelfarb, *The Idea of Poverty*, 118. Here Himmelfarb is quoting from Malthus's sixth edition, IV.III.6, and I.II.6 (moral agent).
149  Ibid., 119.
150  For an interesting thesis on the shifting understanding of motion, see Simon Oliver, *Philosophy, God, and Motion* (New York: Routledge, 2005).
151  An important point made by Himmelfarb, *The Idea of Poverty*, 126.
152  Ibid., 126, citing William Hazlitt, *The Spirit of the Age* (New York: Dolphin, 1825), 44.
153  Ibid.
154  Ibid. Thomas Carlyle refers to utilitarianism as "pig philosophy" (ibid., 12).
155  Ibid., 126.
156  Himmelfarb notes that primary victims of the Poor Law of 1601 were not the poor. While the poor were victims of the lack of education put upon them by upper classes, and while the Poor Laws were aimed at alleviating the pains of the poor, it was the class right above the poor that suffered the most under these dictates (ibid., 120).

# Chapter 6

1  Jeremy Bentham, *The Works of Jeremy Bentham*, ed. John Bowring (London, 1838–1843; Reprinted New York, 1962); "An Introduction to the Principles of Legislation and Morals," ch. 1, part 1.
2  See David Hume, *A Treatise of Human Nature*, ed. L. A. Selby-Bigge (Oxford: Clarendon, 1896), https://oll.libertyfund.org/titles/hume-a-treatise-of-human-nature. All citations will be to this volume and will be referenced as Book.Part.Section.Paragraph. See David Hume, *An Enquiry Concerning Human Understanding*, 2nd ed., ed. Eric Steinberg (Indianapolis, IN: Hackett Publishing Company, 1977).

3   Rene Descartes, *Discourse on Method and Meditations on First Philosophy*, 4th ed. (Indianapolis, IN: Hackett Publishing, 1998), 7.
4   Catherine Pickstock, *After Writing: The Liturgical Consummation of Philosophy* (Oxford: Blackwell, 1998), 58.
5   Matthew Jones, *The Good Life in the Scientific Revolution: Descartes, Pascal, Leibniz and the Cultivation of Virtue* (Chicago: The University of Chicago Press, 2006). See also David Rapport Lachterman, *The Ethics of Geometry: A Genealogy of Modernity* (New York: Routledge, 1989), and Amos Funkenstein, *Theology and the Scientific Imagination from the Middle Ages to the Seventeenth Century* (Princeton, NJ: Princeton University Press, 1986).
6   Thomas Hobbes, *Leviathan*, ed. Richard Tuck (New York: Cambridge University Press, 1991), 89.
7   John Locke, *An Essay Concerning Human Understanding*, ed. Kenneth P. Winkler (Indianapolis, IN: Hackett Publishing), 95.
8   John Locke, *Two Treatises of Government*, ed. Peter Laslett (New York: Cambridge University Press, 1988), 350. (Second Treatise, no. 123).
9   Ibid., 323. (Second Treatise, no. 87).
10  Bacon, *The New Organon*. For an excellent review of medicine as a Baconian project, see Gerald P. McKenny, *To Relieve the Human Estate: Bioethics, Technology, and the Body* (Albany, NY: State University of New York Press, 1997).
11  William Edward Morris and Charlotte R. Brown, "David Hume," *The Stanford Encyclopedia of Philosophy* (Summer 2020 Edition), ed. Edward N. Zalta, https://plato.stanford.edu/archives/sum2020/entries/hume/.
12  Ibid., section 1.
13  Alasdair MacIntyre, *Whose Justice? Which Rationality?* (Notre Dame, IN: University of Notre Dame Press, 1988), 281–8.
14  Frederick Rosen, *Classical Utilitarianism from Hume to Mill* (New York: Routledge, 2003), 20.
15  Pierre Gassendi, *Three Discourses on Happiness, Virtue, and Liberty: Collected from the works of the Learn'd Gassendi*, ed. Mosieur Bernier (London: Awnsham and John Churchill, 1699), 315.
16  For Aristotle, justice is a mean that adjudicates disputes between citizens. It is grounded in the facts of human nature and attempts to remediate the harmed party.
17  Rosen, *Classical Utilitarianism*, 21.
18  Ibid., 29. It should be noted that several scholars suggest that sympathy plays a different role in the earlier *Treatise* than it does in the *Enquiry Concerning Human Understanding*. See Rico Vitz, "Sympathy and Benevolence in Hume's Moral Psychology," *Journal of the History of Philosophy* 42, no. 3 (2004): 261–75.
19  David Hume, *The Letters of David Hume*, 2 vols., ed. J. Y. T. Greig (Oxford: Clarendon Press, 1932), quote from vol. 1, p. 33.
20  David Hume, *An Enquiry Concerning the Principles of Morals*, ed. J. B. Schneewind (Indianapolis, IN: Hackett Publishing, 1983), section 3: part 1.
21  Ibid.
22  Rosen, *Classical Utilitarianism*, 34.
23  See Vitz, "Sympathy and Benevolence."
24  Hume, *An Enquiry Concerning the Principles of Morals*, 43, fn. 19.
25  Rosen, *Classical Utilitarianism*, 41.
26  Ibid., 44.
27  Hume, *An Enquiry Concerning the Principles of Morals*, 24.

28 Ibid., 28.
29 For an excellent discussion of Hume's theory of property see George E. Panichas, "Hume's Theory of Property," in *ARSP: Archiv für Rechts- und Sozialphilosophie / Archives for Philosophy of Law and Social Philosophy* 69, no. 3 (1983): 391–405.
30 Hume, *An Enquiry Concerning the Principles of Morals*, 21.
31 Panichas, "Hume's Theory of Property," 392. See also Hume, *An Enquiry Concerning the Principles of Morals*, 22.
32 Ibid., 393.
33 MacIntyre, *Ethics in the Conflicts of Modernity*, 91–3. It should be noted that MacIntyre also critiques Adam Smith for his individualism in his economics. However, as we shall shortly see, if one reads the *Theory of Moral Sentiments* as a necessary propaedeutic for *Wealth of Nations*, we find that whatever individualism there is in Smith, the centrality of community, the natural origin of the human faculties for community (i.e., sympathy), and the rational ordering of the virtues render Smith less guilty than MacIntyre makes him out to be.
34 Ibid., 79–85.
35 Ibid., 82.
36 Hume, *Treatise*, ii.2.5.1
37 Ibid., ii.2.5.2.
38 MacIntyre, *Ethics in the Conflicts of Modernity*, 82–3. Citing Hume, *Treatise*, ii.2.5.
39 Ibid., 83.
40 MacIntyre, *Whose Justice?*, 313.
41 MacIntyre, *Ethics in the Conflict of Modernity*, 92.
42 See, for example, McCloskey, "Adam Smith," 43–71; and Christopher Bertram, "Jean Jacques Rousseau," *The Stanford Encyclopedia of Philosophy* (Summer 2020 Edition), ed. Edward N. Zalta, https://plato.stanford.edu/archives/sum2020/entries/rousseau/.
43 MacIntyre, *Ethics in the Conflict of Modernity*, 84, 85. See also MacIntyre, *Whose Justice?* 282, 300–7.
44 Bernard Mandeville, *The Fable of the Bees, or Private Vices, Publick Benefits, vol 1. (1732)* (Oxford: Clarendon Press, 1924), https://oll.libertyfund.org/titles/mandeville-the-fable-of-the-bees-or-private-vices-publick-benefits-vol-1. As Polanyi notes in *The Great Transformation*, at the beginning of the eighteenth century, wealth was considered a moral issue, but poverty was not (114).
45 Gertrude Himmelfarb, "Two Enlightenments: A Contrast in Social Ethics," *Proceedings of the British Academy* 117 (2001): 297–324 at 299.
46 Ibid. Mandeville's claim here echoes that of Daniel Defoe, author of *Robinson Crusoe*, who in his 1704 address to Parliament entitled *Giving Alms No Charity and Employing the Poor a Grievance to the Nation* was one of the earliest figures to argue "that if the poor were relieved, they would not work for wages; and that if they were put to manufacturing goods in private institutions, they would merely create more unemployment in private manufactures" (Polanyi, *The Great Transformation*, 114). Defoe's address is available at: https://socialsciences.mcmaster.ca/econ/ugcm/3ll3/defoe/alms. It is notable that these same images appear in our earlier narrative— Robinson Crusoe is invoked by Milton Friedman and the bees by Jonathan Haidt. Tellingly, Hayek lauded Mandeville's ideas about society and politics in *Law, Legislation, and Liberty*, vols. 1–4 (Chicago: University of Chicago Press, 1973–1979) and *Dr. Bernard Mandeville: Lecture on a Master Mind* (Oxford: Oxford University Press, 1966).

47 Jürgen Klein and Guido Giglioni, "Francis Bacon," *The Stanford Encyclopedia of Philosophy* (Winter 2016 Edition), ed. Edward N. Zalta, https://plato.stanford.edu/archives/win2016/entries/francis-bacon/.
48 Tawney, *The Agrarian Problem*, 387.
49 For discussion of Bacon's role in the creation of the 1601 Act for the Relief of the Poor, see the Interlude.
50 The original title is, in fact, *Novum Organum, sive indicia vera de Interpretatione Naturae*, or the New Work, or true directions concerning the interpretation of nature.
51 See especially E. A. Burtt, *The Metaphysical Foundations of Modern Science* (New York: Dover, 2003). Originally published in 1924.
52 Bacon, *The New Organon*, 12–13.
53 Ibid., 13.
54 Ibid., 16.
55 Ibid., 17.
56 Ibid., 21. The word translated here as "harassed" is taken from the Latin *vexare*, to vex or to afflict, or to harass. *Vexatus* is the perfect passive participle of *vexo*, which translates as "*to injure, damage, molest, annoy, distress, plague, trouble, maltreat, abuse, vex, harass, disquiet, disturb, torment, etc*" (Charleton Lewis and Charles Short, *A Latin Dictionary*, http://www.perseus.tufts.edu/hopper/text?doc=Perseus%3Atext%3A1999.04.0059%3Aentry%3Dvexo). The gendered language used here, in the context of such violent imagery, should not be overlooked. See Iddo Landau, "Feminist Criticism of Metaphors in Bacon's Philosophy of Science," *Philosophy* 73, no. 283 (January 1998): 47–61.
57 For the importance of experiment over experience in medicine, see Claude Bernard, *An Introduction to the Study of Experimental Medicine*, trans. Henry Copley Greene (New York: Dover Publications, 1957), 103. See also Jeffrey P. Bishop, *The Anticipatory Corpse: Medicine, Power, and the Care of the Dying* (Notre Dame, IN: University of Norte Dame Press, 2011). See also Heidegger's "Modern Science, Metaphysics, and Mathematics," in *Basic Writings*, ed. David Farrell Krell (New York: HarperCollins, 2008).
58 Bacon, *The New Organon*, 102.
59 Ibid., 106–8.
60 Ibid., 109.
61 Ibid., 103.
62 Paolo Rossi, *Francis Bacon: From Magic to Science*, trans. Sacha Rabinovitch (London: Routledge, 1968), 17. Originally published in Italian, *Francesco Bacone: Dalla Magia Alla Scienza* by Editori Laterza (Bari, 1957).
63 Sophie Weeks, *Francis Bacon's Science of Magic* (PhD dissertation, University of Leeds, 2007), 22.
64 See Burtt, *The Metaphysical Foundations*.
65 Bacon, *The New Organon*, 20, 221 (Book I Aphorism LXXIII, Book II Aphorism LII).
66 In the United States, the statute concerning patents explicitly mentions that patentable information must in some way be useful: one may obtain a patent if and only if one "invents or discovers any new and useful process, machine, manufacture, or composition of matter, or any new and useful improvement thereof" (United States Patent and Trademark Office, "General Information Concerning Patents," October 2015, https://www.uspto.gov/patents-getting-started/general-information-concerning-patents).

67 Bacon, *The New Organon*, 20, 221 (Book I, LXXIII, Book II, LII).
68 See Martin Heidegger, "Question Concerning Technology," in *Basic Writings*, ed. David Farrell Krell (New York: HarperCollins, 2008).
69 See Jacqueline L. Cowan "Francis Bacon's *New Atlantis* and the Alterity of the New World," *Literature and Theology* 25, no. 4 (2011): 407–21.
70 Peter Lucas, "Bacon's *New Atlantis* and the Fictional Origins of Organized Science," *Open Cultural Studies* 2 (2018): 114–21.
71 See McRorie, "The Emptiness of Modern Economics," no. 3, 120–9.
72 See Ryan Patrick Hanley, *Adam Smith and the Character of Virtue* (Cambridge: Cambridge University Press, 2009) on the centrality of the addition of Part VI in the last edition of TMS. See also Samuel Fleischacker, "Sympathy in Hume and Smith: A Contrast, Critique, and Reconstruction," in *Intersubjectivity and Objectivity in Adam Smith and Edmund Husserl: A Collection of Essays*, ed. Christel Fricke and Dagfinn Føllesdal (Berlin: De Gruyter, 2012), 272–311; and Paul Sagar, "Beyond Sympathy: Smith's Rejection of Hume's Moral Theory," *British Journal for the History of Philosophy* 25, no. 4 (2017): 681–705.
73 See Christina McRorie, "Adam Smith, Ethicist: A Case for Reading Political Economy as Moral Anthropology," *Journal of Religious Ethics* 43, no. 4 (December 2015): 677.
74 McRorie, "Adam Smith, Ethicist," 678.
75 McCloskey, "Adam Smith," 51.
76 See Dennis C. Rasmussen, *The Infidel and the Professor: David Hume, Adam Smith, and the Friendship that Shaped Modern Thought* (Princeton: Princeton University Press, 2019), discussed in Taylor McNeil, "An Enlightened Friendship," *TuftsNow*, January 16, 2018, https://now.tufts.edu/articles/enlightened-friendship.
77 Polanyi, *The Great Transformation*, 116.
78 Ibid., 92.
79 Ibid., 129. See Ravallion, "The Two Poverty Enlightenments" 10, fn. 14. See also Himmelfarb, *The Idea of Poverty*.
80 Polanyi, *The Great Transformation*, 116–17.
81 Ibid., 117.
82 See Sagar, "Beyond Sympathy."
83 Blanchard, *The Protestant Ethic*, 67.
84 Sagar, "Beyond Sympathy."
85 Adam Smith, *The Theory of Moral Sentiments*, ed. Joseph Black and James Hutton (London: Alex. Murray & Sons, 1869), at Part II, Section I, Introduction, Paragraph 2, https://oll.libertyfund.org/titles/theory-of-moral-sentiments-and-essays-on-philosophical-subjects. All references for *Theory of Moral Sentiments* will be to this edition and were accessed at the aforementioned website unless otherwise specified. Citations will be to Part.Section.Chapter.Paragraph.
86 McRorie, "Adam Smith, Ethicist," 684. See also Smith, *Theory of Moral Sentiments*, pt. I. sec. I. ch. III. para. 4.
87 McRorie, "Adam Smith, Ethicist," 683. McRorie also makes an interesting point about the shift from the language of "moral anthropology" to "moral psychology." See also Sagar, "Beyond Sympathy"; and Fleischacker, "Sympathy in Hume and Smith."
88 Stephen Darwall, "Sympathetic Liberalism: Recent Work on Adam Smith," *Philosophy and Public Affairs* 28, no. 2 (1999): 139–64.
89 Smith, *The Theory of Moral Sentiments*, pt. I. sec. I. ch. I. para. 10.

90   Ibid., pt. I. sec. I. ch. II. para. 1.
91   Adam Smith, *An Inquiry into the Nature and Causes of the Wealth of Nations*, vol. 2, ed. R. H. Campbell and A. S. Skinner, Glasgow Edition (Indianapolis, IN: Liberty Fund, 1981/1776), 26–7.
92   Robert A. Black, "What Did Adam Smith Say About Self-Love?" *Journal of Markets & Morality* 9, no. 1 (Spring 2006): 7.
93   Samuel Fleischacker, "Adam Smith's Moral and Political Philosophy," *The Stanford Encyclopedia of Philosophy* (Spring 2017 Edition), ed. Edward N. Zalta. https://plato.stanford.edu/archives/spr2017/entries/smith-moral-political/.
94   Sagar, "Beyond Sympathy," 687.
95   Smith, *Theory of Moral Sentiments*, pt. III. sec. I. ch. I. para. 2.
96   Sagar, "Beyond Sympathy," 693.
97   Smith, *Theory of Moral Sentiments*, pt. II. sec. II. ch. III. para. 4.
98   Ibid., *Theory of Moral Sentiments*, pt. III. sec. I. ch. I. para. 2.
99   Ibid., pt. III. sec. I. ch. III. para. 5.
100  Ibid., pt. III. sec. I. ch. III. para. 5.
101  McRorie, "Adam Smith, Ethicist," 685–6.
102  Blanchard, *The Protestant Ethic*, 71.
103  McCloskey, "Adam Smith," 50.
104  Adam Smith, *Correspondence of Adam Smith*, ed. E. C. Mossner and I. S. Ross (Oxford: Clarendon Press, 1977), 320. Quoted in McCloskey, "Adam Smith," 51.
105  Fleischacker, "Adam Smith's Moral and Political Philosophy."
106  Ibid.
107  Brown offers a mixed assessment of Smith's alignment with Aristotle, claiming that in Smith, "*homo oeconomicus* has displaced *Homo politicus*. Aristotle has been inverted, if not buried" (*Undoing the Demos*, Kindle location 1298–313). Yet she moderates this critique by noting the role of interdependence in Smith's work.
108  Blanchard, *The Protestant Ethic*, 73. See also Paul D. Mueller, "Adam Smith's Views on Consumption and Happiness," in *The Adam Smith Review*, ed. Fonna Forman, vol. 8 (New York: Routledge, 2014), 2.
109  Mueller, "Adam Smith's Views," 2.
110  Ibid.
111  Ibid., 4.
112  Smith, *Theory of Moral Sentiments*, pt. II. sec. I. ch. 2. Para. 1.
113  Smith, *An Inquiry into the Nature and Causes of the Wealth of Nations*, 340.
114  Mueller, "Adam Smith's Views," 13–14.
115  Amartya Sen, "Introduction," in *The Theory of Moral Sentiments*, ed. Ryan Patrick Hanley, 250th Anniversary ed. (New York: Penguin Books, 2009), xiii–iv.
116  Ibid., xxi.
117  Smith, *An Inquiry into the Nature and Causes of the Wealth of Nations*, 120.
118  Ibid., 371.
119  Sen, "Introduction," xix, xxiii.
120  Ibid., xxiii. As Sen remarks on p. xxvi, fn. 29: "For Smith's remarks cited here, and to many other remarks on similar lines, see Emma Rothschild and Amartya Sen, 'Adam Smith's Economics,' in *The Cambridge Companion to Adam Smith*, ed. Knud Haakonssen (Cambridge: Cambridge University Press, 2006)."
121  McCloskey's thesis: "I am merely arguing that Smith, in sharp contrast to his great contemporaries in ethical theorizing, was a virtues man, a half-conscious follower

of Plato and Aristotle and therefore of Aquinas, and also of the stoics (though they, I repeat, can be accused of a monism of temperance only), in emphasizing a system of multiple virtues—and indeed precisely five of the seven Aquinian virtues" (McCloskey, "Adam Smith," 58.)
122 Fleischacker, "Adam Smith's Moral and Political Philosophy."
123 Marie A. Martin, "Utility and Morality: Adam Smith's Critique of Hume," *Hume Studies* 16, no. 2 (November 1990): 107–20, 111.
124 Fleischacker, "Adam Smith's Moral and Political Philosophy."
125 Ibid.
126 Fleischacker, in "Adam Smith's Moral and Political Philosophy," notes nearly two-thirds of TMS is devoted to the ways humans cultivate the sentiments.
127 Fleischacker, in "Adam Smith's Moral and Political Philosophy," notes, "[Smith] indeed says explicitly, against the proto-utilitarianism of Hutcheson and Hume, that philosophers in his day have paid too much attention to the consequences of actions, and he wants to focus instead on their propriety: the relation they bear to the motive that inspires them." See also McCloskey, Adam Smith," 45.
128 Martin, "Utility and Morality," 107, 115.
129 Ibid., 111.
130 Ibid., 113.
131 See Lisa Hill, "The Hidden Theology of Adam Smith," *European Journal of the History of Economic Thought* 8, no. 1 (2001): 1–29.
132 Blanchard, *The Protestant Ethic*, 57.
133 See especially Patrick Hanley, *Adam Smith and the Character of Virtue*.

## Concluding Un(neuro)scientific Postlude

1 Fleck, "Crisis in Science."
2 Ibid., 154.
3 Ibid., 156.
4 See Bernard Stiegler, *Technics and Time*, 3 vols. (Stanford, CA: Stanford University Press, 1998, 2009, 2011). See also Stiegler, *The Age of Disruption*; originally published in French as *Dans la disruption. Comment ne pas devenir fou?* By Les Liens qui Libèrent, 2016.
5 Emily Underwood, "U.S. BRAIN Initiative Gets Ethical Advice," *Science Magazine*, May 14, 2014, https://www.sciencemag.org/news/2014/05/us-brain-initiative-gets-ethical-advice.
6 Pierre Gassendi, *Opera omnia*, vol. 1 (Lugduni, Anisson et Devenet, 1658), 92. The Latin reads: "Nihil est in intellectu quod non prius fuerit in sensu."
7 Sady, "Ludwik Fleck," https://plato.stanford.edu/archives/win2021/entries/fleck/.
8 Robert Spaemann, "Ars Longa, Vita Brevis," in *Ethics of Biomedical Research in a Christian Vision: Proceedings of the Ninth Assembly of the Pontifical Academy for Life*, ed. Juan de Dios Vial Correa and Elio Sgreccia (Vatican City: Libreria Editrice Vaticana, 2004), 103.

# Selected Bibliography

Adams, Julia, and David L. Weakliem. "August B. Hollingshead's 'Four Factor Index of Social Status': From Unpublished Paper to Citation Classic." *Yale Journal of Sociology* 8 (Fall 2011): 11–19. https://sociology.yale.edu/sites/default/files/files/yjs_fall_2011.pdf.

Alivisatos, A., Miyoung Chun Paul, George M. Church, Ralph J. Greenspan, Michael L. Roukes, and Rafael Yuste. "The Brain Activity Map Project and the Challenge of Functional Connectomics." *Neuron* 74, no. 6 (June 2012): 970–4.

Alivisatos, A., Miyoung Chun Paul, George M. Church, Ralph J. Greenspan, Michael L. Roukes, and Rafael Yuste. "A National Network of Neurotechnology Centers for the BRAIN Initiative." *Neuron* 88, no. 3 (2015): 445–8.

American Psychiatric Association. *Diagnostic and Statistical Manual of Mental Disorders*. 5th ed. (Washington, DC: American Psychiatric Association, 2013). Online edition. https://doi.org/10.1176/appi.books.9780890425596.

Ardelt, Monika. "Wisdom as Expert Knowledge System: A Critical Review of a Contemporary Operationalization of an Ancient Concept." *Human Development* 47, no. 5 (2004): 257–85.

Åsberg, Marie. "Neurotransmitters and Suicidal Behavior. The Evidence from Cerebrospinal Fluid Studies." *Annals of New York Academy of Sciences* 836 (1997): 158–81.

Ashburner, John, and Karl Friston. "Voxel-based Morphometry—The Methods." *Neuroimage* 11 (2000): 805–21.

Babbie, Earl. *The Practice of Social Research*. 10th ed. Belmont, CA: Wadsworth, 2004.

Bachner-Melman, Rachel, I. Gristenko, L. Nemanov, A. H. Zohar, C. Dina, and R. P. Ebstein. "Dopaminergic Polymorphisms Associated with Self-Report Measures of Human Altruism: A Fresh Phenotype for the Dopamine D4 Receptor." *Molecular Psychiatry* 10, no. 4 (2005): 333–5.

Bacon, Francis. *Instauratio magna. Multi petrasibunt & augebitur Scientia*. https://archive.org/details/instauratiomagna00baco.

Bacon, Francis. *The New Organon*. Edited by Lisa Jardine and Michael Silverthorne. New York: Cambridge University Press, 2000.

Ball, Terence. "James Mill." In *The Stanford Encyclopedia of Philosophy* (Winter 2018 Edition), edited by Edward N. Zalta. https://plato.stanford.edu/archives/win2018/entries/james-mill.

Baltes, Paul B. "The Aging Mind: Potential and Limits." *The Gerontologist* 33 (1993): 580–94.

Baltes, Paul B., Jacqui Smith, and Ursula M. Staudinger. "Wisdom and Successful Aging." *Nebraska Symposium on Motivation* 39 (1991): 123–67.

Baltes, Paul B. and Ursula M. Staudinger. "The Search for a Psychology of Wisdom." *Current Directions in Psychological Science* 2, no. 3 (1993): 75–81.

Baltes, Paul B. and Ursula M. Staudinger. "Wisdom: A Metaheuristic (Pragmatic) to Orchestrate Mind and Virtue Toward Excellence." *American Psychologist* 55, no. 1 (2000): 122–36.

Barbour, Ian G. *Religion and Science: Historical and Contemporary Issues*. San Francisco, CA: Harper Collins, 1997.

Baron-Cohen, Simon. *The Science of Evil: On Empathy and the Origins of Cruelty*. New York: Perseus Books, 2012.

Barraza, Jorge A., Michael E. McCullough, Sheila Ahmadi, and Paul J. Zak. "Oxytocin Infusion Increases Charitable Donations Regardless of Monetary Resources." *Hormones and Behavior* 60, no. 2 (2011): 148–51.

Bartels, Daniel M. and David A. Pizzaro. "The Mismeasure of Morals: Antisocial Personality Traits Predict Utilitarian Responses to Moral Dilemmas." *Cognition* 121, no. 1 (2011): 154–61.

Beatty, John. "Origins of the U.S. Human Genome Project: Changing Relationships between Genetics and National Security." In *Controlling Our Destinies*, edited by Phillip Reid Sloan, 131–53. Notre Dame, IN: Notre Dame Press, 2000.

Beaver, Kevin M., Meghan W. Rowland, Joseph A. Schwartz, and Joseph L. Nedelec. "The Genetic Origins of Psychopathic Personality Traits in Adult Males and Females: Results from an Adoption-Based Study." *Journal of Criminal Justice* 39 (2011): 426–32.

Beck, Bernard. "Bedbugs, Stench, Dampness, and Immorality: A Review Essay on Recent Literature about Poverty." *Social Problems* 15, no. 1 (1967): 101–14.

Becker, Gary. *Accounting for Tastes*. Cambridge, MA: Harvard University Press, 1996.

Becker, Gary. "Crime and Punishment: An Economic Approach." *The Journal of Political Economy* 76 (1968): 169–217.

Becker, Gary. *The Economic Approach to Human Behavior*. Chicago: University of Chicago Press, 2008.

Becker, Gary. "The Economic Way of Looking at Life." *Nobel Prize Lecture*, 1992. https://www.nobelprize.org/uploads/2018/06/becker-lecture.pdf.

Becker, Gary. *The Economics of Discrimination*, 2nd ed. Chicago: University of Chicago Press, 1957.

Becker, Gary. *Human Capital: A Theoretical and Empirical Analysis, with Special Reference to Education*, 2nd ed. New York: National Bureau of Economic Research, 1975.

Becker, Gary. *A Treatise on the Family*. Cambridge, MA: Harvard University Press, 1998.

Becker, Gary and Guity Nashat Becker. *The Economics of Life: From Baseball to Affirmative Action to Immigration, How Real-World Issues Affect Our Everyday Life*. London: McGraw-Hill, 1998.

Becker, Gary, Elizabeth Landes, and Robert T. Michael. "An Economic Analysis of Marital Instability." *Journal of Political Economy* 85 (1977): 1141–88.

Becker, Gary and H. Gregg Lewis. "On the Interaction between the Quantity and Quality of Children." *The Journal of Political Economy* 81 (1973): S279–88.

Becker, Gary and Kevin M. Murphy. "A Theory of Rational Addiction." *Journal of Political Economy* 96, no. 4 (August 1988): 657–700.

Bennett, William, John DiIulio, and John P. Walters. *Body Count: Moral Poverty . . . and How to Win America's War Against Crime and Drugs*. New York: Simon & Schuster, 1996.

Bentham, Jeremy. "An Introduction to the Principles of Morals and Legislation." In *The Works of Jeremy Bentham*, edited by John Bowring. Edinburgh: William Tait, 1838–43. Reprinted New York, 1962.

Bentham, Jeremy. "Principles of Civil Code." In *The Works of Jeremy Bentham*, edited by John Bowring. Edinburgh: William Tait, 1838–43. Reprinted New York, 1962. https://www.laits.utexas.edu/poltheory/bentham/pcc/.

Bentham, Jeremy. *A Table of the Springs of Action*. https://www.laits.utexas.edu/poltheory/bentham/springs/index.html.

Bentham, Jeremy. "To Jaques Pierre Brissot de Warville, 25 November, 1791." In *The Correspondence of Jeremy Bentham, Volume 4: October 1788-December 1793*, edited by A. T. Milne, letter 821, 341–2. In *The Collected Works of Jeremy Bentham*, general editor J. R. Dinwiddy. London: UCL Press, 2017.

Bernard, Claude. *An Introduction to the Study of Experimental Medicine*. Translated by Henry Copley Greene. New York: Dover Publications, 1957.

Bertram, Christopher. "Jean Jacques Rousseau." In *The Stanford Encyclopedia of Philosophy* (Summer 2020 Edition), edited by Edward N. Zalta. https://plato.stanford.edu/archives/sum2020/entries/rousseau/.

Bishop, Jeffrey P. *The Anticipatory Corpse: Medicine, Power, and the Care of the Dying*. Notre Dame, IN: University of Notre Dame Press, 2011.

Black, Donald W. "The Natural History of Antisocial Personality Disorder." *Canadian Journal of Psychiatry* 60, no. 7 (July 2015): 309–14.

Black, Robert A. "What Did Adam Smith Say About Self-Love?" *Journal of Markets & Morality* 9, no. 1 (Spring 2006): 7–34.

Blair, Clancy and C. Cybele Raver. "Poverty, Stress, and Brain Development: New Directions for Prevention and Intervention." *Academy of Pediatrics* 16, no. 3 (April 2016): S30–6.

Blair, James R. "The Amygdala and Ventromedial Prefrontal Cortex in Morality and Psychopathy." *Trends in Cognitive Sciences* 22 (2007): 387–92.

Blair, James R. "Responsiveness to Distress Cues in the Child with Psychopathic Tendencies." *Personality and Individual Differences* 27 (1999): 135–45.

Blakemore, Sarah-Jayne, and Chris Frith. "Self-awareness and Action." *Current Opinion in Neurobiology* 13, no. 2 (2003): 219–24.

Blanchard, Kathryn. *The Protestant Ethic or the Spirit of Capitalism: Christians, Freedom, and Free Markets*. Eugene, OR: Wipf and Stock, 2010.

Blazer, Dan German. *The Age of Melancholy: "Major Depression" and Its Social Origin*. New York: Routledge 2005.

Blonigen, Daniel M., Brian M. Hicks, Robert F. Krueger, William G. Iacono, and Christopher J. Patrick. "Psychopathic Personality Traits: Heritability and Genetic Overlap with Internalizing and Externalizing Psychopathology." *Psychological Medicine* 35 (2005): 637–48.

Bollas, Christopher. *The Shadow of the Object*. New York: Columbia University Press, 1987.

Brown, Scott C. "Learning Across the Campus: How College Facilitates the Development of Wisdom." *Journal of College Student Development* 45, no. 2 (2004): 134–48.

Brown, Scott C. and Jeffrey A. Greene. "The Wisdom Development Scale: Translating the Conceptual to the Concrete." *Journal of College Student Development* 47, no. 1 (2008): 1–19.

Brown, Wendy. *Undoing the Demos: Neoliberalism's Stealth Revolution*. Kindle ed. Cambridge, MA: MIT Press, 2015.

Browning, Don. "Egos Without Selves: A Theological-Ethical Theory of the Family Theory of the Chicago School of Economics." *Annual of the Society of Christian Ethics* 14 (1994): 127–45.

Bruck, Lauryn. "Cunningham on the Poor: 'They're Poor Because They Lack Values, Ethics, and Morals.'" *Media Matters for America*. January 15, 2009. https://www.mediamatters.org/bill-cunningham/cunningham-poor-theyre-poor-because-they-lack-values-ethics-and-morals.

Brugman, Gerard M. "Wisdom and Aging." In *Handbook of the Psychology of Aging*, 6th ed., edited by J. E. Birren and K. Warner Schaie, 445–69. Burlington, MA: Elsevier Academic Press, 2005.

Buckholtz, J. W., J. H. Callicott, B. Kolachana, et al. "Genetic Variation in MAOA Modulates Ventromedial Prefrontal Circuitry Mediating Individual Differences in Human Personality." *Molecular Psychiatry* 13, no. 3 (2008): 313–24.

Burtt, Edwin A. *The Metaphysical Foundations of Modern Science*. New York: Dover, 2003.

Capaldi, Nicholas. *John Stuart Mill: A Biography*. Cambridge: Cambridge University Press, 2004.

Caspi, Avshalom, Joseph McClay, Terrie E. Moffitt, et al. "Role of Genotype in the Cycle of Violence in Maltreated Children." *Science* 297, no. 5582 (2002): 851–4.

Caspi, Avshalom, Karen Sugden, Terrie E. Moffitt, et al. "Influence of Life Stress on Depression: Moderation by a Polymorphism in the 5-HTT Gene." *Science* 301, no. 5631 (2003): 386–9.

Cattell, Raymond. *The Inheritance of Personality and Ability*. New York: Academic Press, 1982.

Choudhury, Suparna, Jennifer R. Fishman, Michelle L. McGowan, and Eric T. Juengst. "Big Data, Open Science and the Brain: Lessons Learned from Genomics." *Frontiers in Human Neuroscience* 8 (2014): 239.

Churchland, Patricia. *Braintrust: What Neuroscience Tells Us about Morality*. Princeton, NJ: Princeton University Press, 2012.

Cirino, Paul T., Christopher E. Chin, Rose A. Sevcik, Maryanne Wolf, Maureen Lovett, and Robin D. Morris. "Measuring Socioeconomic Status: Reliability and Preliminary Validity for Different Approaches." *Assessment* 9 (2002): 145–55.

Cleckley, Harvey M. *The Mask of Sanity: An Attempt to Re-Interpret Some Issues About the So-Called Psychopathic Personality*, 5th ed. St. Louis, MO: Mosby, 1976.

Coccaro, Emil F. "Central Neurotransmitter Function in Human Aggression and Impulsivity." In *Neurobiology and Clinical Views on Aggression and Impulsivity*, edited by Michael Maes and Emil F. Coccaro, 143–68. New York: Wiley, 1998.

Coccaro, Emil F., Larry J. Siever, Howard Klar, Karen Rubenstein, Eric Benjamin, and Kenneth L. Davis. "Diminished Prolactin Responses to Repeated Fenfluramine Challenge in Man." *Psychiatry Research* 22 (1987): 257–9.

Combe, George. *A System of Phrenology*, 5th ed. Edinburgh: MacLachlan and Stewart, 1853.

Cook-Deegan, Robert. *The Gene Wars: Science, Politics, and the Human Genome*. New York: Norton, 1994.

Corry, B. A. "Robbins, Lionel Charles (1898–1984)." In *The New Palgrave Dictionary of Economics*, vol. 4, 2nd ed., edited by Steven N. Durlauf and Lawrence E. Blume. London: Palgrave Macmillan, 2008.

Cowan, Jacquline L. "Francis Bacon's *New Atlantis* and the Alterity of the New World." *Literature and Theology* 25, no. 4 (2011): 407–21.

Crimmins, James E. "Bentham's Metaphysics and the Science of Divinity." *Harvard Theological Review* 79, no. 4 (1986): 387–411.

Crimmins, James E. "Jeremy Bentham." In *The Stanford Encyclopedia of Philosophy* (Summer 2019 Edition), edited by Edward N. Zalta. https://plato.stanford.edu/archives/sum2019/entries/bentham.

Dannlowski, Udo, Patricia Ohrmann, Carsten Konrad, et al. "Reduced Amygdala-prefrontal Coupling in Major Depression: Association with MAOA Genotype and Illness Severity." *International Journal of Neuropsychopharmacology* 12, no. 1 (2009): 11–22.

Darwall, Stephen. "Sympathetic Liberalism: Recent Work on Adam Smith." *Philosophy and Public Affairs* 28, no. 2 (1999): 139–64.

Davies, William. *The Limits of Neoliberalism: Authority, Sovereignty and the Logic of Competition*. London: SAGE Publications, 2014.

Davis, William L. Bob Figgins, David Hedengren, and Daniel B. Klein, "Economic Professors' Favorite Economic Thinkers, Journals, and Blogs." *Econ Journal Watch* 8, no. 2 (2011): 126–46.

Decety, Jean, and Philip L. Jackson. "The Functional Architecture of Human Empathy." *Behavioral and Cognitive Neuroscience Reviews* 3, no. 2 (2004): 71–100.

Decety, Jean, Philip L. Jackson, Jessica A. Sommerville, Thierry Chaminade, and Andrew N. Meltzoff. "The Neural Bases of Cooperation and Competition: An fMRI Investigation." *Neuroimage* 23, no. 2 (2004): 744–51.

DiDomenica, Peter, and Thomas G. Robbins. *Journey from Genesis to Genocide: Hate, Empathy, and the Plight of Humanity*. Pittsburgh, PA: Dorrance Publishing, 2013.

Doty, Robert W. "Neuroscience." In *The History of the American Physiological Society: The First Century, 1887–1987*, edited by John R. Brobeck, Orr E. Reynolds, and Toby A. Appel, 427–34. New York: Oxford University Press, 1988.

Douglas, Charles. *John Stuart Mill: A Study of His Philosophy*. Edinburgh: William Blackwood and Sons, 1895.

Douglas, Thomas. "Moral Enhancement." *Journal of Applied Philosophy* 25, no. 3 (2008): 228–45.

Dutton, Diana B. *Worse than the Disease: Pitfalls of Medical Progress*. New York: Cambridge University Press, 1988.

Eaves, Lindon, Hans Eysenck, and Nicholas Martin. *Genes, Culture, and Personality: An Empirical Approach*. London: Academic Press, 1989.

Elder, Larry. *Stupid Black Men: How to Play the Race Card and Lose*. New York: St. Martin's Press, 2008.

Emmett, Ross. "De Gustibus Est Disputandum: Frank H. Knight's Reply to George Stigler and Gary Becker's 'De Gustibus Non Est Disputandum' With an Introductory Essay." *Journal of Economic Methodology* 13, no. 1 (2006): 97–111.

Emmett, Ross. "Did the Chicago School Reject Frank Knight? Assessing Frank Knight's Place in the Chicago School of Economics Tradition." In *Frank Knight and the Chicago School in American Economics*, edited by Ross Emmett, 145–55. London: Routledge, 2009.

Emmett, Ross. "Frank H. Knight and The Economic Organization." James Madison College. Michigan State University Working Papers Series, Working Paper no.: 0405-01 (April 2005). https://papers.ssrn.com/sol3/papers.cfm?abstract_id=922531.

Emmett, Ross. "Frank Knight and the Chicago School." Presented at the Becker Friedman Institute for Economic Research, The University of Chicago "The Legacy of Chicago Economics." (October 5, 2015).

Emmett, Ross. *The Passage from Classical to Neo-Liberalism: Frank H. Knight's Role Re-Considered*. March 6, 2011. https://papers.ssrn.com/sol3/papers.cfm?abstract_id=1779102.

Fallon, James. *The Psychopath Inside: A Neuroscientist's Personal Journey into the Dark Side of the Brain*. New York: Current, 2013.

Faraone, Stephen V., Alysa E. Doyle, Eric Mick, and Joseph Biederman. "Meta-Analysis of the Association between the 7-Repeat Allele of the Dopamine D(4) Receptor Gene and Attention Deficit Hyperactivity Disorder." *American Journal of Psychiatry* 158, no. 7 (2001): 1052–7.

Fishman, Leo, ed. *Poverty Amid Affluence*. New Haven, CT: Yale University Press, 1966.
Fleck, Ludwik. "Crisis in Science." In *Cognition and Fact: Materials on Ludwik Fleck*, edited by Robert S. Cohen and Thomas Schnelle, 153–60. Dordrecht: D. Reidel Publishing, 1986.
Fleck, Ludwik. *Genesis and Development of a Scientific Fact*. Edited by T. J. Trenn and R. K. Merton. Chicago: University of Chicago Press, 1979.
Fleischacker, Samuel. "Adam Smith's Moral and Political Philosophy." In *The Stanford Encyclopedia of Philosophy* (Spring 2017 Edition), edited by Edward N. Zalta. https://plato.stanford.edu/archives/spr2017/entries/smith-moral-political/.
Fleischacker, Samuel. "Sympathy in Hume and Smith: A Contrast, Critique, and Reconstruction." In *Intersubjectivity and Objectivity in Adam Smith and Edmund Husserl: A Collection of Essays*, edited by Christel Fricke and Dagfinn Føllesdal, 272–311. Berlin: De Gruyter, 2012.
Florence Heller Graduate School for Advanced Studies in Social Welfare. *Colloquia: 1963–1964, Poverty and Dependency*. Waltham, MA: Brandeis University, 1965.
Flory, Janine D., Stephen B. Manuck, and Matthew F. Muldoon. "Retest Reliability of Prolactin Response to dl-Fenfluramine Challenge in Adults." *Neuropsychopharmacology* 26 (2002): 269–72.
Flory, Janine D., Stephen B. Manuck, James M. Perel and Matthew F. Muldoon. "A Comparison of d, l-Fenfluramine and Citalopram Challenges in Healthy Adults." *Psychopharmacology* 174 (2004): 376–80.
Foucault, Michel. *The Birth of Biopolitics: Lectures at the College de France 1978–1979*. Edited by Michel Senellart. Translated by Graham Burchell. New York: Palgrave MacMillan, 2008.
Frederick, Shane and George Loewenstein. "Hedonic Adaptation." In *Well-Being: The Foundations of Hedonic Psychology*, edited by Daniel Kahneman, Ed Diener, and Norbert Schwarz, 351–401. New York: Russell Sage Foundation, 1999.
Freeman, Louis A., Joyce L. Kornbluh, and Alan Haber, eds. *Poverty in America*. Ann Arbor, MI: University of Michigan Press, 1965.
Friedman, Milton. *Capitalism and Freedom*. Kindle ed. Chicago: University of Chicago Press, 2002.
Friedman, Milton. "The Methodology of Positive Economics." In *Essays in Positive Economics*, edited by Milton Friedman, 3–43. Chicago: University of Chicago Press, 1966.
Friedman, Milton. "Neoliberalism and Its Prospects." *Farmand* 2 (1951): 89–93.
Friedman, Milton, and Rose Friedman. *Free to Choose: A Personal Statement*. New York: Houghton Mifflin Harcourt, 1980.
Funkenstein, Amos. *Theology and the Scientific Imagination from the Middle Ages to the Seventeenth Century*. Princeton, NJ: Princeton University Press, 1986.
Gassendi, Pierre. *Opera Omnia*, vol. 1. Lugduni: Lugduni, Anisson et Devenet, 1658.
Gassendi, Pierre. *Three Discourses on Happiness, Virtue, and Liberty: Collected from the Works of the Learn'd Gassendi*. Edited by Monsieur Bernier. London: Awnsham and John Churchill, 1699.
Gianaros, Peter J., Jeffrey A. Horenstein, Sheldon Cohen, Karen A. Matthews, Sarah M. Brown, Janine D. Flory, Hugo D. Critchley, Stephen B. Manuck, and Ahmad R. Hariri. "Perigenual Anterior Cingulate Morphology Covaries with Perceived Social Standing." *Social Cognitive and Affective Neuroscience* 2 (2007): 161–73.
Gianaros, Peter J., Jeffrey A. Horenstein, Ahmad R. Hariri et al. "Potential Neural Embedding of Parental Social Standing." *Social Cognitive and Affective Neuroscience* 3 (2008): 91–6.

Gianaros, Peter J., and Stephen B. Manuck. "Neurobiological Pathways Linking Socioeconomic Position and Health." *Psychosomatic Medicine* 72, no. 5 (2010): 450–61.

Giroux, Susan Searls. "Sade's Revenge: Racial Neoliberalism and the Sovereignty of Negation." *Patterns of Prejudice* 44, no. 1 (2010): 1–26.

Goodson, Teddy. "Does Charity Breed Poverty?" *Blue Virginia*, May 23, 2010. https://bluevirginia.us/2010/05/does-charity-breed-poverty.

Gordon, Margaret S., ed. *Poverty in America*. San Francisco: Chandler, 1965.

Gramsci, Antonio. *Selections from the Prison Notebooks*. Translated by Quintin Hoare and Geoffrey Nowell Smith. London: Lawrence & Wishart, 1971.

Haidt, Jonathan. *All Minus One: John Stuart Mill's Ideas on Free Speech*. New York: Heterodox Academy, 2018.

Haidt, Jonathan. *The Happiness Hypothesis: Finding Modern Truth in Ancient Wisdom*. New York: Basic Books, 2006.

Haidt, Jonathan. *The Righteous Mind: Why Good People are Divided by Politics and Religion*. New York: Pantheon Books, 2012.

Haidt, Jonathan, and Greg Lukianoff. *The Coddling of the American Mind: How Good Intentions and Bad Ideas are Setting up a Generation for Failure*. New York: Penguin, 2018.

Haidt, Jonathan, Clark McCauley, and Paul Rozin. "Individual Differences in Sensitivity to Disgust: A Scale Sampling Seven Domains of Disgust Elicitors." *Personality and Individual Differences* 16, no. 5 (1994): 701–13.

Hammond, J. Daniel. "Milton Friedman [Ideological Profiles of the Economics Laureates]." *Econ Journal Watch* 10, no. 4 (September 2013): 325–32.

Hanley, Ryan Patrick. *Adam Smith and the Character of Virtue*. Cambridge: Cambridge University Press, 2009.

Harrington, Michael. *The Other America: Poverty in the United States*. New York: Scribner's, 1962.

Harris, Sam. *The End of Faith: Religion, Terror, and the Future of Reason*. New York: W.W. Norton, 2004.

Harris, Sam. *Free Will*. New York: Free Press, 2011.

Harris, Sam. *The Moral Landscape: How Science Can Determine Human Values*. New York: Free Press, 2010.

Harris, Sam. *Waking Up: A Guide to Spirituality without Religion*. New York: Simon and Schuster, 2014.

Harris, Sam, and Mark S. Cohen. "The Functional Neuroanatomy of the Belief." Society for Neuroscience Annual Meeting, San Diego, CA, October 25, 2004.

Harris, Sam, Jonas T. Kaplan, Ashley Curiel, Susan Y. Bookheimer, Marco Iacoboni, and Mark S. Cohen. "The Neural Correlates of Religious and Nonreligious Belief." *PLoS ONE* 4, no. 10 (2009): e7272.

Harris, Sam, and Maajid Nawaz. *Islam and the Future of Tolerance: A Dialogue*. Cambridge, MA: Harvard University Press, 2015.

Harris, Sam, Sameer A. Sheth, and Mark S. Cohen. "Functional Neuroimaging of Belief, Disbelief, and Uncertainty." *Annals of Neurology*, 63, no. 2 (2008): 141–7.

Harrison, Peter. *The Territories of Science and Religion*. Oxford: Oxford University Press, 2015.

Harvey, David. *A Brief History of Neoliberalism*. Oxford: Oxford University Press, 2008.

Haycock, Dean A. *Murderous Minds: Exploring the Criminal Psychopathic Brain*. New York: Pegasus Books, 2014.

Hazlitt, William. *The Spirit of the Age*. New York: Dolphin, 1825.
Healy, David. *The Creation of Psychopharmacology*. Cambridge, MA: Harvard University Press, 2002.
Heidegger, Martin. *Basic Writings*. Edited by David Farrell Krell. New York: HarperCollins, 2008.
Heinz, Andreas, Deiter F. Braus, Michael N Smolka et al. "Amygdala-prefrontal Coupling Depends on a Genetic Variation of the Serotonin Transporter." *Nature Neuroscience* 8, no. 1 (2005): 20–1.
Henrich, Joseph, Steven J. Heine, and Ara Norenzayan. "The Weirdest People in the World?" *Behavioral and Brain Sciences* 33, no. 2–3 (2010): 61–83.
Hilfiker, David. *Urban Injustice: How Ghettos Happen*. New York: Seven Stories Press, 2003.
Hill, Lisa. "The Hidden Theology of Adam Smith." *European Journal of the History of Economic Thought* 8, no. 1 (2001): 1–29.
Himmelfarb, Gertrude. *The Idea of Poverty*. New York: Alfred A. Knopf, 1983.
Himmelfarb, Gertrude. "Two Enlightenments: A Contrast in Social Ethics." *Proceedings of the British Academy* 117 (2001): 297–324.
Hirschman, Albert O. *The Rhetoric of Reaction: Perversity, Futility, Jeopardy*. Cambridge, MA: Belknap Press, 2004.
Hitchens, Christopher, Richard Dawkins, Sam Harris, and Daniel Dennet. *The Four Horsemen: Conversations that Sparked an Atheist Revolution*. New York: Random House, 2019.
Hobbes, Thomas. *Leviathan*. Edited by Richard Tuck. New York: Cambridge University Press, 1991.
Hollingshead, August B. "Commentary on 'The Indiscriminate State of Social Class Measurement.'" *Social Forces* 49 (1971): 563–7.
Hollingshead, August B. "Four Factor Index of Social Status." *Yale Journal of Sociology* 8 (2011): 21–52. https://sociology.yale.edu/sites/default/files/files/yjs_fall_2011.pdf.
Hollingshead, August B. and Frederick C. Redlich. *Social Class and Mental Illness: A Community Study*. New York: John Wiley & Sons, 1958.
Horwitz, Allan V. "How an Age of Anxiety Became an Age of Depression." *The Milbank Quarterly* 88, no. 1 (2010): 112–38.
Hume, David. *An Enquiry Concerning Human Understanding*, 2nd ed. Edited by Eric Steinberg. Indianapolis, IN: Hackett Publishing, 1977.
Hume, David. *An Enquiry Concerning the Principles of Morals*. Edited by J. B. Schneewind. Indianapolis, IN: Hackett Publishing, 1983.
Hume, David. *The Letters of David Hume*, 2 vols. Edited by J. Y. T. Greig. Oxford: Clarendon Press, 1932.
Hume, David. *A Treatise of Human Nature*. Edited by L. A. Selby-Biggs. Oxford: Clarendon Press, 1896. https://oll.libertyfund.org/titles/hume-a-treatise-of-human-nature.
Humphrey, Hubert H. *War on Poverty*. New York: McGraw-Hill, 1964.
Inbar, Yoel, David Pizarro, Ravi Iyer, and Jonathan Haidt. "Disgust Sensitivity, Political Conservatism, and Voting." *Social Psychological and Personality Science* 3, no. 5 (2012): 537–44.
Jang, Kerry L., Robert R. McCrae, Alois Angleitner, Rainer Riemann, and W. John Livesley. "Heritability of Facet-Level Traits in a Cross-Cultural Twin Sample: Support for the Hierarchy Model of Personality." *Journal of Personality and Social Psychology* 74 (1998): 1556–65.

Jason, Leonard A., Arne Reichler, Caroline King, Derryk Madsen, Jennifer Camacho, and Wendy Marchese, "The Measurement of Wisdom: A Preliminary Report." *Journal of Community Psychology* 29, no. 5 (2001): 585–98.
Jones, David Stedman. *Masters of the Universe: Hayek, Friedman, and the Birth of Neoliberal Politics*. Princeton, NJ: Princeton University Press, 2013.
Jones, Matthew. *The Good Life in the Scientific Revolution: Descartes, Pascal, Leibniz and the Cultivation of Virtue*. Chicago: The University of Chicago Press, 2006.
Joyce, Richard and Richard Garner, eds. *The End of Morality: Taking Moral Abolitionism Seriously*. New York: Routledge, 2019.
Kandel, Eric R., James H. Schwartz, and Thomas M. Jessell. *Principles of Neural Science*. New York: McGraw Hill, 2000.
Kay, Lily E. "A Book of Life? How a Genetic Code Became a Language." In *Controlling Our Destinies*, edited by Phillip Reid Sloan, 99–124. Notre Dame, IN: Notre Dame Press, 2000.
Keyes, Corey L. M. and Jonathan Haidt, eds. *Flourishing: Positive Psychology and the Life Well-Lived*. Washington, DC: American Psychological Association, 2002.
Kiehl, Kent A. "A Cognitive Neuroscience Perspective on Psychopathy: Evidence for Paralimbic System Dysfunction." *Psychiatry Research* 147 (2006): 107–28.
Kiehl, Kent A. *The Psychopath Whisperer: The Science of Those Without Conscience*. New York: Crown Publishers, 2014.
Kim, Jim Yong, Joyce V. Millen, Alec Irwin, and John Gershman, eds. *Dying for Growth: Global Inequality and the Health of the Poor*. Monroe, ME: Common Courage Press, 2000.
Kinghorn, Warren. "Combat Trauma and Moral Fragmentation: A Theological Account of Moral Injury." *Journal of the Society of Christian Ethics* 32, no. 2 (2012): 57–74.
Klein, Daniel B., William L. Davis, Bob G. Figgins, and David Hedengren. "Characteristics of the Members of Twelve Economic Associations: Voting, Policy Views, and Favorite Economists." *Econ Journal Watch* 9, no. 2 (May 2012): 149–62.
Klein, Daniel B., and Ryan Daza. "Gary Becker." *Econ Journal Watch* 10, no. 3 (September 2013): 285–91.
Klein, Jürgen, and Guido Giglioni. "Francis Bacon." In *The Stanford Encyclopedia of Philosophy* (Winter 2016 Edition), edited by Edward N. Zalta. https://plato.stanford.edu/archives/win2016/entries/francis-bacon/.
Knight, Frank. *The Economic Organization*. New York: Augustus M. Kelley, 1951.
Knight, Frank. "Ethics and the Economic Interpretation." *The Quarterly Journal of Economics* 36, no. 3 (1922): 454–81.
Knight, Frank. "The Ethics of Competition." In *Selected Essays by Frank H. Knight*, edited by Ross Emmett, 61–93. Chicago: University of Chicago Press, 1999.
Knight, Frank. *The Ethics of Competition*. New York: Routledge, 2017.
Knight, Frank. *Risk, Uncertainty, and Profit*. New York: Houghton Mifflin Co., The Riverside Press, 1921.
Knight, Frank. *Selected Essays by Frank H. Knight*, vol. 1. Edited by Ross Emmett. Chicago: University of Chicago Press, 1999.
Kramer, Peter. *Against Depression*. New York: Viking, 2004.
Krugman, Paul. "Who Was Milton Friedman?" *The New York Review of Books*. February 15, 2007.
Lachterman, David Rapport. *The Ethics of Geometry: A Genealogy of Modernity*. New York: Routledge, 1989.
Landau, Iddo. "Feminist Criticism of Metaphors in Bacon's Philosophy of Science." *Philosophy* 73, no. 283 (January 1998): 47–61.

Leitner, Chris. "Frank Knight's Economic and Social Theology." *Le Québécois Libre* 326 (November 15, 2014). http://www.quebecoislibre.org/14/141115-8.html.

Lenoir, Timothy, and Marguerite Hays. "The Manhattan Project for Biomedicine." In *Controlling Our Destinies*, edited by Phillip Reid Sloan, 29–62. Notre Dame, IN: Notre Dame Press, 2000.

Lepenies, Philipp H. "Of Goats and Dogs: Joseph Townsend and the Idealisation of Markets—A Decisive Episode in the History of Economics." *Cambridge Journal of Economics* 38, no. 2 (2014): 447–57.

Lester, David. "The Concentration of Neurotransmitter Metabolites in the Cerebrospinal Fluid of Suicidal Individuals: A Meta-Analysis." *Pharmacopsychiatry* 28, no. 2 (1995): 45–50.

Liao, S. Matthew. *Moral Brains: The Neuroscience of Morality*. Oxford: Oxford University Press: 2016.

Livianos-Aldana, Lorenzo, Luis Rojo-Moreno, and Pilar Sierra-SanMiguel. "Gall and the Phrenological Movement." *The American Journal of Psychiatry* 164, no. 3 (2007): 414.

Loehlin, John. *Genes and Environment in Personality Development*. Newbury Park, CA: Sage, 1992.

Loehlin, John, Lee Willerman, and Joseph Horn. "Personality Resemblances in Adoptive Families: A 10-year Follow-up." *Journal of Personality and Social Psychology* 42 (1987): 1089–99.

Lowe, Naomi, Aiveen Kirley, Ziarih Hawi et al. "Joint Analysis of the Drd5 Marker Concludes Association with Attention-Deficit/Hyperactivity Disorder Confined to the Predominantly Inattentive and Combined Subtypes." *American Journal of Human Genetics* 74, no. 2 (2004): 348–56.

Lucas, Peter. "Bacon's *New Atlantis* and the Fictional Origins of Organized Science." *Open Cultural Studies* 2 (2018): 114–21.

Lyons, Sherrie L. *Species, Serpents, Spirits, and Skulls: Science at the Margins in the Victorian Age*. Albany, NY: New York Press, 2009.

Lysaught, M. Therese. "Love Your Enemies: Life Sciences in the Ecclesially-Based University." In *The Ecclesially-Based University in a Liberal Democratic Society*, edited by John Wright and Michael Budde, 109–27. Grand Rapids, MI: Brazos Press, 2004.

Lysaught, M. Therese. "That Jagged Little Pill and the Counter-Politics of the Community of the Expelled Sacramentality and Psychiatric Medications." *Christian Bioethics* 24, no. 3 (2018): 246–64.

MacIntyre, Alasdair. *After Virtue: A Study of Moral Theory*. Notre Dame, IN: University of Notre Dame Press, 1984.

MacIntyre, Alasdair. *Ethics in the Conflict of Modernity: An Essay on Desire, Practical Reasoning, and Narrative*. New York: Cambridge University Press, 2016.

MacIntyre, Alasdair. *Whose Justice? Which Rationality?* Notre Dame, IN: University of Notre Dame Press, 1988.

Macleod, Christopher. "John Stuart Mill." In *The Stanford Encyclopedia of Philosophy* (Summer 2020 Edition), edited by Edward N. Zalta. https://plato.stanford.edu/archives/sum2020/entries/mill/.

Malone, Kevin M., Elizabeth M. Corbitt, Shuhua Li and J. John Mann. "Prolactin Response to Fenfluramine and Suicide Attempt Lethality in Major Depression." *British Journal of Psychiatry* 168 (1996): 324–28.

Malthus, Thomas. *An Essay on the Principle of Population: Or a View of Its Past and Present on Human Happiness*, 7th ed. London: Reeves and Turner, 1872.

Malthus, Thomas. *Essay on the Principle of Population.* http://www.econlib.org/library/Malthus/malPlongCover.html.
Mandeville, Bernard. *The Fable of the Bees, or Private Vices, Publick Benefits, Vol 1. (1732).* Oxford: Clarendon Press, 1924. https://oll.libertyfund.org/titles/mandeville-the-fable-of-the-bees-or-private-vices-publick-benefits-vol-1.
Manuck, Stephen B., Maria E. Bleil, Karen L. Petersen et al. "The Socioeconomic Status of Communities Predicts Variation in Brain Serotonergic Responsivity." *Psychological Medicine* 35 (2005): 519–28.
Manuck, Stephen B., Janine D. Flory, Robert E. Ferrell, and Matthew F. Muldoon. "Socioeconomic Status Covaries with Central Nervous System Serotonergic Responsivity as a Function of Allelic Variation in the Serotonin Transporter Gene-linked Polymorphic Region." *Psychoneuroendocrinology* 29 (2004): 651–68.
Manuck, Stephen B., Janine D. Flory, Jeanne M. McCaffery, Karen A. Matthews, J. John Mann, and Matthew F. Muldoon. "Aggression, Impulsivity, and Central Nervous System Serotonergic Responsivity in a Nonpatient Sample." *Neuropsychopharmacology* 19 (1998): 287–99.
Marshall, Catherine, and Gretchen B. Rossman. *Designing Qualitative Research*, 5th ed. Thousand Oaks, CA: Sage, 2011.
Martin, Marie A. "Utility and Morality: Adam Smith's Critique of Hume." *Hume Studies* 16, no. 2 (November 1990): 107–20.
Mattan, Bradley D., Kevin Y. Wei, Jasmin Cloutier, and Jennifer T. Kubota. "The Social Neuroscience of Race-Based and Status-Based Prejudice." *Current Opinion in Psychology* 24 (December 2018): 27–34.
Matthews, Karen A., Janine D. Flory, Matthew Muldoon, and Stephen B. Manuck. "Does Socioeconomic Status Relate to Central Serotonergic Responsivity in Healthy Adults?" *Psychosomatic Medicine* 62 (2000): 231–7.
McCloskey, Deirdre. "Adam Smith, the Last of the Former Virtue Ethicists." *History of Political Economy* 40, no. 1 (2008): 47–31.
McKenny, Gerald P. *To Relieve the Human Estate: Bioethics, Technology, and the Body.* Albany, NY: State University of New York Press, 1997.
McLeod, Christa. "Why California Got it Right: Assessing Psychopaths Before Release." *Rutgers Law Record* 45 (2017–2018): 145–69. https://lawrecord.com/files/45_Rutgers_L_Rec_145.pdf.
McRorie, Christina. "Adam Smith, Ethicist: A Case for Reading Political Economy as Moral Anthropology." *Journal of Religious Ethics* 43, no. 4 (December 2015): 674–96.
McRorie, Christina. "The Emptiness of Modern Economics: Why the Dismal Science Needs a Richer Moral Anthropology." *The Hedgehog Review* 16, no. 3 (Fall 2014): 120–9.
Mecklenburger, Ralph D. *Our Religious Brains: What Cognitive Science Reveals about Belief, Morality, Community and Our Relationship with God.* Nashville, TN: Jewish Lights Press, 2012.
Medema, Steven G. "Adam Smith and the Chicago School." In *The Elgar Companion to Adam Smith*, edited by Jeffery Young, ch. 19. Cheltenham: Edward Elgar Publishers, 2010.
Meeks, Suzanne, Shruti N. Shah, and Sarah K. Ramsey. "The Pleasant Events Schedule–Nursing Home Version: A Useful Tool for Behavioral Interventions in Long-term Care." *Aging and Mental Health* 13, no. 3 (2009): 445–55.
Meeks, Thomas W., and Dilip V. Jeste. "Neurobiology of Wisdom: A Literature Overview." *Archives of General Psychiatry* 66, no. 4 (2009): 355–65.

Meissener, Hannah H., ed. *Poverty in the Affluent Society*. New York: Harper and Row, 1966.
Meyer-Lindenberg, Andreas, Joshua W. Buckholtz, Bhaskar Kolachana et al. "Neural Mechanisms of Genetic Risk for Impulsivity and Violence in Humans." *Proceedings of the National Academy of Sciences USA* 103, no. 16 (April 17, 2006): 6269–74.
Milbank, John. *Being Reconciled: Ontology and Pardon*. London: Routledge, 2003.
Milbank, John. *Theology and Social Theory: Beyond Secular Reason*, 2nd ed. Oxford: Blackwell, 2006.
Mill, John Stuart. *The Autobiography of John Stuart Mill*. Rockville, MD: Arc Manor, 2008.
Mill, John Stuart. *Essays on Some Unsettled Questions of Political Economy*, 2nd ed. London: Longmans, Green, Reader & Dyer, 1874.
Mill, John Stuart. *An Examination of Sir William Hamilton's Philosophy and of the Principal Philosophical Questions Discussed in his Writings*. Edited by J. M. Robson. Toronto: University of Toronto Press, 1979.
Mill, John Stuart. "On the Definition of Political Economy, and on the Method of Investigation Proper to It." *London and Westminster Review*, October 1836.
Mill, John Stuart. *A System of Logic, Ratiocinative and Inductive: Being a Connected View of the Principles of Evidence and the Methods of Scientific Investigation*, 8th ed. New York: Harper and Brothers, 1882.
Mill, John Stuart. *Utilitarianism*, 2nd ed. Edited by George Sher. Indianapolis, IN: Hackett Publishing, 2001.
Miller, Joan G., David M. Bersoff, and Robin L. Harwood. "Perceptions of Social Responsibilities in India and in the United States: Moral Imperatives or Personal Decisions?" *Journal of Personality and Social Psychology* 58, no. 1 (1990): 33–47.
Moffitt, Terrie, and Avshalom Caspi. "Evidence from Behavioral Genetics for Environmental Contributions to Antisocial Conduct." In *The Explanation of Crime: Context, Mechanisms, and Development*, edited by Per-Olof H. Wikström and Robert J. Sampson, 108–52. Cambridge: Cambridge University Press, 2006.
Moll, Jorge, Frank Krueger, Roland Zahn, Matteo Pardini, Ricardo de Oliveira-Souza, and Jordan Grafman. "Human Fronto-Mesolimbic Networks Guide Decisions About Charitable Donation." *Proceedings of the National Academy of Sciences USA* 103, no. 42 (2006): 15623–8.
Moll, Jorge, Ricardo de Oliveira-Souza, and P.J Eslinger. "Morals and the Human Brain: A Working Model." *Neuroreport* 14, no. 3 (2003): 299–305.
Morris, Arthur D. "The Reverend Joseph Townsend MA MGS (1739–1816) Physician and Geologist—'Colossus of Roads.'" *Proceedings of the Royal Society of Medicine* 62, no. 5 (May 1969): 471–7.
Morris, William Edward, and Charlotte R. Brown. "David Hume." In *The Stanford Encyclopedia of Philosophy* (Summer 2020 Edition), edited by Edward N. Zalta. https://plato.stanford.edu/archives/sum2020/entries/hume/.
Narvaez, Darcia, and Allan Schore. *Neurobiology and the Development of Human Morality: Evolution, Culture, and Wisdom*. New York: W. W. Norton & Company, 2014.
Nelson, Robert. "Frank Knight and Original Sin." *The Independent Review* 6, no. 1 (Summer 2001): 5–25.
Ng, Irene C. L., and Lu-Ming Tseng. "Learning to be Sociable: The Evolution of *Homo Economicus*." *The American Journal of Economics and Society* 67, no. 2 (2008): 265–86.
Oakley, Barbara. *Evil Genes: Why Rome Fell, Hitler Rose, Enron Failed, and My Sister Stole My Mother's Boyfriend*. Amherst, NY: Prometheus Books, 2008.

Oldham, John M. "The Alternative DSM-5 Model for Personality Disorders." *World Psychiatry* 14, no. 2 (June 2015): 234–6.

O'Reilly, Bill. "The O'Reilly Factor." In *"O'Reilly: "[I]rresponsible and Lazy . . . That's What Poverty Is."* Media Matters for America, edited by Gabe Wildau. June 18, 2004. https://www.mediamatters.org/bill-oreilly/oreilly-irresponsible-and-lazy-thats-what-poverty.

Panichas, George E. "Hume's Theory of Property." *ARSP: Archiv für Rechts- und Sozialphilosophie / Archives for Philosophy of Law and Social Philosophy* 69, no. 3 (1983): 391–405.

Passamonti, Luca, Francesco Fera, Angela Magariello et al. "Monoamine Oxidase-A Genetic Variations Influence Brain Activity Associated with Inhibitory Control: New Insight into the Neural Correlates of Impulsivity." *Biological Psychiatry* 59, no. 4 (2006): 334–40.

Perner, Josef, and Birgit Lang. "Development of Theory of Mind and Executive Control." *Trends in Cognitive Sciences* 3, no. 9 (1999): 337–44.

Persky, Joseph. "Retrospectives: The Ethology of *Homo Economicus*." *The Journal of Economic Perspectives* 9, no. 2 (Spring, 1995): 221–31.

Persson, Ingmar, and Julian Savulescu. "Getting Moral Enhancement Right: The Desirability of Moral Bioenhancement." *Bioethics* 27, no. 3 (2011): 124–31.

Persson, Ingmar, and Julian Savulescu. "The Perils of Cognitive Enhancement and the Urgent Imperative to Enhance the Moral Character of Humanity." *Journal of Applied Philosophy* 25, no. 3 (2008): 162–77.

Persson, Ingmar, and Julian Savulescu. *Unfit for the Future: The Need for Moral Enhancement*. Oxford: Oxford University Press, 2012.

Petty, Richard E., John T. Cacioppo, and David Schumann. "Central and Peripheral Routes to Advertising Effectiveness: The Moderating Role of Involvement." *Journal of Consumer Research* 10, no. 2 (1983): 135–46.

Pezawas, Lukas, Andreas Meyer-Lindenberg, Emily M. Drabant et al. "5-HTTLPR Polymorphism Impacts Human Cingulate-amygdala Interactions: A Genetic Susceptibility Mechanism for Depression." *Nature Neuroscience* 8, no. 6 (2005): 828–34.

Pickstock, Catherine. *After Writing: The Liturgical Consummation of Philosophy*. Oxford: Blackwell, 1998.

Plomin, Robert, John C. DeFries, Valerie S. Knopik, and Jenae M. Neiderhiser. *Behavioural Genetics*, 4th ed. New York: Freeman, 2001.

Polanyi, Karl. *The Great Transformation: The Political and Economic Origins of Our Time*. Boston, MA: Beacon Press, 2001.

Poovey, Mary. *A History of the Modern Fact: Problems of Knowledge in the Science of Wealth and Society*. Chicago: University of Chicago Press, 1998.

Quinn, Michael. "Mill on Poverty, Population, and Poor Relief: Out of Bentham by Malthus?" *Revue d'études Benthamiennes* 4 (2008). https://doi.org/10.4000/etudes-benthamiennes.185.

Raine, Adrian. *The Anatomy of Violence: The Biological Roots of Crime*. New York: Vintage, 2014.

Raine, Adrian. "From Genes to Brain to Antisocial Behavior." *Current Directions in Psychological Science* 17, no. 5 (2008): 323–8.

Raine, Adrian. *The Psychopathology of Crime: Criminal Behavior as a Clinical Disorder*. Cambridge, MA: Academic Press, 1997.

Raine, Adrian. "Schizotypal Personality: Neurodevelopmental and Psychosocial Trajectories." *Annual Review of Clinical Psychology* 2 (2006): 291–326.

Rapport, Maurice M., Arda Alden Green, and Irvie H. Page. "Serum Vasoconstrictor, Serotonin; Isolation and Characterization." *Journal of Biological Chemistry* 176, no. 3 (1948): 961–9.

Rasmussen, Dennis C. *The Infidel and the Professor: David Hume, Adam Smith, and the Friendship that Shaped Modern Thought*. Princeton, NJ: Princeton University Press, 2019.

Ravallion, Martin. "The Two Poverty Enlightenments: Historical Insights from Digitized Books Spanning Three Centuries." The World Bank Development Research Group. Director's Office. January 2011.

Rayo, Luis, and Gary Becker. "Evolutionary Efficiency and Happiness." *Journal of Political Economy* 115, no. 2 (2007): 302–37.

Rayo, Luis, and Gary Becker. "Habits, Peers, and Happiness: An Evolutionary Perspective." *American Economic Review* 97, no. 2 (2008): 487–91.

Reeves, Richard. *John Stuart Mill: Victorian Firebrand*. London: Atlantic Books, 2004.

Reiss, Julian. "Review of *The Methodology of Positive Economics: Reflections on the Milton Friedman Legacy*, ed. Uskali Mäki." *Erasmus Journal for Philosophy and Economics* 3, no. 2 (Autumn 2010): 103–10.

Ricardo, David. *On the Principles of Political Economy and Taxation*. London: John Murray, 1821. Library of Economics and Liberty. http://www.econlib.org/library/Ricardo/ricP2.html.

Rilling, James K., Andrea L. Glenn, Meeta R. Jairam et al. "Neural Correlates of Social Cooperation and Non-Cooperation as a Function of Psychopathy." *Biological Psychiatry* 61, no. 11 (2007): 1260–71.

Robbins, Lionel. *Essay on the Nature and Significance of Economic Science*. London: Macmillan, 1932.

Robson, Arthur J. "The Biological Basis of Economic Behavior." *Journal of Economic Literature* 39, no. 1 (2001): 11–33.

Rogers-Vaughn, Bruce. "Blessed are Those Who Mourn: Depression as Political Resistance." *Pastoral Psychology* 63 (2014): 503–22.

Rogers-Vaughn, Bruce. *Caring for Souls in a Neoliberal Age*. London: Palgrave-MacMillan, 2016.

Rokeach, Milton. *The Open and Closed Mind: Investigations into the Nature of Belief Systems and Personality Systems*. New York: Basic Books, 1960.

Rosen, Frederick. *Classical Utilitarianism from Hume to Mill*. New York: Routledge, 2003.

Rosenbloom, Michael. "Chlorpromazine and the Psychopharmacologic Revolution." *JAMA* 287, no. 14 (2002): 1860–1.

Ross, Don. "Game Theory." In *The Stanford Encyclopedia of Philosophy* (Fall 2021 Edition), edited by Edward N. Zalta. https://plato.stanford.edu/archives/fall2021/entries/game-theory/.

Rothschild, Emma, and Amartya Sen. "Adam Smith's Economics." In *The Cambridge Companion to Adam Smith*, edited by Knud Haakonssen, 319–65. Cambridge: Cambridge University Press, 2006.

Rozin, Paul, Jonathan Haidt, and Clark McCauley. "Disgust." In *Handbook of Emotions*, edited by Michael Lewis, Jeannette Haviland-Jones, and Lisa Barrett, 757–76. 3rd ed. New York: The Guilford Press, 2008.

Rozin, Paul, Laura Lowery, Sumio Imada, and Jonathan Haidt. "The CAD Triad Hypothesis: A Mapping Between Three Moral Emotions (Contempt, Anger, Disgust) and Three Moral Codes (Community, Autonomy, Divinity)." *Journal of Personality and Social Psychology* 76, no. 4 (1999): 574–86.

Sachs, Joe. "Aristotle: Ethics." *The Internet Encyclopedia of Philosophy.* https://www.iep.utm.edu/aris-eth/.
Sadeh, Naomi, Shabnam Javdani, Joshua J. Jackson et al. "Serotonin Transporter Gene Associations with Psychopathic Traits in Youth Vary as a Function of Socioeconomic Resources." *Journal of Abnormal Psychology* 119, no. 3 (2010): 604–9.
Sadler, John Z. *Values and Psychiatric Diagnosis. International Perspectives in Philosophy and Psychiatry.* New York: Oxford University Press, 2005.
Sady, Wojciech. "Ludwik Fleck." In *The Stanford Encyclopedia of Philosophy* (Winter 2021 Edition), edited by Edward N. Zalta. https://plato.stanford.edu/archives/win2021/entries/fleck/.
Sagar, Paul. "Beyond Sympathy: Smith's Rejection of Hume's Moral Theory." *British Journal for the History of Philosophy* 25, no. 4 (2017): 681–705.
Sahakian, Barbara, and Julia Gottwald. *Sex, Lies, and Brian Scans: How fMRI Reveals What Really Goes on in Our Minds.* Oxford: Oxford University Press, 2017.
Sansone, Randy A., and Lori A. Sansone. "Personality Disorders: A Nation-Based Perspective on Prevalence." *Innovations in Clinical Neuroscience* 8, no. 4 (April 2011): 13–18.
Schildkraut, Joseph J. "The Catecholamine Hypothesis of Affective Disorders: A Review of Supporting Evidence." *American Journal of Psychiatry* 122, no. 5 (1965): 509–22.
Schnall, Simone, Jonathan Haidt, Gerald L. Clore, and Alexander H. Jordan. "Disgust as Embodied Moral Judgment." *Personality and Social Psychology Bulletin* 34, no. 8 (2008): 1096–109.
Schultz, Theodore W. "Investment in Human Capital." *The American Economic Review* 51, no. 1 (1961): 1–17.
Seitz, Rüdiger, Janpeter Nickel, and Nina Azari. "Functional Modularity of the Medial Prefrontal Cortex: Involvement in Human Empathy." *Neuropsychology* 20, no. 6 (2006): 743–51.
Seligman, Martin. *Authentic Happiness: Using the New Positive Psychology to Realize Your Potential for Lasting Fulfillment.* New York: Atria Books, 2004.
Seligman, Martin, and Christopher Peterson. *Character, Strengths, and Virtues: A Handbook in Classification.* Oxford: Oxford University Press, 2004.
Selikoff, Irving J., and Edward H. Robitzek. "Tuberculosis Chemotherapy with Hydrazine Derivatives of Isonicotinic Acid." *Dis Chest* 21, no. 4 (1952): 385–438.
Semple, Janet. *Bentham's Prison: A Study of the Panopticon Penitentiary.* Oxford: Oxford, 1993.
Shermer, Michael. *The Science of Good and Evil.* New York: Henry Holt, 2004.
Shostak, Arthur B., and William Gomberg, eds. *New Perspectives on Poverty.* Englewood Cliffs, NJ: Prentice-Hall, 1965.
Simpson, David. "Francis Bacon (1561–1626)." *Internet Encyclopedia of Philosophy.* https://www.iep.utm.edu/bacon/.
Simpson, Donald. "Phrenology and the Neurosciences: Contributions of F. J. Gall and J. G. Spurzheim." *ANZ Journal of Surgery* 75 (2005): 475–82.
Sinnott-Armstrong, Walter, and Christian B. Miller, eds. *Moral Psychology: The Evolution of Morality: Adaptations and Innateness,* vol. 1. Cambridge, MA: MIT Press, 2007.
Sinnott-Armstrong, Walter, and Christian B. Miller, eds. *Moral Psychology: The Cognitive Science of Morality: Intuition and Diversity,* vol. 2. Cambridge, MA: Bradford Books, 2007.
Sinnott-Armstrong, Walter, and Christian B. Miller, eds. *Moral Psychology: The Neuroscience of Morality: Emotion, Brain Disorders, and Development,* vol. 3. Cambridge, MA: Bradford Books, 2007.

Skloot, Rebeca. *The Immortal Life of Henrietta Lacks*. New York: Broadway Books, 2011.
Smith, Adam. *Correspondence of Adam Smith*. Edited by E. C. Mossner and I. S. Ross. Oxford: Clarendon Press, 1977.
Smith, Adam. *An Inquiry into the Nature and Causes of the Wealth of Nations*, vol. 2. Edited by R. H. Campbell and A. S. Skinner, Glasgow Edition. Indianapolis, IN: Liberty Fund, 1981.
Smith, Adam. *The Theory of Moral Sentiments*. Edited by Joseph Black and James Hutton. London: Alex. Murray & Sons, 1869.
Snarey, John R. "Cross-cultural Universality of Social-moral Development: A Critical Review of Kohlbergian Research." *Psychological Bulletin* 97, no. 2 (1985): 202–32.
Somers, Margaret R., and Fred Block. "From Poverty to Perversity: Ideas, Markets, and Institutions over 200 Years of Welfare Debate." *American Sociological Review* 70, no. 2 (2005): 260–87.
Spaemann, Robert. "Ars Longa, Vita Brevis." In *Ethics of Biomedical Research in a Christian Vision: Proceedings of the Ninth Assembly of the Pontifical Academy for Life*, edited by Juan de Dios Vial Correa and Elio Sgreccia, 102–11. Vatican City: Libreria Editrice Vaticana, 2004.
Spooner, Lysander. *Vices are Not Crimes*. 1875. https://static1.squarespace.com/static/55a 3c833e4b07c31913e6eae/t/55a52368e4b0994cd9068873/1436885864688/Vices+Are +Not+Crimes.pdf.
Squire, Larry. *The History of Neuroscience in Autobiography*, vol. 1. Cambridge, MA: Academic Press, 1998.
Staum, Martin S. *Labeling People: French Scholars on Society, Race and Empire, 1815–1848*. Montreal: McGill-Queen's University Press, 2003.
Stephen, Leslie. *The English Utilitarians*, vol. 1. London: Duckworth and Co., 1902.
Sternberg, Richard J. *Wisdom, Intelligence, and Creativity Synthesized*. New York: Cambridge University Press, 2003.
Stiegler, Bernard. *The Age of Disruption: Technology and Madness in Computational Capitalism*. Cambridge, UK: Polity Press, 2019.
Stiegler, Bernard. *Technics and Time*, 3 vols. Stanford: Stanford University Press, 1998.
Stigler, George J. "Frank Hyneman Knight." Working Paper 37. Working Papers. Chicago, IL: Center for the Study of the Economy and the State, The University of Chicago, 1985.
Stigler, George J., and Gary S. Becker. "De Gustibus non est Disputandum." *The American Economic Review* 67, no. 2 (1977): 76–90.
Stoff, David M., Abner P. Pasatiempo, Jupiter H. Yeung, Wagner H. Bridger, and Harris Rabinovich. "Test-retest Reliability of the Prolactin and Cortisol Responses to d, l-Fenfluramine Challenge in Disruptive Behavior Disorders." *Psychiatry Research* 42 (1992): 65–72.
Stone, Michael H. *The Anatomy of Evil*. Amherst, NY: Prometheus Books, 2009.
Stone, Michael H., and Gary Brucato. *The New Evil: Understanding the Emergence of Violent Crime*. Amherst, NY: Prometheus Books, 2019.
Tancredi, Laurence. *Hardwired Behavior: What Neuroscience Reveals About Morality*. Cambridge: Cambridge University Press, 2005.
Tawney, Richard H. *The Agrarian Problem in the Sixteenth Century*. Introduction by Lawrence Stone. New York: Harper Torchbooks, 1967.
Tawney, Richard H. *Religion and the Rise of Capitalism: An Historical Study*. London: John Murray, 1922.
Taylor, Charles. *Modern Social Imaginaries*. Durham, NC: Duke University Press, 2007.

Thompson, John B. *Studies in the Theory of Ideology*. Berkeley, CA: University of California Press, 1984.
Tomczak, Stephen Monroe. "From Townsend to Malthus to the Poor Law Report: An Examination of the Ideas Concerning the Relationship of Public Aid and Reproduction on Policy Development, 1786–1834." *Journal of Sociology and Social Work* 3, no. 2 (December 2015): 27–38.
Townsend, Joseph. *A Dissertation on the Poor Laws, By a Well-Wisher to Mankind*. 1786. https://socialsciences.mcmaster.ca/econ/ugcm/3ll3/townsend/poorlaw.html.
Trout, J. D. *Why Empathy Matters: The Science and Psychology of Better Judgement*. New York: Penguin Group, 2010.
Unger, Rhoda K., Richard D. Draper, and Michael L. Pendergrass. "Personal Epistemology and Personal Experience." *Journal of Social Issues* 42, no. 2 (1986): 67–79.
van der Kolk, Bessel. *The Body Keeps the Score: Brain, Mind, and Body in the Healing of Trauma*. London: Penguin Books, 2015.
van Wyhe, John. "The Authority of Human Nature: The *Schädellehre* of Franz Joseph Gall." *BJHS* 35 (2002): 17–42. http://www.historyofphrenology.org.uk/texts/2002van_wyhe.htm.
van Wyhe, John. "The History of Phrenology." *The Victorian Web*. http://www.victorianweb.org/science/phrenology/intro.html.
van Wyhe, John. "Reading Phrenology." *The History of Phrenology on the Web*. http://www.historyofphrenology.org.uk/literature.html.
Viding, Essi, James R. Blair, Terrie E. Moffitt, and Robert Plomin. "Evidence for Substantial Genetic Risk for Psychopathy in 7-Year-Olds." *Journal of Child Psychology and Psychiatry* 46 (2005): 592–7.
Viding, Essi, and Uta Frith. "Genes for Susceptibility to Violence Lurk in the Brain." *Proceedings of the National Academy of Sciences* 103, no. 16 (April 2006): 6085–6.
Vitz, Rico. "Sympathy and Benevolence in Hume's Moral Psychology." *Journal of the History of Philosophy* 42, no. 3 (2004): 261–75.
Vohs, Kathleen, and Jonathan Schooler. "The Value of Believing in Free Will." *Psychological Science* 19, no. 1 (2008): 49–54.
Walker, Mark. "Enhancing Genetic Virtue: A Project for Twenty-First Century Humanity." *Politics and the Life Sciences* 28, no. 2 (2009): 27–47.
Wang, Eric, Y.-C. Ding, P. Flodman et al. "The Genetic Architecture of Selection at the Human Dopamine Receptor D4 (Drd4) Gene Locus." *American Journal of Human Genetics* 74, no. 5 (2004): 931–44.
Washington, Harriet A. *Medical Apartheid: The Dark History of Medical Experimentation on Black Americans from Colonial Times to the Present*. New York: Anchor, 2008.
Wegner, Daniel. *The Illusion of Conscious Will*. Cambridge, MA: MIT Press, 2002.
Werrett, Simon. "Potemkin and the Panopticon: Samuel Bentham and the Architecture of Absolutism in Eighteenth Century Russia." *Journal of Bentham Studies* 2 (1999): 1–25.
Wheatley, Thalia, and Jonathan Haidt. "Hypnotic Disgust Makes Moral Judgments More Severe." *Psychological Science* 16, no. 10 (October 2005): 780–4.
Wilensky, Harold L., and Charles N. Lebeaux. *Social Welfare and Industrial Society*. New York: Free Press, 1965.
Will, Robert E., and Harold G. Vatter, eds. *Poverty in Affluence*. New York: Harcourt, Brace, and World, 1965.
Williams, Leanne M., Justine M. Gatt, Stacey A. Kuan et al. "Polymorphism of the MAOA Gene Is Associated with Emotional Brain Markers and Personality Traits on an Antisocial Index." *Neuropsychopharmacology* 34 (2009): 1797–809.

Yuste, Rafael, and Cori Bargmann. "Toward a Global BRAIN Initiative." *Cell* 168, no. 6 (2017): 956–9.

Zak, Paul J. *The Moral Molecule: The Source of Love and Prosperity.* New York: Dutton Adult, 2012.

Zak, Paul J. *Trust Factor: The Science of Creating High-Performance Companies.* New York: AMACOM, 2017.

Zak, Paul J., Angela A. Stanton, and Sheila Ahmadi. "Oxytocin Increases Generosity in Humans." *PloS ONE* 2, no. 11 (2007): e1128.

# Index

5-hydroxyindoleacetic acid   34
1601 Poor Law   105, 159–60, 199
1662 Act of Settlement   105

Abiodun, Sade J.   219, 224, 230, 237
acedia   210, 211
adaptation   61–2, 84, 98, 133–4
addiction   114, 120, 121, 124, 139, 202
adrenaline   33
African-Americans   7, 43–4, 104, 221, 226, 228, 244
agency   6, 59, 76, 80, 87, 92, 94, 95, 98, 103, 109, 110, 114, 139, 156, 164–7, 178, 180, 195, 202
altruism   12, 61, 66–8, 83, 94–6
American Physiological Society   4
American Psychiatric Association (APA)   47–9
amygdala   27, 31, 33, 37, 38, 51–2, 55, 65, 67, 72
anterocingulate gyrus   37–8
antisocial behavior   5, 6, 8–9, 11–13, 16–18, 31–9, 45, 51–5, 59–68, 71–5, 143, 198, 203–6
antisocial personality disorder (ASPD)   46–50, 70, 122, 198
Aquinas, Thomas   176, 212–13
Ardelt, Monika   61–4
Aristotle   118, 135, 171, 176, 181–2, 190–2
artifactual being   125, 194–5, 197–206
authority/subversion   82, 83

Babbie, Earl   40–2, 44
Bachner-Melman, Rachel   67–8
Bacon, Francis   71, 110, 144, 147, 168–73, 175–87, 189–95, 198–203, 209
Baltes, P.B.   61–4
Baron-Cohen, Simon   15
Becker, Gary   103, 110, 113–26, 128–40, 150, 190, 194–8, 202–4
benevolence   57, 172–4

Bentham, Jeremy   80, 105–6, 109–10, 143–58, 164–6, 168, 170, 178–9, 195, 200–4
Bentham, Samuel   156
bifurcated anthropology   105, 136, 170, 200–2
biopolitics   4, 12, 17, 26, 71, 140, 143, 151, 152, 160, 204, 206
*bios*   17, 71, 93, 166, 184, 197, 204–6
Blanchard, Kathryn   124, 129, 136, 186, 189, 190, 194
bottom-up   55, 76, 78, 81, 147, 203
BRAIN Initiative   3, 56, 77
Brown, Scott   61–4
Brown, Wendy   10–11, 101, 117, 143, 150, 220, 263
Browning, Don   246

capitalism   86, 125–9, 185, 219, 239, 242–4, 249
care/harm   82, 83, 85
carnal scourge   20–5
Caspi, Avshalom   52, 53, 55, 81, 203
Cassirer, Ernst   207
catecholamine   46
Catholic   106–7, 145, 210
central nervous system (CNS)   34–6
charity   160, 174, 177, 180, 194, 199, 200, 218, 260
Chicago School of Economics   18, 101, 113, 115, 125
Cleckley, Hervey   48, 237
cognitive   1, 3, 20–3, 33, 54, 56, 62–6, 80, 187, 196
competition   66, 125, 128
Comte, August   145, 205
conceptual
    apparatus   20, 40, 47, 129
    definition   40, 41, 45, 58–64
    formation   21
    funneling   32, 40–4, 49–50, 56, 59, 63, 69, 75, 86

cortex   27, 31, 37, 51–2, 67, 76, 78
   medial prefrontal (MPC)   66, 68
   prefrontal (PFC)   27, 55, 65, 66, 72, 91
corticolimbic area   33, 37
   system   34–5, 37–8, 51, 54–5, 65
crime   1, 31, 46, 57–8, 74–5, 108–9, 116, 121–2, 142, 202
Cunningham, Bill   7, 9, 43

Darwin, Charles   84, 105, 145, 161, 170
Decety, Jean   66
*De Gustibus Non Est Disputandum*   119–22, 136
demand curve   120, 202
dementia   58
*Denkkollectiv*   23
desire   6, 13, 48, 81, 83, 90–6, 120, 130, 133–6, 146–50, 166–7, 175–6, 208–14
Diagnostic and Statistics Manual (DSM)   8, 11, 16, 40, 47–50, 55, 58, 72
disgust   80–3, 204
dopamine   33, 34, 46, 65, 67–8, 95

Eagleman, David   15
East India Company   144, 160, 191
economic imaginary   7, 100–9
economics   7–11, 15–18, 41, 55–6, 93, 100–4, 113–19, 122–40, 142–4, 157–71, 184–206
Elizabeth I   105, 179, 199
Emmett, Ross   119, 132, 137–8
emotional homeostasis   60, 64–5, 69, 72, 232
enclosure of the commons   106–7, 179
English Reformation   107
environment   8, 11, 16, 17, 25, 31–3, 35, 37–9, 52, 53, 55, 56, 59, 62, 74–6, 93, 140, 146, 198, 204
epinephrine   95
esoteric community   23–8, 42–4, 75, 97, 138, 203
estate   12, 71, 92, 156, 159, 169, 179, 182–4, 195, 197, 203
ethology   147, 148
evolution   7, 111
exoteric community   16, 24–8, 39, 78

Fable of the Bees   177, 184, 202, 204, 261. *See also* hive
fairness/cheating   79, 82, 83, 85, 236
fellow-feeling   190
fenfluramine   34–6
fictitious entities   18, 108, 116, 143, 149–51, 153–4, 175–7
Fleck, Ludwik   14–17, 20–8, 42, 44, 75, 77, 85, 196, 207, 209, 210
Fleischacker, Simon   190–3
fMRI   1–3, 36–9, 44, 60, 66, 69, 71, 77, 93
Foucault, Michel   12, 26, 27, 102, 103, 114–16, 124, 126, 128, 130, 140, 143, 157, 217
Freakonomics   100, 115, 122, 138
freedom   122, 125, 127–30, 189, 190, 202, 210
free will   6, 11–12, 17, 87–92, 98, 114, 124, 129, 148, 177–8, 204
Friedman, Milton   101–3, 125–40, 202
Friedman, Rose D.   126
Frith, Uta   15, 31, 51–4, 58, 70, 72, 182, 204
*Fuga finis*   210–11

GABA   46
Gall, Franz Joseph   57, 58, 60
game theory   130
Gassendi, Pierre   171–2
Genetic Virtue Project   70, 204
Gianaros, Peter   32–41, 44–6, 50–2, 55, 56, 119, 203, 204
governmentality   12, 124, 157
Greene, Jeffrey   61–4

habits   55, 76, 118–23, 134, 158, 190–2
Haidt, Jonathan   78–88, 93–5, 98, 113, 140, 152, 204–5
happiness   79, 89–92, 118–23, 148–9, 151–5, 172, 191
happiness function   118–23, 177, 202
Hare, Robert   48, 72
Harrington, Michael   43
Harris, Sam   78, 87–95, 98, 139, 204, 205
Harvey, David   10–11, 140
Hayek, Frederick   86, 102, 126, 132
Henry VIII   106–7
Himmelfarb, Gertrude   162, 164–5, 167, 177, 225, 257, 258

hive   84, 86, 177, 204
Hobbes, Thomas   151, 163, 169, 207
Hollingshead, August B.   43, 44, 47, 53, 58, 104, 203, 204
Hollingshead Four Factor Index of Social Status   43, 44
*Homo capitalus*   12, 17–19, 100, 110, 113, 114, 116, 118, 124, 125, 130–3, 139, 142, 144, 195–6, 203–6
*Homo economicus*   16–19, 109, 110, 113–16, 124–5, 129–33, 135–6, 138–44, 149–50, 167–8, 170, 192, 201–3
human capital   103, 113, 115–17, 124, 130, 132, 140, 150
Human Genome Project   2
Human oxytocin mediated empathy (HOME) circuit   95
human science(s)   32–3, 39–45, 104–5, 197, 206–10
Hume, David   9, 18–19, 86–7, 110, 149–54, 161, 167–95, 198–204, 211–12
hunger   156, 163–6, 184
Hutcheson, Frances   86, 151–2, 155, 172, 177, 190, 193
hypothalamic-pituitary-adrenal (HPA) axis   33–5, 37–9, 44, 93

idle   19, 150, 155–7, 178, 184, 201
idleness   109, 158–60, 162, 177, 203
impartial spectator   187–9, 192–3
inductive science   180
industry house(s)   156–7, 167
iron law of wages   157, 159, 160, 163, 166, 201
is-ought distinction   118, 134, 138, 197

Jason, L.A.   61, 63, 64
Jeste, Dilip   58–72
Jones, David Stedman   9, 169
journal science   14
joy   210
justice   153, 171, 172, 175, 188, 200

Kant, Immanuel   9, 80, 90, 151, 154, 170, 192
Keynesianism   10, 102–3

Knight, Frank   114, 119, 124–7, 130–40, 143, 149–51, 201–2
Krugman, Paul   127, 131
Kuhn, Thomas   20, 24

liberty/oppression   82, 84, 85, 150, 169
life   64, 86, 136, 169, 172
limbic structures   51
limbic system   65, 68
loyalty/betrayal   82, 83
lust   25, 157, 158, 160, 165, 200

MacArthur Scale of Subjective Social Status   37
McCloskey, Dierdre   151, 185, 190, 194
MacIntyre, Alasdair   9, 18, 87, 134, 148, 154, 171, 175, 176, 185, 195
McRorie, Christina   184, 187
Malthus, Thomas   150, 156–68, 200, 201, 203, 204
Mandeville, Bernard   177, 184, 195, 199–202
Manuck, Stephen   32–46, 50–2, 55–6, 119, 203–4
market price of labor   159, 160
marriage   109, 116, 139, 159, 161–5, 200, 256, 257
Marshall, Catherine   40–2
Martin, Marie   9, 42, 58, 192–3
Meeks, Thomas   58–72
Meyer-Lindenberg, Andreas   15, 31, 51–5, 71
Milbank, John   146
Mill, James   143, 153, 158, 160
Mill, John Stuart   18–19, 143–53, 166–7, 195, 201–2
mirror neurons   66, 84
monoamine oxidase-a (maoa)   31, 46, 51–4, 65, 228, 229
moral
 anthropology   5, 6, 19, 55, 76, 86, 108, 114, 138, 170, 186, 190, 196–7
 enhancement   5, 17, 70
 foundation(s)   82, 86, 98, 113, 204
 molecule   12, 28, 93, 96, 203
 physics   87–8, 90–3, 152, 155
 psychology   1, 80–3, 94, 175, 176, 200

sense(s)   48, 58, 82, 86, 89, 152, 168, 172, 176, 178, 195
sentiment(s)   9, 19, 86–7, 175–6, 185–8, 190–5, 200, 202, 236, 260, 264
taste(s)   78, 80, 82–7, 93, 110, 184, 189, 193
Moynihan, Daniel Patrick   43

natural price of labor   158
neoliberalism   9–12, 47–9, 101–4, 109–10, 113–16, 125–6, 128, 138–40, 166–7, 184–5, 202–6, 209–10, 214
neurobiology   27, 58, 59, 64
neuroeconomics   4, 7, 67, 93, 95, 203, 240
neurohormones   33, 93
neuroscience
　and biopolitics   26
　definition of   4, 15, 20, 26–7, 44, 143, 206
　history of   4–5
　of morality   4, 6, 13–14, 17, 27, 36, 58, 69, 70, 77, 87–8, 98–100, 109, 125, 131, 143, 166, 171, 184, 194–8, 203–6, 209
　and naturalization   11, 204
　and neoliberalism   11–12, 139–40
　popular   76, 92, 104, 134
　and thought communities   26–7
　and types of science   14–15
　of wisdom   64, 198
neurotechnology   1–4, 56, 69–71, 124, 182–3
neuroticism   34
neurotransmitter(s)   3, 13, 17, 33, 34, 40, 46, 51–3, 59, 64–7, 69, 72, 75, 84
New Atlantis   170, 180, 183, 184, 195, 199
new work   179–80, 182–3, 199
Nobel Prize for Economics   115, 116, 125, 130
norepinephrine   34, 46

Obama, Barack   1, 2
obligation   153
operational definition   41, 55, 63
operations   41, 64, 78, 86

Ordoliberal   101–2
oxytocin   84, 95–9, 123, 203, 205
oxytocin virtuous cycle (OVC)   95

panopticon   110, 151, 155–7, 184, 200, 203
pauper   105, 108, 156, 177
perversity thesis   257
PET   3
Peterson, Christopher   58
phrenology   4, 57–60, 64, 70, 71, 201
Pinochet, Augusto   103
pleasure and pain   78, 87–92, 110, 124, 152–5, 168, 171–4, 178, 184, 187, 192, 195, 200, 202, 212
Polanyi, Karl   105–8, 116, 156, 160, 163, 176, 186, 190, 203
*polis*   13, 17, 71, 91, 93, 166, 169, 170, 174, 175, 180, 184, 195, 197, 200, 201, 204, 212
political economy   3–5, 13, 17–19, 71, 75, 76, 88, 93, 97, 100, 101, 103, 105, 106, 110, 113, 115, 127, 128, 130, 131, 142–4, 149–51, 157, 158, 160, 165, 166, 170, 176, 184, 185, 195, 200, 202, 204, 205
polymorphism   31, 35, 36, 39, 51–3, 67, 68, 72
Poor Law Reform of 1834   143, 144, 157, 158, 166
Poor Laws   9, 42, 105, 108, 142, 151, 157, 159–63, 165, 186, 191, 202
Poovey, Mary   42, 152
popularizers   7, 15, 17, 26, 76–9, 87, 98–100, 103, 104, 115, 134, 171, 184, 185, 198, 203, 205
popular science   14, 15
population growth   158, 161–3
positive science   18, 114, 127, 140, 146, 148–9, 152
positivism   128, 145, 152, 171, 201
positivist science   18, 110, 167, 168
Posner, richard   115
poverty   7–9, 16–17, 35–6, 38, 42–5, 56, 73, 97, 103–5, 110, 140, 142–3, 156, 160, 161, 163, 164, 166, 167, 174, 177–8, 191, 201, 203, 204
poverty enlightenment   42, 105, 225–6

power ontology  179, 184, 185, 194, 195, 203
Presidential Commission for the Study of Bioethical Issues  3
Price theory  100, 132, 137, 138
Principle of population  150, 162, 164, 165
Principles of legislation  18, 157, 168, 201
Principles of morals  18, 168, 172, 173, 201
prolactin  33
property  10, 36, 44, 46, 105, 107, 109, 110, 117, 141, 163, 169, 170, 172, 174–6, 188, 200, 201, 203, 211
prosocial behavior(s)  8, 12, 13, 32, 59, 62, 63, 66, 67, 69, 72, 73, 84, 96, 97, 198
prosociality  62, 67, 68, 72, 73, 84, 85, 139, 205
proxies  5, 8, 32, 77, 198
  for vice  12, 16, 32, 55, 59, 110, 115, 122, 139
  for virtue  12, 16, 59, 61, 115
Prozac  47
prudence  69, 149, 159, 185, 190, 194, 213
psychiatry  15, 16, 26, 27, 32, 40, 44, 46–9, 57, 58, 72, 74
psychology  1, 12, 14, 15, 17, 18, 27, 44, 47, 57–64, 72, 78–83, 85, 93, 94, 100, 124, 143–7, 153, 166, 175, 176, 195, 200–2
psychopath(s)  1, 53–4, 74, 81, 91, 92, 226, 237
psychopathology  8, 17, 49, 68, 71
psychopathy  48, 67, 72, 74, 81, 198

quest  13, 16, 17, 20, 28, 125, 183, 197, 203–7
Quetelet, Adolph  164

race  9, 43, 44, 158, 218, 219, 224, 226, 243, 244, 257
  racism  116, 219, 222
Raine, Adrian  4, 54, 69, 71, 204
Ravallion, Martin  42, 225–6
Reagan, Ronald  10

reproduction  7, 124, 201, 256
Ricardo, David  105, 157–60, 166, 178, 186, 200–1
Robinson Crusoe  129, 137, 163, 249, 260
Rogers-Vaughn, Bruce  10, 47, 104, 218, 228, 247
Rossman, Gretchen  41, 42

Sachs, Jeffrey  73, 75
Sadeh, Naomi  38, 53–5, 81, 203
Sady, Wojciech  23, 25, 210
sanctity/degradation  82, 83
Science of Virtue  8
self-interest  9, 61, 76, 84, 94, 96–7, 109, 124, 135–7, 167, 188–92, 199
Seligman, Martin  58
Sen, Amartya  191
serotonin (5-HT)  34–6, 46, 53
  transporter gene (5-HTT)  35–6
sex  1, 7, 26, 43, 58, 73, 74, 80, 93, 96, 97, 99, 109, 150, 157, 162, 164, 167, 199, 203, 238, 256
Smith, Adam  8–9, 18–19, 97, 110, 113, 131–2, 137, 168, 170, 176, 184–94, 200, 211–12
social
  apparatus  140, 149, 184
  engineering  18, 144, 151, 155–7, 163, 164, 209
  imaginary  3, 5, 9, 14, 17–18, 25–8, 125, 171, 177, 179, 194–8, 205–9, 212
  sciences  15, 18, 32, 34, 39, 41–2, 60, 143–5, 149, 152, 206
sociobiology  56, 123
socioeconomic  11, 17, 32, 38–9, 54, 56, 72, 103, 206, 234, 235
  position (SEP)  16, 36–41, 44–5, 52, 55–6, 110, 115, 119, 139, 143, 225
  status (SES)  8–9, 16, 32–48, 52–5, 59, 73, 104, 110, 115, 119, 139, 143, 202–4, 219
sociology  9, 15, 27, 201–2
sociopathy  5, 49, 52–4, 65, 67, 198
Spaemann, Robert  210–14
Spooner, Lysander  142–3
Spring(s) of action  18, 152–67
SSRI  47

state of nature   125–8, 169, 176, 207
Sternberg, Richard   61–2, 64
Stigler, George   113, 115, 119–20, 124–5, 132, 136–9, 150, 190, 204
*summum bonum*   213
sympathy   173, 186–9

Tawney, R.H.   106, 109, 243
Taylor, Charles   3, 14, 17, 25–6, 28, 99
teleology   12, 55, 62, 122, 148–9, 182, 192–4, 199, 204, 209, 214
temperance   58–9, 69, 185, 190, 192, 213
testosterone   95
textbook science   14
Thatcher, Margaret   10
thought-collective (collectives)   21, 23, 24, 27–8, 102
thought-community (communities)   5, 15–16, 23–8, 31–4, 207–10
thought-style   14, 16, 23–4, 27–8, 32, 39–42, 56, 64, 98–9, 207–10
top-down   76, 147, 148, 193, 212
Townsend, Joseph   18, 144, 158, 160–7
*Treponema pallidum*   21, 26, 27
Trust game   94–6

ultimatum game   96
utilitarianism   9, 18, 90, 129, 138, 148, 155, 171, 201

utility   9, 50, 115–25, 128, 136, 139, 141, 150–3, 157, 170–9, 181, 184, 186, 188, 191, 193, 195, 200–3
utility maximizing behavior   115, 116, 119, 121–4, 128, 139, 141, 189–91

*vademecum* science   14–15
vagrancy   105–6, 243
validation   41, 44, 48, 50, 64
value relativism   60, 88–9
values   2, 133
Viding, Essi   15, 31, 51–4, 58, 70, 72, 182, 204
violence   31, 34, 43, 46, 51, 52, 54–5, 58, 70–3, 88, 104, 107, 169, 215, 220–1, 223, 228–9, 242, 247
virtue   7–13, 16–18, 57–61, 68–74, 76, 87, 115, 118–19, 153–4, 171–7, 186–7, 190–4, 198–202, 210–14

WEIRD societies   19, 82, 85, 205, 207, 211, 237
well-being   2, 45, 56, 59, 78, 88, 90, 92, 140, 160, 190, 206, 214
wisdom   58–65, 68–9, 72–3, 79, 139, 198, 213–14, 224

Zak, Paul   78, 93–9, 124, 140, 176, 203–5

www.ingramcontent.com/pod-product-compliance
Lightning Source LLC
Chambersburg PA
CBHW052206300426
44115CB00011B/1669